ECONOMICS THROUGH THE LOOKING-GLASS

Alice tried another question. "What sort of people live about here?"

"In *that* direction," the Cat said, waving its right paw round, "lives an Old Conservative economist and in *that* direction," waving the other paw, "lives a New Labour economist. Visit either you like: they're both mad."

"But I don't want to go among mad people," Alice remarked.

"Then you shouldn't have come here," said the Cat.

(With apologies to Lewis Carroll)

Economics Through the Looking-Glass

Reflections on a Perverted Science

R.A. RAYMAN

Ashgate

Aldershot • Brookfield USA • Singapore • Sydney

Published by
Ashgate Publishing Limited
Gower House
Croft Road
Aldershot
Hants GU11 3HR
England

Ashgate Publishing Company
Old Post Road
Brookfield
Vermont 05036
USA

British Library Cataloguing in Publication Data
Rayman, R.A.
Economics through the looking-glass : reflections on a perverted science
1.Economics 2.Economics - Philosophy
I.Title
330.1

Library of Congress Cataloging-in-Publication Data
Rayman, R.A.
Economics through the looking-glass : reflections on a perverted science / R.A. Rayman.
p. cm.
Includes bibliographical references and index.
ISBN 1-84014-419-X (hb)
1. Economics. 2. Economics–History. 3. Economic policy. 4. Economic history. 5. Great Britain–Economic policy–1945-
I. Title.
HB171.R37 1998
330–dc21 98-3171
CIP

ISBN 1 84014 419 X

Printed in Great Britain by The Ipswich Book Company, Suffolk

CONTENTS

PART IV: WHAT'S WRONG WITH ECONOMIC THEORY?

PART V: ECONOMICS THROUGH THE LOOKING-GLASS

PART VI: BACK TO THE FUTURE

INFLATION, UNEMPLOYMENT AND THE SOCIAL CONTRACT

"All the members of human society stand in need of each other's assistance."
Adam Smith

In societies where the division of labour has been carried so far in the interests of the community as a whole that each member is economically dependent on every other, it is an implied term of the social contract that every individual who is willing to work should have the right to do so. It is also an implied term of the social contract, in societies where monetary claims are used as a means of exchange, that those claims should be fully honoured.

Inflation and unemployment are breaches of the social contract.

Just as assault and theft are crimes by individuals against society, so inflation and unemployment are crimes by society against individuals.

Unemployment robs them of their income.
Inflation robs them of their savings.

The Hottest Non-Political Issues of Politics

Although there are times when political debate appears to be concerned with little else, unemployment and inflation are not legitimate problems of politics any more than are measles and whooping-cough.

On some economic issues, there are wide divergencies of view between different shades of political opinion. On the subjects of inflation and unemployment, there is no controversy. No one is in favour; everyone is against.

Inflation and unemployment occupy the centre of the political arena, because economic policy, though it can suppress each one separately, cannot provide a lasting cure for both of them together. If the treatment of measles and whooping-cough had been equally lamentable, medicine, not economics, would be the focus of questions in Parliament, comments in the press, and interviews on radio and television.

The failure of economic policy is the responsibility, not of the politicians, but of their economic advisers. Its root cause is a fatal flaw of logic deeply embedded in the foundations of economic theory.

Economists of the World — United!

In the 1960s, economic theory was a battlefield. "Keynesians" and "Monetarists" fought to the death. No quarter was asked; none was given.

Today, the guns are silent and the battlefield is deserted.

> "In most areas of public policy, such as crime or education, governments at least have the excuse that experts give conflicting advice. Not so with unemployment. Economists disagree about a lot of things but not about how to get people back to work. Labour markets, they say, need to clear and the best way to ensure they do is to keep them flexible." [*The Economist*, April 5th 1997].

According to the economics textbooks, unemployment cannot occur in the ideal conditions of perfectly competitive market-clearing equilibrium. Apart from temporary fluctuations, the level of unemployment is explained as a *natural rate* caused by various forms of imperfection in the market structure.

It follows from the "natural rate hypothesis" that the only effective cure for unemployment is to get rid of the imperfections by encouraging competition. The greater the flexibility of markets, the closer the economy can move to market-clearing equilibrium. By the same token, a policy of monetary restriction is recommended as a safe method of controlling inflation. For it also follows from the "natural rate hypothesis" that any *artificial* depression of the volume of employment, which is not *naturally* caused by some structural market imperfection, can be dismissed as a "temporary side-effect".

The New "Single-Gear" Orthodoxy

The "natural rate hypothesis" has become the New Economic Orthodoxy. The economy is treated as a "single-gear" machine which requires (1) the lubrication of competition to operate at its full employment potential and (2) a strictly regulated supply of monetary fuel to prevent inflationary overheating.

For the problem of unemployment, the watchword is *market flexibility*.

For the problem of inflation, the watchword is *monetary control*.

The Global Economic Revolution

During the 1980s, under the banner of Market-Freedom, the New Single-Gear Orthodoxy swept the world. It affected capitalist and communist countries alike. Where no markets existed, new markets were created. Where markets existed, they were liberalised. Private enterprise was encouraged, and the role of the state was reduced.

The pace of economic liberalisation varied from country to country. Some regimes embraced the New Orthodoxy with enthusiasm; others tolerated it with reluctance. For ruthless determination in liberalising markets, in encouraging competition, in attacking restrictive practices, and in curbing the role of the state, few could match Britain in the 1980s.

The results were sensational:–

Taxes, Prices, Jobs, and Growth in the United Kingdom

Nineteen-Sixties	1960	1961	1962	1963	1964	1965	1966	1967	1968	1969	AVERAGE
	%	%	%	%	%	%	%	%	%	%	%
Taxation[1]	28.1	29.3	30.5	29.5	29.1	30.4	31.6	33.4	34.6	36.3	31.8
Inflation[2]	1.0	3.6	4.1	2.1	3.2	4.8	3.9	2.4	4.7	5.5	3.5
Unemployment[3]	1.3	1.2	1.6	2.0	2.6	2.0	2.1	3.1	3.1	2.9	2.2
Economic Growth[4]	4.6	3.0	0.8	4.5	5.4	2.5	1.9	2.3	4.1	2.1	3.1
Nineteen-Seventies	1970	1971	1972	1973	1974	1975	1976	1977	1978	1979	AVERAGE
	%	%	%	%	%	%	%	%	%	%	%
Taxation	36.9	35.1	33.2	32.5	35.8	36.3	35.6	34.9	33.6	34.3	34.7
Inflation	6.4	9.4	7.1	9.2	15.9	24.2	16.5	15.9	8.2	13.5	12.5
Unemployment	3.0	3.6	4.0	3.0	2.9	4.3	5.6	6.0	5.9	5.0	4.3
Economic Growth	2.3	2.0	3.5	7.4	-1.7	-0.7	2.8	2.4	3.5	2.8	2.4
Nineteen-Eighties	1980	1981	1982	1983	1984	1985	1986	1987	1988	1989	AVERAGE
	%	%	%	%	%	%	%	%	%	%	%
Taxation	36.0	38.2	38.7	38.5	38.6	38.3	37.6	37.0	36.8	36.6	37.6
Inflation	18.0	11.9	8.6	4.6	5.0	6.1	3.4	4.1	4.9	7.8	7.4
Unemployment	6.4	9.8	11.3	12.4	11.7	11.2	11.2	10.3	8.6	7.2	10.0
Economic Growth	-2.2	-1.3	1.7	3.7	2.3	3.8	4.3	4.8	5.0	2.2	2.4
Nineteen-Nineties	1990	1991	1992	1993	1994	1995	1996	1997	1998	1999	AVERAGE
	%	%	%	%	%	%	%	%	%	%	%
Taxation	36.9	36.3	34.9	34.0	34.6	35.9	36.0				35.5
Inflation	9.5	5.9	3.7	1.6	2.4	3.5	2.4				4.1
Unemployment	6.9	8.8	10.1	10.4	9.6	8.7	8.2				9.0
Economic Growth	0.4	-1.9	-0.5	2.0	3.8	2.5	2.2				1.2

1. Taxation (total revenue from taxation as a % of money GDP). *United Kingdom National Accounts: The Blue Book*. London: ONS.
2. Inflation (annual % change in the Consumer Price Index). *International Financial Statistics Yearbook*. New York: IMF.
3. Unemployment (standardised annual unemployment rates as a % of the total labour force). *Quarterly Labour Force Statistics*. Paris: OECD.
4. Economic Growth (annual % change in GDP at constant prices). *International Financial Statistics Yearbook*. New York: IMF.

The 1980s merit not just one entry in the record books but two:–
(1) the highest peacetime level of taxation in the whole of British history;
(2) the highest level of unemployment since the Second World War.

The Great Economic Conundrum

Economic policy had been conducted strictly "according to the book". Market flexibility had been increased beyond recognition. The role of the state had been reduced to a degree previously unimaginable. Instead of a record-breaking reduction in the level of unemployment and the burden of taxation, there had been a record-breaking increase.

Milton Friedman, one of the co-authors of the "natural rate hypothesis", had always been frank in admitting that an increase in unemployment would be one of the "side-effects of ending inflation", but he had promised that, though "inevitable", it would be only "temporary" [1974a, p.17]. In the event, the rise in unemployment was massive, widespread, and prolonged. To the millions languishing in the world's dole queues, "temporary side-effect" must have seemed a peculiar choice of words.

From the 1960s to the 1990s: "Temporary Side-Effect" or "Change of Gear"?

	INFLATION[1]				UNEMPLOYMENT[2]				ECONOMIC GROWTH[3]			
	1960s %	1970s %	1980s %	1990-96 %	1960s %	1970s %	1980s %	1990-96 %	1960s %	1970s %	1980s %	1990-96 %
Britain	3.5	12.5	7.4	4.1	2.2	4.3	10.0	9.0	3.1	2.4	2.4	1.2
Canada	2.5	7.3	6.5	2.5	4.8	6.7	9.3	10.1	5.2	4.7	3.1	1.2
France	3.9	8.9	7.2	2.4	1.7	3.8	9.0	11.0	5.7	3.7	2.3	1.3
Germany	2.4	4.9	2.9	1.7	0.8	2.3	5.9	6.7	5.2	3.1	1.8	3.6
Italy	3.4	12.3	11.2	5.1	5.0	6.3	9.5	10.7	6.3	3.9	2.4	1.2
Japan	5.4	9.0	2.5	1.4	1.3	1.7	2.5	2.6	10.5	5.2	4.0	2.3
United States	2.3	7.1	5.5	3.4	4.7	6.1	7.2	6.2	4.1	2.8	2.5	1.9

1. Inflation (annual % change in the Consumer Price Index). *International Financial Statistics Yearbook*. New York: IMF
2. Unemployment (standardised annual unemployment rates as a % of the total labour force). *Quarterly Labour Force Statistics*. Paris: OECD.
3. Economic Growth (annual % change in GDP at constant prices). *International Financial Statistics Yearbook*. New York: IMF.

Edmund Phelps, another co-author of the "natural rate hypothesis", was forced to concede that he was "unable to explain persuasively why . . . unemployment in many countries rose so stubbornly well into the mid-1980s" [1994, p.ix]. In an attempt to rescue the hypothesis, he found it necessary to argue that the natural rate of unemployment had been driven up by an increase in market inflexibility so dramatic that it amounted to a "structural slump". But this flew in the face of the facts. It was communism that had collapsed, not capitalism. As a result of the "liberal revolution" during the 1980s, economies throughout the world had become more flexible than ever before — not less. Instead of the lower unemployment and faster growth predicted by the New Single-Gear Orthodoxy, however, the actual result was higher unemployment and slower growth.

There is a much simpler explanation. It is that the conventional "single-gear" view is totally false. What the tables show are not single-gear economies whose lubrication has experienced nearly two decades of neglect, but well-lubricated multi-gear economies which have suffered *a downward change of gear*.

The "Single-Gear" Fallacy

It is perfectly true that structural imperfections of the market are responsible for the "natural rate of unemployment" — the shortfall below the potential market-clearing equilibrium. It is also true that the "natural rate" can move as the degree of imperfection changes. What orthodox theory fails to recognise is that the underlying *market-clearing equilibrium* itself is not fixed; it can shift away from full employment. The economy is, in other words, a "multi-gear" machine.

Because it is based on the fallacy that there are no gears to shift, the New Orthodoxy is fatally blind to the danger that monetary restriction can cause a downward shift in the economic gear-lever. This leads to the absurd self-contradiction of orthodox policy: a *laissez-faire* micro-economic policy coupled with an interventionist macroeconomic policy.

Two principles are sacred to the New Economic Orthodoxy: one is the freedom of all markets to operate without outside interference; the other is the supreme importance of money. In the words of Milton Friedman himself, "when it gets out of order, it throws a monkey wrench into the operation of all the other machines" [1968, p.12].

Of all the markets in the economy, which one does the New Orthodoxy single out for "control"? — the market for money! Instead of the quantity of money and its price (the rate of interest) being determined by the forces of a freely competitive market, one or the other is to be "controlled" (a euphemism for "rigged") by a "monetary authority".

It has now become the hallmark of what is regarded as "responsible" macroeconomic policy to keep the economy operating *below* its market potential by throwing a spanner into its monetary works. Inflation is curbed by monetary restrictions which prevent economic activity from reaching the natural level that would otherwise be determined by market forces. At the first signs of economic growth, interest rates are raised *above the market level* from fear of inflation.

When the only policy on offer is stabilisation of the price level by strangulation of the economy, is it any wonder that unemployment continues to soar above its natural market rate?

1984 and All That

Faced with an outcome which was almost the exact opposite of what their theory had predicted, the "economic experts" took refuge in a Newspeak worthy of George Orwell's Ministry of Truth:

FAILURE IS SUCCESS.

The economic policy recommended by the experts had delivered unacceptably high unemployment, miserably low growth and crushingly heavy taxation. To contemplate the possibility of a fundamental error in the textbooks of economic theory was unthinkable. Instead, any government which achieved record levels of unemployment as a result of playing strictly "according to the book" was applauded by the economic experts for the brilliance of its management of the economy.

So successful was the propaganda that *The Economist*, in its issue of September 28th 1991, was able to publish an extraordinary, but entirely accurate, observation:

> "Despite having anything up to one worker in ten on the dole, many a government in Europe can now expect not merely to survive, but to win re-election boasting of its economic prowess."

In 1992, Britain's Conservative Government did just that. The Labour Opposition was left with no choice. It announced its conversion to the New Economic Orthodoxy. The result? — rapturous applause from the economic experts for its new-found economic wisdom. "The party [is] at long last, beginning to sound economically literate" [*The Economist*, May 6th 1995]. An essential pre-condition for its landslide victory in the election of May 1997 was a pledge, not to abandon the disastrous monetary policy of its predecessor, but to maintain it.

New Labour: Same Old Economics?

Within a week of taking office, the new Chancellor had accomplished what the monetarist zealots could only dream of: the privatisation of interest-rate policy under an independent committee of the Bank of England. Responsibility for throwing spanners into the monetary works was taken away from politicians liable to be deflected by short-term electoral considerations; it was delivered into the safe-keeping of unelected experts less likely to flinch from inflicting serious long-term damage on the economy.

Economic Trench Warfare

During the 1914-18 War, the generals were similarly blind to the senselessness of their military strategy. The enormous casualties spurred them on, not to abandon the strategy, but to pursue it even more relentlessly. Eventually, the lessons were learned and the appalling mistakes of the First World War were not repeated during the Second.

Seventeen years of high unemployment and low growth are, however, not sufficient to persuade "expert" economic opinion to question the strategy of throwing monetary spanners into the economic works. On the contrary, now that unemployment has been "reduced" to only three times what used to be regarded as intolerably high, and economic growth has "increased" to less than half of what used to be regarded as miserable, the strategy is hailed by its sponsors as a brilliant success.

A bird trapped in a greenhouse displays similar acumen. When the strategy of hurling itself through the glass succeeds only in causing injury, it dashes its body against the panes with even greater ferocity. Eventually, after battering itself senseless, it sinks exhausted to the ground. As it drags its shattered body to freedom — through the doorway which has been open all the time — it celebrates the success of its strategy (no doubt to a chorus of approval from the IMF).

Such is the nature of the logic, by which "expert" economic opinion is able to persuade the politicians to continue:–

(1) throwing monetary spanners into the works;

and (2) trying to lubricate the economy out of second gear.

The Stranglehold of Classical "Single-Gear" Economics

The analogy drawn in Keynes's *General Theory* "between the sway of the classical school of economic theory and that of certain religions" [1936, p.350] is something of an understatement. Economics is not *like* a religion; it *is* a religion.

The classical "single-gear" view that unemployment cannot occur in the ideal conditions of perfectly competitive market-clearing equilibrium has become an Article of Religious Faith which is shared by *all* shades of economic opinion — Orthodox and non-Orthodox. It is true that the policy conflicts between the rival sects can be extremely bitter; but they are disputes over the *relevance* of the theory to the real world — not over its *logic*. That the logic of the theory is not questioned even by Keynes is made clear in his declaration that "our criticism of the accepted classical theory of economics has consisted not so much in finding logical flaws in its analysis as in pointing out that its tacit assumptions are seldom or never satisfied" [1936, p.378].

The object of *Economics Through the Looking-Glass* is to break the stranglehold of classical "single-gear" economics by proving that there *is* a logical flaw in its analysis. The fundamental error lies in the failure to recognise that a monetary economy is a "multi-gear" machine.

Unemployment *can* occur in ideal conditions of perfectly competitive market-clearing equilibrium. In addition to the *natural rate* of unemployment which varies with the degree of market imperfection, there is a possibility of an *equilibrium rate* of unemployment — in the genuine *market-clearing* sense.

According to classical "single-gear" theory, unemployment is a problem because we do not live in a Utopia of continuous market-clearing equilibrium free from what Phelps calls "informational and organizational imperfections" [1994, p.247n]. According to the "multi-gear" alternative, unemployment would still be a problem *even if we did!*

The policy implications are enormous. In order to operate at its full employment potential, the multi-gear economy requires more than the lubrication of competition; it needs to be in top gear. The danger of monetary restriction as a remedy for inflation is its power to shift the gear-lever downwards.

In terms of economic potential, the British economy is one of the most powerful in the world. It is better lubricated than at any time during the last half century. It is also better lubricated than many other economies (including the Japanese). Britain's disappointing performance during the 1980s and 1990s *in spite of vast improvements in market flexibility* illustrates a simple fact of life. No economy, however industrious its work-force, however enterprising its business managers, can avoid being overtaken, if it is handicapped by a macroeconomic policy that keeps it stuck in second gear.

The British economy will never realise its enormous potential until it is released from the stranglehold of "single-gear" economics.

Plan of the Book

The disastrous consequences of the New Economic Orthodoxy are described in Part I — ***the Dismal Science***. The cost of throwing spanners into the monetary works during the 1980s is put at *more than double* the cost of the property destruction inflicted on the British mainland by enemy action during the whole of the Second World War. So catastrophic was the effect on the economy that, had it not been for the windfall of North Sea Oil, Britain's average rate of growth during the 1980s would have been *negative*. One consequence is that, throughout the 1980s, Britain suffered the greatest burden of taxation ever experienced during the whole of its peacetime history.

Part II — ***Religion and the Rise of "Monetarism"*** — chronicles the development of economics, not as a science, but as a religion devoted to the false doctrine of the economy as a single-gear machine.

Part III is ***A Young Person's Guide to Economic Theory*** which explores (without the aid of complex mathematics) the microeconomic foundations of macroeconomic theory, and shows that, on the contrary, a monetary economy is a multi-gear machine. The Orthodox view that "the theory of unemployment ... requires a non-Walrasian model in which there is no Walrasian auctioneer continuously clearing commodity and labor markets" [Phelps (1968) p.30] is proved to be false by a simple demonstration that unemployment can occur *even if a Walrasian auctioneer is in charge*.

Part IV answers the question ***What's Wrong with Economic Theory?*** by identifying the various errors in Classical, Keynesian, and Monetarist economics.

A fresh start is made in Part V with the unravelling of the religious mythology — from modern monetarism all the way back to Adam Smith — in an examination of ***Economics Through the Looking-Glass*** which reveals that most of the labels mean the opposite of what they say.

Part VI continues the Looking-Glass journey ***Back to the Future*** in order to demonstrate that greater progress can be made by travelling *backwards* in time from Adam Smith to the "multi-gear" economic realism of the seventeenth century than by travelling *forwards* to the "single-gear" economic fallacies of the twentieth.

The Epilogue ***Is Full Employment Dead?*** comes to the optimistic conclusion that it is not. But, before it can be fully restored to life, "monetarist" interventionism must be repudiated and its place taken by a *laissez-faire* economic policy for ***Full Employment Without Inflation in a "Multi-Gear" Economy*** — which is the title of the next volume.

It is not possible to investigate the multi-gear alternative, however, until the flaws in the single-gear theory of the New Economic Orthodoxy have been clearly exposed. That is the task of this volume.

Before venturing into the Looking-Glass world of Orthodox economic theory, the reader is given fair warning. Economics may be a glorious religion, but, as Thomas Carlyle is supposed to have remarked, it is a "Dismal Science".

PART I

THE DISMAL SCIENCE

CHAPTER 1

THE END OF ECONOMIC CIVILIZATION AS WE KNOW IT

On 10th April 1975, the following obituary appeared in the columns of the *Times* newspaper. "The age of full employment is over ... the price ... quite simply ... accelerating and ultimately explosive inflation ... is too high."

What looked at the time like a brilliant triumph for Marxist propaganda was secured, not by the authors of some sinister conspiracy to discredit the free enterprise system, but by the most passionate of the self-proclaimed disciples of Adam Smith.

So successful were their efforts, that the average percentage of the total labour force out of work throughout the OECD countries in the 1980s was more than double its level of the 1960s. The damage to British industry caused by high unemployment during the 1980s was almost double the cost of the destruction caused by enemy bombing during the whole of the Second World War.*

The achievement is all the more remarkable in view of the difficulty in finding any political party which is actually in favour of high unemployment. On the contrary, one of the few issues over which there is wide agreement across the whole political spectrum is the desirability of full employment without inflation. If an effective policy for price stability and full employment were available, there would be no shortage of politicians eager to pursue it. However strenuously economists seek to evade responsibility, the failure of economic policy is directly attributable, not to lack of will on the part of politicians, but to errors of logic in the textbooks of economic theory.

Economic theory is often criticised on the ground that it applies to an ideal world of perfectly competitive markets — a world which is far removed from the experience of real life. Yet there is no harm in assuming ideal conditions — however completely they are divorced from reality. In the natural sciences, successful theories have been developed on the assumption of perfect vacuums, zero gravity, and frictionless bearings — even though no such phenomena are experienced in the real world. The problems of economics remain unsolved, not because economists are preoccupied with an ideal world, but because their explanation of the ideal world is hopelessly mistaken.

---

* See p.26 below.

In the face of a critical shortage of labour, which is becoming progressively more acute for the demographic reason of an ageing population, any waste of labour in unemployment is criminally irresponsible. It is like pouring away precious water in a desert.

The obituary needs to be rephrased more honestly. "The age of full employment is over … the vested intellectual interest in false economic theory is too powerful."

Errors of logic in the textbooks of economic theory are more than a matter of academic regret; they are directly responsible for two of the most serious violations of economic law and order — unemployment and inflation.

CHAPTER 2

THE BREAKDOWN OF LAW AND ORDER

It all seemed to be going so well.

The nineteen-thirties had not been without their economic difficulties; but there were two economic essentials upon which Britain could always depend: Bank rate at 2% and Scotch Whisky at 12/6d a bottle.

In the period following the Second World War,* unemployment seemed to have found a natural level of just over 1% of the labour force. After a hiccup in the early 1950s caused by the Korean War, inflation (expressed as an annual change in the consumer price index) settled down below 2%.

Then came 1956 and the Suez Crisis. The effect on the British economy was cataclysmic. Inflation soared to 4%. Wages went through the roof — to a weekly average in manufacturing industry of no less than £9.18.6. With Scotch Whisky approaching £2 a bottle, the natives began to fear that the End of the World was Nigh. Their worst fears were confirmed in the panic of September 1958 when Bank rate was raised to the crisis level of 7%. Unemployment got completely out of hand; at almost 2% of the labour force, there were over 450,000 people on the dole. Marxists gleefully proclaimed the beginning of the Collapse of Capitalism.

But there was one abiding comfort. No civilised government would let unemployment rise above half-a-million. The Marxists had no answer to that; for, deep down in their hearts, they knew it was true.

Unemployment was no longer a political issue. Economic science had the problem under control. The bad old days of the 1920s and 1930s were gone for ever.

The Bad Old Days

In the decade following the First World War, unemployment at 7%, 8%, or 9% of the total labour force became common.† But that was before the discovery of macroeconomics.

---

* The six year altercation with some of our European partners produced in the economic statistics what would now be called a "blip". It may, however, bear some responsibility for the first great post-war economic trauma: the 1949 devaluation of the £ sterling from $4.03 to $2.80.

† The high levels of unemployment during the 1920s were the result of *bad* economic management and should, on no account, be confused with the even higher levels during the 1980s which were (so we are told) the result of *good* economic management.

Table 2.1
Inflation and Unemployment in the United Kingdom from 1900 to 1959

1900s	1900	1901	1902	1903	1904	1905	1906	1907	1908	1909	AVERAGE
	%	%	%	%	%	%	%	%	%	%	%
Inflation	5.3	0.4	0.1	0.2	-0.1	0.3	0.0	1.3	0.3	0.6	0.8
Unemployment	2.5	3.3	4.0	4.7	6.0	5.0	3.6	3.7	7.8	7.7	4.8
1910s	**1910**	**1911**	**1912**	**1913**	**1914**	**1915**	**1916**	**1917**	**1918**	**1919**	**AVERAGE**
	%	%	%	%	%	%	%	%	%	%	%
Inflation	0.8	0.1	3.0	-0.4	-0.3	12.6	18.0	25.3	22.0	10.1	8.7
Unemployment	4.7	3.0	3.3	2.1	3.3	1.1	0.4	0.6	0.8	3.4	2.3
1920s	**1920**	**1921**	**1922**	**1923**	**1924**	**1925**	**1926**	**1927**	**1928**	**1929**	**AVERAGE**
	%	%	%	%	%	%	%	%	%	%	%
Inflation	15.4	-8.6	-14.0	-6.0	-0.8	0.4	-0.7	-2.4	-0.2	-0.9	-2.0
Unemployment	2.0	11.3	9.8	8.1	7.2	7.9	8.8	6.8	7.5	7.3	7.7
1930s	**1930**	**1931**	**1932**	**1933**	**1934**	**1935**	**1936**	**1937**	**1938**	**1939**	**AVERAGE**
	%	%	%	%	%	%	%	%	%	%	%
Inflation	-2.8	-4.3	-2.6	-2.1	-0.1	0.7	0.7	3.4	1.5	6.4	0.0
Unemployment	11.2	15.1	15.6	14.1	11.9	11.0	9.4	7.8	9.3	5.8	11.1
1940s	**1940**	**1941**	**1942**	**1943**	**1944**	**1945**	**1946**	**1947**	**1948**	**1949**	**AVERAGE**
	%	%	%	%	%	%	%	%	%	%	%
Inflation	16.6	10.8	7.2	3.3	2.7	2.9	3.1	7.1	6.2	2.3	6.1
Unemployment	3.3	1.2	0.5	0.4	0.4	0.5	1.9	1.4	1.3	1.2	1.2
1950s	**1950**	**1951**	**1952**	**1953**	**1954**	**1955**	**1956**	**1957**	**1958**	**1959**	**AVERAGE**
	%	%	%	%	%	%	%	%	%	%	%
Inflation	2.6	9.4	6.0	2.0	1.9	3.5	4.6	3.4	2.7	0.6	3.6
Unemployment	1.3	1.1	1.6	1.5	1.2	1.0	1.1	1.3	1.9	1.9	1.4

Source: Inflation (annual % change in consumer prices); Unemployment (% of the total labour force): C.H.Feinstein, *National Income, Expenditure and Output of the United Kingdom 1855-1965*, Cambridge: 1972.

So great was the progress made by economic science during the 1930s, however, that after the Second World War it was possible to avoid the mistakes made in the aftermath of the First.

Then in the 1960s came a major theoretical breakthrough.

Historically, unemployment had normally been accompanied by falling prices, and inflation had normally been accompanied by falling unemployment. It was either one thing or the other — inflation or unemployment. But the new economics made possible, throughout the 1980s, the consistent achievement of both together — a feat which has been hailed in some quarters as the "economic miracle".

The Economic Miracle

During the past thirty years, the British economy has experienced an unremitting cycle of inflation and unemployment.

Table 2.2
Inflation and Unemployment in the United Kingdom from 1960

1960s	1960	1961	1962	1963	1964	1965	1966	1967	1968	1969	AVERAGE
	%	%	%	%	%	%	%	%	%	%	%
Inflation [1]	1.0	3.6	4.1	2.1	3.2	4.8	3.9	2.4	4.7	5.5	3.5
Unemployment [2]	1.3	1.2	1.6	2.0	2.6	2.0	2.1	3.1	3.1	2.9	2.2
1970s	**1970**	**1971**	**1972**	**1973**	**1974**	**1975**	**1976**	**1977**	**1978**	**1979**	**AVERAGE**
	%	%	%	%	%	%	%	%	%	%	%
Inflation	6.4	9.4	7.1	9.2	15.9	24.2	16.5	15.9	8.2	13.5	12.5
Unemployment	3.0	3.6	4.0	3.0	2.9	4.3	5.6	6.0	5.9	5.0	4.3
1980s	**1980**	**1981**	**1982**	**1983**	**1984**	**1985**	**1986**	**1987**	**1988**	**1989**	**AVERAGE**
	%	%	%	%	%	%	%	%	%	%	%
Inflation	18.0	11.9	8.6	4.6	5.0	6.1	3.4	4.1	4.9	7.8	7.4
Unemployment	6.4	9.8	11.3	12.4	11.7	11.2	11.2	10.3	8.6	7.2	10.0
1990s	**1990**	**1991**	**1992**	**1993**	**1994**	**1995**	**1996**	**1997**	**1998**	**1999**	**AVERAGE**
	%	%	%	%	%	%	%	%	%	%	%
Inflation	9.5	5.9	3.7	1.6	2.4	3.5	2.4				4.1
Unemployment	6.9	8.8	10.1	10.4	9.6	8.7	8.2				9.0

Sources: 1. Inflation (annual % change in the Consumer Price Index). *International Financial Statistics Yearbook*. New York: IMF.
2. Unemployment (standardised annual unemployment rates as a % of the total labour force). *Labour Force Statistics*. Paris: OECD.

The labels "unemployment" and "inflation" are perhaps misleading; they suggest diseases which societies "catch" by chance or by "infection" from abroad. There are other labels which might be more appropriate.

Just as assault and theft are crimes by individuals against society, so inflation and unemployment are crimes by society against individuals. Unemployment robs them of their income; inflation robs them of their savings.

Inflation: The Sting

Individuals who wish to get themselves mugged, do not have to venture out into the streets. It can be arranged in the comfort of their own home. All they have to do is invest their savings in any bank, building society, life insurance company, or financial institution of their choice.

According to *A Survey of Britain's Savings Institutions* made by *The Economist* [November 29, 1975, p.4], "in the 18 months to mid-1975 Britons with any savings lost a quarter of the real value of their personally-held financial wealth. Over 35 billion was taken from them by inflation."

£35,000 million sounds rather a lot. As a matter of fact, it is rather a lot. It is the equivalent of 17,500 Great Train Robberies — or one every three-quarters of an hour, throughout the whole of the 18 month period.* Keynes refers to inflation as "taxation by currency depreciation" [1923, p.9]. By comparison, the whole of the revenue from both personal and corporate taxation levied *openly* during the same period amounted to less than £20,000 million.

Now, that £35,000 million — and all the other millions which preceded and followed — did not simply disappear from the face of the earth. Inflation is not like unemployment. Wealth is not lost; it is merely redistributed. To the community as a whole, the cost is zero. One person's loss of purchasing power is another person's gain. It is "merely" redistribution — just like mugging. The main operators are burglars and the financial institutions. But, on the whole, the financial institutions are more skilful.†

According to Section 16 of the Theft Act 1968:-

"(1) A person who by any deception dishonestly obtains for himself or another any pecuniary advantage shall on conviction on indictment be liable to imprisonment for a term not exceeding five years.

(2) The cases in which a pecuniary advantage within the meaning of this section is to be regarded as obtained for a person are cases where —

(a) any debt or charge for which he makes himself liable or is or may become liable (including one not legally enforceable) is reduced or in whole or in part evaded or deferred; ..."

One of the less publicised success stories of the past twenty-five years is the extent to which the savings institutions and other organisations have managed, in the words of the Theft Act, to "reduce or evade" the debt for which they are liable. The "Pecuniary Advantage" secured for property investors at the expense of small savers reached its peak in 1973-1975 with the £35,000 million mentioned by *The Economist* — not a bad haul for 18 months' work.

* For those too young to remember, the Great Train Robbers were a bunch of amateurs who, in 1963, got away with a measly £2 million.

† In spite of massive productivity gains achieved during the 1980s (which were the envy of all other sectors of the economy), British burglars still lagged way behind the financial institutions. According to the Association of British Insurers, estimated insurance claims in the UK for 1989 (at current prices) were:- Commercial Theft £167.9 million, Domestic Theft £276.4 million, and Motor Theft £290.8 million [*Insurance Statistics 1985-89* p.30].

But there was always the threat of prosecution under section 16 paragraph (2)(a) of the Theft Act. Changes in English Law normally take a generation to accomplish — if not centuries. In this case, a remedy was found with unaccustomed speed. The offending paragraph was repealed by section 5(5) of a new Theft Act, which came into force on 20th October 1978. Section 2(2) of the new Act restricted "liability" to mean "legally enforceable liability". The managers of other people's savings could, once again, sleep easily in their beds.

The lawyers may have moved with commendable speed, but the politicians moved even faster.

Inflation: The Cover-Up

The advantage to the government of "inflation as a method of taxation" is obvious. "A Government can live by this means when it can live by no other. It is the form of taxation which the public find hardest to evade and even the weakest Government can enforce, when it can enforce nothing else" [Keynes (1923) p.41]. It is a means which has been exploited by both the major political parties when in office and condemned by both the major political parties when in opposition. But it is essential to the success of this type of operation that its true extent is concealed from the general public. "The owners of small savings suffer quietly, as experience shows, these enormous depredations, when they would have thrown down a Government which had taken from them a fraction of the amount by more deliberate but juster instruments" [Keynes (1923) p.65]. "Inflation has been irresistibly attractive to sovereigns because it is a hidden tax ... that can be imposed without specific legislation. It is truly taxation without representation" [Friedman (1974a) p.13].

It was therefore of the utmost importance to prevent the electorate from receiving accurate information on the enormity of the consequences. Unfortunately, the Accounting Standards Steering Committee (representing the British Professional Accountancy bodies) was about to spill the beans. Its *(Provisional) Statement of Standard Accounting Practice No.7*, entitled "Accounting for changes in the purchasing power of money", was already in the hands of the printers. One of the main features of its recommended system of "Current Purchasing Power accounting" would have been to report the effect of "taxation by currency depreciation". Worse still, savers would inevitably have demanded the same right as companies to deduct purchasing-power losses from their taxable income.

To forestall this dire threat to National Security, the government took decisive action to nip it in the bud. In January 1974, a Committee of Enquiry was set up under the chairmanship of F.E.P.Sandilands to consider the question of Inflation Accounting. The Committee was appointed by a Conservative administration with the approval of the Labour opposition. Its report was accepted by a Labour administration with the approval of the Conservative opposition.

The Sandilands Committee did its work well — though not without some anxious moments. It had got off to an admittedly shaky start when it let slip that "the value (or 'purchasing power') of money as a medium of exchange changes in inverse proportion to the changes in price of the items on which it is spent" [para.40]. But it recovered quickly and was able to recommend a system of accounting which maintained the principle that "the value of £5,000 cash is always £5,000, and no gain or loss arises in isolation from holding it through time" [para.429].

Neither the £35,000 million taken from the British public during the 18 months to mid-1975 would therefore have to be reported, nor would the "enormous depredations" suffered both before and since. The consequences of inflation were to be concealed "at a stroke". What is more, the system of accounting necessary to engineer so complete a cover-up had taken the Committee only 17 months to construct.

Changes to the system of accounting normally take even longer than changes to English law. The traditional system of "Historical Cost accounting" goes back to the fifteenth century, and unsuccessful calls for reform have been continuing, on and off, ever since. It is not surprising that a report produced at such a relatively breakneck speed should have one or two rough edges. The Sandilands Committee does, in fact, concede that there are exceptional circumstances in which its recommended system of accounting is unsafe: "in times of rising prices" [para.478] and "when prices are rising" [para.544].*

The *Report on Inflation Accounting* makes a valuable point which is not always properly appreciated. It is absolutely true that "the value of £5,000 cash is always £5,000"; and, provided that people don't do anything silly, it is also true that "no gain or loss arises in isolation from holding it through time." As long as the money is used for something sensible like papering the ceiling or lighting cigars, then £5,000 will always cover the same area of ceiling or (provided that the notes are kept dry) light the same number of cigars. It is only if money is used for peculiar purposes — like buying things — that the possibility of a loss in purchasing power arises. To be fair to the Committee, paragraph 40 of the *Report* does make an exception in cases where money is used "as a medium of exchange".

---

* It may sound carping to criticise, but in some quarters this is regarded as a serious handicap for a system which purports to account for inflation.

Nevertheless, there are individuals misguided enough to save money with the object of spending it in the future, and for them the purchasing power loss can be extremely distressing.

It is not simply a question of the ravages of double-digit inflation — "£1 to a penny in 20 years" would require a 26% per annum rate of inflation. Single-digit inflation, though undoubtedly preferable to the double-digit variety, can do plenty of damage.

Some idea of the destructive power of inflation is given in Table 2.3.

Table 2.3: The Destructive Power of Inflation

Annual Rate of Inflation	Time that it Takes to Reduce the Purchasing Power of Money:– by 1/4	by 1/3	by 1/2	by 2/3	by 3/4
%	*years*	*years*	*years*	*years*	*years*
2½	11¾	16½	28	44½	56
5	6	8¼	14¼	22½	28½
10	3	4¼	7¼	11½	14½
15	2	3	5	8	10
20	1½	2¼	3¾	6	7½
25	1¼	1¾	3	5	6¼

At 10% per annum, inflation takes only 7¼ years to deprive money of half of its purchasing power, and 14½ years to reduce it by three-quarters. At 5% per annum, it takes just over 14 years to cut the purchasing power of money in half. If inflation is "held down" to what during the 1997 election emerged as the "consensus" target rate of 2½% per annum, any money saved will have lost a quarter of its purchasing power in less than 12 years; by the end of a 45 year career, it will have lost as much as two-thirds.

But these figures are hypothetical. Table 2.4, which shows what has *actually* happened to "the pound in your pocket", is, if anything, even more frightening.

£1 put in the pocket in 1950 would, if spent in 1990, have bought no more than 7p (less than 1/6d) would have bought in 1950; it had lost 93% of its purchasing power.

More to the point, the table shows that, during both the 1950s and the 1960s, the destruction of purchasing power was about one-third, but during the 1970s it was nearly three-quarters. The 1980s saw a vast improvement compared with the 1970s, but, even so, in spite of desperate efforts to cure inflation, the purchasing power of money was almost halved.

Table 2.4: "The Pound in Your Pocket"

Date when £1 was "put in the pocket"	Purchasing Power of the same £1 (in terms of prices when the £1 was "put in the pocket")			
	Jan.1960	Jan.1970	Jan.1980	Jan.1990
January 1950	67p	46p	13p	7p
January 1960		69p	20p	10p
January 1970			28p	15p
January 1980				52p

Source: *Retail Prices 1914-1990*. London: Central Statistical Office, 1991.

Figure 2.1: Inflation in the United Kingdom

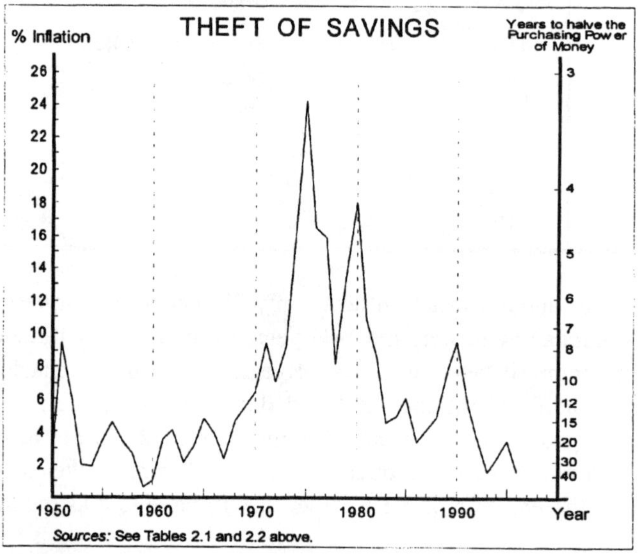

Another period like the 1980s, never mind the 1970s, and £ notes really would have been the cheapest way of papering the ceiling. That, presumably, is why the £1 note was withdrawn from circulation and replaced by a coin.*

By comparison with previous periods, the 1990s have experienced a great improvement. There is now a serious danger that the electorate can be hoodwinked into believing that inflation kept down to a target of 2½% per annum is not merely acceptable but a triumph of economic policy. To rob savings of half of their purchasing power does not turn into

* The £1 coin was introduced on April 21st 1983, and the £1 note was withdrawn on 11th March 1988.

a justifiable policy simply because the process now takes as long as 28 years.

The losses inflicted on law-abiding citizens by criminal activity cannot match the amounts stolen from them by inflation — even when the annual rate is as "low" as 2½%.

There is no doubt about it: inflation is ***a bad thing***. It causes an unjust redistribution of wealth within the community. But unemployment is worse since it causes loss of wealth to the community as a whole. Indeed, the ultimate evil of inflation is that, because it makes the holding of existing real wealth more profitable than the production of new wealth, it eventually leads to an increase in the level of unemployment.

Inflation causes the cake to be sliced unfairly; unemployment reduces its size.

Inflation, like mugging, makes sense — to those who benefit.

Unemployment, by contrast, makes no sense at all. No one gains; everyone loses. The waste of economic potential represents wanton destruction of wealth. It is sheer economic vandalism.

CHAPTER 3

IT CAME FROM OUTER SPACE

There is something rather odd about unemployment. Nobody knows where it came from.

It seems to have started in the mid-'seventies and infected the big industrial economies, almost without exception. Table 3.1 summarises the experience of "The Group of Seven" countries during the last three decades.

Table 3.1: Inflation and Unemployment in "The Group of Seven"

	INFLATION[1]				UNEMPLOYMENT[2]			
	1960s %	1970s %	1980s %	1990-96 %	1960s %	1970s %	1980s %	1990-96 %
Britain	3.5	12.5	7.4	4.1	2.2	4.3	10.0	9.0
Canada	2.5	7.3	6.5	2.5	4.8	6.7	9.3	10.1
France	3.9	8.9	7.2	2.4	1.7	3.8	9.0	11.0
Germany	2.4	4.9	2.9	1.7	0.8	2.3	5.9	6.7
Italy	3.4	12.3	11.2	5.1	5.0	6.3	9.5	10.7
Japan	5.4	9.0	2.5	1.4	1.3	1.7	2.5	2.6
United States	2.3	7.1	5.5	3.4	4.7	6.1	7.2	6.2

1. Inflation (annual average % change in the Consumer Price Index). *International Financial Statistics Yearbook.* New York: IMF.

2. Unemployment (standardised annual unemployment rates as a % of the total labour force). *Quarterly Labour Force Statistics.* Paris: OECD.

In every single country in the Group of Seven, unemployment was higher in the 1970s than in the 1960s, and it was higher in the 1980s and 1990s than it was in the 1970s.

The explanation favoured by most world leaders is that the higher unemployment experienced in their countries is not the fault of their own economic policy; it is the result of a phenomenon called "the world recession". Since categorical assurances have been given (on the very highest authority) that this phenomenon is not the responsibility of any government on Earth, it can only be the result of Extra-Terrestrial forces engaged in a brutal orgy of inter-galactic destruction.

Due, no doubt, to its exposed position on the Earth's crust, Britain has been particularly vulnerable to this form of cosmic attack. Japan, which has the good fortune to be situated in a sheltered area of the globe, has been well shielded.

There are scientists who are hoping that careful analysis of the incidence of unemployment in various countries will enable them to pinpoint precisely the part of the universe from which it emanates. Others are working on the theory that it is seeping through the hole in the ozone layer. The only practicable solution so far considered, however, is to relocate the British Isles out of harm's way — somewhere in the Pacific where there is plenty of room. But, for obvious reasons, this is out of the question: it would infringe the Treaty of Rome and jeopardise Britain's membership of the European Union.

Fortunately, empirical research has come to the rescue.

Figure 3.1 provides conclusive proof of the "ozone layer theory of unemployment". As the hole in the ozone layer increased from the mid-seventies to the mid-eighties, so did unemployment. The empirical evidence is irrefutable. As soon as the offending chlorofluorcarbons were removed from the nation's hair-sprays, the effect on unemployment was an immediate and dramatic fall.

Figure 3.1: Unemployment in the United Kingdom

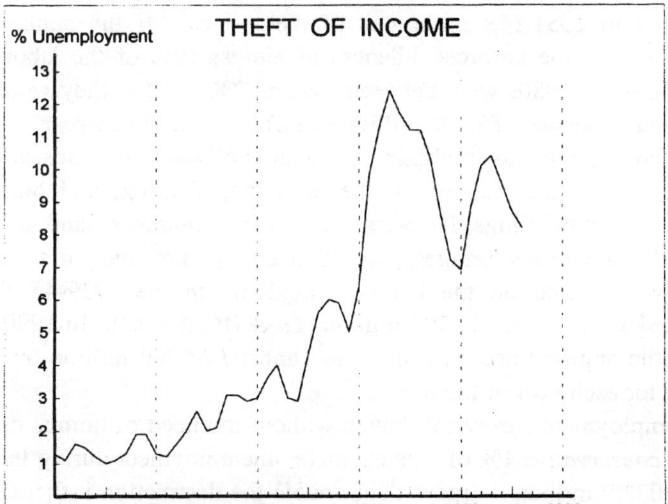

Sources: See Tables 2.1 and 2.2 above.

We now have the definitive solution to the problem of unemployment. It was there all the time, if only we had known it — in our aerosol cans.

Unemployment: The Sting

The economic cost of unemployment is almost impossible to measure.

It is a simple matter to add up all the social security payments made to those out of work. The advantage of this method is that the total can be calculated accurately to the last penny. Unfortunately, that total is not a measure of the real cost of unemployment; it is simply the sum of the transfer payments made by the employed section of the community to those who have no jobs. The real cost to the community as a whole is the output which is lost — the goods and services which would have been produced if the unemployed had been at work. Fortunately for the politicians, it is impossible to put a precise figure on what-might-have-been-but-wasn't. Any attempt to do so is pure speculation; and the trouble with pure speculation is that it can too easily be dismissed as pure speculation.

Since there is no other method available, it may be worth giving pure speculation a try.

According to Table 1.1 of the *United Kingdom National Accounts* published in *The Blue Book 1997*, Gross Domestic Product in 1990 amounted to £551,118 million at market prices. If the annual losses resulting from the enforced idleness of almost 10% of the labour force throughout the 1980s were between 1% and 2% of GDP, they would have amounted to between £5,000 million and £10,000 million a year.

In a book written to emphasise the ravages of war, the "colossal amount of damage on land caused by the bombing, shelling, and burning of houses, public buildings, factories, warehouses, churches, land and crops, railways, waterworks, bridges, gas and electricity stations, ports, and other property" inflicted on the United Kingdom "in the 1939-45 War" is estimated at just under £1,300 million [Enock (1951) p.108]. In 1990 prices, that is the approximate equivalent to almost £24,000 million, or £4,000 million for each year of the war.

Unemployment can wreak havoc without the need of bombs or shells. On the *conservative* 1% of GDP estimate, unemployment during the 1980s cost £50,000 million — more than *double* the destruction inflicted on the British mainland by enemy action during the whole of the Second World War.

Part of the bill has been paid openly: during the 1980s, Britain suffered the greatest increase in taxation in its peacetime history:-

Figure 3.2: The Ever-Increasing Tax Burden

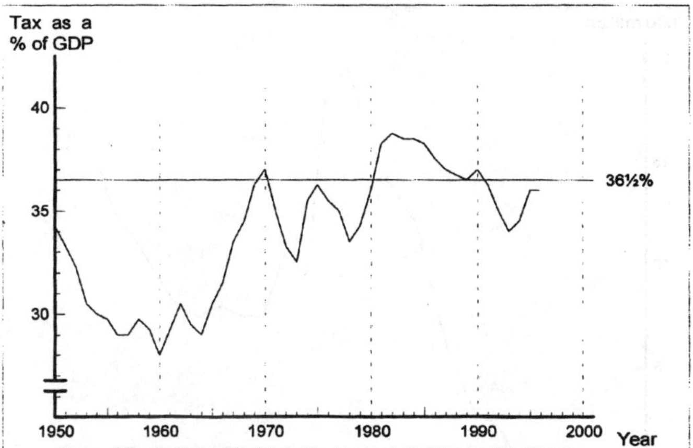

Source: Office for National Statistics. *The Blue Book 1997* (and earlier editions).

The record increase in the tax burden is remarkable because it occurred under an administration dedicated to reducing the economic role of the state. It is even more remarkable that, in spite of being an all-time record, it is actually understated. It has been camouflaged by a significant shift of responsibility (for services like health and education) from the public sector to private individuals. Such a shift would otherwise have produced a significant *fall* in the tax burden.

But the true extent of the damage has been covered-up by the greatest windfall in British history.

Unemployment: The Cover-up

The name of the cover-up is North Sea Oil.

The contribution made by "Extraction of Mineral Oil and Natural Gas" to the Gross Domestic Product was negligible before 1976. But it constituted over 4% of GDP throughout the 1980s. Expressed in terms of 1990 GDP, it was worth well in excess of £20,000 million a year.

Figure 3.3: Contribution of North Sea Oil and Gas to United Kingdom GDP

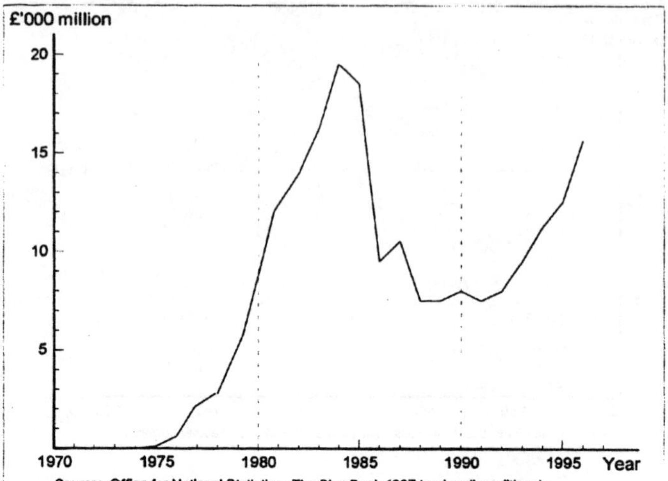

Source: Office for National Statistics. *The Blue Book 1997* (and earlier editions).

Whose Fault is it Anyway?

Politicians can be irritating people — often intensely so. But, appearances notwithstanding, they do not set out deliberately to inflict wilful economic damage on the national economy.

If it is not the fault of the politicians, whose fault is it?

Before the discovery that unemployment came from outer space, there was a quaint but persistent rumour, admittedly far-fetched, that unemployment had something to do with economic policy.

The shocking truth can now be revealed.

Britain has fallen into the hands of a tiny minority of wreckers, subject to no form of democratic election and owing allegiance to alien dogma … the "Economists".

CHAPTER 4

THE DISMAL SCIENCE

"Cur'd yesterday of my disease, I died last night of my physician."
Matthew Prior *The Remedy Worse than the Disease*

To most of us, a dirty nappy is the natural by-product of a normal healthy baby. To an economist, it is a serious health hazard. If nothing is done, it can breed infection and in extreme cases may even result in death.

The first priority is to devise a cure.

But economists are a notoriously quarrelsome breed. During the 1960s, controversy was at its height.

The "monetarists", after painstaking empirical research, had discovered a close correlation between the amount of food fed in at one end of the baby and the amount of mess expelled at the other. With impeccable logic, they recommended control of the baby's food supply by careful monitoring of significant food aggregates (which went under esoteric labels like F_1, F_2, and F_3).

The "prices-and-incomes-controllers" disagreed. Cutting down baby's food supply had undesirable side-effects: it cut down baby's growth. Their alternative was not to stop feeding the baby but to prevent the unpleasant consequences from emerging by clamping its legs together. Although this approach avoided starving the baby, it was not without its drawbacks. By restricting the baby's movement, it hampered its development. Worse still, it was only a temporary expedient. The nappy could be kept clean for a time, but, when the internal pressure could no longer be contained, the consequences were explosive.

Nappy changing was naturally rejected out of hand by the economists as a superficial expedient which merely treated the symptoms and did nothing to remove the cause. The debate could therefore be continued over fundamental issues — namely, which end of the baby should be blocked up.

The outcome of the debate was a choice of evils — between distorting the child's development and stunting its growth.

Professional economists are rarely consulted on matters of child care. That is good news for babies; but it is bad news for economies.

Economies also dirty their nappies, particularly during periods of rapid technological progress (like the transition from agriculture to manufacturing and from manufacturing to services) which cannot be accomplished without fairly drastic social change. Conflict may arise over relative shares, as badly placed individuals (or countries) seek to "catch up" and well placed individuals (or countries) seek to "maintain differentials"; and it may manifest itself in the desire of the community as a whole to consume more than it produces.

The mess can seep out in various ways. In economies under highly centralised control, it shows up in shortages, queues, rationing, and black markets. In tightly regimented societies whose members "know their place", or in communities able to take advantage of underprivileged groups, the seepage may be contained. Where scope is allowed for market forces, educational opportunity, and political freedom, the result is a more or less rapid rise in the general level of prices. And the mess in the nappy is called "inflation".

There is a temptation to regard price stability as normal. But that is contradicted by historical experience. Such periods are exceptional. During the 1970s, however, the fact that many foreign nappies were much cleaner than ours caused acute distress to those whose main preoccupation was with the laundry bills. From the point of view of the long term health of the child, it may be worth inquiring whether clean nappies are a sign of good economic manners or whether they are a symptom of social or political constipation.

To attempt to cure a dynamic economy of inflation is rather like trying to cure it of its capacity for responding to social and economic change. It may be that the real problem is not how to prevent inflation but how to allow it to continue.

That may sound absurd. Inflation can be a killer, if it gets out of control. It is held at least partly responsible for the collapse of societies from Imperial Rome to the Weimar Republic.

The infection must not be allowed to spread. But why has it not occurred to the economists that, instead of trying to "cure" their baby of its "disease", they may do less damage by changing its nappy?

The reason is faulty economic analysis.

The legacy of faulty economic theory is faulty economic policy. Ever since the end of the Second World War, the United Kingdom economy has been riding on a merry-go-round of monetary restriction, alternating with prices and incomes control. Over forty years of riding this merry-go-round have produced the acute economic nausea of ever-increasing circles of unemployment and inflation.

The case against government controls over prices and incomes or government controls over the money supply is not that they will not work. The case against them is that they work only too well. They are temporary expedients which suppress the symptoms of inflation without providing a long term cure.

The result is the popular (but mistaken) belief that an annual rate of growth more than 3% is "unsustainable". Had it not been for the misguided policy of containing inflation by strangling economic growth, it might have become clear that an annual rate of growth of less than 5% is "unsustainable" because it falls too far short of Britain's economic potential.

Is Economics a Science?

That is a favourite question to put to students of economics.

The question, however, is meaningless. There is nothing inherent in any subject which confers upon it the status of a "science". It depends entirely on the attitude of its practitioners.

"Is medicine a science?" It all depends. Do the surgeons paint their faces blue, conduct frenzied dances around the patient, and rely on incantations? Or do they use the latest techniques of microsurgery?

Learned economic journals are filled with the equivalent of mediaeval medical disputes over the best way of bleeding the patients to rid them of fever.

As the new millennium approaches, there is a subject of anxious debate: can Britain any longer afford to meet the aspirations of its citizens for improvements in education, transport, health-care, or pensions?

It is a score on which there should be no anxiety. Not only is the British economy fundamentally sound, but it probably has greater potential per capita (in terms of natural resources, climate, cultural and political heritage) than any other — including Japan, Germany, and the United States of America. Its stunted growth is caused not by any disease but by its physicians. For there is no economy on Earth which is powerful enough to withstand the remedies administered by the doctors of the New Economic Orthodoxy.

If Britain had not been held back, bound up in the monetary shackles of curiously misnamed "sound finance", it could easily have managed an average annual growth rate of 4% during the 1980s and 1990s. Its GDP would be 50% higher. 50% more would be available for better roads, schools, hospitals, and pensions. It is at least arguable that the losses inflicted on the British people by faulty economic thinking during the past two decades have exceeded the whole of the losses inflicted by deliberate criminal activity during the past two millennia.

Over half a century ago, Keynes pointed out “the analogy between the sway of the classical school of economic theory and that of certain religions” [1936, p.350].

Today, the analogy seems more appropriate than ever.

PART II

RELIGION AND THE RISE OF MONETARISM

INTRODUCTION

According to orthodox economic opinion, the economy is a single-gear machine which will operate at its full employment potential so long as it is well-oiled with the lubricant of competition. There is no appreciation of the danger that the economy may be in too low a gear, because the orthodox belief is that there are no gears to change.

It is impossible to view the conventional economic wisdom in a proper perspective, however, unless its history is understood, not as the development of a science, but as the establishment of a religion. The history of economic thought makes sense, only when it is recognised as a process of Divine Revelation.

CHAPTER 5

THE REVELATION

The name of the religion is Free Trade. The part of Moses is played by Adam Smith. Mount Sinai is a little place in Scotland called Kirkcaldy.

After wandering in an economic wilderness where human life was governed by the vagaries of the harvest and was haunted by the ever-present spectre of famine and starvation, Mankind was about to enter the Promised Land of the Industrial Revolution. But, first, the People had to cast aside their pagan beliefs. For they were surrounded on every side by idolaters called "Mercantilists" who worshipped at the altar of Protectionism.

The message, revealed to Adam Smith in 1776, is inscribed in the Five Books of his *Inquiry into the Nature and Causes of the Wealth of Nations*.

And These are the Five Books of Smith:*

Book I	Of the Causes of Improvement in the productive Powers of Labour, and of the Order according to which its Produce is naturally distributed among the different Ranks of the People;
Book II	Of the Nature, Accumulation, and Employment of Stock;
Book III	Of the different Progress of Opulence in different Nations;
Book IV	Of Systems of Political Economy;
Book V	Of the Revenue of the Sovereign or Commonwealth.

In the Beginning ...

"In that rude state of society in which there is no division of labour, in which exchanges are seldom made, ... every man provides everything for himself" [II, Introduction]. "Among the savage nations of hunters and fishers, every individual who is able to work, is more or less employed in useful labour, and endeavours to provide, as well as he can, the necessaries and conveniences of life, for himself, or such of his family or tribe as are either too old, or too young, or too infirm to go a hunting and fishing. Such nations, however, are ... miserably poor" [Introduction].

Specialisation and the Division of Labour

"Among civilised and thriving nations, on the contrary, ... a workman, even of the lowest and poorest order, ... may enjoy a greater share of the

* In deference to the Biblical stature of the *Wealth of Nations*, quotations are identified by a Book reference (in Roman numerals) followed by a Chapter reference (in Arabic numerals).

necessaries and conveniences of life than it is possible for any savage to acquire" [Introduction]. "The division of labour ... occasions, in every art, a proportionable increase of the productive powers of labour. ... Each individual becomes more expert in his own peculiar branch, more work is done upon the whole, and the quantity of science is considerably increased by it" [I.1].

Exchange: the Essential Pre-requisite for the Division of Labour

"The separation of different trades and employments from one another seems to have taken place in consequence of this advantage" [I,1]. "But without the disposition to truck, barter, and exchange, every man must have procured to himself every necessary and conveniency of life which he wanted" [I,2]. "As it is the power of exchanging that gives occasion to the division of labour, so the extent of this division must always be limited by the extent of that power, or, in other words, by the extent of the market" [I,3].

"When the division of labour has been once thoroughly established, it is but a very small part of a man's wants which the produce of his own labour can supply. He supplies the far greater part of them by exchanging that surplus part of the produce of his own labour, which is over and above his own consumption, for such parts of the produce of other men's labour as he has occasion for. Every man thus lives by exchanging" [I,4].

Money: the Medium of Exchange

"But if [one man who wishes to purchase the produce of another] should chance to have nothing that [the other] stands in need of, no exchange can be made between them. ... In order to avoid the inconveniency of such situations, every prudent man ... must naturally have endeavoured to ... have at all times by him ... a certain quantity of some one commodity or other, such as he imagined few people would be unlikely to refuse in exchange for the produce of their industry" [I,4].

"In all countries, however, men seem at last to have been determined by irresistible reasons to give the preference, for this employment, to metals above every other commodity. Metals can not only be kept with as little loss as any other commodity, scarce anything being less perishable than they are, but they can likewise, without any loss, be divided into any number of parts, ... the common instrument of commerce [being] gold and silver among all rich and commercial nations. ... The inconveniency and difficulty of weighing those metals with exactness gave occasion to the institution of coins. ... It is in this manner that money has become in all civilised nations the universal instrument of commerce, by the intervention of which goods of all kinds are bought and sold, or exchanged for one another" [I,4].

"Money, therefore, [is] the great wheel of circulation" [II,2].

"The substitution of paper in the room of gold and silver money, replaces a very expensive instrument of commerce with one much less costly, and sometimes equally convenient. Circulation comes to be carried on by a new wheel, which it costs less both to erect and maintain than the old one" [II,2].

Self-Interest: the Motivation for Exchange

Exchange, upon which thriving commerce depends, cannot take place unless it is to the mutual advantage of each party. "It is not from the benevolence of the butcher, the brewer, or the baker, that we expect our dinner, but from their regard to their own interest. We address ourselves, not to their humanity but to their self-love, and never talk to them of our own necessities but of their advantages" [I,2].

Chapter 2 of the Fourth Book of Smith contains the famous Revelation: "Every individual is continually exerting himself to find out the most advantageous employment for whatever capital he can command. It is his own advantage, indeed, and not that of the society, which he has in view. ... He generally, indeed, neither intends to promote the public interest, nor knows how much he is promoting it. ... He intends only his own gain, and he is in this, as in many other cases, led by an invisible hand to promote an end which was no part of his intention. ... By pursuing his own interest he frequently promotes that of the society more effectually than when he really intends to promote it" [IV,2].

The Wealth of Nations remains the Bible of free enterprise.

The story of Adam Smith's encounter with the Holy Spirit of the Market is related in the Economic Scriptures.

"And the Spirit of the Market called Adam Smith up to the top of the mount; and Adam Smith went up. And the Spirit of the Market spake all these words, saying,

1) I am the Spirit of the Market, which have brought thee out of the land of Protectionism, out of the house of bondage. Thou shalt have no other Economic Systems before me.
2) Thou shalt not take unto thee any other Economic Systems, thou shalt not participate in them, nor serve them: for I the Spirit of the Market am a jealous Spirit, visiting poverty and decline upon them that ignore me; and bestowing growth and prosperity upon them that follow me, and keep my commandments.

3) Thou shalt not take the name of the Spirit of the Market in vain; for the Spirit of the Market will not hold him guiltless that taketh his name in vain.
4) Remember the working day, to keep it busy. Six days shalt thou labour and do all thy work. Not until the Sabbath day shalt thou rest. For six days did the Spirit of the Market reserve for production distribution and exchange: wherefore the Spirit of the Market blessed the working week and hallowed it.
5) Provide for thy children and thy grandchildren: that their days may be prosperous in the Economic System which the Spirit of the Market giveth thee.
6) Thou shalt not restrict competition.
7) Thou shalt not raise artificial barriers against international trade.
8) Thou shalt not inflate the supply of money.
9) Thou shalt not levy unjust taxes.
10) Thou shalt not brook any interference in the market place, thou shalt not brook any interference from the government, nor from trades unions, nor from business corporations, nor from professional associations, nor from any thing that interferes with the market.

And all the people saw the wheelings, and the dealings, and the noise of commerce: and when they saw it, they removed, and stood afar off. And they said unto Smith, Speak thou with us, and we will hear: but let not the Spirit of the Market move freely amongst us, lest our economy perish from domestic and foreign competition. And Smith said unto the people, Fear not: for the Spirit of the Market is come to bring ye wealth, if ye sin not."

These ten commandments are The Law of Competition; all the rest is commentary.

The First Commandment: Free-Market Competition

The First Commandment establishes that the most effective forum for transmitting information from the consumer to the producer is the market place. The greater the freedom of competition, the better the communication.

"In general, if any branch of trade, or any division of labour, be advantageous to the public, the freer and more general the competition, it will always be the more so" [II,2]. "The prejudices ... against shopkeepers and tradesmen are altogether without foundation. ... Their competition ... can never hurt either the consumer or the producer; on the contrary, it must tend to make the retailers both sell cheaper and buy dearer than if the whole trade was monopolised by one or two persons" [II,5].

The Second Commandment: against False Alternatives

The second commandment contains a warning against falling into the temptation of believing false claims that there are alternative information systems which can surpass the free play of market forces.

Builders of graven images who bow down before the false god of central planning and worship it above the Spirit of the Market are threatened with retribution "unto the third and fourth generation of them that ignore me" — a threat which, according to believers, was visited, even after 70 years, upon the Union of Soviet Socialist Republics.

"Every system which endeavours, either by extraordinary encouragements to draw towards a particular species of industry a greater share of the capital of the society than what would naturally go to it, or, by extraordinary restraints, force from a particular species of industry some share of the capital which would be otherwise employed in it, is in reality subversive of the great purpose which it means to promote. It retards, instead of accelerating, the progress of the society towards real wealth and greatness; and diminishes instead of increasing, the real value of its land and labour" [IV,9].

Third Commandment: Taking the name of the Market in Vain

The greatest sins against Spiritual religion are those committed in its own name — by those who preach hate in the name of love. The Economic religion is not immune from this type of subversion. The Third Commandment is a warning to beware of those who use freedom to compete as a licence to exploit monopoly — particularly when they claim to be upholding the public interest.

"The pretence that corporations are necessary for the better government of the trade is without any foundation. The real and effectual discipline which is exercised over a workman is not that of his corporation, but that of his customers" [I,10]. "Monopoly, besides, is a great enemy to good management, which can never be universally established but in consequence of … free and universal competition" [I,11].

The Fourth Commandment: the Work Ethic

Like its counterpart in the Old Testament, the Fourth Commandment has fallen into disuse. It is regarded as a quaint anachronism which is highly approved of in principle, provided that its application is restricted in practice — preferably to other people.

The Fifth Commandment: Accumulation of Capital

Adam Smith's Fifth Commandment is as popular with the owners of capital as the Biblical Commandment is with the parents of children. For it reveals that the path of economic righteousness lies through saving and the accumulation of capital.

"Capitals are increased by parsimony, and decreased by prodigality and misconduct. Whatever a person saves from his revenue he adds to his capital, and either employs it himself ... or enables some other person to do so, by lending it to him for an interest. ... As the capital of an individual can be increased only by what he saves, ... so the capital of a society, which is the same with that of all the individuals who compose it, can be increased only in the same manner. Parsimony, and not industry, is the immediate cause of the increase of capital" [II,3].

"An augmentation of fortune is the means by which the greater part of men propose and wish to better their condition. ... The most likely way of augmenting their fortune is to save and accumulate. ... Every prodigal appears to be a public enemy, and every frugal man a public benefactor" [II,3].

To counter the pagan belief of the "mercantilists" that saving may cause unemployment, Smith points out that "what is annually saved is as regularly consumed as what is annually spent, and nearly in the same time too; but it is consumed by a different set of people" [II,3].

"Almost all loans at interest are made in money, either of paper, or of gold and silver. But what the borrower really wants, and what the lender really supplies him with, is not the money, but the money's worth, or the goods which it can purchase. ... By means of the loan, the lender, as it were, assigns to the borrower his right to a certain portion of the annual produce of the land and labour of the country to be employed as the borrower pleases" [II,4].

Smith assumes that capital saved is either invested by the saver himself or else lent to others better able to create and exploit opportunities for employing it more effectively. This, in his view, is the engine of economic growth.

"The annual produce of the land and labour of any nation can be increased in its value by no other means but by increasing either the number of its productive labourers, or the productive powers of those labourers. ... The productive powers of ... labourers cannot be increased, but in consequence either of some addition and improvement to those machines and instruments which facilitate and abridge labour; or of a more proper division and distribution of employment. In either case an additional capital is almost always required" [II,3].

"Capital has been silently and gradually accumulated by the private frugality and good conduct of individuals, by their universal, continual, and uninterrupted effort to better their own condition. It is this effort, protected by law and allowed by liberty to exert itself in the manner that is most advantageous, which has maintained the progress of England towards opulence and improvement in almost all former times, and which, it is to be hoped, will do so in all future times" [II,3].

The Sixth Commandment: Against Restriction of Competition

The First Commandment is hard to obey for those who enjoy monopoly advantages as the result of protection from competition. It is easier for a camel to go through the eye of a needle, than for a monopolist to enter into the kingdom of Free Competition.

That is reason for the Sixth Commandment. It contains a specific injunction against the evil of monopoly and restrictive practices.

"People of the same trade seldom meet together, even for merriment or diversion, but the conversation ends in a conspiracy against the public, or in some contrivance to raise prices" [I,10].

The Seventh Commandment: Against Protectionism

Liberalism begins at home, but it does not end there. Economic freedom in international trade is essential to promote the wealth of the nation. The Seventh Commandment prohibits protection against foreign competition.

"It is the maxim of every prudent master of a family never to attempt to make at home what it will cost him more to make than to buy. The tailor does not attempt to make his own shoes, but buys them of the shoemaker. ... What is prudence in the conduct of every private family can scarce be folly in that of a great kingdom. If a foreign country can supply us with a commodity cheaper than we ourselves can make it, better buy it of them with some part of the produce of our own industry employed in a way in which we have some advantage" [IV,2].

"In the restraints upon the importation of all foreign commodities which can come into competition with those of our own growth or manufacture, the interest of the home consumer is evidently sacrificed to that of the producer" [IV,8].

The Eighth Commandment: Against Inflation of the Money Supply

The Eighth Commandment warns against undue increases in the quantity of money lest they reduce its purchasing power.

"Any increase in the quantity of silver, while that of the commodities circulated by means of it remained the same, could have no other effect than to diminish the value of that metal. The nominal value of all sorts of goods would be greater, but their real value would be precisely the same as before. They would be exchanged for a greater number of pieces of silver; but the quantity of labour which they could command, the number of people whom they could maintain and employ, would be precisely the same" [II,4].

The Ninth Commandment: Against Unjust Taxation

Smith premises his examination of taxation with "the four following maxims with regard to taxes in general.

I. The subjects of every state ought to contribute towards the support of the government, as nearly as possible, in proportion to their respective abilities; that is, in proportion to the revenue which they respectively enjoy under the protection of the state. ... In the observation or neglect of this maxim consists, what is called, the equality or inequality of taxation. ...

II. The tax which each individual is bound to pay ought to be certain, and not arbitrary. The time of payment, the manner of payment, the quantity to be paid, ought all to be clear and plain to the contributor, and to every other person. ...

III. Every tax ought to be levied at the time, or in the manner, in which it is most likely to be convenient for the contributor to pay it.

IV. Every tax ought to be so contrived as both to take out and to keep out of the pockets of the people as little as possible, over and above what it brings into the public treasury of the state" [V, 2, pt.II].

The Tenth Commandment: Against (Government) Interference

All interference is bad, but government interference is probably the gravest threat to individual liberty.

"What is the species of domestic industry which his capital can employ, and of which the produce is likely to be of the greatest value, every individual, it is evident, can, in his local situation, judge much better than any statesman or lawgiver can do for him. The statesman who should attempt to direct private people in what manner they ought to employ their capitals would not only load himself with a most unnecessary attention, but assume an authority which could safely be trusted, not only to no single person, but to no council or senate whatever, and which would nowhere be so dangerous as in the hands of a man who had folly and presumption enough to fancy himself fit to exercise it" [IV,2].

"The sovereign is completely discharged from a duty, in the attempting to perform which he must always be exposed to innumerable delusions, and for the proper performance of which no human wisdom or knowledge could ever be sufficient; the duty of superintending the industry of private people and of directing it towards the employments most suitable to the interest of the society" [IV, 9].

"It is the highest impertinence and presumption, ... in kings and ministers, to pretend to watch over the œconomy of private people, and to restrain their expence, either by sumptuary laws, or by prohibiting the importation of foreign luxuries. They are themselves always, and without any exception, the greatest spendthrifts in the society. Let them look well after their own expence, and they may safely trust private people with theirs. If their own extravagance does not ruin the state, that of their subjects never will" [II,3].

The Creed: Liberalism

"All systems either of preference or of restraint, therefore, being thus completely taken away, the obvious and simple system of natural liberty establishes itself of its own accord. Every man, as long as he does not violate the laws of justice, is left perfectly free to pursue his own interest his own way, and to bring both his industry and his capital into competition with those of any other man, or order of men" [IV,9].

The road is hard, the flesh is weak, it is only too easy to yield to temptation. "The member of parliament who supports [those who seek protection] is sure to acquire not only the reputation of understanding trade, but great popularity and influence. ... If he opposes them, [he is subject to] real danger arising from the insolent outrage of furious and disappointed monopolists" [IV,2].

The Covenant with the Faithful

The Free-Trade religion, like many others, has undergone a process of modernisation; it has been condensed. Particular emphasis is placed on three commandments: competition, accumulation, and sound money.

Competition promises the blessing of full employment; accumulation promises the blessing of economic growth; sound money promises the blessing of stable prices.

The reward for hearkening diligently to the words of Adam Smith and obeying his Free-Trade commandments is that entry into the Promised Land of economic prosperity is open to all classes of society.

"It is the great multiplication of the productions of all the different arts, in consequence of the division of labour, which occasions, in a well-governed society, that universal opulence which extends itself to the lowest ranks of the people" [I,1].

That was the Good News.

The Bad News was still to come.

CHAPTER 6

THE CLASSICAL DOCTRINE

And it came to pass, after the death of Smith, exactly as his opponents had predicted: milk and honey for some, misery and deprivation for others.

The social upheaval following the industrial revolution had created a class of capitalists who owned the means of production and a class of labourers who owned only their own labour power. Many of the dispossessed proletariat were living in conditions of such misery and squalor that they were worse off than feudal peasants.

Those who reaped the rewards, eagerly embraced the new faith. Those who suffered the penalties, despised it.

The priests themselves were divided.

Criticism of the evils of competition came both from supporters who wished to make the free market system work as Smith envisaged and from opponents who wished to overthrow it.

Reform, or revolution: that was the question.

Political economy was at its most political.

Defender of the Faith

John Stuart Mill was a staunch believer in Smith's Free Market Religion. He set out the principles of the Faith in his *Principles of Political Economy* [1848], and he took upon himself the burden of defending the religion against its Socialist critics.

"I do not pretend that there are no inconveniences in competition, or that the moral objections urged against it by Socialist writers, as a source of jealousy and hostility among those engaged in the same occupation, are altogether groundless. But if competition has its evils, it prevents greater evils. ... Instead of looking upon competition as the baneful and anti-social principle which it is held to be by the generality of Socialists, I conceive that, even in the present state of society and industry, every restriction of it is an evil, and every extension of it, even if for the time injuriously affecting some class of labourers, is always an ultimate good" [1848, p.793].

Like Smith, he condemned the hypocrisy of the Pharisees who loudly proclaimed the sanctity of free competition while making sure that they themselves started with an advantage. He therefore insisted that Smith's commandment on competition could not be properly observed unless there was equality of opportunity.

"Impartiality between competitors would consist in endeavouring that they should all start fair, and not in hanging a weight upon the swift to diminish the distance between them and the slow. Many, indeed, fail with greater efforts than those with which others succeed, not from difference of merits, but difference of opportunities; but if all were done ... to diminish this inequality of opportunities, the differences in fortune arising from people's own earnings could not justly give umbrage" [p.808].

It was entirely consistent with his liberal philosophy that he should have been one of the first to advocate "the opening of industrial occupations freely to both sexes. ... The ideas and institutions by which the accident of sex is made the groundwork of an inequality of legal rights, and a forced dissimilarity of social functions, must ere long be recognised as the greatest hindrance to moral, social, and even intellectual improvement" [pp.759,760].

This was economic liberalism in its holiest manifestation. Free competition meant competition without restriction. It must be genuinely open to all, regardless of class, race, or sex.

The Wages of Imperfect Competition is Unemployment

But a pestilence was cast over the face of the earth to try the faithful and put their faith to the test. Fat years were followed by lean years. And the righteous were no less sorely afflicted by these *trade cycles* than were the wicked.

The injustice was manifest. It did not seem to matter how highly competitive were the markets or how strictly the word of the Law revealed to Smith was obeyed. Even the most free-enterprise of free-enterprise economies were, from time to time, plunged into deep depression. They were forced to endure periodic "commercial crises" (now known as "recessions") which brought unemployment and distress to all classes of society.

In his pastoral role, Mill sought to give comfort to his flock by explaining away unemployment as a "temporary derangement of markets" [p.561]. "Production is not excessive, but merely ill assorted" [p.559], or else, "it is simply the consequence of an excess of speculative purchases" [p.561].

The message from the pulpit was clear, and it was a message that even the least observant member of the congregation could understand.

If firms maintained prices which were too high, they would be unable to sell the whole of their output. If unions of workers demanded wages which were too great, they would be unable to find jobs for all their members. If businessmen took risks and misjudged the market, they would suffer losses. If industries were slow to respond to changes in consumer tastes or production technology, they would go into decline.

All this the congregation could readily accept.

Nevertheless there were doubters. Restrictive practices and mistakes of foresight were obvious facts of economic life. But they occurred in good times as well as bad. Was it not possible that unemployment might have some additional cause?

Ancient pagan beliefs, which appealed to the natural instincts of the common people, began to reassert themselves. In the days before the Revelation to Smith, tribal elders like Sir William Petty and François Quesnay (who were revered both as healers and as economic advisers) had instilled into the hearts of the people a mortal fear of hoarding. There was one old-fashioned belief to which simple folk still clung: if everyone kept their money under the bed, it did not matter how faithful they were to the spirit of competition, very little business would be transacted.

The re-emergence of such heresy, every time a trade recession occurred, was a threat to the very foundations of the religion. It needed to be exorcised — and the only way to do so was by "proving" that unemployment was the consequence of market imperfection and *nothing but* market imperfection. It had to be clearly demonstrated that the curse of unemployment was the penalty, not of observing the Religion, but of violating its strict Moral Code.

Mill refused to entertain the pagan beliefs. "The permanent decline in the circumstances of producers, for want of markets, … is a conception to which the nature of a commercial crisis gives no support" [p.561].

Free competition in the market place would be enough to produce a cure, if only the multitude had sufficient faith to put their trust in Smith's Holy Law.

How the Free Market Provides Salvation

In Book III on Exchange, Mill explains how the market value — the price — of any commodity is determined by the forces of supply and demand.

"Let us suppose that the demand at some particular time exceeds the supply, that is, there are people ready to buy, at the market value, a greater quantity than is offered for sale. Competition takes place on the side of the buyers, and the [market] value rises … [until] the demand becomes equal and no more than equal to the supply" [pp.446,447].

"The converse case is equally simple. Instead of a demand beyond the supply, let us suppose a supply exceeding the demand. The competition will now be on the side of the sellers: … the [market] value falls. … Demand and supply, the quantity demanded and the quantity supplied, will be made equal. If unequal at any moment, competition equalizes them, and the manner in which this is done is by an adjustment of the [market] value" [p.447,448].

"Demand and supply always rush to an equilibrium" [p.456].

To the crucial question: "Is it possible that there should be a deficiency of demand for all commodities ... ?" [p.557], Mill gives a firm answer. The answer is "no!", and Mill acknowledges "that the merit of having placed this most important point in its true light belongs principally, on the Continent, to the judicious J. B. Say" [p.562].

Say's Law

What is now known as "Say's Law" is derived from the following passage in the *Treatise on Political Economy* by Jean-Baptiste Say.

"A man who applies his labour to the investing of objects with value by the creation of utility of some sort, can not expect such a value to be appreciated and paid for, unless where other men have the means of purchasing it. Now, of what do these means consist? Of other values of other products, likewise the fruits of industry, capital, and land. Which leads us to a conclusion that may at first sight appear paradoxical, namely, that it is production which opens a demand for products. ... A product is no sooner created, than it, from that instant, affords a market for other products to the full extent of its own value. ... Thus, the mere circumstance of the creation of one product immediately opens a vent for other products" [1803, pp.133-135].

"Even when money is obtained with a view to hoard or bury it, the ultimate object is always to employ it in a purchase of some kind ... for money, as money, has no other use than to buy with" [p.133n].

Mill gives the "authorised version" of "Say's Law" in Book III of his *Principles*. "Whoever brings additional commodities to the market, brings an additional power of purchase; ... he brings also an additional desire to consume; since if he had not that desire, he would not have troubled himself to produce" [1848, p.559].

Mill concedes that "there are persons who produce and accumulate ... their savings because they have nothing on which they care to expend them. ... But these do not in the smallest degree affect our conclusion. For, what do these persons do with their savings? They invest them productively; that is, expend them in employing labour. In other words, having a purchasing power belonging to them more than they know what to do with, they make over the surplus of it for the general benefit of the labouring class" [p.560].

Mill appreciates that this point is not immediately obvious.

"To the vulgar, it is not at all apparent that what is saved is consumed. To them, every one who saves appears in the light of a person who hoards" [p.71]. But what is saved "is not, generally speaking, hoarded, but (through savings banks, benefit clubs, or some other channel) re-employed as capital, and consumed" [p.70].

The mechanism which makes all this possible is the market for loanable funds. As long as there is free competition in the market for loanable funds, there is no obstruction to the flow of money from savers to spenders.

"The rate of interest will be such as to equalize the demand for loans with the supply of them. It will be such, that exactly as much as some people are desirous to borrow at that rate, others shall be willing to lend. If there is more offered than demanded, interest will fall; if more is demanded than offered, it will rise; and, in both cases, to the point at which the equation of supply and demand is re-established" [pp.637,638].

What is saved is lent.
What is lent is borrowed.
What is borrowed is spent.

In the words of the Prophet: "What is annually saved is as regularly consumed as what is annually spent, and nearly in the same time too" [Smith (1776) II,3].

Mill has no doubt as to the culprit responsible for the resurgence of paganism.

"It is the intervention of money which obscures, to an unpractised apprehension the true character of these phenomena" [1848, p.72]. So convinced is Mill of the damage that this causes to the Free Trade religion that he dedicates himself to the mission of proving conclusively that money makes no difference to real economic transactions, but merely facilitates them. His noble object is to protect the religion from the accusation that the hoarding of money might cause unemployment even in the most highly competitive economy.

Mill's Doctrine

Mill's Doctrine that "money makes no difference" is based on the belief that there is no essential difference between a barter economy and a monetary economy.

"Great as the difference would be between a country with money, and a country altogether without it, it would be only one of convenience; a saving of time and trouble" [p.6]. "Exchanging things for one another by first exchanging a thing for money, and then exchanging the money for something else, makes no difference in the essential character of transactions" [p.487]. "Things which by barter would exchange for one another, will, if sold for money, sell for an equal amount of it" [p.488].

So strong is Mill's conviction that "it is the intervention of money which obscures ... the true character of [economic] phenomena" [p.72] that, for almost 500 pages, he conducts his argument in "real" terms. When he finally does bring money into the discussion, he insists that "the introduction of money does not interfere with any of the Laws of Value laid down in the preceding chapters ... [which] are as applicable to a money system as to a system of barter" [p.488].

He moves inexorably to his triumphal conclusion.

"There cannot, in short, be intrinsically a more insignificant thing, in the economy of society, than money; except in the character of a contrivance for sparing time and labour. It is a machine for doing quickly and commodiously, what would be done, though less quickly and commodiously, without it: and like many other kinds of machinery, it only exerts a distinct and independent influence of its own when it gets out of order" [p.488].

According to Mill's Doctrine, therefore, money does not affect the direction or volume of economic activity, it simply affects the level of prices at which the "real" activity takes place.

The Influence of Money on Prices

Chapter 4 of the Second Book of Smith contains a crude quantity theory of money. "Any increase in the quantity of silver, while that of the commodities circulated by means of it remained the same, could have no other effect than to diminish the value of that metal. The nominal value of all sorts of goods would be greater, but their real value would be precisely the same as before. They would be exchanged for a greater number of pieces of silver; but the quantity of labour which they could command, the number of people whom they could maintain and employ, would be precisely the same."

The message was spread by the evangelists — first by Jean-Baptiste Say, then by David Ricardo. "No government has the power of increasing the total national money otherwise than nominally. The increased quantity of the whole reduces the value of every part; and *vice versa*" [1803, p.227]. "Whether a bank lent one million, ten million, or a hundred millions, ... they would alter only the value of the money which they thus issued" [1817, p.246].

Mill was full of concern for the simpler souls among the congregation — those whose faith was strong but whose intellect was weak. He feared that they might misinterpret the message and fall into the error of believing that the level of prices was determined by the quantity of money. So he was careful to make it absolutely clear that "money acts upon prices in no other way than by being tendered in exchange for commodities" [1848, p.524]. "Money not in circulation has no effect on prices. The converse, however, is a much commoner case; people make purchases with money not in their possession" [p.524]. "Credit, in short, has exactly the same purchasing power with money" [p.532].

The Article of Faith

Such was Mill's authority that his Doctrine was incorporated into the Religion as an Article of Faith. In a competitive economy, according to Mill's doctrine, monetary changes affected only the level of prices; they could have no more than a temporary effect on the volume of employment. The "real" economy was determined by tastes and technology.

The beautiful simplicity of this doctrine gave the Religion a strong intellectual appeal. The impact on real output of changes in tastes and technology could be considered separately from the impact on prices of monetary changes. Real analysis was segregated from monetary analysis. It was the beginning of a theoretical apartheid.

Mill's *Principles* answered a spiritual need and gained acceptance as the Authorised Version of the Free Trade Bible. It provided a wealth of material for Sermons delivered by a whole generation of orthodox priests with a vocation to spread the Gospel of Free Trade. There is no doubt of their sincerity. They sought to uphold the authority of their Church at a time when it was under attack from the false accusations of Satan (whose messenger on Earth was a blasphemous heretic by the name of Karl Marx).

Acceptance of Mill's doctrine meant that free competition could be advertised as the solution to *all* economic problems. The invisible hand could now be worshipped as the guarantor not only of the direction of activity but also of full employment.

John Stuart Mill was surely entitled to inherit the mantle of Adam Smith. He could justly claim the title of Defender of the Faith.

The Moral Code

Mill regarded his *Principles* as "a work similar in its object and general conception to that of Adam Smith, but adapted to the more extended knowledge and improved ideas of the present age" [1848, p.xxviii].

The message of the *Principles* is the same as that of the *Wealth of Nations*:

for full employment	–	free competition.
for stable prices	–	sound money.
for economic growth	–	thrift.

Mill's repetition of Adam Smith's view that "saving … enriches, and spending impoverishes, the community along with the individual" [1848, pp.72,73] is the Classical Doctrine which sets the Holy Seal of approval on free-enterprise Capitalism.

The Dissenters

But all was not well. In justifying his Classical Doctrine, Mill had relied on the assertion that "persons who produce and accumulate … their savings because they have nothing on which they care to expend them invest them productively; that is, expend them in employing labour. In other words, having a purchasing power belonging to them more than they know what to do with, they make over the surplus of it for the general benefit of the labouring class" [1848, p.560].

It is true that he was simply repeating the words of the Master. "What is annually saved is as regularly consumed as what is annually spent, and nearly in the same time too" [Smith (1776) II,3].

But that only made matters worse. For the assertion was so clearly contradicted by the facts of experience that it laid the Religion wide open to the derision of its bitterest enemies.

Karl Marx took full advantage of the opportunity.

"Nothing can be more childish than the dogma, that because every sale is a purchase, and every purchase a sale, therefore the circulation of commodities necessarily implies an equilibrium of sales and purchases. … Its real purport is to prove that every seller brings his buyer to market with him. Nothing of the kind. … No one can sell unless someone else purchases. But no one is forthwith bound to purchase, because he has just sold" [1867, p.113].

This criticism proved so embarrassing for the orthodox clergy that it was proscribed as a heresy and was forbidden even to be mentioned in respectable God-fearing circles. The remedy to bolster the faith was repetition of the catechism — twice as often as before and three times more loudly.

The congregation accepted the Classical Doctrine without question. But the more thoughtful priests remained uncomfortable. They were frequently embarrassed by members of their flock whose vigorously expressed beliefs seemed to be founded on superstition rather than faith.

It came as a great relief when the True Faith was restored by a miracle of Divine Inspiration.

CHAPTER 7

THE IMMACULATE CONCEPTION

The second half of the nineteenth century saw the rise of the religious seminaries. Chairs of Economics were established at universities, where learned professors devoted themselves to interpretation of the Holy Scripture. Commentaries appeared in vast numbers — with claims to be the true meaning of the words of the prophets. Fierce theological disputes broke out, most of which were quite incomprehensible to the laity. Perhaps the most significant development was the translation of the doctrine from the ancient tongues into the modern scientific language of mathematics. Theoretical propositions could then be supported by rigorous mathematical proof.

Unfortunately, the algebra became so complicated that much of the theology became inaccessible not only to the lay members of the congregation but also to quite a number of the clergy.

The "Marginalist" Theology

One of the pioneers in the application of mathematics to economic theory was the French economist, Augustin Cournot. His *Researches into the Mathematical Principles of the Theory of Wealth* [1838] included the use of calculus in marginal analysis, derivation of the demand curve, and the effect of restricted and unrestricted competition on the behaviour of producers. In Cournot's opinion, "the employment of mathematical symbols is perfectly natural when the relations between magnitudes are under discussion ... if they are able to facilitate the exposition of problems, to render it more concise, to open the way to more extended developments, and to avoid the digressions of vague argumentation. ... Any one who understands algebraic notation, reads at a glance in an equation results reached arithmetically only with great labour and pains" [1838, pp.3,4].

It is a sad fact of life that anyone who does *not* understand algebraic notation, reads an *equation* only with great labour and pains, and frequently abandons the enterprise without ever reaching the results.

Possibly for that reason, Cournot's work was neglected, and it took another 30 years for the "marginalist revolution" to be achieved. The leaders were Stanley Jevons with *The Theory of Political Economy* [1871] and Carl Menger, founder of the "Austrian School", with his *Principles of Economics* [1871].

From their work are derived the fundamental "laws" of consumer psychology and production technology.

The "law of diminishing marginal utility" and the "law of diminishing returns" remain the foundation of modern microeconomic theory:

"Utility denotes satisfaction. More precisely, it refers to the extent to which goods and services are preferred by consumers. … The law of diminishing marginal utility states that, as the amount of a good consumed increases, the marginal utility [the extra utility added by the last unit consumed] of that good tends to diminish" [Samuelson & Nordhaus (1995) pp.73,74].

"The law of diminishing returns holds that we will get less and less extra output when we add additional doses of an input while holding other inputs fixed" [p.96].

These "laws" constitute the assumptions about tastes and technology which form the basis of the familiar demand and supply curves which proliferate in the modern textbooks of economic theory.

The mathematical approach was taken a stage further by Léon Walras, a French economist who occupied the Chair of Political Economy at the University of Lausanne. The general equilibrium analysis which he presented in his *Elements of Pure Economics* [1874] moved economic theory into a new dimension.

The Walrasian Utopia

In commenting on the economic crises which afflict the real world, Walras offers the advice that "the more we know of the ideal conditions of equilibrium, the better we shall be able to control or prevent these crises" [1874, p.381].

To most economists, "ideal conditions" mean "perfect competition" implying large numbers of "economically rational" competitors with complete knowledge of all available opportunities and with absolute freedom (within the law) to pursue their own self-interest. (Large numbers are necessary to prevent any individual competitor from gaining monopolistic power. Complete knowledge implies total awareness of all economic opportunities as soon as they arise. Rationality and freedom imply willingness and ability to take immediate advantage of those opportunities.)

These requirements are so stringent that they are rarely, if ever, satisfied. Nevertheless, they are not good enough for Walras.

The ideal conditions envisaged by Walras are those of a very special kind of auction:

"The whole world may be looked upon as a vast general market. ... We shall suppose that the market is perfectly competitive, just as in pure mechanics we suppose, to start with, that machines are perfectly frictionless" [p.84]. "The markets which are best organized from the competitive standpoint are those in which purchases and sales are made by auction, through the instrumentality of stockbrokers, commercial brokers or criers acting as agents who centralize transactions in such a way that the terms of every exchange are openly announced and an opportunity is given to sellers to lower their prices and to buyers to raise their bids" [pp.83,84].

Market prices are established by a "tâtonnement" process of "groping" towards equilibrium. Provisional bids are made by means of "tickets" or "bons" used "to represent the successive quantities [of products and services] at prices first cried at random and then raised or lowered according as there is an excess of demand over offer or vice versa, until the two become equal" [p.242]. Not until the Walrasian auctioneer has balanced his books and announced the final "market clearing" prices do the bids become final. Only then do any transactions actually take place.

Since there is an exact balance between quantities demanded and quantities supplied, all markets "clear". There are no unsold supplies or unsatisfied demands in any market. Every market is "in equilibrium".

"For the market to be in a state of equilibrium ... it is necessary and sufficient that at these prices the effective demand for each commodity equal its effective offer" [p.172]. "The term *effective offer* [applies] to any offer made ... of a definite amount of a commodity at a definite price ... [and] the term *effective demand* [applies] to any such demand for a definite amount of a commodity at a definite price" [pp.84,85].

The Walrasian auctioneer is therefore a co-ordinator of bids who works with lightning speed so that all the operations involved in the "tâtonnement" process "take place simultaneously" [p.477]. The result is perfect price flexibility.

The Walrasian auction is a Utopia in the literal sense of the Greek "ou topos" (meaning "no place"). The "tâtonnement" process is an automatic form of "recontracting" which excludes the possibility of any transactions taking place at non-equilibrium prices. With its infinitely flexible price mechanism capable of instantaneous response to change, the Walrasian Utopia is the economic equivalent of the perfectly frictionless engine. It does not exist in real life, but it is useful as an indication of the theoretical ideal.

The outstanding feature of the *Elements*, however, is the way in which the complex interrelationships and interdependencies of economic life are brought into the analysis.

General Economic Equilibrium

If the demand for tea were a function of a single variable like the price of tea, it could be adequately represented in two dimensions, with the quantity of tea demanded plotted against various different prices of tea. But the demand for tea is a function of many variables, including the prices of close substitutes like coffee. In the *Elements*, the demand for each commodity is explicitly recognised as a function of many variables including the prices of all other commodities. Equilibrium is therefore a multi-dimensional phenomenon which cannot adequately be represented in a diagram of only two dimensions. Consequently, the problem has to be formulated as a series of simultaneous equations.

The advantage of general equilibrium analysis over partial equilibrium analysis is that, once the problem has been formulated correctly, relationships cannot be overlooked. The disadvantage is that it requires masses of complicated algebraic formulae which present a formidable obstacle to the non-mathematician. Nevertheless, the Walrasian system is an overwhelming justification for Cournot's belief that "the employment of mathematical symbols ... facilitate the exposition of problems ... open the way to more extended developments, and ... avoid the digressions of vague argumentation" [1838, pp.3,4].

A case in point is the way in which Walras manages to integrate money into the analysis.

The Place of Money in Orthodox Theology

By developing his concept of the "desired cash balance" [1874, p.321], Walras introduces money into the system of general economic equilibrium as a commodity like any other. And, like any other commodity, money is desired for its own particular characteristics.

The peculiarity of money which distinguishes it from other commodities arises directly from its function as a medium of exchange or as a store of value. In the words of Adam Smith, "it is not for its own sake that men desire money, but for the sake of what they can purchase with it" [IV,1]. (The term used by Keynes is " "real" balances (*i.e.* balances, in hand or at the bank, measured in terms of purchasing power" [1923, p.83].) Consequently, it is not the face value of a sum of money (the "nominal" balance) which matters, but its purchasing power (the "real" balance). And the power of money to purchase goods and services depends on the level of prices.

In an economy where the nominal quantity of money is fixed by the government (or "monetary authority"), changes in the "desired cash balance" have an impact on the general level of prices through what is now known as the "real-balance effect". If there is a general increase in the desire to hoard money, then, in the words of the Swedish economist Knut Wicksell, "nobody will succeed in realising the object at which he is aiming — to increase his cash balance; for the sum of individual cash balances is limited by the amount of the available stock of money, or rather is identical with it. On the other hand, the universal reduction in demand and increase in supply of commodities will necessarily bring about a continuous fall in all prices. This can only cease when prices have fallen to the level at which the cash balances are regarded as *adequate*" [1898, p.40].

The "real-balance effect" argument enables Wicksell to confirm the orthodox view of the role of money. "Money as such ... is of significance in the economic world only as an intermediary" [p.29].

There is no departure from Mill's doctrine that real transactions are determined by tastes and technology. Apart from temporary disturbances, money does not affect the transactions themselves, but only the prices at which they are carried out.

Apartheid in Economic Theory: the Segregation of Real and Monetary Factors

The "scientific" proof that money did not affect real transactions but only the prices at which they were completed sanctioned the segregation of "real" from "monetary" factors in the orthodox theology. It confirmed the habit of analysing economic problems in terms of fundamentals. Money was regarded as little more than a veil which could be drawn aside to reveal the real transactions beneath.

Although money features in the Walrasian system of simultaneous equations, it does so mainly as a unit of account or *numéraire*. "The commodity in terms of which the prices of all the others are expressed is the '*numéraire*' [or *standard commodity*]" [1874, p.161]. "In general ... the commodity which serves as the *numéraire* serves also as money and acts as a medium of exchange" [p.189].

It is a rather peculiar form of apartheid. Money is on the electoral register; it has a vote, so to speak, but no influence on real economic events.

The acceptance of segregation between real and monetary factors became endemic in economic literature and exercised a decisive influence on the orthodox classical attitude to saving and economic growth.

The Classical Theory of Capital and Interest

"In loans, as in all other money transactions, … the money which passes," is regarded by Mill, "only as the medium, and commodities as the thing really transferred — the real subject of the transaction" [1848, p.644]. The theory of capital and interest developed by the "Austrian School" is a literal interpretation of this view. According to Eugen von Böhm-Bawerk (one of Menger's most distinguished and influential disciples), "a loan is nothing else than a real and true exchange of present goods for future goods" [1888, p.285].

The classical theory of interest is based on the exchange between "present goods" and "future goods". Böhm-Bawerk identifies three factors responsible for the premium (or "agio") which present goods command over future goods. "These three factors are: The difference in circumstances of provision between present and future; the underestimate, due to perspective, of future advantages and future goods; and, finally, the greater fruitfulness of lengthy methods of production" [p.273].

In the language of Irving Fisher's elegant restatement of this theory in his *Theory of Interest* [1930], the first two factors are responsible for each individual's subjective "marginal rate of time preference"; the third factor is responsible for the "marginal rate of return over cost" from the available investment opportunities. If there is a perfectly competitive capital market, investment will be pushed to the point at which "the marginal rate of return over cost … and the marginal rate of time preference … will, each of them, be equal to the market rate of interest" [1930, p.270].

Equilibrium is achieved through movements in the rate of interest.

An individual who is strongly influenced by Böhm-Bawerk's second factor may wish to live now and pay later. If his marginal rate of time preference is greater than the market rate of interest, he will borrow and consume until his (diminishing) marginal rate of time preference becomes equal to the market rate of interest. Any individual with investment opportunities promising a marginal rate of return over cost (due to the third factor) higher than the market rate of interest will borrow and invest until the (diminishing) marginal rate of return over cost becomes equal to the market rate of interest.

These are sources of *demand* for loanable funds.

An individual who is strongly influenced by Böhm-Bawerk's first factor may wish to save for a rainy day. If his marginal rate of time preference is less than the market rate of interest, he will abstain from consumption and lend until his (increasing) marginal rate of time preference becomes equal to the market rate of interest.

This is a source of *supply* of loanable funds.

The market rate of interest will move until the demand and supply of loanable funds are equal.

In the classical theory, the real rate of interest is a price like any other. There are no special problems. In Böhm-Bawerk's view "the exchange of present goods for future, … is only a special case of the exchange of goods in general" [1888, p.375]. A change in the demand for present consumption is like a change in the demand for oranges. Other things being equal, the former results in a change in the rate of interest, the latter results in a change in the price of oranges.

The treatment of the capital market in "real" terms as an exchange between present and future consumption has the full approval of Walras. "It is clearly seen now that the key to the whole theory of capital is to be found in thus eliminating capital loans *in the form of numéraire* so that attention is directed exclusively to the lending of capital *in kind*" [1874, p.290].

This confirms the favourable view held by Smith and Mill of thrift as the key to economic progress.

Thrift: the Noblest Economic Virtue of All

An increase in the desire to save, for example, is reflected in shift of demand away from present goods (consumption) towards future goods (investment). The premium on present goods (the real rate of interest) will fall, and investment spending will increase at the expense of consumption.

The economic reality behind saving money is simply that the saver postpones his consumption: instead of consuming now, he consumes later. Resources which would have been devoted to consumption (present goods) are diverted towards investment (future goods); the result is the accumulation of capital. Loans of money are simply the means by which resources are made available by their owners to those able to invest them to the best advantage.

Since investment spending results in the accumulation of future goods, thrift is regarded by Walras as the key to economic growth. "According as the excess of income over consumption in the aggregate is greater or less than the excess of consumption over income in the aggregate, an economy is either progressive or retrogressive" [1874, p.269].

Present Sacrifice reaps a Future Reward. No less an authority than Adam Smith himself identifies the accumulation of capital as the principal cause of "progress … towards opulence and improvement" [II,3] — in short, the very foundation of the Wealth of Nations.

The Apotheosis of the Market Place

In the *Elements*, Walras achieves what has come to be venerated as an "immaculate conception". His general equilibrium theory is revered as the holiest manifestation of doctrinal purity, and it has never been seriously challenged.

By contrast with the mathematically unsophisticated "flat earth" theories involving the "partial analysis" of individual markets in isolation, Walrasian general equilibrium analysis encompasses a full planetary system: all the inter-relationships between all markets are properly observed. The paths of the heavenly bodies in this economic universe are determined solely by tastes and technology. Real factors are dominant. Money remains on the periphery; as long as it does not "get out of order", it has no effect on the orbits.

The Walrasian Utopia has been sanctified as the apotheosis of a free market economy working to the ultimate degree of perfection. The doctrine that it guarantees full employment has been incorporated into the Holy Scripture as an Article of the True Faith. It cannot be questioned. To do so would be sheer blasphemy — a vile and wicked heresy.

Theological debate did not end with Walras, but his vision of the free market Paradise remains unchallenged. The Walrasian Utopia is still the model of the ideal free market system. Subsequent theological disputes have been over the extent to which theoretical conclusions drawn from this Heavenly Paradise can be applied to the Real World. But the nature of the Paradise itself remains sacrosanct.

Modern writers on the subject of unemployment do not literally bow towards the altar and make the sign of the cross. But they are anxious to affirm their belief in the immaculate conception. As a mark of respect to Walras, their remarks are usually prefaced with the almost obligatory declaration that, in the ideal conditions of Walrasian General Equilibrium, unemployment is a sheer impossibility.

The orthodox doctrine that equilibrium guarantees full employment has been elevated to the status of Holy Writ.

From Religion to Science

The immaculate conception gave new hope to those who believed in the free market religion. It certainly came as a great relief to the clergy. Mill's *Principles* had left them on the defensive. They were able to maintain the Classical Doctrine only by relying on an act of faith. This was just about adequate for preaching to the converted, but it was highly vulnerable to socialist criticism. Walras' *Elements* enabled them to take the offensive once more; they could go out into the world on an evangelical mission to spread the free-trade gospel. Even if they could not follow the mathematics themselves, they had the reassurance that the old propositions were no longer dependent on an act of faith; they could be supported by rigorous scientific proof.

There is no essential doctrinal difference between Mill's *Principles* and Walras' *Elements*. In both, money has no real significance except as an intermediary. In both, therefore, a perfectly competitive monetary economy generates the same real economic activities as a perfectly competitive barter economy. According to both Mill and Walras, unemployment is a phenomenon of "maladjustment" due to some kind of imperfection or rigidity in the market mechanism. According to both, there is only one effective cure — removal of the imperfection. Both extol the virtues of thrift as the engine of economic growth and progress.

The only significant difference between the two is scientific respectability.

The introduction of mathematical techniques improved the appearance of the theology. It gave the religion a modern and "scientific" aura.

Once the ancient beliefs had been supported by modern scientific proof, there was no longer any room for dissent. All was harmony. The Immaculate Conception ushered in a Golden Age of Economic Theory.

CHAPTER 8

THE GOLDEN AGE OF CLASSICAL ORTHODOXY

"It was," as Charles Dickens might have written, "the best of times. … It was the age of wisdom, … it was the epoch of belief, … it was the season of Light. … It was clearer than crystal … that the principles of Economic Theory were settled for ever."

In 1821, Colonel Robert Torrens had confidently predicted that "with respect to Political Economy the period of controversy is passing away, and that of unanimity rapidly approaching. Twenty years hence there will scarcely exist a doubt respecting any of its fundamental principles" [p.xiii]. It had taken a little longer than expected, but, by the first quarter of the twentieth century, it was beyond question that the prophecy had been amply fulfilled.

It is true that there were arguments over detail (and the more petty the detail, the fiercer the argument). But the fundamental principles were no longer in dispute.

John Stuart Mill had been similarly premature in announcing, "happily there is nothing in the laws of Value which remains for the present or any future writer to clear up; the theory of the subject is complete: the only difficulty to be overcome is that of so stating it as to solve by anticipation the chief perplexities which occur in applying it" [1848, p.436]. But, after Walrasian general equilibrium analysis had been incorporated into the theology, it was accepted that the theory was settled. All that remained was to apply it to the real world.

On the behaviour of the Utopian ideal, Walras became the acknowledged master; and he has remained unchallenged ever since.

Economists were able to pride themselves that economics had become a science. In an age of scepticism, it was far more comfortable to be a scientist than a priest.

The New Scientists

Economists began to enjoy prestige as successful physicians who had mastered the anatomy of the economy. Economic diseases were still prevalent. To prescribe the correct cure was still difficult. But it was regarded mainly as a problem of diagnosis. The difficulty lay in ascertaining how close the real world came to the theoretical model. Economic science was not unlike medical science; the fact that the economy was a highly complex patient merely served to enhance the reputation of professional economists.

They had remedies for all the most serious economic problems. They could prevent unemployment, they could cure inflation, and they had a prescription for economic growth. When closely examined, the new pills were not much different from the ones prescribed by Adam Smith, but, instead of coming in old-fashioned jars, they were vacuum-sealed in complex mathematical formulae — and that made them seem much more hygienic.

These developments enhanced the reputation of the profession, and the dismal science became not only respectable but even popular. In response, a significant effort was made to bring economics to the masses.

Economic Theory Made Simple

By the end of the nineteenth century, the "marginalist" approach had become established as the highest expression of orthodox theology. It was codified and refined by Alfred Marshall in his *Principles of Economics* [1890] which gained acceptance throughout the English speaking world as the Revised Version of the Free Trade Bible.

Marshall took the view that "the chief use of pure mathematics in economic questions seems to be in helping a person to write down quickly, shortly and exactly, some of his thoughts for his own use. ... But when a great many symbols have to be used, they become very laborious to any one but the writer himself. ... It seems doubtful whether any one spends his time well in reading lengthy translations of economic doctrines into mathematics, that have not been made by himself" [1890, p.ix].

The subject was made more accessible, by the relegation of complex mathematics to appendices and by the use of simple diagrams. The concept of market equilibrium was easier to understand in terms of Marshall's supply and demand curves than in terms of a series of Walrasian simultaneous equations.

The Equilibrium of Demand and Supply

An abridged version of the *Principles* published to cater for "the needs of junior students", contains a simple explanation of the operation of market equilibrium. "In our typical market ... we assume that the forces of demand and supply have free play; that there is no combination among dealers on either side; but each acts for himself, and there is much *free competition*; that is, buyers generally compete freely with buyers, and sellers compete freely with sellers. ... In such a market there is a definite demand price for each amount of the commodity. … The more of a thing is offered for sale in a market, the lower is the price at which it will find purchasers; or, in other words, the demand price for each unit diminishes with every increase in the amount offered. … In like way there is a supply price. … As the … amount produced increases, the supply price increases, if nature is offering a sturdy resistance to man's efforts to wring from her a larger supply. … To represent the equilibrium of demand and supply geometrically we may draw the demand and supply curves together as in [Figure 8.1]" [1892, pp.196,199].

Figure 8.1

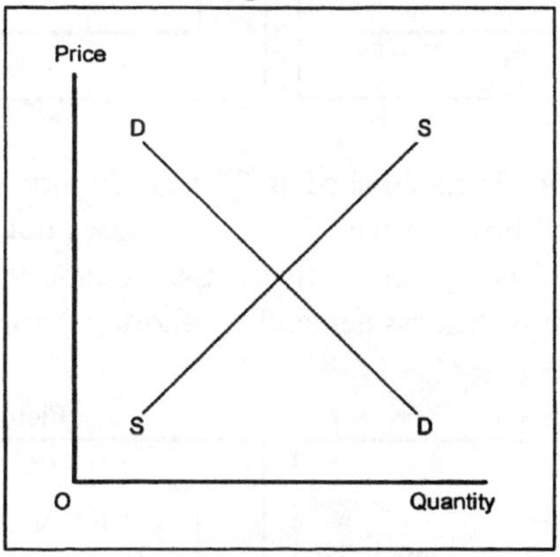

For the reasons given by Marshall, the conventional demand curve, *DD*, slopes downwards from left to right; the conventional supply curve, *SS*, slopes upwards. (As the precise shape of the curves is not material to the argument, they are shown as straight lines.)

If the market price is established at P_H, as in Figure 8.2, it is "too high". The market does not "clear": the quantity demanded, OQ_D, is smaller than the quantity supplied, OQ_S. Consequently, there is "excess supply" (a surplus) amounting to Q_DQ_S.

In these circumstances, there are sellers with unsold supplies who would be willing to sell at a lower price. If there is free competition among them, they will drive the price down to *P* in Figure 8.3 where the quantity that sellers are willing to sell, *OQ*, is exactly equal to the quantity that buyers are willing to buy, so that there is no longer any excess supply. *P* is the "equilibrium price" at which the market "clears".

Figure 8.2

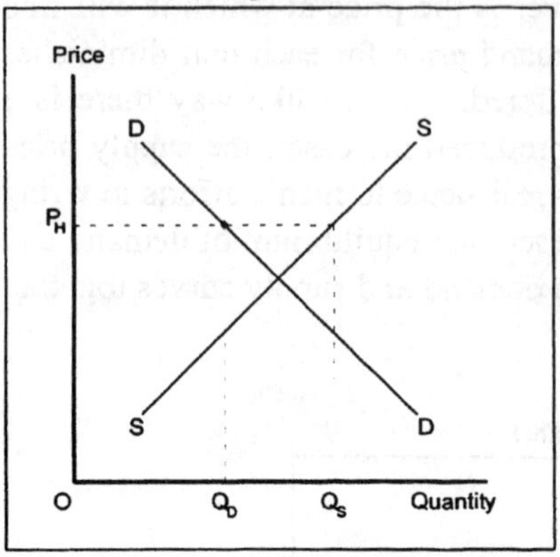

Figure 8.3

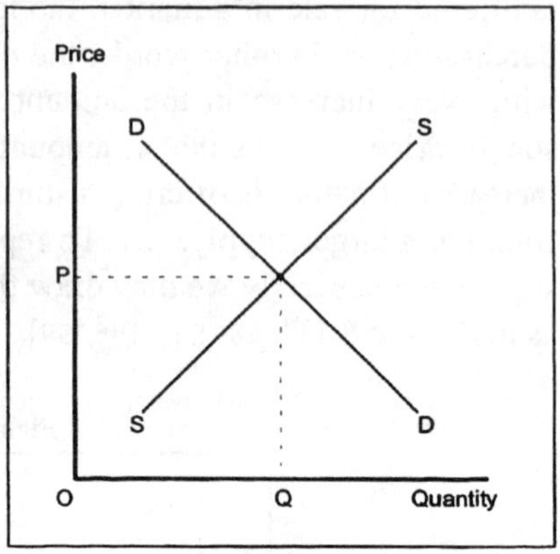

If the market price is established at P_L, as in Figure 8.4, it is "too low". It is below the equilibrium price. The market does not clear: the quantity demanded, OQ_D, is greater than the quantity supplied, OQ_S. Consequently, there is "excess demand" (a shortage) amounting to Q_SQ_D.

Figure 8.4

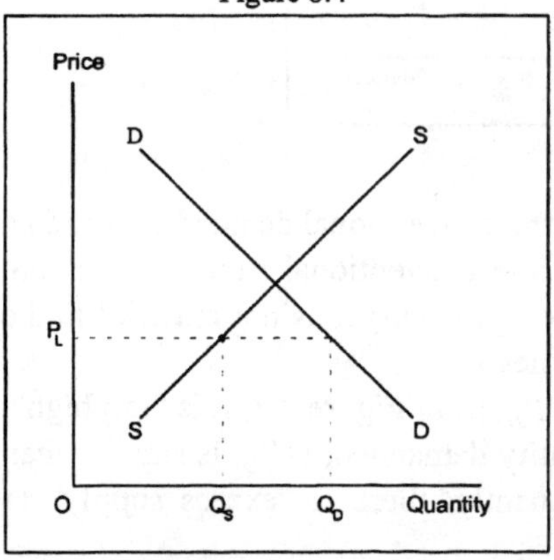

Figure 8.5

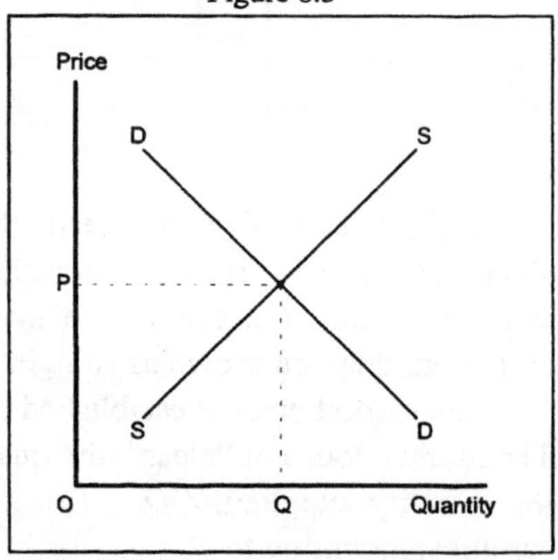

In these circumstances, there are unsatisfied buyers who would be willing to pay a higher price. If there is free competition among them, they will drive the price up to *P* in Figure 8.5 where the quantity that buyers are willing to buy is equal to the quantity that sellers are willing to sell, so that there is no longer any excess demand.

The "equilibrium price", *P*, at which the market "clears" is established at the intersection between the supply curve and the demand curve.

Changes in Supply or Demand

In chapter XIII of Book V of the Principles, Marshall deals with the effect of changes in supply or demand conditions, which he represents by "shifts" in the curves.

Figure 8.6 illustrates the effect of an "increase in supply". The supply curve shifts downwards to the right from S_1S_1 to S_2S_2. "Other things being equal" (particularly the shape and position of the demand curve), the result will be a fall in the equilibrium price from P_1 to P_2.

Figure 8.6

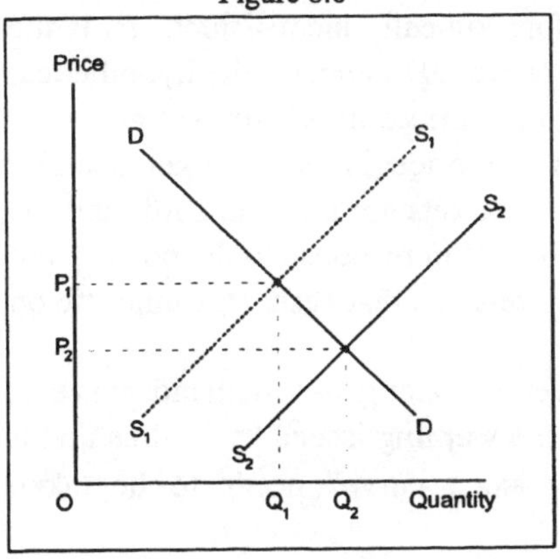

Figure 8.7

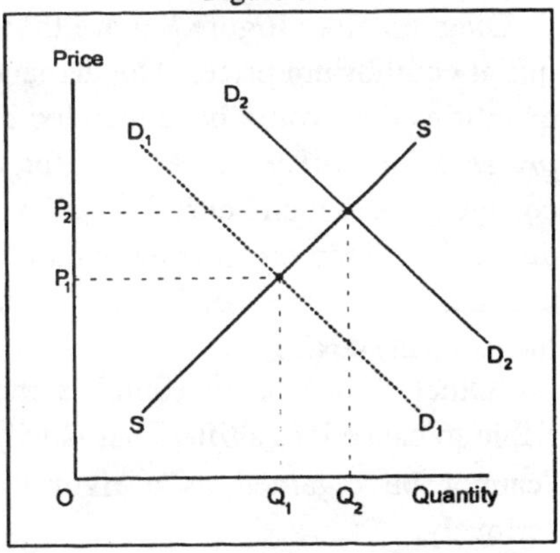

If there is an "increase in demand", the demand curve shifts upward to the right (as shown in Figure 8.7). "Other things being equal" (particularly the shape and position of the supply curve), the result will be a rise in the equilibrium price from P_1 to P_2.

The Perilous World of "Supply" and "Demand"

The habit of subjecting so many economic problems to this type of analysis lends credence to the anonymous view that "you can make even a parrot into a learned economist; all it must learn are the two words "supply" and "demand" " [quoted in Samuelson and Nordhaus (1992) p.48].

Ricardo is not so sure. "The opinion that the price of commodities depends solely on the proportion of supply to demand, or demand to supply, has become almost an axiom in political economy, and has been the source of much error in that science" [1817, p.382].

Walras gives the reason why. In a paper published in 1890, and incorporated in later editions of the *Elements*, he explicitly criticises the use of "*supply and demand curves* which a number of English economists, following the lead of Mr. Marshall of Cambridge, are wont to employ. ...

The *demand* curve ... representing the *quantity sold* as a function of the *selling price*, cannot be regarded as a rigorously exact curve. The quantity sold of any product is a function not only of its own selling price, but also of the selling prices of all other products and the prices of all productive services. ... The selling prices of products and the prices of productive services are mutually interrelated. Whenever the price of a given product is changed, the prices of productive services and consequently the selling prices of the other commodities are also changed. ... [The] *supply* or *cost of production curve*, ... which is drawn as a function of the *quantity of output* is not admissible either" [quoted in Walras (1874) pp.483,484,486].

Diagrams like Figure 8.6 are therefore logically inconsistent. P_1 is the initial equilibrium price. The demand curve *DD* indicates the hypothetical quantities that would be demanded at other prices in *this* market *given the prices in all other markets*. But, if the price in *this* market actually changes, the demand curves in *all other* markets are liable to shift; and the demand curve in *this* market is liable to shift in response to the consequent changes in the prices in those *other* markets. In that case, P_2 cannot lie on the same curve as P_1.

"Other things being equal" a movement along *any* demand curve is liable to cause it to shift. That is why the warning issued by Walras that it "cannot be regarded as a rigorously exact curve" needs to be taken seriously.

It is not the much maligned *ceteris paribus* clause which is at fault. It is perfectly legitimate to assume that all other *independent variables* (e.g. tastes and technology in all other markets) remain unaltered. What is not legitimate is to assume that *dependent variables* will not change. The assumption that "other things being equal" the demand curve will not shift is a straightforward error of logic. "Other things being equal" it will.

The standard textbook use of demand and supply curves would be less misleading if the phrase "other things being equal" were supplemented with something like "and ignoring other things which are not equal". The dangers of the supply and demand apparatus would then be clear. It is risky even for "partial analysis" (e.g. of the market for tea) when the repercussions are not normally significant; it can be fatal for "general analysis" (e.g. of the market for labour) where changes in the variable under consideration may be linked so directly with changes in other significant variables that the repercussions are enormous.

Nevertheless, the temptation provided by the convenience and simplicity of the supply and demand apparatus has proved hard to resist. Instead of being restricted to the microeconomic analysis of individual markets, it is routinely pressed into service for analysing macroeconomic problems affecting the economy as a whole.*

Economic Policy Made Simple

Supply and demand analysis makes economic problems delightfully simple. A cure for inflation and unemployment can be worked out in a few minutes.

The classical view of unemployment is still presented in modern textbooks in terms of the now traditional supply and demand analysis applied to the market for labour.

"[Figure 8.8] shows the usual picture of competitive supply and demand, with a market equilibrium at point E and a wage of W. … Wages move up or down to clear the labor market. All unemployment is voluntary. … [Figure 8.9] shows what happens if wages do not adjust to clear the labor market. At the too-high wage at W_H, OL_D workers are employed, but L_DL_S workers are involuntarily unemployed" [Samuelson & Nordhaus (1995) pp.564,565]. L_DL_S represents the excess supply of labour.

Figure 8.8

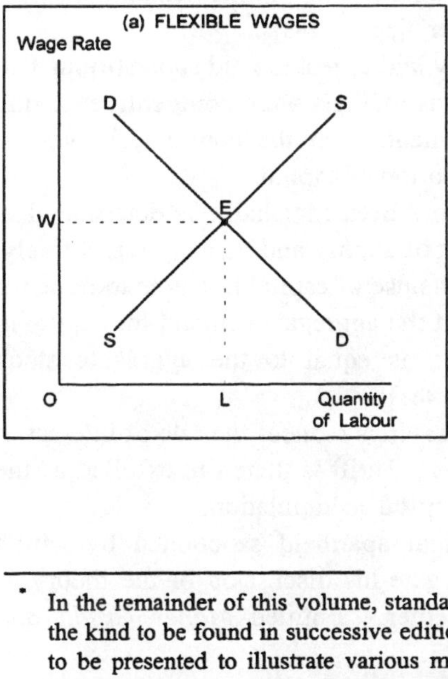

Figure 8.9

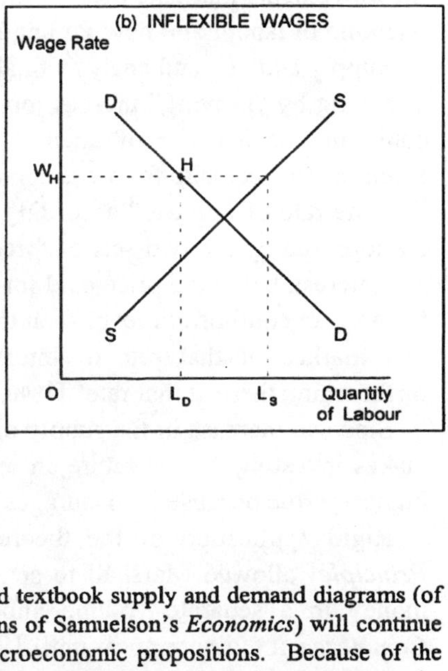

* In the remainder of this volume, standard textbook supply and demand diagrams (of the kind to be found in successive editions of Samuelson's *Economics*) will continue to be presented to illustrate various macroeconomic propositions. Because of the logical inconsistency inherent in the drawing of the curves, these diagrams cannot be regarded as *proof* of any macroeconomic proposition. They are, nevertheless, extremely useful as a simple indication of what the proposition is. However, it is not safe to regard any macroeconomic proposition as valid, unless it is proved to follow logically from microeconomic foundations based on individual preferences.

This is a perfect illustration of the orthodox classical point of view adopted by Arthur Pigou, one of the most eminent of the young Cardinals in Marshall's entourage.

Pigou was an ardent advocate of John Stuart Mill's view of unemployment. "Unemployment is *wholly* caused by maladjustment between wage-rates and demand" [1913, p.51]. "Unemployment is likely to be greater, the more rigidly wage-rates are maintained in the face of variations in the demand for labour" [p.77]. "Unemployment is likely to be present, if any workpeople have to be paid a rate of wage artificially raised above that which the free play of economic forces tends to bring about. ... Any attempt on the part of a particular Trade Union to force up the wages of its members above those current in the general run of similar occupations is a cause of unemployment, and the abandonment of that policy is, *pro tanto*, a remedy for it. ... When humanitarian considerations lead, in effect, to the establishment of a minimum wage below which no worker will be engaged, the existence of a large body of persons not worth this minimum wage is a cause of unemployment. ... Some measure of unemployment will necessarily be present, so long as wage-rates are lacking in plasticity, and fail to move ... in conformity with the movements that take place, from time to time, in the demand, now for one kind of labour and now for another" [pp.242,243].

Supply and demand analysis finally laid to rest the old superstitious fear of saving by "proving" that, as long as markets were competitive, saving could not be a cause of unemployment. On the contrary, it was an essential pre-requisite for the accumulation of capital.

"The rate of interest," according to Alfred Marshall, "is determined in the long run by the two sets of forces of supply and demand respectively. ... Interest, being the price paid for the use of capital in any market, tends towards an equilibrium level such that the aggregate demand for capital in that market, at that rate of interest, is equal to the aggregate stock forthcoming there at that rate" [1890, p.443].

Since an increase in the supply of savings reduces the rate of interest, it makes investing for the future cheaper. Thrift is therefore extolled as the highest virtue because it encourages capital accumulation.

Rigid application of the theoretical apartheid sanctioned by Mill's *Principles* allowed Marshall to segregate his discussion of the theory of money in a separate volume altogether. Entitled *Money Credit and Commerce*, it did not appear until 1923.

The Moral Code

Scientific advances in the presentation of the theological principles did not shake confidence in the old moral code. On the contrary, the application of scientific principles provided a much more secure foundation for the religion. The principles of economic theology became more widely disseminated among the laity.

Those with an interest in the Free-Trade religion no longer had to commit themselves to an act of faith. They had rational scientific grounds for their beliefs.

Smith's Commandments became scientific Laws. Perfect competition was the guarantor of full employment; capital accumulation was the engine of economic growth; and sound money was the protector of price stability.

The ethic of hard work and thrift had an appeal not just to the soul but also to the mind.

It was, indeed, the Golden Age of Classical Orthodoxy.

And yet there were still a few awkward individuals who persisted with the irritating habit of questioning the doctrine of the established Church.

The Dissenters

From the ranks of the clergy there arose a new leader. He was an orthodox priest whose reputation had been established by his work on the nature of money and the working of the monetary system. He had become well-known among the people as the result of his fulminations against governments which allowed inflation to destroy the savings of their citizens.

"Inflation [is] a method of taxation. … A Government can live by this means when it can live by no other. It is the form of taxation which the public find hardest to evade and even the weakest Government can enforce, when it can enforce nothing else."

He was so outraged by indoctrination of the faithful with the Dogma that "money did not matter" that he was driven by his conscience to Protest. He called for a Reformation of the "old orthodoxy" and a return to the true Faith of Adam Smith. For he firmly believed that "the advantage to efficiency of the decentralisation of decisions and of individual responsibility is even greater, perhaps, than the nineteenth century supposed; and the reaction against the appeal to self-interest may have gone too far."

Imagine the consternation of the orthodox clergy when this turbulent priest published his Confession and nailed it to the door of his Church.

His message was the importance of money.

CHAPTER 9

THE KEYNESIAN REFORMATION

The name of this turbulent priest was John Maynard Keynes.

His sermons fulminating against the evils of inflation (published as a series of newspaper articles) made him popular with the laity. They were subsequently collected in *A Tract on Monetary Reform* [1923], which constitutes probably the most blistering attack ever written on the folly of irresponsible monetary policy. His monetary credentials had been established with *Indian Currency and Finance* [1913]. His codification of orthodox theory and policy in a two volume work of scholarship, *A Treatise on Money* [1930], confirmed his orthodox credentials with the clergy. By the 1930s, he was generally acknowledged as the leading authority on monetary economics.

Then came an event which shook the world.

The Deluge

It started slowly at first with a trickle. Then, for forty days and forty nights, it rained financial experts from the skyscrapers of Wall Street. "In the week or so following Black Thursday, the London penny press told delightedly of the scenes in downtown New York. Speculators were hurling themselves from windows; pedestrians picked their way delicately between the bodies of fallen financiers" [Galbraith (1954) p.148].

Following the Great Crash of October and November 1929, the Great Depression of the 1930s brought a Great Flood of Unemployment over the face of the earth. In Britain alone, three million jobs were swept away in the deluge. The People were sorely afflicted and cried out in their distress. The Princes of the Church solemnly insisted that it was Divine Retribution for falling into the evil ways of restrictive practices. There would be no relief until true Repentance had been shown by a sincere return to the righteous path of pure Competition.

Arthur Pigou, the young cardinal, had become Pope. From the Holy City of Cambridge, he issued the following encyclical:

"Such unemployment as exists at any time is due wholly to the fact that changes in demand conditions are continually taking place and that frictional resistances prevent the appropriate wage adjustments from being made instantaneously" [1933, p.252].

There was no mistaking this unequivocal reaffirmation of the orthodox faith.

What troubled even the most faithful was the insistence of the clergy that Mill's "temporary derangements" or Pigou's "frictional resistances" were the *sole* cause of unemployment. All the evidence pointed in the opposite direction. Production and employment had an awkward habit of sinking into depression, not just temporarily, but for years on end — without any discernible increase in the imperfection of the markets. On the contrary, economic adversity provided a stimulus for markets to become more competitive not less. Haunted by the spectre of bankruptcy and unemployment, firms were much readier to cut their prices, and employees were more willing to accept lower wages. An economic depression had very little to be said in its favour, but there was nothing like it for concentrating minds wonderfully on cutting out inefficiency and waste.

The zeal which the priests of the Orthodox Church displayed in preaching the Gospel of Free Trade was undiminished. But they were no longer able to carry conviction even among the faithful. The Religion itself was in serious jeopardy, not from its Socialist critics, but from the inability of free markets to afford protection from the scourge of unemployment. The common people began to lose faith in a God which seemed to have forsaken them. There was a serious risk that they might turn to the false idols of protectionism, or, Heaven forbid, sell their soul to the Marxist Devil.

Maynard Keynes saw that the Church would not survive unless it was reformed. In order to return to the purity of Smith, the theology had first to be rid of the false dogma that money did not matter. In his *General Theory of Employment, Interest and Money* [1936], he set out to challenge "the conviction ... that money makes no real difference except frictionally" [p.19].

The Road to Damascus

This required nothing less than a total repudiation of the "classical orthodoxy" upon which his own reputation had been established. In an extraordinary public recantation, he renounced the policy of monetary control which he had recommended in his *Treatise on Money* [1930] as a method of preserving the stability of the price level by confessing that he "had not then understood that ... the system could be in equilibrium with less than full employment" [1936, p.243].

The vision which inspired Keynes's dramatic conversion was the revelation that money was far more than "a machine for doing quickly and commodiously, what would be done, though less quickly and commodiously, without it" [Mill (1848), p.488]. It had a real significance of its own.

Segregation had to be abolished. Money had to be integrated into the analysis of the real economy; it could no longer be left in solitary confinement; it had to be brought within the fold.

The substance of Keynes's *General Theory* is contained in a single paragraph: "An act of individual saving means — so to speak — a decision not to have dinner to-day. But it does *not* necessitate a decision to have dinner or to buy a pair of boots a week hence or a year hence or to consume any specified thing at any specified date. Thus it depresses the business of preparing to-day's dinner without stimulating the business of making ready for some future act of consumption. It is not a substitution of future consumption-demand for present consumption-demand, — it is a net diminution of such demand" [1936, p.210].

This declaration is in direct conflict with the orthodox tradition. "What is annually saved is," according to the classical economists, "as regularly consumed as what is annually spent" [Smith, II,3]. It "is not, generally speaking, hoarded, but (through savings banks, benefit clubs, or some other channel) re-employed as capital and consumed. ... In other words [persons who produce and accumulate ... their savings because they have nothing on which they care to spend them] ... invest them productively" [Mill (1848) pp.70,560].

Who but a miser would hoard idle cash balances beyond the relatively small amounts needed for day-to-day transactions? No rational person would do so when money could be lent out at interest. Thrift was to be encouraged, because it led to the accumulation of capital. The fear that a shortage of spending might cause unemployment was a pagan belief founded on ignorance and superstition; those who foolishly entertained such a notion were disparaged by Mill as "the vulgar" [p.70].

It was to dispose of the fallacy of this classical argument that Keynes enunciated the doctrine of "liquidity preference". He identified three motives for holding cash: "(i) the transactions-motive, *i.e.* the need of cash for the current transaction of personal and business exchanges; (ii) the precautionary-motive, *i.e.* the desire for security as to the future cash equivalent of a certain proportion of total resources; and (iii) the speculative-motive, *i.e.* the object of securing profit from knowing better than the market what the future will bring forth" [1936, p.170].

The first two motives were recognised by the classical economists but "assumed to absorb a quantity of cash which is not very sensitive to changes in the rate of interest" [p.171]. The "speculative-motive", by contrast, absorbs a quantity of cash which is highly sensitive to changes in the rate of interest. The novelty of Keynes's approach was to suggest a motive for holding idle cash which was consistent with rational business behaviour and which, in certain circumstances, could lead to hoarding on a massive scale.

The acceptance of hoarding as a rational economic activity had a revolutionary impact on economic theory. It challenged the classical view that money made no difference except frictionally, and established that money could have a real significance of its own.

The Impact of Hoarding on Effective Demand

To the question "can effective demand be deficient?", Mill had given the unequivocal answer "no!". To the same question, Keynes gave an equally unequivocal "yes!".

If savers carry out their intention of increasing future consumption, not by ordering goods for future delivery (as the classical economists imply), but by hoarding money, then, instead of revealing their preferences in the market place, they are concealing them.

The possibility of a deficiency of effective demand suggests an additional cause of unemployment which is not recognised in the classical theology. It is the third of the three categories of unemployment which are identified in the *General Theory*.

"Frictional unemployment" is attributed to "various inexactnesses of adjustment which stand in the way of continuous full employment: for example, unemployment due to a temporary want of balance between the relative quantities of specialised resources as a result of miscalculation or intermittent demand; or to time-lags consequent on unforeseen changes; or to the fact that the change-over from one employment to another cannot be effected without a certain delay, so that there will always exist in a non-static society a proportion of resources unemployed 'between jobs' " [1936, p.6].

"Voluntary unemployment" is attributed to "the refusal or inability of a unit of labour, as a result of legislation or social practices or of combination for collective bargaining or of slow response to change or of mere human obstinacy, to accept a reward corresponding to the value of the product attributable to its marginal productivity" [p.6].

These first two categories include all the imperfections and frictional resistances which cause disequilibrium. Keynes is therefore in complete harmony with the classical economists in holding these maladjustments and frictional resistances responsible for unemployment.

The focus of Keynes's criticism of the classical economists is their failure to "admit of the possibility of the third category" which he calls "involuntary unemployment" [p.6].

"The amount of labour N which the entrepreneurs decide to employ depends on the sum (D) of two quantities ... the amount which the community is expected to spend on consumption, and ... the amount which it is expected to devote to new investment. D is ... the *effective demand*. ... [If effective demand is deficient], the economic system may find itself in stable equilibrium with N at a level below full employment" [pp.29,30].

Keynes's three categories of unemployment can be illustrated in terms of the familiar supply and demand diagram.

Figure 9.1: The "Multi-Gear" Economy

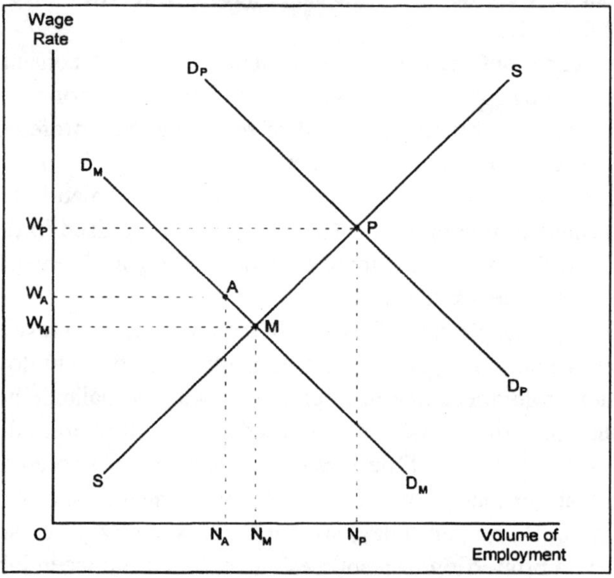

Figure 9.1 is a modified version of Figure 8.9 above.* The willingness for employment is represented by the supply curve *SS* showing that, the higher the real wage, the greater the supply of labour. As the diagram is drawn in terms of the money wage rate, it is clearly based on the assumption that one of the "other things assumed to be equal" is the level

* This type of diagram, adapted from *Economics* [Samuelson & Nordhaus (1995) p.565], is extremely useful for *identifying* propositions. For the reasons given in the previous chapter, however, these diagrams are not legitimate for *proving* propositions, particularly in the context of general equilibrium.

Throughout this volume, supply and demand diagrams are used to illustrate propositions made in the text. Analytical proof (throughout Parts III, and IV) is provided in the Appendix where the microeconomic foundations are based on individual preferences.

of prices. The potential demand for labour is represented by the demand curve D_PD_P. It shows the demand for labour as it would be derived from the intentions to spend money on both present goods (consumption) and future goods (investment).

The intersection of the two curves at the point *P* indicates that the potential equilibrium volume of employment is equal to ON_P.

But, if potential consumers of future goods bypass the market by hoarding money instead of placing orders for forward delivery, the demand revealed in the market place in the form of actual bids, D_MD_M, will fall short of the potential demand, D_PD_P, which is intended. Even if there is a Walrasian auctioneer to take charge of the proceedings, he is no more than a co-ordinator of bids. If the bids actually made in the market place are represented by the demand curve D_MD_M, then the most he can do is get to the intersection at point *M*. The market equilibrium volume of employment will be no greater than ON_M.

If, in addition, the market is of less than Utopian perfection, the wage rate may fail to move far enough or fast enough to reach even the market equilibrium at point *M*. It may stick at W_A so that the actual disequilibrium volume of employment is determined at point *A*. The wage rate W_A is above the market equilibrium rate W_M, and the actual disequilibrium volume of employment, ON_A, is below the market equilibrium volume, ON_M.

The *equilibrium rate of unemployment* by which the market equilibrium volume of employment falls short of the potential equilibrium volume is equal to the distance N_MN_P. It is caused by deficiency of effective demand: the bids are simply not made. The disequilibrium rate of unemployment by which the actual disequilibrium volume of employment falls short of the market equilibrium volume is equal to the distance N_AN_M. It is caused by any of the various possible forms of market imperfection: the bids are either "rigged" or else they are not properly and instantly co-ordinated.

The *disequilibrium rate of unemployment* is composed of the first two of Keynes's categories ("voluntary" and "frictional" unemployment). It is the only type recognised by the classical economists and includes Mill's "maladjustments" and Pigou's "frictional resistances". It would be cured by the appointment of a Walrasian auctioneer.

The *equilibrium rate of unemployment*, which corresponds to Keynes's third category ("involuntary" unemployment), is not recognised by the classics at all. Its significance is that, if it really exists, it is not susceptible to classical remedies. Since it is unrelated to the degree of market imperfection, it could occur even in a Walrasian Utopia. For a deficiency of effective demand implies, not that there is no auctioneer to co-ordinate the bids, but that there are insufficient bids to co-ordinate.

Why Money Matters

Keynes's emphasis on the importance of money is not a denial of the immaculate conception of the Walrasian planetary system. The orbits of the heavenly bodies are determined by tastes and technology as revealed in the market place through effective demand and effective offer. The point of the *General Theory* is that demand can be made effective only by the spending of money; there is no other way in a market economy. The saving of money renders the intended future demand ineffective.

The characteristic feature of a monetary economy in which savings need not be spent is that the demand for future consumption need not be transmitted through the market system. Even if markets have the perfection of a Walrasian Utopia, a monetary economy need not be fully employed. This is not because the mythical auctioneer is failing to co-ordinate the bids, but because the bids for future consumption are not being made in the first place.

The Keynesian Reformation

The Keynesian reformation was popular with a large section of the clergy, because he was careful not to offend the dignity of the priests. "Our criticism of the accepted classical theory of economics has consisted not so much in finding logical flaws in its analysis as in pointing out that its tacit assumptions are seldom or never satisfied" [1936, p.378].

The disclaimer is a little disingenuous in view of Keynes's declared intention to "argue that the postulates of the classical theory are applicable to a special case only and not to the general case, the situation which it assumes being a limiting point of the possible positions of equilibrium" [p.3]. To a classical fundamentalist, the claim that there might be more than one position of economic equilibrium was not simply revolutionary, it was heretical.

Nevertheless, it made it possible for the clergy to embrace the new theology without too much embarrassment. After all, the speculative motive could not have emerged as such a powerful influence until the development of highly sophisticated financial markets in the twentieth century. The *General Theory*, with its Liquidity Preference Doctrine, could be hailed as a revolutionary advance in empirical relevance rather than in theoretical significance. Unemployment could be explained without the necessity of sacrificing cherished theological beliefs.

Keynes had bestowed upon professional economists a precious gift which enabled them to execute one of the most difficult manoeuvres known to mankind — a U turn without serious loss of face.

Here, at last, was what they had been seeking with increasing desperation — a theology which for the first time appeared to give a rational explanation for the economic depression which, according to orthodox theology, could not occur. It came as a welcome relief to be spared the embarrassment of having to preach sermons which denied the possibility of a phenomenon which was not only an obvious fact of experience but one which vitally affected every single member of the congregation.

Most of the priests easily squared their consciences. The classical economists had clearly implied that hoarding would be a bad thing. They had merely argued that it could safely be dismissed as the irrational behaviour of misers who wanted to hold money for its own sake. Keynes had done no more than to point out that the real world had changed since the days of Smith and Mill so that hoarding money could be regarded as the rational behaviour of enterprising businessmen. The acceptance of Keynes's liquidity preference doctrine as an empirical advance involved no crisis of conscience. There was no theological conflict. No principles had to be compromised. The eighteenth-century Free Trade Religion was simply being brought up to date by the introduction of an awareness of the realities of twentieth-century commercial life.

The Reaction of the Zealots

Keynes's protest was not against the Religion itself but against what he saw as the corruption of the Priests. For he remembered "Bonar Law's mingled rage and perplexity in face of the economists, because they were denying what was obvious" [1936, p.350].

The fundamentalists among the orthodox clergy, however, were not deceived by the charm. In their eyes, what Keynes was leading was not simply a reformation but a revolution. To the orthodox clergy, steeped in the Classical Doctrine, the *General Theory* was an inflammatory document.

For Keynes to recognise what was merely an obvious fact of economic life as a theoretical possibility was the height of bad manners. To admit that there might be a cause of unemployment beyond Mill's "temporary disturbances" and Pigou's "frictional resistances" was an outrage. To conclude that "the economic system may find itself in stable equilibrium ... at a level below full employment" [1936, p.30] was sheer blasphemy.

That kind of thinking could shake the Church to its very foundations.

And so it did.

The Revolution in Economic Policy

The beauty of the orthodox doctrine lay in its simplicity.

According to classical theory, the sole cause of unemployment was market imperfection. It followed that the sole cure was removal of the barriers to free competition. Other than that, there was nothing that a government could do. Any further interference, however well-intentioned, was likely to do more long term harm than short term good, since it obstructed the working of the free-market mechanism.

The trouble with the Keynesian alternative was that it abandoned the certainties of the old orthodoxy.

According to Keynes's theory, unemployment had an additional cause; it was also due to deficiency of effective demand. It followed that removal of the barriers to free competition, though essential for curing the disequilibrium element of unemployment caused by market imperfection, was totally inadequate to deal with the equilibrium element caused by insufficiency of demand. If market freedom was not enough to maintain the level of effective demand, Government intervention might be necessary.

And this is precisely what Keynes was proposing. "The State will have to exercise a guiding influence on the propensity to consume partly through its scheme of taxation, partly by fixing the rate of interest, and partly, perhaps, in other ways. Furthermore, it seems unlikely that the influence of banking policy on the rate of interest will be sufficient by itself to determine an optimum rate of investment. I conceive, therefore, that a somewhat comprehensive socialisation of investment will prove the only means of securing an approximation to full employment" [1936, p.378].

The admission of the government into sacrosanct areas of the market-place from which it had been absolutely prohibited by Adam Smith horrified the Elders of the Church. It was anathema to the Religion of Free Trade. But it became popular with the masses and their political representatives.

Policies of public spending had already achieved practical success under Roosevelt's "New Deal" in the United States. The adoption of "Keynesian" economic policy after the Second World War enabled the nations of the Free World to avoid most of the disastrous economic mistakes which had been made in the aftermath of the First.

The *General Theory* opened a whole new branch of "macroeconomics" devoted to the question of the level of activity throughout the economy.

"Demand management" by means of the government's fiscal policy became all the rage.

Even more embarrassing for the clergy, the *General Theory* confirmed what had seemed obvious to the man in the street. Massive increases in unemployment had occurred without any discernible increase in market imperfection. The ordinary man had been right all along; it was the economic experts who were wrong.

In the summer of 1942, the dissenter was elevated to the House of Lords as the 1st Baron Keynes of Tilton.

The Legacy of the Keynesian Reformation

In stating that his "criticism of the accepted classical theory of economics ... consisted not so much in finding logical flaws in its analysis as in pointing out that its tacit assumptions are seldom or never satisfied, with the result that it cannot solve the economic problems of the real world" [1936, p.378], Keynes made clear that his intention was not to establish a new Religion but simply to protest against the intellectual corruption of the old.

Although Lord Keynes presented himself as a reformer not as a revolutionary, his disciples hailed him as a Messiah whose New Testament on macroeconomics was a further Revelation to be revered alongside the Old Testament on microeconomics handed down by Adam Smith.

The message was spread among the gentiles by the great apostles. Vast numbers of converts were attracted to the cause of Keynesian economics by the Gospel according to St. John Hicks [1937] and the Gospel according to St. Alvin Hansen [1953]. By virtue of assiduous missionary work and evangelical zeal, the Keynesian Reformation became established in academic and political circles all over the world. The old classical orthodoxy was eventually eclipsed.

After the death of its great visionary in 1946, a new generation of priests set to work on the doctrine of counter-cyclical fiscal policy. The revolutionary policy recommendation was that the Government should regulate the volume of activity by "fine-tuning" its fiscal policy, through the chosen instruments of taxation and government spending. Monetary policy, which had been the instrument of control in the days of the old orthodoxy, became subordinate.

Government intervention in the economy, which had grown to an unprecedented extent to meet the emergency of the Second World War, was continued. And it achieved notable success in the post-war period. The practice of Keynesian economics coincided with a period of economic growth and full employment. The era of prosperity following the Second

World War contrasted vividly with the economic devastation which followed the First.

Keynesian economics was triumphant; the Reformation was complete.

The Prohibition

Then, as is often the way, supporters of the cause adopted views which were more extreme than those of their departed leader. Converts to the Keynesian Reformation became more Keynesian than Keynes. In their eyes, the *General Theory* was the guide to economic salvation. Such was the fervour of some of the more fanatical devotees that they began to look upon Keynes's New Testament not as a supplement to Smith's Old Testament but as a replacement. It was the arrogance of these zealots which was largely responsible for provoking the subsequent counter-reformation.

Those who still kept faith with the strict traditions of the classical religion, in which they had been brought up, were excluded from positions of influence in the Councils of the Established Church. Their most cherished beliefs were treated with contempt. Reviled and ridiculed as fanatics and cranks, branded as narrow-minded reactionaries, they were persecuted and cast out. The only way of surviving in this hostile climate was to submit. So they suppressed their private opinions and swore the new oath of allegiance: "We are all Keynesians now".

Keynesian economics became the new orthodoxy. The old orthodoxy was driven underground. Its adherents were forced to eke out their existence in an underworld.

Classical economics entered an era of Prohibition.

CHAPTER 10

THE NEO-CLASSICAL COUNTER-REFORMATION

"By the waters of Michigan, there we sat down, yea, we wept, when we remembered the Land Promised to Adam Smith."

[*Old Monetarist Hymnal*, Psalm 137]

But the spirit of free enterprise did not die. The flame was kept alive by a shattered remnant of the faithful who still clung to their orthodox traditions. To escape persecution by the Keynesians, they were forced into exile.

The Exile

The place they chose for their long sojourn in the wilderness during the Prohibition of classical economics was the Underworld of Chicago where illicit shrines were set up and dedicated to the secret worship of Adam Smith.

The Godfather

The Godfather was Don Patinkin, undisputed boss of the movement for the rehabilitation of classical economics and an acknowledged master of abstract theory. Out of the "real-balance effect" argument, he managed to fashion an automatic weapon so devastating that it was destined to wreak terrible havoc among his Keynesian opponents and to achieve a Neo-classical Counter-reformation.

The logic of his demonstration of the relationship between price flexibility and full employment was irresistible. If prices and wages are perfectly flexible, the deficiency of effective demand identified by Keynes as the cause of involuntary unemployment simply cannot occur. Competitive pressure from those unable to obtain work will drive down wages and prices; the real purchasing power of cash balances will therefore rise beyond the currently "desired" level, and spending will increase. This process cannot cease until effective demand has risen to absorb all those willing to work for the market wage rate. For, as long as competition is unrestricted, "there always exists a sufficiently low price level such that full employment is generated" [1948, p.262].

The real-balance effect argument can be presented in terms of the "multi-gear" diagram used in the previous chapter. D_PD_P represents the potential demand for labour derived from the intended demand for consumption (both present and future). If future consumption demand manifests itself not as specific orders for future consumption but in the form of the hoarding of money, the market demand for labour as revealed in the market place (D_MD_M) is derived from present consumption demand only.

Figure 10.1: The "Multi-Gear" Economy

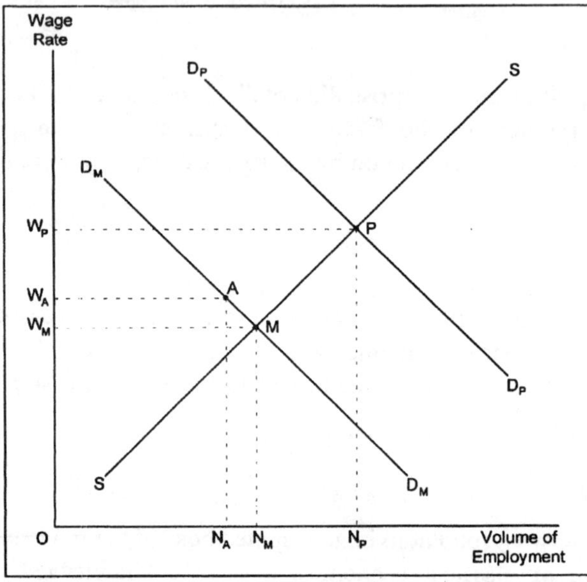

Keynes's argument is that the market equilibrium volume of employment ON_M will be below the potential equilibrium volume of employment ON_P.

Patinkin's riposte is that the real-balance effect prevents the market demand curve represented by D_MD_M from remaining in its initial position. The fall in wages and prices causes the real purchasing power of money balances to rise thus satisfying the demand for future consumption and causing the market demand curve to rise towards the potential demand curve.

If that is true, then Keynes is guilty of a major theoretical error.

In order to answer "the question of how this set of forces could have been overlooked by Keynesian economists, in general, and Keynes himself, in particular", Patinkin found it "instructive to trace through the exact chain of errors in Keynes's reasoning which caused him to overlook these factors" [1948, p.269]. "The last link in the chain of errors [occurred] when Keynes began to examine the effects of increased cash balances … , he did not even consider their possible influence on consumption" [p.270].

In defiance of the Keynesian doctrine that deficiency of effective demand could occur even in a fully operating market economy, Patinkin was therefore able to reaffirm the old orthodoxy. "*Involuntary* unemployment can, *by definition,* exist only if there are wage rigidities ... [or some other form of disequilibrium due to] the dynamic workings of the system" [pp.282,283]. The notion of an equilibrium rate of unemployment was a contradiction in terms. There could be no such thing. "The possibility of the coexistence of underemployment equilibrium and flexible prices ... is," according to Patinkin, "an indefensible position" [pp.278,279].

Classical economists before Keynes had been forced to dismiss the problem of hoarding money on the ground that it would not normally occur on a significant scale. Armed with Patinkin's real-balance effect argument, neo-classical economists after Keynes were able to argue that, even if it occurred, hoarding would have no effect on the volume of employment *unless markets were imperfect.* Unemployment could therefore be blamed once again on imperfections or rigidities in the market structure.

The Dark Days of Prohibition

Within his own family of theorists, Don Patinkin was respected and feared; he was the Godfather — the one who had masterminded the theory behind the neo-classical counter-reformation. The other Chicago gang bosses acknowledged his leadership. Harry G. Johnson, a Canadian who had made it to the very top of the organisation, gave the thumbs-up to the real-balance effect argument. It "finally disposes of the Keynesian contention that under-employment equilibrium does not depend on the assumption of wage-rigidity. It does" [1958, p.119].

Johnson was able to get the message of the neo-classical counter-reformation on to the streets. "It turns out that Keynes's theory is a special case of the classical — or rather of the neo-classical theory, since a satisfactory 'classical' theory was not worked out until after the Keynesian revolution. ... Keynes's theory started from an empirically relevant special assumption, derived some important meaningful results from it, and provided an approach which has since proved its usefulness for a wide range of problems" [p.120].

The challenge to the Keynesian authorities was obvious. Although the *General Theory* was highly praised for the relevance of its empirical assumptions, that was all. If the *General Theory* was acclaimed as a major and trail-blazing advance in *empirical* relevance — but no more, the clear implication was that it had no claim to *theoretical* significance. Keynes was damned with great praise.

Keynes's fundamental theoretical proposition — equilibrium with less than full employment — was therefore dismissed as a fallacy; it was allowed no place in the new theology. The creed of the neo-classical counter-reformation was orthodox classical theory bolstered with Keynesian empirical assumptions.

But what was needed most of all was a hit-man to turn abstract theory into practical policy — someone who could convert a scheme into a going-concern — someone able not only to defy the Keynesian authorities but also to stand up against rival gangs. The Enforcer was a ruthless mathematician from the lower East side of New York.

The Enforcer

Like many other members of the Organisation, he came from a humble background. Born in Brooklyn, New York, the son of poor immigrants, he was irresistibly drawn to the Chicago Underworld where he was able to put his talent for mathematics to good use working the numbers racket — a painstaking empirical investigation into the historical relationship between money and prices. This research was carried out so brilliantly that he soon rose to be head of a notorious gang of zealots known to the public as the "Chicago School".

The name of the Enforcer, destined to strike terror into the hearts of his Keynesian opponents, was Milton Friedman.

What really gave him his big break was the prohibition of classical economics imposed by the Keynesian authorities.

Friedman was an extremely smart operator. From Smith's ancient distillery in Scotland, classical spirit was smuggled into the United States and transported to Chicago where it was mixed with large quantities of local moonshine from illicit stills. The bottles were labelled so cleverly that they were difficult to tell from the genuine article. But, whereas Smith's pure Scotch, which had been matured for years in the wood, was smooth and mellow, Friedman's bootleg variety was almost raw spirit; it was rough and fiery. There was no doubt about its effectiveness in producing an instant feeling of inebriation, but it left its victims with a terrible hangover. That they might lose their jobs in the short run, as a "temporary side-effect", was never denied. That this condition would persist in the long run was ingeniously covered up.

In the course of the vicious gang wars which broke out in the learned journals, Friedman and his henchmen were able to terrorise their opponents with the sheer ruthlessness of their logic. The only way to buy

Protection for scholarly reputations was by accepting and retailing Friedman's bootleg brand of classical economics.

Few had the stomach to resist. Friedman and the Chicago School soon took over the south side of the City — the stockyards, the waterfront, and, most important of all, the University. Then they took over the north side, and it was not long before they had sewn up the whole of the East Coast and started to muscle-in on the West Coast as well.

It is true that the general public deplored the strong-arm tactics used by Friedman and the Chicago mob, and many onlookers were shocked at the number of innocent scholars who perished in the cross-fire. But classical free-enterprise economics had been popular before Prohibition; and it was highly addictive. Customers were reluctant to give up their freedom of choice, and businessmen found it difficult to resist the temptation to make a fast buck. Witnesses were unwilling to testify. In consequence, although some of the small-time operators were put away, Friedman himself was never convicted. He remained at large distributing the spirit of free enterprise and undermining the Keynesian faith in government intervention.

In the eyes of law-abiding Keynesians, Milton Friedman became Public Enemy Number One. The Keynesian authorities were powerless to stop the illicit dissemination of the bootleg economics. It was not long before the whole country was saturated in the classical economic spirit.

Nor did it stop there. Intellectual family connections with the old country made the classical revival a world-wide phenomenon. What gave the impetus to its irresistible spread was the strict code of "non-omerta" — volubility. No opportunity was missed for propagating the message through the communications media. Press, radio, and television were all used to advertise the case for free markets. The classical revival was unstoppable.

The Keynesian authorities, finding themselves powerless to enforce the Prohibition against Classical economics, bowed to the inevitable. Prohibition was repealed. Milton Friedman and the rest of the Chicago mob turned legitimate. The long exile was over.

The Return

Don Patinkin, the great theologian behind the rehabilitation of classical economics, returned to the Promised Land. Out of Zion went forth the Law and the word of Classical Orthodoxy from Jerusalem: "Equilibrium means full employment, or, equivalently, unemployment means disequilibrium" [1956, p.328].

Back in Chicago, even Milton Friedman had become respectable and he was accepted back into the Church. When the persistent growth of government expenditure and monetary expansion resulted in a Great Inflation, it was regarded as Divine Retribution for the wasted years of Prosperity and Full Employment inflicted on the unsuspecting masses by unprincipled Keynesianism.

The Puritans, who longed for the good old days of unemployment when the unions knew their place, were looking for a strong leader to impose the stern discipline of free competition and to uphold the strict orthodox traditions.

The choice was obvious. Friedman's underworld origins were quietly forgotten, and he was elected to the Holy See. The kid from Brooklyn had made it.

A sad postscript to this chapter mourns the passing of the outstanding monetary theorist of the second half of the twentieth century — perhaps of all time:

Don Patinkin, born Chicago January 8th 1922, died Jerusalem August 7th 1995.

CHAPTER 11

MONETARISM *IN EXCELSIS*

The first task of the new Pontiff on taking over the Holy Office was to purge the Established Church of all vestiges of the Keynesian heresy.

In a sermon delivered on the occasion of his consecration as President of the American Economic Association, Milton Friedman spelled out the principles of a fundamentalist revival and a return to the old orthodoxy of the classical tradition. Founded with the objective of wiping out the iniquities of Keynes and his followers, the new movement came to be known as "Monetarism".

Monetarism is a child of the Counter-Reformation. Its theological basis is Patinkin's argument that Keynes is guilty of having overlooked the "real-balance effect" and that the very notion of an equilibrium rate of unemployment is a contradiction in terms. According to Patinkin, there can be no such thing. "The possibility of the coexistence of underemployment equilibrium and flexible prices ... is an indefensible position" [1948, pp.278,279].

Friedman's verdict is that the real-balance effect argument "did undermine Keynes' key theoretical proposition, namely, that even in a world of flexible prices, a position of equilibrium at full employment might not exist. Henceforth, unemployment had again to be explained by rigidities or imperfections, not as the natural outcome of a fully operative market process" [1968, p.3].

The "Natural Rate" of Unemployment

Wrapped in the mantle, which once graced the shoulders of John Stuart Mill, as Defender of the Faith, Milton Friedman is the symbol of a belief in classical theology that is uncompromising. His attitude to economic policy derives from a strict fundamentalist interpretation of the neo-classical counter-reformation.

At the heart of his Monetarist theology is the notion of a "natural rate of unemployment" defined as "the level that would be ground out by the Walrasian system of general equilibrium equations, provided there is embedded in them the actual structural characteristics of the labor and commodity markets, including market imperfections, stochastic variability in demands and supplies, the cost of gathering information about job vacancies and labor availabilities, the costs of mobility, and so on" [1968, p.8].

The "natural rate of unemployment" is therefore equal to the disequilibrium rate which would occur if the market were left to itself; it is the natural outcome of market forces operating free from outside interference. Consequently, it is determined only by whatever imperfections are present within the market.

The supply and demand curves for labour, S_1S_1 and D_1D_1 in Figure 11.1, are a reflection of production technology and consumer tastes. Potential full employment equilibrium is determined, in Figure 11.1(a), by the intersection of the two curves at E.

Figure 11.1: The "Natural Rate of Unemployment"

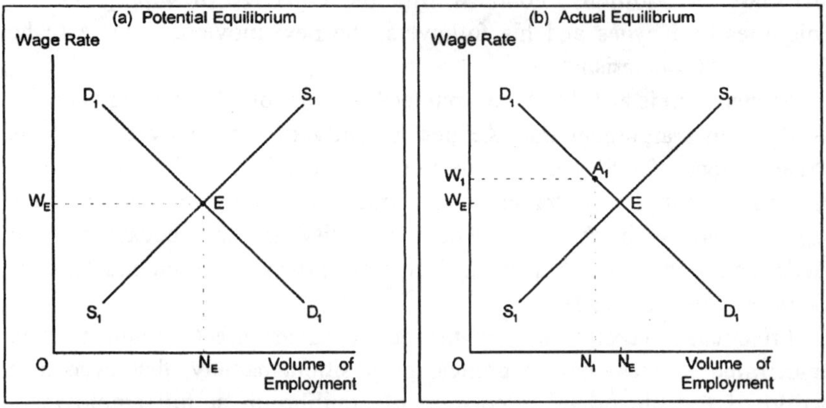

Whether or not potential full employment equilibrium is actually achieved depends on the perfection of the market.

In a Walrasian Utopia of perfect wage and price flexibility, the pressure of competition pushes the wage rate to its "market-clearing" equilibrium level at W_E, so that potential full employment amounting to ON_E is achieved.

But the real world is subject to what Friedman calls "the actual structural characteristics of the labor and commodity markets, including market imperfections, stochastic variability in demands and supplies, the cost of gathering information about job vacancies and labor availabilities, the costs of mobility, and so on" [1968, p.8]. These imperfections prevent the wage rate falling to the market clearing level: in Figure 11.1(b), potential full employment equilibrium at E is not achieved. There is insufficient competitive pressure to force the wage rate down to its "market-clearing" equilibrium level at W_E: it is kept up at W_1 by monopoly power and restrictive practices. Consequently, the economy finds itself in a position of disequilibrium at A_1, where the actual volume of employment ON_1 is below the equilibrium full employment level ON_E.

Because the market is imperfect, potential full employment equilibrium is not achieved. "The actual structural characteristics of the labor and commodity markets" cause the actual level of employment to fall short (by the distance, N_1N_E) of the full employment potential.

N_1N_E is the "natural rate of unemployment" caused by the imperfection of the market. "Many of the market characteristics that determine its level are man-made and policy made. ... Legal minimum wage rates ... and the strength of labor unions all make the natural rate of unemployment higher than it would otherwise be" [p.9].

Tackling market imperfection, however, can be a dangerous business. It often involves a politically risky confrontation with powerful vested economic interests. A weak government may prefer to embark on a policy of monetary expansion in an attempt to conceal the consequences of the "natural rate of unemployment" without removing the causes.

"Let us assume that the monetary authority tries to peg the "market" rate of unemployment at a level below the "natural rate", ... [and] increases the rate of monetary growth. This will be expansionary. By making nominal cash balances higher than people desire, it will tend initially ... to stimulate spending. [The demand curve for labour will shift upwards from D_1D_1 in Figure 11.1 to D_2D_2 in Figure 11.2.] ... Producers will tend to react to the initial expansion in aggregate demand by increasing output, employees by working longer hours, and the unemployed, by taking jobs now offered at former nominal wages" [pp.9,10].

Figure 11.2: The Effect of Monetary Expansion

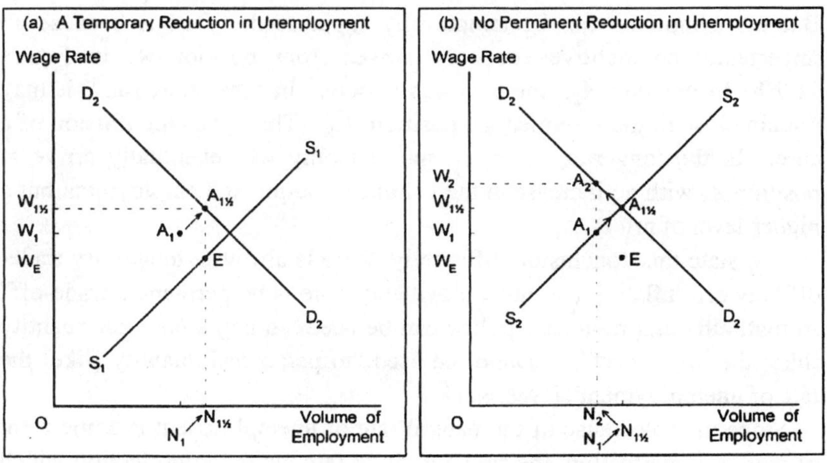

Stimulated by the extra demand, the level of wages and the volume of employment will both be higher than before. In the imperfect world of Figure 11.2(a), the point of actual unemployment disequilibrium moves up from A_1 to $A_{1\frac{1}{2}}$, and the volume of employment increases from N_1 to $N_{1\frac{1}{2}}$.

But the matter does not end there.

$A_{1\frac{1}{2}}$ turns out to be only an intermediate position.

The supply curve for labour S_1S_1 showing the relationship between output and prices is, as Friedman points out, "at the earlier price level" [1968, p.8]. But the supply of labour depends, not on the nominal money wage, but on the real wage. If the willingness of employees to supply labour at various levels of real wage remains unchanged, the supply curve shifts upwards in nominal terms so that the same real wage as before corresponds to each level of employment.

It is because the supply curve of labour remains unchanged in terms of the real wage that, in Figure 11.2(b), it shifts upwards from S_1S_1 to S_2S_2 in terms of the money wage.

In the imperfectly competitive economy of Figure 11.2(b), the new disequilibrium is established at A_2, where the volume of employment is ON_2, and the wage rate is OW_2. The final result is that employment eventually returns to its initial volume but at a higher level of wages and prices.

"It takes time for people to adjust to a new state of demand" [p,10]. But, when sufficient time has elapsed, the increase in money prices and wages in response to the rise in nominal demand "will tend to return unemployment to its former level" [p.10].

The "natural rate of unemployment" cannot be reduced by this means. But the symptoms can be temporarily suppressed. That is because an imperfectly competitive economy moves from position A_1 in Figure 11.2(b) to position A_2; but it moves slowly. In "the short run", it may remain close to the intermediate position $A_{1\frac{1}{2}}$. That gives the illusion of a cure. In the long run, however, the economy will eventually arrive at position A_2 with no increase in the volume of output and employment but a higher level of prices.

"To state this conclusion differently, there is always a temporary trade-off between inflation and unemployment; there is no permanent trade-off" so that, although monetary policy can be used "to peg a nominal quantity [like] the price level", it cannot be used "to peg a real quantity [like] the rate of unemployment" [1968, p.11].

Since the sole cause of the natural rate of unemployment is some form of market imperfection, the sole cure is to remove the imperfection which prevents the wage rate from moving quickly to its equilibrium level. "Improvements in employment exchanges, in availability of information about job vacancies and labor supply, and so on, would tend to lower the natural rate of unemployment" [p.9].

The moral which Friedman draws from this story is that well-intentioned Keynesian policies of expansion can produce temporary increases in the level of employment. But, they "cannot peg the rate of unemployment for more than very limited periods" [p.5]. It is only a matter of time before they work through into prices.

The inflationary process described in Figure 11.2 is an illustration of "demand-pull" inflation which is stimulated when a nation attempts to increase its consumption (through private or government spending) faster than it is willing or able to increase its production.

Unfortunately, once the inflationary process has been allowed to become established, it cannot be simply switched off.

From Demand-Pull to Cost-Push

The initial weakness opens a Pandora's Box of inflationary expectations.

Even if the government has learned its lesson and does not initiate further rounds of monetary expansion, it may find that its hand is forced.

Encouraged by the success of the previous round of wage claims, union leaders may be tempted to try again and repeat the process. That leads to "cost-push" inflation, where the supply curve (in Figure 11.3) is shifted upwards to S_3S_3.

Figure 11.3: The Inflationary Spiral — Cost-Push

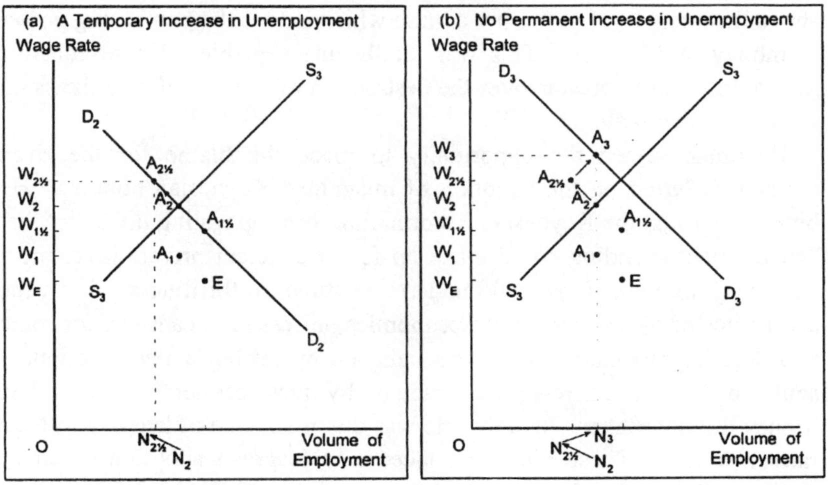

This reduces the level of employment (in Figure 11.3(a)) even further (to $ON_{2½}$) as workers "price themselves out of jobs". Simply to prevent unemployment rising above its "natural rate", governments (often under as much pressure from employers as from unions) are encouraged to expand the money supply to finance the latest round of wage claims. If the government succumbs, the result is a shift in demand to D_3D_3 (in Figure 11.3(b)), and the economy moves to A_3. The result confirms the monetarist argument. The economy returns to its "natural rate of unemployment" at ON_3. But the price level has moved up by one more ratchet.

Demand-pull and cost-push pressures are not isolated. They feed on each other as demand and supply chase each other up the inflationary spiral.

That, in very simple terms, is the theory behind Monetarism. How does it work in practice?

The Great Inflation

In an influential book entitled *The Great Inflation: 1939-1951*, "the inflation of 1939-51" is described as "in any sense one of the greatest, if not the greatest, in the history of the world economy" [Brown (1955) p.v]. But that period included both the Second World War and the Korean War. During the 1950s, to the consternation of professional economists, the rate of price inflation reached the alarming rate of over 3% per annum.

By the end of the 1960s, the rate of price inflation was high and accelerating rapidly. In both Britain and the United States, it had risen above the crisis level of 5% per annum which halves the purchasing power of money in 14 years. This was totally unacceptable. No responsible government could preside over the destruction of savings of its citizens on such a massive scale.

Friedman seized the opportunity to place the blame for the *Even Greater Inflation* on the adoption of misguided Keynesian policies. He bitterly attacked the Keynesian Reformation for propagating the belief that "government spending could make up for insufficient private investment [and that] tax reductions could undermine stubborn thriftiness. The wide acceptance of these views in the economics profession meant that for some two decades monetary policy was believed by all but a few reactionary souls to have been rendered obsolete by new economic knowledge. Money did not matter. Its only role was the minor one of keeping interest rates low ... . These views produced a widespread adoption of cheap money policies after the war. And they received a rude shock when these policies failed in country after country. ... Inflation, stimulated by cheap money policies, not the widely heralded postwar depression, turned out to be the order of the day" [1968, p.2].

Keynes was thus exposed as a false Messiah, branded as the architect of inflation and creeping state control, and condemned as an economic illiterate who committed the unpardonable sin of believing that "money did not matter".

Price stability could be achieved only by a return to the principles of sound money based on strict adherence to orthodox classical tradition.

The Monetarist Program for Monetary Correction

Friedman's "Program for Monetary Stability" is a reaffirmation of "the conviction", criticised by Keynes, "that money makes no real difference except frictionally" [1936, p.19]. Using Mill's famous analogy of money as "a machine for doing quickly and commodiously, what would be done, though less quickly and commodiously, without it," the lesson which Friedman draws from his own studies of monetary history is that "monetary policy can prevent money itself from being a major source of economic disturbance" by ensuring that "the machine" does not "get out of order", and it can "provide a stable background for the economy" by keeping "the machine well oiled". His policy "prescription" is that "the monetary authority should guide itself by magnitudes that it can control" and "avoid sharp swings in policy" "by adopting publicly the policy of achieving a steady rate of growth in a specified monetary total" [1968, pp.12-16].

A steady rate of monetary growth tailored to the long term growth potential of the real economy would maintain stability in the level of prices. If an improvement in productivity causes an increase in production of, say, 4%, a compensating increase in the wage rate permits an increase in consumption of 4% without causing prices to rise. As long as a wage increase is earned by a corresponding increase in production, an increase in the money supply is appropriate for financing the increased volume of business at the existing level of prices.

In Friedman's opinion, "the precise rate of growth, like the precise monetary total, is less important than the adoption of some stated and known rate. [The] rate that would on the average achieve rough stability in the level of prices of final products, which [Friedman himself has] estimated would call for something like a 3 to 5 per cent per year rate of growth in currency plus all commercial bank deposits or a slightly lower rate of growth in currency plus demand deposits only" [1968, p.16].

Monetary expansion to finance a rise in real wages earned as the reward for an increase in productivity is therefore to be welcomed. An improvement in living standards of this type is a characteristic feature of the economic progress which impressed Adam Smith.

A monetarist policy of keeping monetary expansion in line with real expansion would also have the effect of preventing the monetary system from being put out of order by government interference. It is therefore advertised as a policy of non-intervention designed to allow the economy to realise its fullest practicably attainable potential (at the "natural rate" of unemployment) with a reasonable promise of price stability.

Control over the money supply is recommended not only for preventing inflation but also as a cure. "Monetary policy can hold any inflationary dangers in check by a slower rate of monetary growth than would otherwise be desirable" [p.14].

The inflationary dangers caused by irresponsible monetary expansion to finance wage claims which are not justified by increased productivity have been demonstrated in Figures 11.2 and 11.3.

The monetarist answer is firm monetary discipline.

Faced with inflationary pressure of the kind illustrated in Figure 11.4(a) (which is a reproduction of Figure 11.3(a)), the government must stand firm. If it refuses to finance inflationary wage claims by monetary expansion, the demand curve will remain at D_2D_2. Instead of following the path described in Figure 11.3(b), the economy will remain at $A_{2\frac{1}{2}}$. This halts the wage price spiral, but the volume of employment will remain depressed at $ON_{2\frac{1}{2}}$. Unemployment will rise above its "natural rate" to an extent indicated by the distance $N_{2\frac{1}{2}}N_2$ in Figure 11.4(a).

Figure 11.4: The Inflationary Spiral — Monetarist Resistance

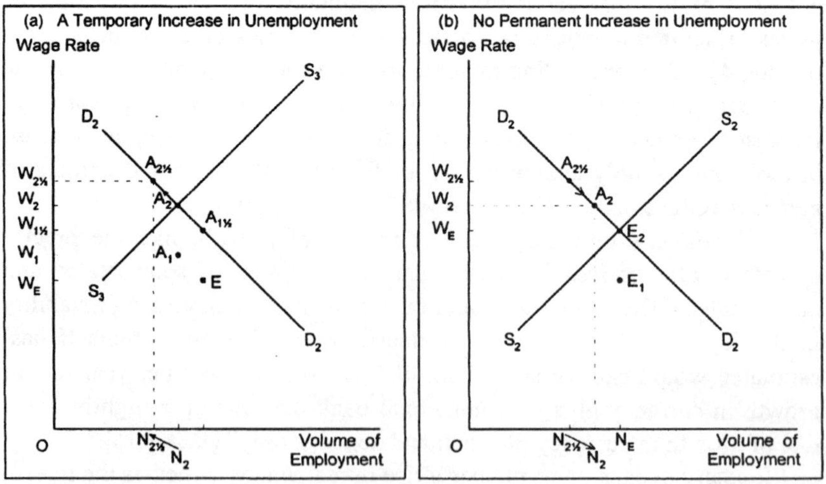

"Unemployment is an inevitable side effect of an effective policy to damp down inflation ... — because of the time that it takes for the tapering off of total demand to be recognised by employers and employees for what it is, and for contractual arrangements to be readjusted to the new situation" [1974(b)].

But once "the tapering off of total demand" actually has been "recognised by employers and employees for what it is", "contractual arrangements" are "readjusted to the new situation" by the return of the supply curve to its previous position at S_2S_2.

The vicious spiral, in which demand-pull and cost-push inflation continuously feed upon each other, can be broken. But governments must display the "political will" to endure the pain at $A_{2½}$, until the tide is turned and inflationary expectations are "squeezed out" of the economy.

Monetarism and the Unions

Presented like this, the battle against inflation looks like a struggle between the monetary authority (as the force for good) and the unions (as the forces of evil). Critics have therefore raised objections to monetarism on the grounds that it is anti-union, that it blames union leaders for causing inflation, and that it seeks to use unemployment or the threat of unemployment as a punishment to deter such anti-social behaviour.

This is unfair and reflects a misunderstanding of Friedman's argument.

Milton Friedman is certainly no friend of labour unions (or any other sort of union — business or professional), and he holds them responsible for many economic evils. But inflation is not one of them.

It is monetary irresponsibility on the part of the government which Friedman identifies as the culprit. Inflationary wage claims are not, in his view, the cause of inflation, but one of its symptoms. If the government allows the supply of money to expand faster than the volume of real output, any responsible union leader has a duty to make wage claims to cover the inevitable rise in prices.

Friedman's attitude is clearly explained in a letter to *The Economist*.

"In my view, neither unemployment nor the threat of unemployment is a tool for damping down wage inflation or strikes" [1974b]. "The recession and unemployment that typically accompany the reduction of inflation are not the cure but a side-effect" [1974a, p.15]. "I have been dismayed, even in my few days in London, at the widespread support of "union-bashing" as a way to attack inflation. Unions do much harm, primarily by restricting the employment opportunities available to the more disadvantaged of your citizens. But they do not produce and have not produced inflation. On the contrary, one of the unfortunate effects of inflation has been to strengthen unions. Blaming unions for inflation leads to wrong policy, to evasion of the real problem and, even more tragically, to weakening the political fabric of your society" [1974b].

Monetarism and the Government

Friedman is commendably honest about the bitterness of the monetarist pill, and the consequent difficulty in persuading the patient to take the cure.

"There is no technical problem about how to end inflation .... The real obstacles are political, not technical." For "ending inflation would also have the side-effect of producing a temporary, though perhaps fairly protracted, period of economic recession or slowdown and of relatively high unemployment. The political will is today lacking to accept that side-effect" [1974a, p.9]. "Such side effects constitute, I believe, the most important political obstacle to ending inflation, given, first, the commitment on the part of the US, UK and most other governments to 'full employment', secondly the failure of the public at large to recognise the inevitable if temporary side-effects of ending inflation, and, thirdly, the unwillingness or inability of political leaders to persuade the public to accept these side-effects" [pp.17,18].

Old-fashioned classical morality is vindicated. A return to sound money is the monetarist prescription for squeezing inflation out of the system. In the real world of imperfect markets, however, monetary changes are not translated instantaneously into prices. That is why the monetarist cure for inflation comes with the warning that "unemployment is an inevitable side effect of an effective policy to damp down inflation ... — because of the time that it takes for the tapering off of total demand to be recognised by employers and employees for what it is, and for contractual arrangements to be readjusted to the new situation" [1974b].

If governments have the resolution to resist inflationary pressure by restricting monetary expansion, the upward shifting supply curve of labour meets a demand curve which is not obligingly accommodating. The immediate effect is a temporary increase in the level of unemployment. The ultimate reward is a reduction in unemployment to its natural rate and a significant slowdown in the rate of price inflation.

"We are all Monetarists now ..."

The experience of the British economy (set out in Table 11.1) is an object lesson in monetarist theory.

In retrospect, it is easy to see where Keynesianism failed.

While it is perfectly true that Keynesian policies of monetary expansion achieved low levels of unemployment during the 1950s and early 1960s, these were purely temporary as economies moved from positions like A_1 to positions like $A_{1\frac{1}{2}}$ (in Figure 11.2). But these low levels could not be sustained indefinitely. Eventually, in confirmation of the monetarist theory, they worked through into prices as economies moved from $A_{1\frac{1}{2}}$ to A_2.

Bearing out Friedman's contention that "one of the unfortunate effects of inflation has been to strengthen unions" [1974(b)], the supply curve for labour was shifted upwards along the path indicated in Figure 11.3. In the late 'sixties and early 'seventies, the level of unemployment doubled as the economy moved to $A_{2\frac{1}{2}}$. Government efforts to get the level of unemployment down led to the massive inflation of the mid-seventies. That is how, in monetarist theology, the temporarily full employment of the 1950s and 1960s led to the inflation and unemployment of the 1970s.

Table 11.1: Inflation and Unemployment in the United Kingdom

1950s	1950	1951	1952	1953	1954	1955	1956	1957	1958	1959	AVERAGE
	%	%	%	%	%	%	%	%	%	%	%
Inflation [1]	2.6	9.4	6.0	2.0	1.9	3.5	4.6	3.4	2.7	0.6	3.6
Unemployment [2]	1.3	1.1	1.6	1.5	1.2	1.0	1.1	1.3	1.9	1.9	1.4
1960s	**1960**	**1961**	**1962**	**1963**	**1964**	**1965**	**1966**	**1967**	**1968**	**1969**	**AVERAGE**
	%	%	%	%	%	%	%	%	%	%	%
Inflation	1.0	3.6	4.1	2.1	3.2	4.8	3.9	2.4	4.7	5.5	3.5
Unemployment	1.3	1.2	1.6	2.0	2.6	2.0	2.1	3.1	3.1	2.9	2.2
1970s	**1970**	**1971**	**1972**	**1973**	**1974**	**1975**	**1976**	**1977**	**1978**	**1979**	**AVERAGE**
	%	%	%	%	%	%	%	%	%	%	%
Inflation	6.4	9.4	7.1	9.2	15.9	24.2	16.5	15.9	8.2	13.5	12.5
Unemployment	3.0	3.6	4.0	3.0	2.9	4.3	5.6	6.0	5.9	5.0	4.3
1980s	**1980**	**1981**	**1982**	**1983**	**1984**	**1985**	**1986**	**1987**	**1988**	**1989**	**AVERAGE**
	%	%	%	%	%	%	%	%	%	%	%
Inflation	18.0	11.9	8.6	4.6	5.0	6.1	3.4	4.1	4.9	7.8	7.4
Unemployment	6.4	9.8	11.3	12.4	11.7	11.2	11.2	10.3	8.6	7.2	10.0
1990s	**1990**	**1991**	**1992**	**1993**	**1994**	**1995**	**1996**	**1997**	**1998**	**1999**	**AVERAGE**
	%	%	%	%	%	%	%	%	%	%	%
Inflation	9.5	5.9	3.7	1.6	2.4	3.5	2.4				4.1
Unemployment	6.9	8.8	10.1	10.4	9.6	8.7	8.2				9.0

Sources: 1. Inflation (annual % change in the Consumer Price Index). *International Financial Statistics Yearbook*. New York: IMF.
2. Unemployment (standardised annual unemployment rates as a % of the total labour force). *Labour Force Statistics*. Paris: OECD.

By the middle of the 1970s, "double-digit" inflation had become widespread in the OECD countries. In 1975, Great Britain experienced an inflation rate of almost 25% per annum. At that rate, it takes only 3 years to halve the purchasing power of money. The announcement made by *The Economist* in its issue of November 29, 1975, (quoted once before in chapter 2 above) was typical of press comment at the time. "In the 18 months to mid-1975 Britons with any savings lost a quarter of the real value of their personally-held financial wealth. Over £35 billion was taken from them by inflation." Few politicians had the will *not* to take the monetarist cure.

Country after country adopted policies of "sound money". In the OECD countries, between 1975 and 1985, the rate of inflation was halved, but the level of unemployment was doubled. World inflation was curbed at the expense of a world recession.

It was then that the political beauty of monetarism became manifest in all its glory.

Governments responsible for introducing these policies proudly claimed success, on the ground that the cut in the rate of inflation was permanent and was the result of their own policies. The increase in unemployment was dismissed as "temporary" and, although admitted by Friedman himself to be "inevitable", it was explained away as an Act of God known as "the world recession".

Monetarist theory was vindicated.

Adopting the orthodox classical view that money does not matter, except frictionally, Friedman had argued that monetary policy could be used "to peg a nominal quantity [like] the price level", but it could not be used "to peg a real quantity [like] the rate of unemployment" [1968, p.11].

And he had been proved right.

As a weapon against unemployment, monetary expansion was shown to be both ineffective and unsafe. The reduction in the level of unemployment was only temporary, whereas the increase in the level of prices was permanent.

By the same token, as a weapon against inflation, monetary restriction was shown to be not only effective but also safe. The reduction in the rate of inflation was permanent, but the reduction in the volume of employment was only temporary.

The Moral Code

The message of Monetarism is the same as that of Mill's *Principles* and Adam Smith's *Wealth of Nations*.

The sole cause of unemployment is imperfection in the market structure. Consequently, the only effective long-term cure is the removal of obstacles to free competition. The sole cause of inflation is monetary irresponsibility. Consequently, the only effective long-term cure is sound money.

The moral code is the one recommended by the classical economists:

for full employment – free competition,
for stable prices – sound money,
for economic growth – thrift.

The success of the neo-classical counter-reformation both in theory and in practice caused the fundamentalist religious revival to spread far beyond the ranks of the monetarists and led to the development of a New Orthodoxy.

We are all monetarists now … .

CHAPTER 12

THE NEW ORTHODOXY

The claim that "we are all monetarists now" may sound a trifle extravagant. Not everyone is a "monetarist". There are many economists proud to call themselves "Keynesian". To them, Milton Friedman is an abomination.

Yet, however much it may sound like a contradiction in terms, it is to the most dedicated opponents of monetarism that the claim "we are all monetarists now" applies most particularly.

The Resurgence of Fundamentalism

The great religious revival generated by the counter-reformation in economic theory has inspired a return to the fundamentals of the True Religion.

In the Free-Market version of the Lord's Prayer, "Our Father which art in heaven" is Adam Smith; "Thy Kingdom come" looks forward to a Walrasian Utopia; "Thy Will be done" is an appeal for perfect competition; "Lead us not in to Temptation" is a plea for freedom from monopoly and restrictive practices — and, most particularly, for deliverance from government interference.

The immaculate conception of Walras is enshrined in the word of the divine law from the lips of the Prophet Patinkin. "Equilibrium means full employment, or, equivalently, unemployment means disequilibrium" [1956, p.328].

That is the Holy Writ — the modern version of "Say's Law" — to which all believers pledge unquestioning obedience. It is a return to the Classical Doctrine of Mill's *Principles*; and the Classical Doctrine has re-established itself as the New Orthodoxy.

The New Orthodoxy owes its acceptance to the public recantation made by the leaders of the Keynesian reformation.

The Return of the Keynesian Prodigals

Under the theoretical onslaught of the counter-reformation, the Keynesians simply capitulated. The exposure of Keynes's fundamental theoretical error left them with little choice.

According to Patinkin, "the fundamental argument of Keynes is directed against the belief that price flexibility can be depended upon to generate full employment automatically. The defenders of the classical tradition, on the other hand, still insist upon this automaticity as a basic tenet" [1948, p.252].

Unable to offer any resistance to Patinkin's real-balance effect argument, the Keynesians unconditionally surrendered to the classical view. They were forced to accept Patinkin's conclusion that "the possibility of the coexistence of underemployment equilibrium and flexible prices ... is an indefensible position" [1948, pp.278,279].

Sinners who had been led astray by Keynes's *General Theory* repented of their iniquity and prayed for absolution. They were able to return to the fold following public confessions made by some of the most distinguished Keynesian theologians.

"There is every reason to doubt," admitted Axel Leijonhufvud "that Keynes ever set out on the quixotic quest of reconciling perfect price-flexibility with unemployment of resources" [1968, p.53n]. "Involuntary unemployment is a disequilibrium phenomenon," agreed James Tobin (winner of the Nobel Prize for Economics in 1981), "what Keynes calls equilibrium should be viewed as persistent disequilibrium" [1972, pp.2,4].

With the capitulation of the "Keynesians", the influence of the neo-classical counter-reformation spread far beyond the enclaves of the fundamentalist zealots. The old classical doctrine that equilibrium means full employment was reinstated as the "new orthodoxy".

Following the restoration of classical orthodoxy, there was a great ingathering of exiles as all true believers in the Free Trade Religion returned to the bosom of the Holy Mother Church.

The New Bible

It is only to be expected that the New Orthodoxy in economic theology should have its very own bible.

The New Bible is not simply a modern translation of the old one. Written by Paul Samuelson (winner of the Nobel Prize for Economics in 1970), and entitled simply "Economics", it is rather like a manual which is continually updated to keep abreast of the latest fashions in economic thought. New editions appear every three or four years — the first having been published in 1948, the fifteenth (with W.D. Nordhaus as joint author) in 1995. It has been extremely successful because it provides an accurate reflection of the current trends and changing fashions among the leading theologians, and it is presented in language which is easily accessible to the lay members of the Church.

Such has been the pace of change in economic thinking during the last fifty years (which encompass the Keynesian Reformation and the subsequent Monetarist Counter-Reformation) that, on the crucial question of unemployment, the modern editions, which reflect the New Orthodoxy, bear hardly any resemblance to the first.

Perhaps the most striking aspect of the New Orthodoxy is that, on the vital question of unemployment, it is a reversion to the Classical Doctrine laid down by John Stuart Mill.

The Resurrection of the Classical Doctrine

The explanation of unemployment in the 15th edition of the New Bible could easily have been written by Mill or Pigou. It is presented in terms of the now traditional supply and demand analysis applied to the market for labour.

"The left-hand panel [of Figure 12.1] ... shows the usual picture of competitive supply and demand, with a market equilibrium at point *E* and a wage of *W*. ... In (a), wages move up or down to clear the labor market. All unemployment is voluntary. Part (b) shows what happens if wages do not adjust to clear the labor market. At the too high wage at W_H, OL_D workers are employed, but L_DL_S workers are involuntarily unemployed" [Samuelson & Nordhaus (1995) pp.564,565].

Figure 12.1: Unemployment According to the "New Orthodoxy"

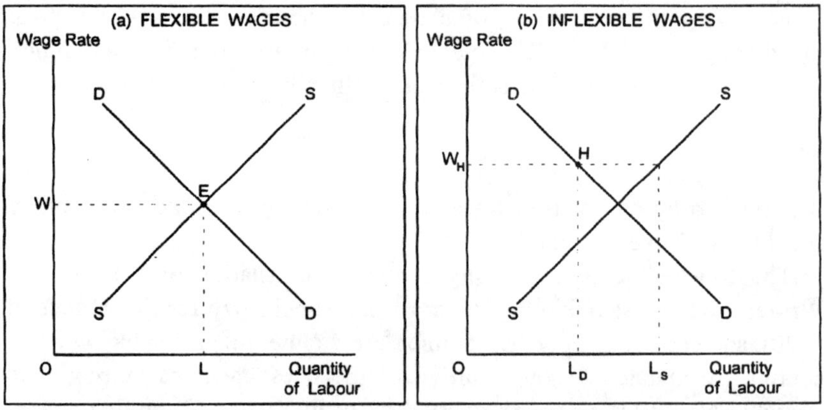

The point is made extremely clearly in the previous edition. "A labor market characterized by perfectly flexible wages will not contain involuntary unemployment. Prices and wages simply float up or down until the markets are cleared. In any economy with perfectly flexible wages, widespread unemployment such as that in the 1930s or 1980s would simply not exist" [Samuelson & Nordhaus (1992) p.578].

The classical doctrine that equilibrium means full employment is unchallenged as the central tenet of the New Orthodoxy. Church unity is safe, and the debate on equilibrium economics is at an end.

Colonel Torrens (whose 1821 prophecy has been quoted on p.63 above) is finally vindicated: with respect to the economics of equilibrium, at least, the period of controversy has passed away, and that of unanimity has arrived. There scarcely exists a doubt respecting any of its fundamental principles.

Policy disputes among the rival sects are as fierce as ever. But they cannot be attributed to embarrassing conflicts over fundamental theory; they are the result of legitimate differences of opinion about the nature of the real world.

As long as they derive from a shared theology, empirical differences are no threat to the unity of the Orthodox Church. They are therefore openly admitted by the New Bible.

Sectarian Conflict: the "Keynesians" and the "Monetarists"

"At the heart of the classical view is the belief that prices and wages are flexible and that wage-price flexibility provides a self-correcting mechanism that quickly restores full employment and always maintains potential output. ... Keynes' *General Theory* offered an alternative macroeconomic theory. ... Whereas the classical approach assumed flexible prices and wages ... the Keynesian approach insisted on price and wage inflexibility. ... Keynes and his followers emphasized that because wages and prices are inflexible, there is no economic mechanism that will quickly restore full employment and ensure that the economy produces at full capacity" [Samuelson & Nordhaus (1995) pp.602,603].

Following their triumph (chronicled in the previous chapter) on the theoretical front, the Monetarists have, in recent years, made a significant advance on the empirical front by taking full advantage of what has become known as the "rational expectations hypothesis".

Monetarism and "Rational Expectations"

Monetarists believe that, although positions like $A_{1\frac{1}{2}}$ (in Figure 12.2, which is a reproduction of Figure 11.2) can be achieved temporarily, they are not sustainable in the long run. Some of the more zealous members of the sect argue that such positions are not sustainable even in the short run.

The extreme form of this belief is based on what has come to be known as the "rational expectations hypothesis".

The "rational expectations hypothesis" does not imply that people never make mistakes; it implies merely that they do not normally continue to repeat the same mistakes over and over again. On the contrary, they learn from them. As Confucius might have said: "Man who stubs toe on edge of bath ... treads more warily in future."

This provides some justification for the belief that, even if the labour market is riddled with the imperfections symptomatic of monopoly "collective" bargaining between big unions and big business, its reactions to situations which have been encountered on previous occasions may be surprisingly fast.

Figure 12.2: The Effect of Monetary Expansion

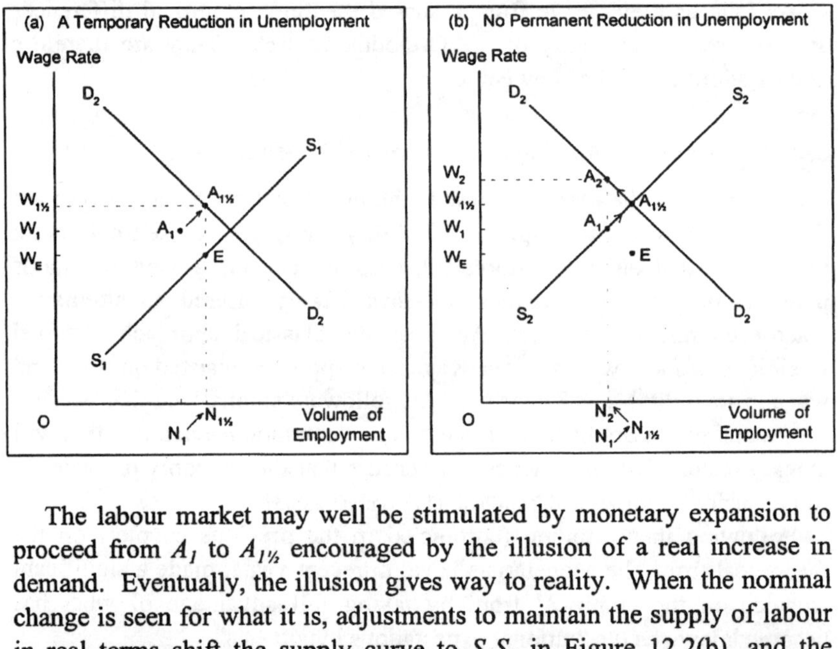

The labour market may well be stimulated by monetary expansion to proceed from A_1 to $A_{1½}$ encouraged by the illusion of a real increase in demand. Eventually, the illusion gives way to reality. When the nominal change is seen for what it is, adjustments to maintain the supply of labour in real terms shift the supply curve to S_2S_2 in Figure 12.2(b), and the market moves towards A_2. Next time round, experience of the previous occasion leads to the expectation of a similar outcome. The illusion does not last so long. Consequently, the shift in the supply curve takes place more quickly. Once the market has got used to Keynesian policies of monetary expansion, monetary injections become a habit. The drug loses its effect. The economy spends less time at positions like $A_{1½}$ and moves more directly to positions like A_2. Larger and larger doses produce a smaller and smaller effect. Each time, the addict requires a larger fix.

Unions which learn from their experience of government policy cease to be fooled by the illusion of real gains; they adjust rapidly to the inflationary reality. Expansionary monetary policy is a signal to unions to incorporate inflationary expectations in their wage and salary claims; it is an encouragement to firms to grant them, in the knowledge that government policy will finance such claims even though they have not been earned by real increases in productivity.

Monetarists are prepared to concede the initial success of Keynesian policies in moving the economy towards positions like $A_{1½}$. But they point out that success in maintaining low levels of unemployment with low rates of inflation for prolonged periods has usually been achieved with the aid of direct intervention through wage and price controls in an effort to prevent the supply curve from shifting upwards in response to the rise in prices.

Sectarian Consensus

The New Bible presents the source of conflict between the rival sects as empirical rather than theoretical.

"One of the precepts of Keynesian economics is that prices and wages are "sticky". While generally accepting the view that there is *some* inertia in wage-price setting, … monetarists think that Keynesian economists exaggerate the economy's wage-price stickiness. … The disputes today are ones of emphasis rather than of fundamental beliefs" [1995, p.608].

This account of the nature of the conflict upholds the unity of the New Orthodox Church. Both sides of the controversy between the Keynesians and the Monetarists can claim to be true guardians of the Orthodox Faith. They can appeal to the New Bible for confirmation that what separates them is not a theoretical dispute at all; it is simply that they hold different views of the nature of the real world.

After fifty years, the great debate between Keynes and the Classics is no longer a Sectarian Conflict; it has turned into a Sectarian Consensus.

The Sectarian Consensus is that the economy is a single-gear machine.

CHAPTER 13

THE SINGLE-GEAR ECONOMY

> "It was a beautiful spring morning. Uncle Milton was driving along in his motor car. Only one thing spoilt his enjoyment. He kept being overtaken by other vehicles. This irritated him so intensely that he went straight back home and did an enormous amount of research. He made the remarkable discovery that oil has the property of making machines operate more efficiently. So he set to work and carefully lubricated every single part of his motor car.
>
> Things were a little better, but not much.
>
> Poor old Uncle Milton never realised that it was possible to change out of first gear."
>
> [from *The Tragic Tale of Milton's Motor*]

The central tenet of the New Orthodoxy is that the economy is a single-gear machine.

The SIZE of the engine is determined by *tastes and technology*. Consequently, the size is not permanently fixed. It changes as tastes and technology change. An economy with a large population of thrifty, hard-working, enterprising, inventive, and well-educated individuals, with the good fortune to inherit a wealth of natural resources or manufactured constructions, has a much larger engine with a much greater output potential than an economy which lacks these advantages.

The machine, whatever its size, cannot operate efficiently unless it is well-oiled. LUBRICATION is provided by *competition*. The freer the competition, the lower the frictional resistance. If competition were perfectly Utopian, the machine would be absolutely frictionless.

The machine cannot operate without fuel. The FUEL is *money*. There is an optimum quantity of money which will drive the machine with stable prices: too little money will cause the price level to fall, too much will cause it to rise.

Whether the economy has a high or a low potential depends on tastes and technology.

Whether or not the economy reaches its full potential, depends on the degree of competition.

Whether or not prices will be stable depends on the quantity of money.

That, in short, is the New Orthodoxy.

The Single-Gear Economy

The New Orthodoxy is conditioned by the belief that the economy is a single-gear machine.

The size of the engine, as determined by tastes and technology, is reflected in the supply and demand curves of Figure 13.1. Full employment potential is determined by the intersection at *M*. The New Orthodoxy does not accept the possibility of a deficiency of effective demand. Unlike the "multi-gear" diagram of Figure 9.1, there is no divergence between potential demand and effective demand revealed in the market place. Consequently, market equilibrium is the same as potential equilibrium. Since the gear ratio is fixed and cannot change, market equilibrium cannot diverge from potential equilibrium. Point *M* and point *P* (which diverge in the "multi-gear" diagram) coincide. They are, according to the New Orthodoxy, one and the same.*

Figure 13.1: The "Single-Gear" Economy

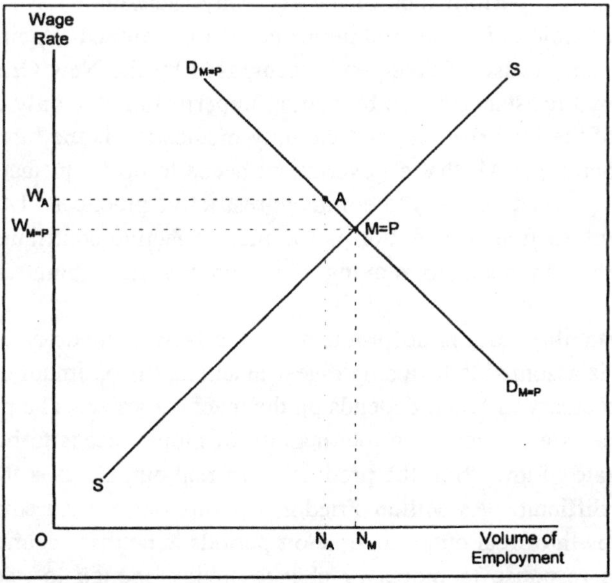

The only possible cause of failure of a single-gear economy to achieve full employment potential is some form of market imperfection. Frictional resistance prevents the engine from achieving its full potential. In

* The diagram is drawn in terms of the volume of employment. Improvements in technology which increase productivity mean that a given level of employment will produce an increasing volume of output.

Figure 13.1, frictional resistance takes the form of a wage rate, W_A, maintained at a level higher than the market-clearing rate W_M. The actual disequilibrium level of employment ON_A falls short of the potential equilibrium level ON_M, and unemployment is equal to N_AN_M.

Better lubrication in the form of more perfect competition would move point *A* closer to point *M* at which the market clears. This also happens to coincide with point *P* at which the economy reaches its full potential.

Price Stability and Full Employment in a Single-Gear Economy

If the government wishes to achieve full employment without inflation, its scope for action (or inaction) is clear. It is clear precisely because the economy is regarded by the New Orthodoxy as a single-gear machine.

(a) Few Technical Problems ...

Full employment is no problem for the New Orthodoxy. The object is to bring the actual performance of the economy (determined at point *A*) as close as possible to its potential performance (determined at point *M* = *P*). Since the only cause of divergence recognised by the New Orthodoxy is the frictional resistance set up by market imperfection, the only cure is the removal of the imperfection, and the only medication is the lubrication of free competition. All that a government needs to do — in fact, the only useful thing it can do — is to eliminate restrictive practices. Dismantling any barriers to free competition is the most effective contribution that a government can make to moving the economy from point *A* towards point *M*.

Price stability, too, is no problem for the New Orthodoxy. Since the economy is assumed to be a single-gear machine, the optimum quantity of money necessary to fuel it depends on the machine's size. The principle is simple: the rate of growth in the quantity of money needs to be matched with the rate of growth in the production of real output. It is the practice which is difficult. As Milton Friedman points out, measurement of the rate of growth of real output over short periods is neither accurate enough nor is the response to monetary changes quick enough to permit "fine tuning" of the money supply. It is like steering an oil tanker; there is a tendency towards over-correction — "too much, too late". That is why he recommends that "the monetary authority should ... avoid sharp swings in policy ... by adopting publicly the policy of achieving a steady rate of growth in a specified monetary total" [1968, pp.12-16].

To the New Orthodoxy, the economic prescription poses no problem. "The real obstacles are," in Friedman's words, "political, not technical" [1974a, p.9].

(b) ... Plenty of Political Problems

It is all very well for the priests of the New Orthodoxy to agree that the only effective step that the government can take towards full employment is to increase the freedom to compete by using its power and influence to reduce market imperfection. Barriers to competition have to be dismantled in order to discourage monopoly concentrations of economic power. But the political risks can be enormous. Restrictive practices are powerfully entrenched on both sides of industry and in the professions. To defy vested economic interests takes political courage.

The political risks in pursuing a "sound money" policy are no less intimidating. Friedman himself admits that "ending inflation would also have the side-effect of producing a temporary, though perhaps fairly protracted, period of economic recession or slowdown and of relatively high unemployment" [1974a, p.9]. The political acceptability of his policy depends heavily on the interpretation of "temporary, though perhaps fairly protracted". To the man in the dole queue, the definition of "the short run" given in Friedman's "key propositions of monetarism" is not entirely reassuring. "In the short run, which may be as much as five or ten years, monetary changes affect primarily output" [1970, p.23].

Commenting on inflation in the USA in mid-1974, Friedman declared that "an effective policy to end inflation would entail as a side-effect a considerably more severe and protracted recession than we experienced in 1970. The political will to accept such a recession, without reversing policy and re-stimulating inflation, is simply not present" [1974a, p.18].

It is little wonder that politicians have often preferred the easy option of succumbing to what the New Orthodoxy regards as the Keynesian delusion.

Failure of Political Will: The Keynesian Delusion

When a single-gear economy is in danger of being overtaken because it is insufficiently competitive, there is a temptation to try and make it keep up with the rest of the field by pumping in more fuel. Inflating the money supply in an effort to move the economy from point *A* to point *M* avoids the electoral unpopularity of slowing down and applying proper lubrication. A temporary burst of speed caused by the excessive use of fuel creates the illusion that the machine is more efficient than it really is. But the illusion cannot last. The over-revving of a poorly lubricated engine inevitably causes overheating as it puts a strain on bearings clogged up with the frictional resistances imposed by restrictive practices. Efforts to sustain the illusion by suppressing the consequences only make matters worse in the long run.

The illusion of non-inflationary growth can be maintained by "statutory price and wage controls", which Friedman observes, "have consistently been introduced to cover up an inflationary monetary and fiscal policy. That was true in the United States in 1971 and in Britain in 1972. The apparent initial success of the controls is an illusion, reflecting partly the suppression of inflationary symptoms and partly the time lag before the inflationary policy produces its inevitable effects, as documented by the subsequent price and wage explosion in both our countries [the UK and the USA]" [1974b].

The Sectarian Consensus

The Sectarian Consensus achieved by the New Orthodoxy is an ecumenical triumph. Belief in the resurrection of the Classical single-gear view of the economy is universal. Equilibrium means full employment, and the only way to approach that Heavenly Paradise is to apply the lubricant of free competition.

There is still fierce Sectarian conflict over the practical difficulties of making the economic machine operate efficiently in the conditions of imperfect lubrication which are normally encountered in the Real World. But there is no serious disagreement that unemployment is Divine Retribution visited upon those who stray from the straight and narrow path of competition into the sinful ways of monopoly and trade restriction.

In an Age of Conformism in economic theory, the scope for diversity in economic policy is extremely limited.

If the economy is afflicted by unemployment, the machine is badly lubricated and there is no alternative to freeing competition. If the economy is afflicted by inflation, the machine is overheating and there is no alternative to controlling the fuel supply even though it may produce a temporary, if prolonged, slowdown. That is the economic logic of the single-gear economy; and it is embraced not only by "Monetarists" but also by "Keynesians" who are unwilling to jeopardise their recent membership of the New Orthodox Church.

To the monetarists, the inflationary experience of the late 1970s came as an unmistakable sign from Heaven. It confirmed their vision of the economy as a single-gear machine which had been allowed to overheat through monetary irresponsibility. It also lent weight to their complaint that failure to achieve price stability and full employment was due to lack of political resolve to follow the teachings of the Prophets of the New Orthodoxy.

Towards the New Jerusalem

With the restoration of the true economic faith of Adam Smith, however, doubt became certainty, and weakness became strength. The meek went forth to inherit the Earth.

And they were joined enthusiastically by the not-so-meek.

Politicians in many countries, desperately searching for salvation from their economic troubles, clutched at the New Economic Bible. Grasping it firmly in both hands, they set out, with all the zeal of recent converts, on the long march towards the New Jerusalem.

CHAPTER 14

REALITY AND THE FALL OF MONETARISM

The Great Crusade

In 1979, after years of co-operation between governments of both parties and the trade unions had culminated in unemployment and inflation, the unions were rejected by many of their own members and a new British Government was elected with a commitment to the Free Enterprise Capitalism of Adam Smith.

Armed with the New Economic Bible, it set off on a crusade towards the New Jerusalem. A huge bonfire was built for the destruction of restrictive practices, whether carried on by big business, powerful unions, or secretive professions.

A Holy War was declared on Inflation and Unemployment:

unemployment would be cured by competition;
inflation would be cured by sound money.

After a ruthless campaign, which included a number of bloody massacres in the field of industrial relations, victory over the infidels was celebrated and thanks offered to the Almighty Spirit of the Market. Hearts may not have been captured, but minds certainly were. As the Free-Market Juggernaut crushed everything in its path, even the most implacable of erstwhile political opponents fought to clamber on board — claiming all along to have been true believers in the Almighty God of Market Forces.

In the New Jerusalem, an Orthodox economic theocracy was established. Brought in to run it was a new breed of fundamentalist priests whose souls burned with free-market idealism and whose lives were dedicated to the strict enforcement of the Law handed down by Adam Smith.

However much they deplored the methods, even the most reluctant converts were forced to acknowledge the progress made by the Great Crusade towards its main objective. By the end of the 1980s, unions had become far less intransigent, firms had become significantly more responsive, and even the professions had become slightly more open. Market flexibility was still far from perfect, but no one could deny its dramatic improvement.

The New Jerusalem?

In its chronicle of the Entry into the Promised Land, the 1989 version of the New Economic Bible reflects the confident monetarist spirit of the 1980s.

"A nation cannot push unemployment below the natural rate for long without igniting an upward spiral of wage and price inflation. ... It can steel itself for a period of austerity, induce a recession, and thereby reduce inflation to a lower level. ... In the short run, ... there is a tradeoff between inflation and unemployment. In the long run, ... as long as the unemployment rate is below the natural rate, inflation will tend to rise continually" [1989, pp.335,336].

"The latest test of the theory came over the last decade in Thatcher's Britain and Reagan's United States. Both countries suffered deep recessions as means of reducing unacceptably high inflations. Both countries subsequently found clear and substantial declines in inflation, much as predicted by the modern inflation theory just outlined" [p.336].

But that victory was not achieved without considerable sacrifice. The New Bible refers to "the cruel dilemma of needing high unemployment to contain inflation. ... Current estimates indicate that a substantial recession, reducing GNP by $100 to $225 billion below its potential is necessary to slow inertial inflation by 1 percentage point" [p.341].

In Britain, the cost was financed partly out of the consumption of the "windfall" discovery of huge oil reserves in the North Sea and partly by the highest peacetime tax burden in the nation's history.* In the United States, it was financed by a current account deficit of unprecedented proportions. Both countries paid a price in economic resources which was comparable to the cost of their participation in the two World Wars.

On the question of whether or not it has all been worthwhile, however, it is possible to detect a certain uneasiness.

The economic problems of the 1990s do not appear to be so different from those of the late 1970s — and this prompts some disturbing questions. Is this really the Promised Land? Or have we, perhaps, taken a wrong turning?

The Crisis in Orthodox Economics

It is the success of Orthodox *laissez-faire* microeconomic policy in making markets significantly more flexible which has made the failure of Orthodox interventionist macroeconomic policy so embarrassingly obvious.

---

* See chapter 3 above.

For many years, Orthodox theorists found it difficult to come to terms with reality. Excuses of ever increasing ingenuity were invented to explain why a country like Britain, with markets more flexible than at any time in its recent history, instead of enjoying a dramatic decrease in unemployment, had suffered a massive and sustained increase [see Table 2.2 above].

At last, however, has come an admission of the failure of Orthodox monetary theory; and it has come from one of its most distinguished pioneers.

Edmund Phelps, who is acknowledged in the New Economic Bible [1995, p.589] as the co-author with Milton Friedman of the *natural rate hypothesis*, has admitted being "unable to explain persuasively why ... unemployment in many countries rose so stubbornly well into the mid-1980s" [1994, p.ix]. "The neoclassical theory has thus far failed to show that it can plausibly account for the peculiar features of the 1980s slump in much of the world any better than it could account for the depression of the 1930s" [p.231]. "The monetary approach, though still an indispensable perspective on high-frequency fluctuations, cannot plausibly explain the long swings in the unemployment rate" [p.245].

However, the belated admission that "the longer booms and slumps must be explained largely as *displacements of the equilibrium path of unemployment itself*, not as deviations of unemployment around an impervious equilibrium path" [p.x] does not signal a conversion to multi-gear economics. On the contrary, it is part of an effort to protect the natural-rate hypothesis by recognising that "the natural rate moves!" [p.vii]. Phelps's "moving-natural-rate theory" [p.2] is not a rejection of the "natural rate hypothesis" but an attempt to save it.

Such an heroic enterprise requires desperate measures — and none are more desperate than having to change the meaning of words. Phelps confesses that "some of the terms of discourse have undergone a change of meaning. The term "equilibrium" is a case in point. ... Labor-market equilibrium is not defined by market clearing" [pp.9,10]. That he is not alone in this view* does not make his reference to a "non-market-clearing equilibrium" [p.245] any less extraordinary.

Even Humpty-Dumpty (famous for using words to mean just what he chose them to mean) might have balked at the use of the term "equilibrium" to describe the condition of a market which failed to clear!

---

* "The level of unemployment at which inflation stabilizes is the *equilibrium* level of unemployment. This concept of equilibrium has nothing to do with the concept of 'market-clearing' ... . It simply represents the state to which the system will return after a disturbance" [Layard, Nickell, & Jackman (1991) pp.9,10].

Once the odd use of terms is appreciated, it becomes clear that Phelps's "structuralist theory of unemployment" is a "single-gear" theory. The "moving-natural-rate theory" [p.2] attributes adverse movements to the increase in structural imperfections like "the investment cost incurred in providing a new worker with the firm-specific training, or breaking-in, needed to transform the worker into a functional employee, able to be productive within the firm" [p.69] and to the fact that "the enterprise economy is riddled with informational imperfections in every market" [p.86]. His "reasons for dubbing the approach *structuralist* ... [are that] it sees informational and organizational imperfections and features at the bottom of unemployment" [p.247 n.14].

Since it is proclaimed as a "market imperfection" theory, the claim that "one can think of the structuralist theory ... as reconstructing the classical model" [p.352] can hardly be denied. But, in that case, it is difficult to see how it differs in principle from any other classical "market imperfection theory of unemployment". Nor is there any evidence for the additional claim that, in "reconstructing the classical model", the structuralist theory manages "*to make it work*" [p.352].

There can be little objection to the view that "we would like a theory to do well at explaining the data at the big opportunities — to illuminate the major movements" [p.336]. Whether the "structuralist theory" offers a convincing explanation of the jumps during the last 15 years *even with hindsight* is for the reader to decide. However, it is fair to point out that multi-gear economics had no difficulty in predicting the effect of the "monetarist experiment" several years *before* it was started. "Even if markets were Utopian and free from any vestige of frictional resistance, the economy could still be in equilibrium at much less than full employment. The side-effects of a successful monetary policy could be far from temporary. ... The cure it produces may be worse than the disease" [Rayman (1975) pp.14,15].

Multi-gear economics requires no redefinition of terms — "equilibrium" means equilibrium in the genuine market-clearing sense. All it requires is recognition that the economy is a multi-gear machine and that an interventionist monetary policy has the power to change the gear.

Orthodoxy's Last Stand?

The *structuralist theory of unemployment* is a noble last-ditch effort to salvage the single-gear core of Orthodox Economics. It is true that the natural rate moves; it is also true that Orthodox remedies will reduce unemployment by lowering the natural rate. But, even if the natural rate were reduced to zero, it would still leave unsolved the main problem which is not structural at all: the problem of an economy stuck in too low a gear.

That is why the suggested "Economic Policies to Which the Structuralist Theory Might Lead" [1994, ch.20] are so disappointing. The theory leads up an Orthodox blind-alley and leaves economic policy stranded in the same old classical dead-end.

"Employment subsidies or some instrument performing like them seem the most cost-effective means to counteract low levels of employment" [p.372]. "A balanced-budget cut in transfer payments is perhaps the next best candidate ... ; an across-the-board cut in public expenditures is also a plausible prospect" [p.373]. "In future decades the problem of high unemployment may abate" [p.373]. "If and when the decline of real interest rates and of the welfare state come to pass, economic life will center more nearly on earning wages and remaining employed. Workers will be attracted by decent rates of pay, and the reduced flow of unearned income and transfer income in lieu of wage income will offer less of a temptation not to work. When that happens, employment will have a more significant place in the minds of the population, and the biases toward high turnover, shirking, and the rest, and hence toward swollen rates of unemployment, will be far weaker than in the present day" [p.374].

It may be comforting for economists to blame unemployment on the unemployed. After all, the First World War generals found it convenient to explain away the failure of their own disastrous strategy by criticising the resolution of the troops whose lives were senselessly sacrificed. But, though there may be "shirkers" among the ranks of the unemployed, many are so desperate to obtain any kind of work that some have tragically been driven to take their own lives. To the surviving members of their families, remarks like "the reduced flow of unearned income and transfer income in lieu of wage income will offer less of a temptation not to work" must be grossly offensive.

The question of welfare benefits is a matter of personal political opinion. However, the phenomenon of unemployment is centuries old. Long before the creation of the welfare state, it was a recurring problem. It afflicted the first Elizabethan age as much as it afflicts the second. Even if the welfare state were totally abolished, the problem of unemployment would not disappear.

The End of the Era of Orthodox Economics?

Signs of disenchantment with the New Orthodoxy are clearly discernible in the 1992 version of the New Economic Bible. "The natural-rate theory ... leaves many questions unanswered, such as the reasons for the upward drift in unemployment rates in Europe over the last two decades. … The upward creep in the natural rate came from a mixture of demographic trends, changes in social policies, and increases in structural unemployment" [Samuelson & Nordhaus (1992) p.617].

The Orthodox excuses, however, are wearing rather thin. The demographic trend in much of the developed world is towards an ageing population with relatively fewer active workers having to support a relatively larger number of retired pensioners. That implies a developing *shortage* of labour not an increasing surplus. The social policy excuse is even less convincing. In Britain the changes have been overwhelmingly in the direction recommended by Phelps for *reducing* structural unemployment. Why, then, has unemployment dramatically increased?

Tables 2.1 and 2.2 above trace the history of unemployment in the United Kingdom during this century. For 30 years throughout the 1940s, 1950s and 1960s it averaged less than 2% of the total work force. Suddenly in the mid-1970s it doubled to 5%. Between 1980 and 1982 it doubled again, and for 6 years it remained at over 10% — three times the level of the 1970s and six times the level of the 1960s. In Orthodox Economic scripture, these changes may be passed off as "temporary side-effects" or "upward creep or drift". To those whose faith in Orthodoxy is less than total, they look suspiciously like changes of gear.

Orthodox "single-gear" economic theory has resulted in what the New Bible continues to call "the cruel dilemma of needing high unemployment to contain inflation" [1995, p.597]. It is the conspicuous failure of the Orthodox promise that this could be dismissed as no more than a "temporary side-effect" which has dragged economic policy into the political arena.

Politics or Economics? — That is the Question

Some politicians insist on using the right-hand side of the economic road; others insist on using the left-hand side; and there are those who prefer to drive down the middle. But the side of the road is immaterial, if it happens to be leading in the wrong direction. As long as the only source of "respectable" economic advice is committed to "single-gear" Orthodoxy, the road which all political parties are doomed to travel is not the road to Salvation, it is a circular road which takes them nowhere. The same signs keep coming up over and over again … high inflation … high unemployment … low growth … currency crises. And the passengers keep complaining that surely they've been here before.

Single-gear economic orthodoxy plays into the hands of critics who "find the high unemployment that prevails in North America and Europe to be the central flaw in modern capitalism" [Samuelson & Nordhaus (1995) p.597].

The danger is that disillusionment with the New Jerusalem will lead to the return of policies of wage and price controls, albeit, dressed up in "free market" or "private enterprise" labels. It is already responsible for the world-wide retreat into protectionist clubs disguised as Common Markets, Currency Unions, or Free Trade Areas. The inability of single-gear economics to restore market freedom without spiralling inflation or massive unemployment is also responsible for setting back the cause of democracy in the ex-Communist countries of Eastern Europe and for breeding cynicism and hostility to free trade in some of the developing countries.*

If the New Jerusalem turns out to be somewhat less than Paradise on Earth, there must be something rotten in the state of Economic Theology.

What is wrong is obvious. Economics is a religion when it ought to be a science. Belief in the economy as a single-gear machine is maintained, not as the outcome of rational argument, but as an article of religious faith.

But, if the economy is shown to be a multi-gear machine, it will become clear that the unsuccessful interventionist macroeconomic policy of the New Orthodoxy is operating in direct conflict with its successful *laissez-faire* microeconomic policy.

There is one key fundamental theoretical question, therefore: "Does the economy have only one gear (as the New Orthodoxy insists) or does it have several?". That is a question, however, which it is a heresy to ask. Even to contemplate the possibility of a multi-gear economy is to place the immortal soul in peril of eternal damnation. Adults must stop reading at this point.

Part III is for children only. So, boys and girls, (sorry, young persons) if you are sitting comfortably …

* As Adam Smith observed "after it has been for some time interrupted, … freedom of trade should be restored only by slow gradations, and with a good deal of reserve and circumspection. Were those high duties and prohibitions taken away all at once, cheaper foreign goods of the same kind might be poured so fast into the home market, as to deprive all at once many thousands of our people of their ordinary employment and means of subsistence" [1776, IV,2].

PART III

A YOUNG PERSON'S GUIDE TO ECONOMIC THEORY

INTRODUCTION

In a typical industrial economy, there are literally millions of producers and millions of consumers. They normally never meet. How can the producers possibly know what the consumers want? What kind of goods and services should be produced, at what time, and in what quantities?

This mystery is explored in Part III by means of a guided tour through the "Looking-Glass Economy".

The object of the tour is twofold:

(1) to provide a simple explanation of the microeconomic foundations of macroeconomic theory, and

(2) to expose the fundamental flaw in Orthodox "single-gear" economics.

The error which lies at the heart of the Orthodox Friedman/Phelps "natural rate hypothesis" is the fallacy that "the theory of unemployment ... requires a non-Walrasian model in which there is no Walrasian auctioneer continuously clearing commodity and labor markets" [Phelps (1968) p.30].* The excursion into a Looking-Glass Utopia exposes the Orthodox fallacy by proving that unemployment can occur *even if there is a "Walrasian auctioneer continuously clearing commodity and labor markets"*.†

The conclusion is that, although perfect competition is necessary for full employment, it is not sufficient. Contrary to the message of the New Orthodoxy, it turns out that a monetary economy is a multi-gear machine. The lubrication of competition is essential for maximum efficiency. But it is not enough — if the machine is in the wrong gear.

---

* The "single-gear" fallacy is repeated in Phelps's "structuralist theory of unemployment". "Labor-market equilibrium is not defined by market clearing" [1994, p.10]. "The enterprise economy is riddled with informational imperfections in every market" [p.86]. "The real wage, though flexible in one sense, does not clear the labor market, owing to one or another problem created by deficiencies of information" [p.146].

† The simplifying assumption that the auction is instantaneous (see pp.136,137 below) means that the argument is the equivalent of static equilibrium analysis. A diagrammatical representation is provided in the Appendix.

CHAPTER 15

TWEEDLEDUM AND TWEEDLEDEE

Tweedledum and Tweedledee are twins whose talents for production and preferences for consumption are equal but opposite.

There are only two kinds of product: A and B. Tweedledum is much more efficient at producing Product A than at producing Product B; but, whereas he has a strong desire to consume Product B, he has no desire at all for Product A.

Tweedledee: "contrariwise".

TWEEDLEDUM

	PRODUCT A	PRODUCT B
Ability to Produce	3 units per hour	1 unit per hour
Desire to Consume	Very Weak	Very Strong

TWEEDLEDEE

	PRODUCT A	PRODUCT B
Ability to Produce	1 unit per hour	3 units per hour
Desire to Consume	Very Strong	Very Weak

The Mutual Advantage of Trade

On their own, producing for their own consumption, the brothers can obtain no more than *one* unit of their strongly desired product for each hour of effort. As trading partners, producing for each other's consumption, they can obtain *three.*

Exchange is the key to greater productivity. By enabling each brother to consume what the other produces, it makes possible the "division of labour". Each brother is able to specialise in the activity in which he has a "comparative advantage". If Tweedledum takes over the production of A and Tweedledee takes over the production of B, their joint productivity is multiplied by a factor of three. By taking advantage of each other's productive talents, they are able to achieve three times more output per hour than if they had to produce for themselves.

Because trade is to the mutual advantage of both parties, Uncle Jean-Baptiste optimistically regards it as a force for peace. "Every nation [is interested] in the prosperity of all others: for it is only those who produce much that can readily give ... any thing in exchange. ... Wars, entered into for commerce, will appear so much the more senseless as we become better informed" [Say (1815) pp.105,106].

It is one thing, however, to agree in principle that trade is of mutual benefit. It is quite another to agree on the practical terms on which the trade is to be conducted. For the share of the benefit depends on the relative prices at which the products are exchanged.

The Conflict over the Terms of Trade

Tweedledum is anxious to obtain as much B as possible in exchange for his own output of A; Tweedledee is equally anxious to obtain as much A as possible in exchange for his own output of B. There is a direct conflict. So far from leading to the resolution of their usual quarrels, trade may turn out to be a fertile source for making them worse.

There are, however, limits beyond which the rate of exchange between Product A and Product B cannot be set:

	TWEEDLEDUM		TWEEDLEDEE		
	Produce 1B per hour for Consumption	Produce 3A per hour for Exchange	Produce 1A per hour for Consumption	Produce 3B per hour for Exchange	
	units of B per hour	*units of B per hour*	*units of A per hour*	*units of A per hour*	
RELATIVE PRICES:					
$P_A > 3P_B$	1	>9	1	<1	DISADVANTAGE TO TWEEDLEDEE
$P_A < 3P_B > \frac{1}{3}P_B$	1	<9 >1	1	>1 <9	MUTUAL ADVANTAGE
$P_A < \frac{1}{3}P_B$	1	<1	1	>9	DISADVANTAGE TO TWEEDLEDUM

If the price of A is more than 3 times greater than the price of B, there can be no deal: Tweedledee will not buy. If the price of A is less than ⅓ of the price of B, there can be no deal: Tweedledum will not sell.

As long as the rate of exchange is between these (fairly wide) limits, trade is to their mutual advantage. It pays Tweedledum to specialise in the production of A, even though what he really wants is Product B. The same goes for Tweedledee, who finds that it pays him to specialise in the production of B, even though what he really wants is Product A.

The mechanism for determining prices is discussed in the next chapter. For the time being, however, the price of both products is simply assumed to be £4 per unit. On that basis they make their plans.

Tweedledum's Choices

Suppose that Tweedledum's "available resources" are:
Time (70 hours) + *Real Wealth* (90 units of Product B) + *Money* (£600 cash).

He has the ability to produce Product A at the rate of 3 units per hour. The market price of both Product A and Product B is £4 per unit.

Measured in terms of "potential consumption", his "available resources" are equivalent to 450 units of Product B:–

AVAILABLE RESOURCES	Quantity of Resource	Method of Conversion	Potential Product B
Time	70 hours	{Produce 210 A} {Sell for £840 } {Purchase 210 B}	210 units
Real Wealth	90 units of B	Hold	90 units
Money	£600	Purchase 150 B	150 units
Total			450 units

The allocation decision depends on his assessment of the "desirability" of the various alternatives.

Suppose that he wishes to dispose of his resources by:-

1) consuming 20% in the form of *LEISURE*;
2) consuming $26\frac{2}{3}$% .. .. *CONSUMPTION*;
3) holding 20% .. .. *REAL WEALTH*;
4) holding $33\frac{1}{3}$% .. .. *MONEY.* *

On that basis, his planned allocation of resources is as follows:–

PLANNED ALLOCATION	"Desired" Proportion	Equivalent Product B	Planned Choice
Leisure	20%	90 units	30 hours
Consumption	$26\frac{2}{3}$%	120 units	120 units of B
Real Wealth	20%	90 units	90 units of B
Money	$33\frac{1}{3}$%	150 units	£600
Total	100%	450 units	

* The assumption that preferences can be expressed as proportions of total resources is purely for the sake of simplicity. These proportions are used to illustrate the effects of different types of change. More realistic assumptions would merely add complexity without affecting the principle.

The actual preferences have no significance in themselves. What matters is the extent to which they are transmitted to the market.

For a diagrammatical representation, see Section A of the Appendix.

Whether or not Tweedledum can achieve this plan depends on his "trading partner" Tweedledee.

Tweedledee's Choices

Tweedledee faces exactly the same choices as Tweedledum. The only difference is that Tweedledee is a more efficient producer of Product B and a more eager consumer of Product A. Since the preferences of these otherwise identical twins are equally intense, Tweedledee's plan is precisely the same as Tweedledum's with the sole exception that Products A and B are switched:–

PLANNED ALLOCATION	"Desired" Proportion	Equivalent Product A	Planned Choice
Leisure	20%	90 units	30 hours
Consumption	$26\frac{2}{3}$%	120 units	120 units of A
Real Wealth	20%	90 units	90 units of A
Money	$33\frac{1}{3}$%	150 units	£600
Total	100%	450 units	

The assumed price of £4 per unit for both products has two important properties. With equality of *relative prices*, the amount of Product A that Tweedledum plans to supply matches Tweedledee's demand for Product A, and Tweedledum's demand for Product B matches Tweedledee's supply of Product B. At the *absolute price level* of £4, the money balances held by the two brothers represent precisely the purchasing power which they desire.

£4 per unit for Product A and £4 per unit for Product B are the "equilibrium" prices. Both brothers are able to achieve their plans in full. So there is no pressure for any price change.

Equilibrium and Full Employment

What constitutes "full employment" for the economy as a whole is determined by the economic choices made by its individuals.

The volume of employment "desired" by Tweedledum and Tweedledee is 40 hours each. For their two-person economy, therefore, "full employment" is 80 hours. When their economy is in equilibrium, that is precisely what they achieve.

The results are shown in Table 15.1.

The Gains from Trade

Trade is obviously a good thing for both Tweedledum and Tweedledee. The opportunity for exchange is the equivalent of a threefold increase in their productivity. Working alone "trading" with nature, they can obtain *one* unit of consumption for each hour of effort; trading with each other, they can get *three*.

Table 15.1: "Full Employment Equilibrium"

	TWEEDLEDUM	TWEEDLEDEE
	hours	*hours*
Time Available	70	70
minus		
Leisure	30	30
equals		
Employment	40	40
FLOW OF REAL INCOME	*units*	*units*
Production (Sales)	120 A	120 B
– Consumption (Purchases)	–120 B	–120 A
= SAVING	-0-	-0-
STOCK OF REAL WEALTH	*units*	*units*
Closing Balance	90 B	90 A
– Opening Balance	–90 B	–90 A
= INVESTMENT	-0-	-0-

This ability is identified by Uncle Adam as one of the most fundamental distinguishing characteristics of the human race. "The propensity to truck, barter, and exchange one thing for another ... is common to all men, and to be found in no other race of animals. ... Nobody ever saw a dog make a fair and deliberate exchange of one bone for another with another dog" [Smith (1776) I,II].

The ability to swap means that human beings are not limited to the results of their own efforts. When the consumer does not also have to be the producer, economic progress becomes possible. Cows are still chewing the same old cud as their ancestors, whereas people, on the whole, have moved up in the world.

Once exchange is admitted to the scheme of things, the link between production and consumption is severed. An entirely new dimension is added to the problem. How can scarce resources be allocated in a sensible way, if consumption is divorced from production? How does the producer know what the consumer wants, when the two may never even meet?

Is it possible for the gains from specialisation and the division of labour to be achieved in an economy where there are not just two individuals but several millions?

CHAPTER 16

THE INVISIBLE HAND

The Looking-Glass Utopia

The Looking-Glass Utopia is blessed with 500 sets of twins. Of the 1,000 inhabitants, 500 are Dums (each one a perfect replica of Tweedledum), and 500 are Dees (each one a perfect replica of Tweedledee). Every Dum makes exactly the same choices as Tweedledum in the previous chapter:

Table 16.1: The Planned Allocation of Resources

PLANNED ALLOCATION	"Desired" Proportion	Equivalent Product B	Planned Choice
Leisure	20%	90 units	30 hours
Consumption	$26\frac{2}{3}$%	120 units	120 units of B
Real Wealth	20%	90 units	90 units of B
Money	$33\frac{1}{3}$%	150 units	£600
Total	100%	450 units	

Every Dee makes exactly the same choices as Tweedledee. So the plans of the Dees are the same as the plans of the Dums — except that Products A and B are switched.

These are the choices when the price of both products is £4 per unit. But the interests of the Dums and the Dees are in direct conflict. The Dums would prefer a higher price for Product A which they sell and a lower price for Product B which they buy. The Dees: "contrariwise".

They are about to settle their differences in a typically adult fashion — by preparing for a battle — when along comes Uncle Adam.

Uncle Adam and the "Invisible Hand"

Uncle Adam tells them that there is no need to fight. There is a method of settling their dispute which will make them all better off. It is called "free competition". What makes it particularly attractive is the surprising promise that each individual can pursue his own self-interest. "By directing [his] industry in such a manner as its produce may be of the greatest value, he intends only his own gain, and he is in this, as in many other cases, led by an invisible hand to promote an end which was no part of his intention. ... By pursuing his own interest he frequently promotes that of the society more effectually than when he really intends to promote it" [Smith (1776) IV,2].

The "invisible hand" sounds almost too good to be true. They cannot wait to give it a try. But how can they organise free market competition when there are so many different individuals?

Uncle Léon and the Walrasian Auction

Uncle Léon is the person to ask. "The markets which are best organized from the competitive standpoint are those in which purchases and sales are made by auction, through the instrumentality of stockbrokers, commercial brokers or criers acting as agents who centralize transactions in such a way that the terms of every exchange are openly announced and an opportunity is given to sellers to lower their prices and to buyers to raise their bids" [Walras (1874) pp.83,84].

A competitive auction is just the thing for helping them to find what Uncle Léon calls the "equilibrium" prices. These are the prices at which the quantity of Product B demanded by the Dums will be exactly the same as the quantity offered by the Dees, and the quantity of Product A demanded by the Dees will be exactly the same as the quantity offered by the Dums. The markets for both products will "clear"; all the Dums and all the Dees will get what they want; none of them will have any unsatisfied demands or unwanted supplies.

Uncle Léon agrees to act as the auctioneer.

A "Walrasian Auction" and the "Equilibrium" Prices

The rules of the auction are simple. A set of prices is "announced" by the auctioneer. The Dums and the Dees are free to make bids for whatever quantities they want to buy or sell at that set of prices. If the quantity which sellers offer to sell does not match the quantity which buyers offer to buy *of any single item*, the "books do not balance" and no transactions can take place. Another set of prices is announced, and a new round of bids is invited. No exchange actually takes place until a set of prices has been announced at which the "effective supply" is equal to the "effective demand" *in respect of every single item*.

Uncle Léon insists that he can deal only with "*effective offer*" "of a definite amount of a commodity at a definite price" and "*effective demand*" "for a definite amount of a commodity at a definite price" [Walras (1874) pp.84,85]. The irrelevance of "notional" demand is confirmed by Uncle John Stuart who emphasises that "demand" is "not the mere desire for the commodity" but the desire "combined with the power of purchasing" [Mill (1848) p.445]. This is simply a reminder of Uncle Adam's observation that "the effectual demand ... is different from the absolute demand. A very poor man may be said in some sense to have a demand for a coach and six; he might like to have it; but his demand is not an effectual demand, as the commodity can never be brought to market in order to satisfy it" [Smith (1776) I,7]. Uncle Jean-Baptiste puts it more succinctly: "there is no other effective demand than that which is accompanied by the offer of a price" [Say (1815) pp.27,28].

(a) Relative Prices

The experience of the previous chapter provides a clue as to how the auction will proceed. With the prices of both products at £4 per unit, each Dum plans to supply 120 units of Product A (in return for money income of £480) and to demand 120 units of Product B (in return for money expenditure of £480). Since the plans made by each Dee are equal but opposite, the total quantity of Product A supplied by the Dums is exactly equal to the total quantity demanded by the Dees, and the total quantity of Product B supplied by the Dees is exactly equal to the total quantity demanded by the Dums. Their plans are compatible. There is no excess supply of or excess demand for either product. Both markets are in equilibrium.

A shift in relative prices is likely to disturb the existing equilibrium. An increase in the price of Product A relative to that of Product B moves the "terms of trade" in favour of the Dums and against the Dees. It is an incentive for the Dums to supply more A and to demand more B. It is an incentive for the Dees to demand less A and to supply less B. The likely result is excess supply of Product A and excess demand for Product B. The auctioneer's books would not balance. There would be unsold supplies of Product A and unsatisfied demands for Product B. Similarly, if the price of Product A were set *below* that of Product B, there would be unsold supplies of Product B and unsatisfied demands for Product A. Not until Uncle Léon had brought the price of Product A into equality with that of Product B would the excess demand and excess supply be eliminated.

This result confirms what is intuitively obvious. If equal numbers of Dums and Dees have the same opportunities for producing their own product and equal preferences for consuming the product made by their opposite number, equilibrium requires that the prices of each product must be the same.

Although this explains the determination of *relative* prices, it still leaves open the question of the *absolute* price level.

(b) The Level of Prices

The determination of the absolute price level depends on what Uncle Léon calls the "desired cash-balance" [Walras (1874) p.321]. But the "desirability" of money balances depends, not on their nominal "face value", but on their purchasing power in terms of real goods and services [pp.327,328]. The term used by Uncle Maynard is "real balances" defined as "balances, in hand or at the bank, measured in terms of purchasing power" [Keynes (1923) p.83].

Money is simply a stock of purchasing power; its significance depends on the prices of the goods and services on which it is to be spent. A cash balance of £400 with the relevant price index at 200 has no more purchasing power than a cash balance of only £200 with the price index at 100.

If the Dums and the Dees are free from "money illusion", they are not deceived by the "nominal" face value of their cash holdings. Their desire for money is therefore related, not to its nominal face value, but to its real purchasing power. The demand for money is a demand for "real balances".

Suppose that the auctioneer initially "announces" the prices of both products at £3 per unit. The *tâtonnement* process as the Looking-Glass Utopia "gropes" (in the literal meaning of the French word) or "feels its way" towards equilibrium through successive rounds of bidding and rebidding at a "Walrasian auction" is outlined in Table 16.2.

The initial disequilibrium is shown in the *Round 1* column. At a price level of £3 per unit, the real purchasing power of each individual's £600 cash balance is equivalent to 200 units — making the total of his "available resources" the equivalent of 500 units.

The result of the intention to allocate resources in the "desired" proportions is shown in the "Planned Allocation" section of the table. The total Leisure "desired" by the 1,000 individuals is equivalent to 100,000 units. With productivity at 3 units per hour, that represents 33,333 hours and it implies desired employment of 36,667 hours. Aggregate supply is therefore equal to 110,000 units. Aggregate demand, however, is equal to a total of 143,333 units (133,333 which the 1,000 individuals plan to consume *plus* 10,000 units which they plan to add to their holdings of real wealth). The result in the Product Markets is excess demand of 33,333 units.

If Money holdings are to be maintained at the desired 33⅓% of resources, they must have the purchasing-power equivalent of 166,667 units. But, at the current price of £3 per unit, that requires no more than £500,000 compared with the actual £600,000 which is the total money

Table 16.2: The Movement (*Tâtonnement*) towards Equilibrium

		Round 1	Round 2	Round 3	Round 4	Round 5
PRICE *(per unit)*		£3.00	£3.25	£3.50	£3.75	£4.00
AVAILABLE RESOURCES *('000 equivalent units)*						
Time	(70,000 hours)	210.0	210.0	210.0	210.0	210.0
Real Wealth	(90,000 units)	90.0	90.0	90.0	90.0	90.0
Money	(£600,000/Price)	200.0	184.6	171.4	160.0	150.0
Total		500.0	484.6	471.4	460.0	450.0
PLANNED ALLOCATION *('000 equivalent units)*						
Leisure	(20%)	100.0	96.9	94.3	92.0	90.0
Consumption	(26⅔%)	133.3	129.2	125.7	122.7	120.0
Real Wealth	(20%)	100.0	96.9	94.3	92.0	90.0
Money	(33⅓%)	166.7	161.6	157.1	153.3	150.0
Total		500.0	484.6	471.4	460.0	450.0
PRODUCT MARKET *('000 equivalent units)*						
Demand	(Consumption)	133.3	129.2	125.7	122.7	120.0
	(+ Investment) *	10.0	6.9	4.3	2.0	0.0
Supply	(Time – Leisure)	110.0	113.1	115.7	118.0	120.0
Excess Demand		33.3	23.0	14.3	6.7	0.0

* Investment = Real Wealth Planned – Real Wealth Available

available. It is the collective attempt to spend the "surplus" £100,000 of money which finances the excess demand of 33,333 units in the Product Markets.

Since aggregate demand is 33,333 units greater than aggregate supply, "the books do not balance". No transactions can be allowed. In order to stimulate a reduction in the quantity demanded and an increase in the quantity supplied, the auctioneer needs to raise the price of both products. The technique is simple: "prices [are] first cried at random and then raised or lowered according as there is an excess of demand over offer or vice versa, until the two become equal" [Walras (1874) p.242].

Table 16.2 is based on the assumption that prices are changed in steps of 25 pence. The effect of a price increase to £3.25 for both products is shown in the *Round 2* column. The fall in the purchasing power of the available money causes a corresponding reduction in the total available resources. In order to maintain the desired proportions, the planned allocation has to change. The reduction in leisure increases the supply of output, the reduction in consumption and investment reduces the demand. Consequently, the excess demand is reduced. But it still remains as high as 23,000 units. A further round of bidding is therefore necessary.

Using the same technique as before, the auctioneer increases prices by a further 25p to £3.50. The result is that the excess demand is reduced still further — but it is not eliminated completely. The *tâtonnement* process of "groping" towards equilibrium continues through successive rounds of bidding and rebidding as long as there is disequilibrium.

Not until *Round 5*, when prices have been raised to £4 per unit, is aggregate demand equal to aggregate supply. Only then do the plans of all one thousand individuals become compatible. Every individual is able to achieve his desired level of leisure, consumption and money. Excess supply and demand have been eliminated from every market. The books balance. Equilibrium has been restored. Transactions can go ahead.

At the market-clearing equilibrium prices of £4 per unit for each product, the purchasing power of the £600 money balance held by each individual is exactly equal to the "desired" level of 150 units of product. At higher prices, the real purchasing power of the nominal balance would be below the "desired" level. In order to restore "real balances" to their desired level, each individual would require a larger money balance. The only way for individuals to increase their money balances is by reducing their purchases below their sales. The attempt by every Dum and every Dee to do this would result in excess supply in *both* product markets. This could not be eliminated until the "auctioneer" had lowered the prices of both products far enough for the purchasing power of the existing money balances to have risen to the desired level.

The price level is therefore determined by the supply of money and the demand for "real balances" operating through pressure on supply and demand in the product markets.

Macroeconomic Equilibrium

In the Looking-Glass Utopia, the "Walrasian auctioneer" ensures that no transactions can take place at non-equilibrium prices. Not until excess supply and excess demand have been eliminated from all markets so that "the books balance", does the auctioneer announce the equilibrium set of prices. Only then are transactions allowed to go ahead. The economy achieves market-clearing equilibrium. At this set of prices, all markets clear: there are no unwanted supplies, nor are there any unsatisfied demands.

So Uncle Adam's promise has been fulfilled. A threefold gain in productivity is obtainable even in an economy of one thousand individuals where producers and consumers may never meet. The key is freedom of competition.

The benefits of competition cannot be fully appreciated, however, except by contrast with the disaster of "protectionism".

The Economic Consequences of Protectionism

If the Dums attempt to "protect" their own jobs by prohibiting purchases from the Dees, all trade will cease. This will undoubtedly hurt the Dees; but it will be just as damaging to the Dums, for they will have to satisfy their desire for Product B by making it for themselves. But, since the Dums can manage its production at only 1 unit per hour, they are merely denying themselves the opportunity of taking advantage of the superior productivity of the Dees who are three times more efficient. If their protectionist policy is "successful", the Dums simply cut their own productivity by two thirds and secure for themselves the questionable "benefit" of having to work harder to produce less. It is the sort of boost to employment that can always be achieved by abandoning mechanical diggers in favour of teaspoons.

Uncle Adam leaves no doubt about the self-destructive absurdity of artificial trade restrictions. "By means of glasses, hotbeds, and hotwalls, very good grapes can be raised in Scotland, and very good wine too can be made of them at about thirty times the expence for which at least equally good can be brought from foreign countries. Would it be a reasonable law to prohibit the importation of all foreign wines, merely to encourage the making of claret and burgundy in Scotland?" [1776, IV,2].*

The Invisible Hand and the Gains from Trade

The threefold gain from specialisation and division of labour made possible by trade between the Dums and the Dees can therefore be achieved by millions of unconnected individuals acting in their own self-interest. The essential requirement to allow the "invisible hand" to do its work is the freedom to compete in a perfectly open market.

"It is the great multiplication of the productions of all the different arts, in consequence of the division of labour, which occasions, in a well-

---

* This absurdity is exquisitely caricatured in Frédéric Bastiat's famous petition: "From the Manufacturers of Candles, Tapers, Lanterns, Candlesticks, [etc] ...

To the Honourable Members of the Chamber of Deputies.

Gentlemen: ... We are suffering from the ruinous competition of a foreign rival who apparently works under conditions so far superior to our own for the production of light that he is *flooding* the *domestic market* with it at an incredibly low price; ... and a branch of French industry whose ramifications are innumerable is all at once reduced to complete stagnation. This rival, which is none other than the sun, is waging war on us so mercilessly that we suspect he is being stirred up against us by perfidious Albion. ... We ask you to be so good as to pass a law requiring the closing of all windows, dormers, skylights, ... all openings, holes, chinks, and fissures through which the light of the sun is wont to enter houses, to the detriment of the fair industries with which, we are proud to say, we have endowed the country" [1845, pp.56,57].

governed society, that universal opulence which extends itself to the lowest ranks of the people" [Smith (1776) I,1]. "Differences among individuals increase the power of the collaborating group beyond the sum of individual efforts. Synergetic collaboration brings into play distinctive talents that would have been left unused had their possessors been forced to strive alone for sustenance" [Hayek (1988) p.80].

Full Employment in the Looking-Glass Utopia

In equilibrium, each one of the 1,000 individuals chooses 30 hours of leisure and 40 hours of work. "Full employment" for the whole economy is the "desired" volume of 40,000 hours. "Potential (full employment) output" amounts to 120,000 units.

Table 16.3: "Full Employment Equilibrium"

	Each Individual	Whole Economy
	hours	*hours*
Time Available	70	70,000
minus		
Leisure	30	30,000
equals		
Employment	40	40,000
FLOW OF REAL INCOME	*units*	*units*
Production (Sales)	120	120,000
− Consumption (Purchases)	−120	−120,000
= SAVING	-0-	-0-
STOCK OF REAL WEALTH	*units*	*units*
Closing Balance	90	90,000
− Opening Balance	−90	−90,000
= INVESTMENT	-0-	-0-

The Apotheosis of Free Competition

Uncle Léon is no ordinary auctioneer; he works with such lightning speed that the successive rounds of bidding and rebidding involved in the "tâtonnement" process "take place simultaneously" [Walras (1874) p.477]. Progress towards market-clearing equilibrium can therefore be regarded "as consuming *no* time" [p.75]. The "Walrasian Utopia" is a perfectly flexible market economy capable of instantaneous response to change. Because no transactions take place at non-equilibrium prices, there is no disappointment of expectation — there are no unplanned shortages nor any unplanned surpluses.

The fact that Utopian markets have perfect price flexibility beyond anything capable of being achieved in the real world makes them ideal for isolating the significance of any economic change. None of the results can be attributed to market imperfection or dynamic disequilibrium.

The Looking-Glass Utopia inhabited by 500 sets of twins is therefore an ideal test track for comparing rival economic theories.*

The starting point is the initial equilibrium representing 40,000 hours of employment and a £4 per unit price level. The first question to be considered is the significance of money.

---

* The object is to challenge the Orthodox theory that full employment would be guaranteed by "a "Walrasian auctioneer" assumed to furnish, without charge and without delay, all the information needed to obtain the perfect coordination of the activities (both spot and future) of all traders" [Leijonhufvud (1968) pp.47,48]. A "head-on" challenge is essential in order to expose the fallacy of the Orthodox view that "the theory of unemployment ... requires a non-Walrasian model in which there is no Walrasian auctioneer continuously clearing commodity and labor markets" [Phelps (1968) p.30] and that "involuntary unemployment is a disequilibrium phenomenon" [Tobin (1972) p.2].

The logic of the Orthodox theory is not challenged by calls "to abandon the economist's notion of the economy as a machine, with its attendant concept of equilibrium" [Ormerod (1994) p.151]. Criticism that "the model of competitive equilibrium is a travesty of reality" [p.48], though valid, diverts attention from its fatal weakness as a *travesty of logic*. Similarly, the target of Kaldor's article on "The Irrelevance of Equilibrium Economics" is the unreality of analyses based on static equilibrium positions. "It is the deep underlying belief, common to all economists of the so-called "neo-classical" school, that general equilibrium theory is the one and only starting point for any logically consistent explanation of the behaviour of decentralised economic systems" [1972, p.1238]. In that case, it is not sufficient to dismiss "the rarefied world of Walrasian perfection where markets are *continually* in equilibrium" as irrelevant because "the markets of the real world are not in continuous equilibrium in this sense" [p.1247]. A more effective challenge, surely, is to prove that the neoclassical general equilibrium explanation is logically *in*consistent.

For a diagrammatical representation, see Section B of the Appendix.

CHAPTER 17

MONEY MAKES THE WORLD GO ROUND

PART I: THE SUPPLY OF MONEY

Without exchange, specialisation and the division of labour would be impossible. It is exchange, therefore, which enables human beings to make use of each other's talents. But the instrument which lubricates the process is money.

Without money, exchange would be reduced to barter between pairs of individuals. As Uncle Adam explains, "money has become in all civilised nations the universal instrument of commerce, by the intervention of which goods of all kinds are bought and sold, or exchanged for one another" [Smith (1776) I,IV]. "Money [is] the great wheel of circulation, the great instrument of commerce. … The substitution of paper in the room of gold and silver money, replaces a very expensive instrument of commerce with one much less costly, and sometimes equally convenient. Circulation comes to be carried on by a new wheel, which it costs less both to erect and to maintain than the old one" [1776, II,2].

If money is so beneficial to trade, can printing more of it make an economy even more prosperous?

Not according to Uncle John Stuart.

"There cannot … be intrinsically a more insignificant thing, in the economy of society, than money; except in the character of a contrivance for sparing time and labour. It is a machine for doing quickly and commodiously, what would be done, though less quickly and commodiously, without it. … Things which by barter would exchange for one another, will, if sold for money, sell for an equal amount of it. … The relations of commodities to one another remain unaltered by money" [Mill (1848) p.488].

Uncle Knut agrees. "Money as such … is of significance in the economic world only as an intermediary" [Wicksell (1898) p.29].

So does Uncle Milton. "Consider two societies that are alike except that in one there are twice as many pieces of paper, each labeled one dollar, as in the other. The only effect will be that nominal prices are twice as high in the first as in the second society" [Friedman (1962) p.284].

The Effect of a Change in the Quantity of Money

In order to put his theory to the test, Uncle Milton takes off in a helicopter and, from the sky, drops sufficient banknotes to increase the money balances of every single individual from £600 to £750. The total quantity of money in the Looking-Glass Utopia is increased by 25% from £600,000 to £750,000.*

The Dums and the Dees are delighted with this "windfall". In view of Uncle Milton's well-known objection to the notion of a "free lunch", it comes as an extremely pleasant surprise. At current market prices, everyone seems to have become £150 better off — without the need for any additional productive effort.

Will the extra cash provide anyone with a free lunch?

If their preferences remain unchanged and they still plan to allocate their resources in the same proportions as before, the extra money disturbs the initial equilibrium. Since every individual's total resources are increased by the extra money, each one plans to increase his Leisure, Consumption, Real Wealth, and Money by the *relevant proportion* of the total increase. But money holdings have received the *whole* of the increase. Consequently, all individuals now have more money than they want but not enough of everything else.

The existing equilibrium has been disturbed. In the Looking-Glass Utopia, a new equilibrium is established by competitive bidding at a "Walrasian Auction".

The Walrasian Auction

The initial disequilibrium following the change is shown in the *Round 1* column of Table 17.1 (with the initial equilibrium in the column on the extreme right for purposes of comparison). At the current price level of £4 per unit, the extra £150 raises the real purchasing power of each individual's cash balance by 37½ units, increasing the total of his "available resources" from the equivalent of 450 units to 487½ units.

The result of the intention to allocate resources in the same proportions as before is shown in the "Planned Allocation" section of the *Round 1* column. The planned increase in Leisure implies a cut in the supply of output amounting to 7½ units per individual. The planned increase in consumption demand of 10 units plus the planned increase in investment demand of 7½ units implies an increase in total demand of 17½ units per

* Some of the operations of this particular helicopter flying over the community and dropping dollar bills from the sky feature in an essay on *The Optimum Quantity of Money* [Friedman (1969) p.4].

Table 17.1
The Movement (*Tâtonnement*) towards Equilibrium
following a 25% Increase in the Quantity of Money

	Round 1	Round 2	Round 3	Round 4	Round 5	INITIAL
PRICE *(per unit)*	£4.00	£4.25	£4.50	£4.75	£5.00	£4.00
AVAILABLE RESOURCES						
('000 equivalent units)						
Time (70,000 hours)	210.0	210.0	210.0	210.0	210.0	210.0
Real Wealth (90,000 units)	90.0	90.0	90.0	90.0	90.0	90.0
Money (£750,000/Price)	187.5	176.5	166.7	157.9	150.0	150.0
Total	487.5	476.5	466.7	457.9	450.0	450.0
PLANNED ALLOCATION						
('000 equivalent units)						
Leisure (20%)	97.5	95.3	93.3	91.6	90.0	90.0
Consumption (26⅔%)	130.0	127.1	124.5	122.1	120.0	120.0
Real Wealth (20%)	97.5	95.3	93.3	91.6	90.0	90.0
Money (33⅓%)	162.5	158.8	155.6	152.6	150.0	150.0
Total	487.5	476.5	466.7	457.9	450.0	450.0
PRODUCT MARKET						
('000 equivalent units)						
Demand (Consumption)	130.0	127.1	124.5	122.1	120.0	120.0
(+ Investment) *	7.5	5.3	3.3	1.6	0.0	0.0
Supply (Time – Leisure)	112.5	114.7	116.7	118.4	120.0	120.0
Excess Demand	25.0	17.7	11.1	5.3	0.0	0.0

* Investment = Real Wealth Planned – Real Wealth Available

individual. The increase in demand over supply therefore amounts to 25 units for each individual. For the whole economy of 1,000 individuals, the result in the Product Markets is excess demand of 25,000 units.

If Money holdings are to be maintained at the desired 33⅓% of resources, they must have the purchasing-power equivalent of 162,500 units. But, with prices at £4 per unit, that requires no more than £650,000 compared with the actual £750,000 which is now available. It is the collective attempt to spend the "surplus" £100,000, which finances the excess demand of 25,000 units in the Product Markets.

Since aggregate demand is 25,000 units greater than aggregate supply, "the books do not balance". No transactions can be allowed. In order to stimulate a reduction in the quantity demanded and an increase in the quantity supplied, the auctioneer needs to raise the price of both products.

The *Round 2* column shows the effect of a 25 pence price increase. The purchasing power of the available money falls, with a corresponding reduction in the total available resources. In order to maintain the desired proportions, the planned allocation has to change. The reduction in leisure increases the supply of output, the reduction in consumption and investment reduces the demand. Although the reduction in excess demand is a distinct improvement on *Round 1*, it is still far from equilibrium. A further round of bidding is therefore necessary.

Using the same procedure as before, the auctioneer raises prices by another 25 pence to £4.50. The result is a further reduction in excess demand, but it is not eliminated completely. The *tâtonnement* process of "groping" towards equilibrium continues through successive rounds of bidding and rebidding as long as there is disequilibrium. During each round, the auctioneer raises prices in response to the pressure of the bidding. Each price rise reduces excess demand so that the disequilibrium becomes smaller and smaller until it is totally eliminated.

Not until *Round 5*, when prices have been raised to £5 per unit, is aggregate demand equal to aggregate supply. Only then do the plans of all one thousand individuals become compatible. Every individual is able to achieve his desired level of leisure, consumption and money. Excess supply and demand have been eliminated from every market. The books balance. Equilibrium has been restored. Transactions can go ahead.

The only difference between the new equilibrium in the *Round 5* column and the initial equilibrium (in the extreme right-hand column) is in the level of prices.*

This confirms Uncle Milton's belief that, as long as real preferences remain unchanged, a change in the quantity of money has a purely nominal effect. Money prices and money incomes are increased by 25%, but there is no effect whatever on the "real economy". Output and employment (and therefore real incomes) remain unchanged. An increase in the quantity of money leaves real transactions unaffected, but produces a proportional increase in the level of prices.

As long as the preferences of Dums and the Dees do not alter, the desired proportions between goods and money can be maintained only by pressure to spend. Excess demand in the product markets cannot be eliminated completely, until prices have risen sufficiently to reduce the purchasing power of the money balances (the "real balances") to their initial value. After the 25% increase in their money balances, equilibrium cannot be restored until prices have increased by 25%.

It appears, therefore, that equilibrium following a change in the quantity of money, cannot be restored until there has been a proportional change in the level of prices.

Uncle Milton is delighted. The experience of the Dums and the Dees provides the evidence he needs to support one of his favourite theories.

---

* For a diagrammatical representation, see Section C of the Appendix.

The Quantity Theory of Money

As Great Uncle Gerard used to say, "The *Moneyes of Chriftendome*, which haue their ebbing and flowing, doe fhew their operation vpon Commodities, making by *Plenty*, the price thereof deare, or by *Scarcity* better cheape" [Malynes (1622) p.36].

Uncle Irving's "Equation of Exchange" [Fisher (1911) p.27] looks more scientific:

	the quantity of Money in circulation	(*M*)
multiplied by	*its Velocity of circulation*	(*V*)
is equal to	*the level of Prices*	(*P*)
multiplied by	*the volume of Transactions*	(*T*)
or	$MV = PT.$	

In the Looking-Glass Utopia, aggregate real balances of 150,000 units support aggregate purchases of 120,000 units, so the velocity of circulation is $^4/_5$.

With the quantity of money at its initial total of £600,000, the equation of exchange is:

$$(M)\ £600{,}000 \times (V)\ ^4/_5 = (P)\ £4.00 \times (T)\ 120{,}000.$$

When the aggregate quantity of money is increased to £750,000, the equation becomes:

$$(M)\ £750{,}000 \times (V)\ ^4/_5 = (P)\ £5.00 \times (T)\ 120{,}000.$$

As Uncle Irving explains, "the quantity theory asserts that (provided velocity of circulation and volume of trade are unchanged) if we increase the *number* of dollars … prices will be increased in the same proportion" [p.31].

Uncle Milton congratulates himself on having demonstrated the first law of economics with a perfect object lesson. Pieces of paper, however beautifully engraved, will not enable the Dums and the Dees to consume that which they have not produced. They have to rely on their own efforts. It should be a constant reminder that no government, however well-intentioned, can improve living standards simply by printing and distributing bundles of paper. The only way to economic prosperity is by creating real goods and services through the effort of production.

Provided that markets are perfect, monetary changes make no difference to real production and consumption; they affect only prices.

That, however, is true of changes in the *supply* of money. What about changes in the *demand*?

PART II: THE DEMAND FOR MONEY

Different aspects of the demand for money are traditionally distinguished on the basis of the subjective motives which are the cause.* It may be more useful if the distinction is made on the basis of the objective market choices which are the effect.

In order to isolate different aspects of the impact on the Looking-Glass Utopia, the demand for money is artificially separated into a pure "liquidity demand" and a pure "saving demand".

Table 17.2: The "Liquidity" Demand for Money

PLANNED ALLOCATION OF RESOURCES	INITIAL EQUILIBRIUM	Increase in "Liquidity Demand" for Money	Increase in "Saving Demand" for Money
	% of Total	*% of Total*	*% of Total*
Leisure	20	18 →→	20
		↓	
Consumption	$26\frac{2}{3}$	24 →→ ↓	20 →→
		↓	↓
Real Wealth	20	18 →→ ↓	20 ↓
		↓	↓
Money	$33\frac{1}{3}$	40 ←←	40 ←←
Total	100	100	100

In Table 17.2, the initial preferences of Tweedledum are shown in the first column. A change in the "liquidity demand" for money implies a "pure" change in the desire for money "uncontaminated" by a change in the preference for anything else. The increase in the "liquidity demand" for money (in the second column) is characterised by a shift into Money unaccompanied by any change in relative preferences between Leisure, Consumption, and Real Wealth. The shift into money is drawn proportionally from all the other options.

Saving implies a reduction of present consumption in favour of an increase in future consumption. *Real* saving is accomplished by the accumulation of real wealth. *Monetary* saving is accomplished by the accumulation of money. The increase in the "saving demand" for money (in the third column) is characterised by a shift into Money drawn exclusively from Consumption.

* Time-preference is the basis of the theory of interest of Böhm-Bawerk [1888] and Fisher [1930]. The "psychological and business incentives to liquidity" are the subject of chapter 15 of Keynes's *General Theory* [1936].

For the purpose of isolating the effect of a change in the preference for holding money (unaccompanied by a change in any other preferences), it is the economic impact of an increase in the "liquidity demand" for money which needs to be considered.

The Effect of a Change in the Liquidity Demand for Money

If the "liquidity demand" for money of every individual in the Looking-Glass Utopia increases in exactly the same way as Tweedledum's, each one will plan to allocate his resources in the proportions shown in the second column of Table 17.2. The planned cut in leisure increases effective supply, but the planned cut in consumption and investment reduces effective demand.

The initial disequilibrium following the change is shown in the *Round 1* column of Table 17.3 (with the initial equilibrium in the column on the extreme right for purposes of comparison).

Table 17.3
The Movement (*Tâtonnement*) towards Equilibrium following an Increase in the "Liquidity Demand" for Money

		Round 1	Round 2	Round 3	Round 4	Round 5	INITIAL
PRICE *(per unit)*		£4.00	£3.75	£3.50	£3.25	£3.00	£4.00
AVAILABLE RESOURCES *('000 equivalent units)*							
Time	(70,000 hours)	210.0	210.0	210.0	210.0	210.0	210.0
Real Wealth	90,000 units)	90.0	90.0	90.0	90.0	90.0	90.0
Money	(£600,000/Price)	150.0	160.0	171.4	184.6	200.0	150.0
Total		450.0	460.0	471.4	484.6	500.0	450.0
PLANNED ALLOCATION *('000 equivalent units)*							
Leisure	(18%)	81.0	82.8	84.9	87.2	90.0	90.0
Consumption	(24%)	108.0	110.4	113.1	116.3	120.0	120.0
Real Wealth	(18%)	81.0	82.8	84.9	87.2	90.0	90.0
Money	(40%)	180.0	184.0	188.5	193.9	200.0	150.0
Total		450.0	460.0	471.4	484.6	500.0	450.0
PRODUCT MARKET *('000 equivalent units)*							
Supply	(Time – Leisure)	129.0	127.2	125.1	122.8	120.0	120.0
Demand	(Consumption)	108.0	110.4	113.1	116.3	120.0	120.0
	(– Disinvestment) *	−9.0	−7.2	−5.1	−2.8	0.0	0.0
Excess Supply		30.0	24.0	17.1	9.3	0.0	0.0

* Disinvestment = Real Wealth Available – Real Wealth Planned

The result of the intention to allocate resources in the new proportions is shown in the "Planned Allocation" section of the *Round 1* column. The planned reduction in Leisure implies an increase in the supply of output amounting to 9 units per individual. The planned reduction in consumption demand of 12 units plus the planned reduction in investment demand of 9 units implies a reduction in total demand of 21 units per individual. The increase in supply over demand therefore amounts to 30 units for each individual. For the whole economy of 1,000 individuals, the result in the Product Markets is excess supply of 30,000 units.

Since "the books do not balance", no transactions can be allowed and the auction must continue. In order to stimulate a reduction in the quantity supplied and an increase in the quantity demanded, the auctioneer needs to lower the price of both products.

The *Round 2* column shows the "real-balance effect" of a 25 pence price cut. The purchasing power of the available money rises to 160,000 units, with a corresponding increase in the total available resources. In order to maintain the desired proportions, the planned allocation has to change. The increase in leisure reduces the supply of output, the increase in consumption and investment increases the demand. Consequently, the excess supply is reduced from 30,000 units to 24,000. Although this is a distinct improvement on *Round 1*, it is still far from equilibrium. A further round of bidding is therefore necessary.

The *tâtonnement* process of "groping" towards equilibrium continues until *Round 5*, when prices have been lowered to £3 per unit. Aggregate demand is equal to aggregate supply, and the plans of all one thousand individuals are compatible. Every individual is able to achieve his desired level of leisure, consumption and money. Excess supply and demand have been eliminated from every market. The books balance. Equilibrium has been restored. Transactions can go ahead.

The only difference between the new equilibrium in the *Round 5* column and the initial equilibrium (in the extreme right-hand column) is in the level of prices.*

Because an increase in the "liquidity demand" for money is not accompanied by a change in any other preferences, the necessary adjustments are solely monetary so that the impact is purely nominal. Excess supply in the product markets is eliminated when prices have fallen far enough to raise the purchasing power of the existing quantity of money (the "real balances") to the newly desired level. Real transactions are unaffected, because the new equilibrium is achieved by the "real-balance effect" of a fall in the level of prices.

In terms of the equation of exchange, an increase in the "liquidity demand" for money is equivalent to a reduction in the velocity of circulation. Aggregate real balances with purchasing power of 200,000

---

* For a diagrammatical representation, see Section D of the Appendix.

units support aggregate purchases of 120,000 units, so the velocity of circulation is reduced to $^3/_5$. With the total quantity of money unchanged at its initial aggregate amount of £600,000, the equation of exchange becomes:

$$(M)\ £600{,}000 \times (V)\ ^3/_5 = (P)\ £3.00 \times (T)\ 120{,}000.$$

The conclusion is that a change in the "liquidity demand" for money has a similar economic impact to a change in the supply. Money prices and money incomes alter, but there is no effect whatever on the "real economy". Output and employment (and therefore real incomes) remain unchanged. The Looking-Glass Utopia of the Dums and the Dees experiences a fall in prices of 25%, but it continues to enjoy full employment of 40,000 hours.

The Moral of the Story: Money Doesn't Matter to the Real Economy

Uncle John Stuart has therefore been right all along.

"There cannot ... be intrinsically a more insignificant thing, in the economy of society, than money. ... The relations of commodities to one another remain unaltered by money" [Mill (1848) p.488]. "Great as the difference would be between a country with money, and a country altogether without it, it would be only one of convenience; a saving of time and trouble" [p.6].

There is nothing in the experience of the Dums and the Dees to upset the New Orthodoxy. The use of money does not seem to affect the transactions themselves — only the level of money prices at which they take place.

Money appears to influence the level of prices, but it makes no difference to the volume of employment. Equilibrium, apparently, still means full employment. The New Orthodoxy remains intact.

A strange muffled sound is heard in the distance. It grows louder all the time. It comes from a procession of New Orthodox priests. As they draw nearer, the sound becomes discernible. It is their ritual chant repeated over and over again. "Equilibrium means full employment ... unemployment means disequilibrium" ... "Equilibrium means full employment ... unemployment means disequilibrium" ... "Equilibrium means full employment ... unemployment means disequilibrium" ...

As a means of avoiding all the inconvenience of barter, money is an excellent device. Money really does make the economic world go round. — Or so it seems.

CHAPTER 18

SAVING: THE NOBLEST VIRTUE

> "Annual income twenty pounds, annual expenditure
> nineteen nineteen six, result happiness.
> Annual income twenty pounds, annual expenditure
> twenty pounds ought and six, result misery."
>
> Mr. Wilkins Micawber
> [Charles Dickens, *David Copperfield*, ch.12]

The initial market-clearing equilibrium shown in Table 16.3 above is the macroeconomic outcome of the plans of each individual Dum and each individual Dee. The economy enjoys "full employment" amounting to 40,000 hours, because all the Dums and all the Dees are employed for the length of time which they desire. The enjoyment of leisure amounting to 30,000 hours is purely voluntary. There is no "involuntary unemployment".

On the question of how the Looking-Glass Utopia can become more prosperous, Uncle Adam has some words of advice. "An augmentation of fortune is the means by which the greater part of men propose and wish to better their condition. ... The most likely way of augmenting their fortune is to save and accumulate. ... As the capital of an individual can be increased only by what he saves, ... so the capital of a society, which is the same with that of all the individuals who compose it, can be increased only in the same manner" [Smith (1776) II,3].

What will happen to the initial full employment equilibrium, if the Dums and the Dees follow Uncle Adam's advice, and there is an increase in the general desire to save as the result of a switch in preferences away from present consumption to future consumption? Will there be any effect on the volume of employment?

A Question of Thrift

In providing for the future, the Dums and the Dees have two options. They can save goods, or they can save money. The first alternative involves the accumulation of a stock of real wealth — goods which are held for the purpose of future consumption. The second alternative involves the accumulation of a stock of monetary wealth — purchasing power which is held for the purpose of acquiring real goods and services for future consumption.

Suppose this general desire to save takes the form of a cut in present consumption during the period from $26\frac{2}{3}$% of total resources to 20%. The intention is simply to switch the consumption of $6\frac{2}{3}$% of total resources from the present to the future; *there is no change in the general preference for consumption (present and future) relative to leisure.* The increase in thrift is therefore intended to be "neutral" with respect to employment. The point of this assumption is that any *unintended* impact on the level of employment will be thrown into sharp relief.

Column 1 of Table 18.1 shows the initial preferences before the increase in thrift. *Column 2* is included for purposes of comparison. *Column 3* shows the change in preferences, if the Dums and the Dees choose the first option and accumulate *real wealth.* *Column 4* shows the change in preferences, if they choose the second option and accumulate *money.*

Table 18.1: Real Saving

PLANNED ALLOCATION OF RESOURCES	*(column 1)* INITIAL EQUILIBRIUM	*(column 2)* Increase in the Desire for Liquidity	*(column 3)* Increase in the Desire to Save Real Wealth	*(column 4)* Increase in the Desire to Save Money
	% of Total	*% of Total*	*% of Total*	*% of Total*
Leisure	20	18 →→	20	20
		↓		
Consumption	$26\frac{2}{3}$	24 →→ ↓	20 →→	20 →→
		↓	↓	↓
Real Wealth	20	18 →→ ↓	$26\frac{2}{3}$ ←←	20 ↓
		↓		↓
Money	$33\frac{1}{3}$	40 ←←	$33\frac{1}{3}$	40 ←←
Total	100	100	100	100

The effect on full employment equilibrium depends on which alternative they choose: real saving or monetary saving.

The Effect of Accumulating Real Wealth

Investing in real wealth may take several forms including:

> the storage of *durable* consumption goods (like tins of baked beans or frozen food) for the purpose of future consumption;
>
> the ordering of consumption goods or services for *forward delivery* (like the placing of contracts in the commercial "futures" markets or the advance booking of holidays) for the purpose of future consumption;
>
> the manufacture of *producer goods* (like fishing nets or industrial machinery) in order to make goods for future consumption.

A switch of preferences to any of these forms of investment diverts demand away from "present goods" towards "future goods". In the real world, the resulting disequilibrium would be resolved by a change in relative prices leading to a transfer of economic activity away from catering for present consumption towards catering for future consumption; but it would take time. In the Looking-Glass Utopia, however, transitional effects are eliminated by the efficiency of the "auctioneer", and redistributional effects on the desired volume of employment are precluded by the simplifying assumption that the only form of investment is the storage of Product A or Product B. Consequently, "future goods" necessitate exactly the same productive effort as "present goods".

Consumption is reduced by $6\frac{2}{3}$% of total resources from $26\frac{2}{3}$% to 20%. Real Wealth is increased by $6\frac{2}{3}$% of total resources from 20% to $26\frac{2}{3}$%. The replacement of the cut in consumption spending by an increase in investment spending leaves effective demand unchanged. Apart from the switch from "present goods" to "future goods", equilibrium is undisturbed. Effective demand of 120,000 units remains equal to effective supply of 120,000 units. The economy remains in equilibrium and continues to enjoy full employment — the achievement of the desired volume of employment — of 40,000 hours.

The New Equilibrium

There is only one change between the new equilibrium and the initial equilibrium — a shift between consumption and real wealth. There is no change in the level of prices or in the volume of employment.

The results are summarised in Table 18.2.*

Why Saving is a Good Thing

The moral of the story is clear. In the Looking-Glass Utopia, a "neutral" change in the desire to save makes no difference to the achievement of the desired level of employment *provided that the change takes the form of an increase in the accumulation of real wealth.*

If the additional goods available for future periods are capital instruments for use in production, it is probable that they will enhance future productivity and expand production in subsequent periods. To Uncle Adam, this is one of the most promising of the "causes of the wealth of nations". His enthusiastic encouragement of saving is prompted by the conviction that it will lead to economic growth and expansion.

---

* For a diagrammatical representation, see Section E of the Appendix.

Table 18.2: The Impact of an Increase in the "Saving Demand" for Real Wealth

	INITIAL EQUILIBRIUM	NEW EQUILIBRIUM	CHANGE
Level of Prices	£4 per unit	£4 per unit	*ZERO*
Volume of Employment	40,000 hours	40,000 hours	*ZERO*
FLOW OF REAL INCOME	*units*	*units*	*units*
Production	120,000	120,000	0
– Consumption	–120,000	–90,000	–(30,000)
= SAVING	0	30,000	30,000
STOCK OF REAL WEALTH	*units*	*units*	*units*
Closing Balance	90,000	120,000	30,000
– Opening Balance	–90,000	–90,000	0
= INVESTMENT	0	30,000	30,000

Round brackets indicate negative changes (i.e. reductions).

"As the capital of an individual can be increased only by what he saves, ... so the capital of a society, which is the same with that of all the individuals who compose it, can be increased only in the same manner. Parsimony, and not industry is the immediate cause of the increase in capital. ... Every prodigal appears to be a public enemy, and every frugal man a public benefactor" [Smith (1776) II,3].

The upholders of the New Orthodoxy are equally delighted. Equilibrium, apparently, still means full employment. Their religious beliefs are triumphantly vindicated. The New Orthodoxy remains intact and can be confidently preached.

A strange muffled sound is heard in the distance. It grows louder all the time. It comes from a procession of New Orthodox priests. As they draw nearer, the sound becomes discernible. It is their ritual chant repeated over and over again. "Equilibrium means full employment ... unemployment means disequilibrium" ... "Equilibrium means full employment ... unemployment means disequilibrium" ... "Equilibrium means full employment ... unemployment means disequilibrium" ...

CHAPTER 19

SAVING: THE DEADLIEST SIN

Spending on actual goods for future consumption — accumulating real wealth — is one way of saving. The alternative is to increase the stock of purchasing power necessary to buy the goods — by accumulating monetary wealth.

The decision to take the second option and to save an additional $6\frac{2}{3}$% of total resources by restricting consumption in favour of increasing the holding of money results from the change in preferences indicated in column 4 of Table 19.1.

Table 19.1: Monetary Saving

PLANNED ALLOCATION OF RESOURCES	*(column 1)* INITIAL EQUILIBRIUM	*(column 2)* Increase in the Desire for Liquidity	*(column 3)* Increase in the Desire to Save Real Wealth	*(column 4)* Increase in the Desire to Save Money
	% of Total	*% of Total*	*% of Total*	*% of Total*
Leisure	20	18 →→ ↓	20	20
Consumption	$26\frac{2}{3}$	24 →→ ↓	20 →→ ↓	20 →→ ↓
Real Wealth	20	18 →→ ↓	$26\frac{2}{3}$ ←←	20 ↓
Money	$33\frac{1}{3}$	40 ←←	$33\frac{1}{3}$	40 ←←
Total	100	100	100	100

The planned cut in total consumption again amounts to $6\frac{2}{3}$% of total resources. But, this time, there is no corresponding increase in investment spending. By contrast with an increase in *real* saving (*column 3*) which simply switches $6\frac{2}{3}$% of total resources from one kind of spending (on present consumption) to another kind of spending (on future consumption), an increase in money saving (*column 4*) switches $6\frac{2}{3}$% of total resources out of spending altogether.

That is the only intended difference. *There is no change in the general preference for consumption (present and future) relative to leisure.* The decision to save is "neutral" with respect to employment. The planned volume of employment remains at 40,000 hours, and planned output is still 120,000 units. The problem is that these plans can no longer be achieved.

The Effect of Accumulating Monetary Wealth

The failure to replace consumption spending by investment spending cuts effective demand by 6$\frac{2}{3}$% of total resources. Unlike a switch into real wealth which changes the composition of effective demand, a switch into monetary wealth reduces its volume. With effective demand below effective supply, markets no longer clear.

That is the vital difference between the two forms of saving.

The initial disequilibrium following the change is shown in the *Round 1* column of Table 19.2 (with the initial equilibrium in the column on the extreme right for purposes of comparison).

Table 19.2
The Movement (*Tâtonnement*) towards Equilibrium
following an Increase in the "Saving Demand" for Money

		Round 1	Round 2	Round 3	Round 4	Round 5	INITIAL
PRICE *(per unit)*		£4.00	£3.75	£3.50	£3.25	£3.00	£4.00
AVAILABLE RESOURCES *('000 equivalent units)*							
Time	(70,000 hours)	210.0	210.0	210.0	210.0	210.0	210.0
Real Wealth	(90,000 units)	90.0	90.0	90.0	90.0	90.0	90.0
Money	(£600,000/Price)	150.0	160.0	171.4	184.6	200.0	150.0
Total		450.0	460.0	471.4	484.6	500.0	450.0
PLANNED ALLOCATION *('000 equivalent units)*							
Leisure	(20%)	90.0	92.0	94.3	96.9	100.0	90.0
Consumption	(20%)	90.0	92.0	94.3	96.9	100.0	120.0
Real Wealth	(20%)	90.0	92.0	94.3	96.9	100.0	90.0
Money	(40%)	180.0	184.0	188.5	193.9	200.0	150.0
Total		450.0	460.0	471.4	484.6	500.0	450.0
PRODUCT MARKET *('000 equivalent units)*							
Supply	(Time – Leisure)	120.0	118.0	115.7	113.1	110.0	120.0
Demand	(Consumption)	90.0	92.0	94.3	96.9	100.0	120.0
	(+ Investment) *	0.0	2.0	4.3	6.9	10.0	0.0
Excess Supply		30.0	24.0	17.1	9.3	0.0	0.0

* Investment = Real Wealth Planned – Real Wealth Available

The result of the change in preferences is shown in the "Planned Allocation" section of the *Round 1* column. Since planned Leisure remains unaltered, aggregate supply remains at 120,000 units. Since planned Consumption is cut by 30,000 units *without any compensating increase in investment in Real Wealth*, aggregate demand is reduced to 90,000 units. The result is excess supply of 30,000 units.

The reason for the excess supply in the Product Markets is the attempt to increase holdings of Money to the newly desired purchasing-power equivalent of 180,000 units. With prices at £4 per unit, that requires no less than £720,000 compared with the actual £600,000 which is available. It is the collective attempt to make up the "shortfall" of £120,000, which is responsible for the excess supply of 30,000 units in the Product Markets.

Since aggregate supply is 30,000 units greater than aggregate demand, "the books do not balance". No transactions can be allowed. In order to stimulate a reduction in the quantity supplied and an increase in the quantity demanded, the auctioneer needs to lower the price of both products.

The *Round 2* column shows the effect of a 25 pence price reduction. The purchasing power of the available money rises, with a corresponding increase in the total available resources. In order to maintain the desired proportions, the planned allocation has to change. The increase in leisure reduces the supply of output, the increase in consumption and investment reduces the demand. Although the reduction of excess supply to 24,000 units is a distinct improvement on *Round 1*, it is still far from equilibrium. A further round of bidding is therefore necessary.

The *tâtonnement* process of "groping" towards equilibrium continues through successive rounds of bidding and rebidding as long as there is disequilibrium. During each round, the auctioneer lowers prices in response to the pressure of the bidding. Each price fall reduces excess supply so that the disequilibrium becomes smaller and smaller until it is totally eliminated.

Not until *Round 5*, when prices have been lowered to £3 per unit, is aggregate demand equal to aggregate supply. Only then do the plans of all one thousand individuals become compatible. Every individual is able to achieve his desired level of leisure, consumption and money. Excess supply and demand have been eliminated from every market. The books balance. Equilibrium has been restored. Transactions can go ahead.

The New Equilibrium

There are two differences between the new equilibrium in the *Round 5* column and the initial equilibrium (in the extreme right-hand column). The first is a 25% reduction in the level of prices from £4 per unit to £3. The second is an $8\frac{1}{3}$% fall in the volume of employment which accompanies a corresponding reduction in both aggregate demand and aggregate supply.

The results are summarised in Table 19.3.*

* For a diagrammatical representation, see Section F of the Appendix.

Table 19.3: The Impact of an Increase in the "Saving Demand" for Money

	INITIAL EQUILIBRIUM	NEW EQUILIBRIUM	CHANGE
Level of Prices	£4 per unit	£3 per unit	*25% FALL*
Volume of Employment	40,000 hours	36,667 hours	*8⅓% FALL*
FLOW OF REAL INCOME	*units*	*units*	*units*
Production	120,000	110,000	(10,000)
– Consumption	–120,000	–100,000	–(20,000)
= SAVING	0	10,000	10,000
STOCK OF REAL WEALTH	*units*	*units*	*units*
Closing Balance	90,000	100,000	10,000
– Opening Balance	–90,000	–90,000	0
= INVESTMENT	0	10,000	10,000

Round brackets indicate negative changes (i.e. reductions).

Even though the Looking-Glass Utopia has perfectly flexible markets presided over by a Walrasian auctioneer, so that there is no possibility of market imperfection or dynamic disequilibrium, it suffers from unemployment. The volume of employment desired by the Dums and the Dees remains at the initial level of 40,000 hours. The volume actually achieved is only 36,667 hours.

The culprit, apparently, is the desire to save by accumulating money.

Why Saving is a Bad Thing

The moral of the story is clear. A "neutral" change in the desire to save will have a significant impact on the level of employment, if the change is reflected in a switch from present consumption to the accumulation of uncommitted purchasing power.

The principles of sound finance enunciated by Adam Smith and repeated so succinctly by Mr. Micawber have been followed to the letter by all the Dums and all the Dees. Yet the result of their noble efforts of self-denial in saving for the future is a reduction in the level of output and employment below that which is desired.

The result is particularly disappointing for the upholders of the New Orthodoxy. Equilibrium, apparently, no longer means full employment.

An eerie silence settles over the Looking-Glass Utopia. The procession of New Orthodox Priests is nowhere to be seen or heard.

What can have gone wrong?

CHAPTER 20

MONEY IS THE ROOT OF ALL EVIL

Saving is a noble virtue, when it is an engine of economic growth. When it is a cause of unemployment, it turns into a deadly sin.

The author of the evil transformation is money.

How is it that "the great wheel of circulation, the great instrument of commerce" — which makes the economic world go round in chapter 17 — becomes an economic stumbling-block in chapter 19?

The Market as the Channel of Economic Communication

The solution to the problem of communication between millions of different producers and consumers who normally never meet is a free market. It is through offers to buy and sell in the market-place that individuals are able to reveal their continually changing preferences. That is how the Dums and the Dees manage to achieve the maximum gains from trade in the Looking-Glass Utopia described in chapter 16.

Money as a *medium of exchange* is indispensable for facilitating trade. Without it, commerce would be reduced to barter. The only effective way in which consumers can signal their preferences is by spending money (or promising to spend money). That is how money makes the economic world go round in chapter 17.

There is, however, a snag. Any imperfection in the market — in the channel of communication — can distort the signals or delay their transmission. But there is an effective remedy — freedom of competition. It is the basis of the orthodox belief that price and wage flexibility, by allowing markets to respond quickly and accurately to changes in consumers' intentions, can guarantee full employment.

The Looking-Glass Utopia is the Apotheosis of the Market-Place; — it is the perfectly competitive ideal. The fiction of the "Walrasian Auction" guarantees that the process of adjustment from one "market-clearing equilibrium" to another is instantaneous. There are no transactions at "false" (i.e. non-equilibrium) prices. The perfectly flexible and frictionless markets of the Looking-Glass Utopia are perfect channels of communication. They provide a clinically pure background for identifying the economic impact of various different types of economic change.

Nothing can be attributed to market imperfection.

Perfect Markets and the Deficiency of Effective Demand

In every case summarised in Table 20.1, resources are allocated precisely in accordance with preferences *revealed in the market-place.*

Table 20.1: The Economic Impact of Changes in the Underlying Preferences

	(column 1) INITIAL EQUILIBRIUM (ch.16)	*(column 2)* Increase in the Desire for Liquidity (ch.17)	*(column 3)* Increase in the Desire to Save Real Wealth (ch.18)	*(column 4)* Increase in the Desire to Save Money (ch.19)
PLANNED ALLOCATION OF RESOURCES	*% of Total*	*% of Total*	*% of Total*	*% of Total*
Leisure	20	18 →→ ↓	20	20
Consumption	26$\frac{2}{3}$	24 →→↓ ↓	20 →→ ↓	20 →→ ↓
Real Wealth	20	18 →→↓ ↓	26$\frac{2}{3}$ ←←	20 ↓ ↓
Money	33$\frac{1}{3}$	40 ←←	33$\frac{1}{3}$	40 ←←
Total	100	100	100	100
FLOW OF REAL INCOME	*units*	*units*	*units*	*units*
Production	120,000	120,000	120,000	110,000
− Consumption	−120,000	−120,000	−90,000	−100,000
= SAVING	0	0	30,000	10,000
STOCK OF REAL WEALTH	*units*	*units*	*units*	*units*
Closing Balance	90,000	90,000	120,000	100,000
− Opening Balance	−90,000	−90,000	−90,000	-90,000
= INVESTMENT	0	0	30,000	10,000
LEVEL OF PRICES	£4 per unit	£3 per unit *25% FALL*	£4 per unit *NO CHANGE*	£3 per unit *25% FALL*
VOLUME OF EMPLOYMENT	40,000 hours	40,000 hours *NO CHANGE*	40,000 hours *NO CHANGE*	36,667 hours *8$\frac{1}{3}$% FALL*

Column 1 shows the underlying preferences of the Dums and the Dees in initial full employment equilibrium (discussed in chapter 16). At the market-clearing equilibrium price level of £4 per unit, 40,000 hours of employment are "desired" by the Dums and the Dees. For the Looking Glass Utopia, therefore, *full employment* means 40,000 hours. 40,000 hours is what they want; 40,000 hours is what they get. *There is no unemployment.*

Column 2 shows what happens when there is an increase in the pure "liquidity demand" for money (discussed in chapter 17 above). The increase in the preference for money is not accompanied by a change in any other preferences; — the intensity of the desire for holding money increases, but the intensity of the desire for everything else remains the same. The planned increase in money balances is therefore drawn proportionately from all the other choices (as indicated by the arrows). Consequently, there is no relative change in any of the *real* choices (including Leisure) *revealed in the market-place*. The fall in the desire for everything else relative to money causes a fall in the level of prices. But as the relative *real* preferences *revealed in the market-place* remain unaltered, there is no impact whatever on employment. All the Dums and all the Dees get what they want at the market prices. The "desired" volume of employment of 40,000 hours continues to be achieved; *there is still no unemployment.*

Column 3 shows what happens when there is an increase in the "saving demand" for real wealth (discussed in chapter 18 above). The intention is simply to restrict present consumption in favour of future consumption. There is no change in the preference for Leisure. The switch of spending from Consumption to Real Wealth leaves Leisure's share of the preferences *revealed in the market-place* unaltered at 30%. The result is the intended diversion of employment from catering for present consumption to catering for future consumption; but there is no change in Leisure and therefore no change in the volume of employment. All the Dums and the Dees get what they want at the market prices. The "desired" volume of employment of 40,000 hours continues to be achieved; *there is no unemployment.*

Column 4 shows what happens when there is an increase in the pure "saving demand" for money (discussed in chapter 19 above). The switch from spending on Consumption to holding Money reduces the preferences *revealed in the market-place* thereby increasing Leisure's share of *revealed preferences* to $33\frac{1}{3}$%. The result is an unintended increase in Leisure and a corresponding fall in the volume of employment *below the desired level.* It is the only case where the Dums and the Dees do *not* achieve their desired volume of employment. They do *not* get what they want at the market prices; they get too much leisure. 40,000 hours employment is what they want; 36,667 hours is all that they get. *The result is unemployment.*

Since markets are perfect, market imperfection cannot be responsible! The "natural rate of unemployment" is zero.

The Market as a Revealer of Preferences

The market provides one of the most valuable economic freedoms — the freedom to choose. The choice is exercised by spending money: one £, one vote. As long as the channels of communications are perfect, the bids are transmitted without distortion and without delay. At equilibrium prices, all individuals get what they bid for.

If they do not get what they want, it cannot be the fault of market imperfection. The feature which distinguishes monetary saving in *column 4* from real saving in *column 3* is that, although savers of money get what they bid for, *they do not bid for what they want.*

The villain of the piece is money.

Money as a Concealer of Preferences

If it were not for the availability of money as a *store of value*, savers would have to commit themselves to specific orders for future delivery. They would literally have to purchase "future goods". Money provides them with a means of escape; it releases them from the necessity of having to make decisions in advance.

Although it is true that an open market is the source of one of the most valuable economic freedoms — the freedom to choose — , money is the source of an even more valuable economic freedom — the freedom *not* to choose.

In an exchange economy, the market is the only effective channel of economic communication. Holding money "as a store of value" cuts off the signals. Intentions have no economic impact unless they are supported by actual "bids" — the spending of money or the placing of specific orders — in the market-place. By allowing savers the privilege of concealing their preferences, saving money defeats the whole object of the market as a channel of economic communication.

The market is a device for revealing preferences; saving money is a means of concealing them. In so far as saving money prevents intended demand from being made effective, it is a deadly sin. Market perfection offers no protection from this type of deficiency of effective demand. Even the most perfect channels of communication are useless *if the signals are never transmitted.*

Money is a perfect economic bypass for avoiding the market-place. Because the accumulation of monetary wealth has the property of concealing real preferences, it is responsible for the possibility (denied by Orthodox economic theory) of deficiency of effective demand.

The experience of the Dums and the Dees in their Looking-Glass Utopia provides a perfect illustration of the danger of money as a "concealer of preferences" even in markets so flexible that the economy never deviates from perfectly competitive equilibrium.

A "Concealed Preference" Theory of Unemployment

When saving takes the form of the accumulation of money, the *intended* increase in future consumption amounting to $6\frac{2}{3}$% of total resources is channelled into money. It is therefore concealed from the market. But the market cannot respond to *intentions*. The signal received is the same as if preferences for consumption (present plus future) had fallen relative to leisure. Equilibrium can be restored only if there is a "real" adjustment. Compared with initial full employment equilibrium, consumption has to fall, whereas leisure has to rise — *and, if leisure increases, the level of employment must fall.*

The process of bidding and rebidding that would take place at a "Walrasian auction" is described in the Table 19.2 of the previous chapter. The results, which are summarised in *column 4* of Table 20.1, indicate that two changes must occur before equilibrium can be restored:

(a) a fall in the level of prices, and
(b) a fall in the volume of employment.

The fall in the level of prices increases the purchasing power of the existing quantity of money so that it is equal to the newly desired level of 200,000 units. Although the price level adjustment is strong enough to satisfy the increased demand for "real balances", it is not strong enough on its own to restore equilibrium. The change in the composition of "real" preferences, can be satisfied only by "real" changes. Compared with the initial equilibrium, consumption has to fall by 20,000 units, real wealth has to rise by 10,000 units, and leisure has to rise by 3,333 hours. But, if leisure rises to 33,333 hours, the level of employment must fall to 36,667 hours.

Even though the Looking-Glass Utopia has perfectly flexible markets presided over by a Walrasian auctioneer, so that there is no possibility of market imperfection or dynamic disequilibrium, it suffers from unemployment. At 36,667 hours, the volume of employment actually achieved by the Dums and the Dees falls short of the desired "full employment" level of 40,000 hours.

The culprit is the saving of money.

Saving: Vice or Virtue?

According to Adam Smith, there is no doubt. "As the capital of an individual can be increased only by what he saves, ... so the capital of a society, which is the same with that of all the individuals who compose it, can be increased only in the same manner" [1776, II,3].

The happy experience of the Dums and the Dees in chapter 18 indicates that, if saving takes the form of accumulating *real wealth*, the whole economy will be better-off. But their unfortunate experience in chapter 19 suggests the opposite, if saving takes the form of accumulating *monetary wealth.*

In both cases, the desire to restrict consumption is "neutral" with respect to employment. The amount of leisure which each individual wishes to enjoy remains unaltered. The only difference is that the commitment to specific investment involves actual spending on the acquisition of real output, whereas the desire to keep options open involves the accumulation of monetary claims. The desire to save restricts effective demand for present consumption. The desire to invest replaces that cut by increasing effective demand for future consumption. The desire to hold money leaves effective demand deficient.

Since the benefit from investing in real wealth and the detriment from holding money are both consequences of the same desire to save, it cannot be the act of saving which is responsible for the fall in the level of employment.

The real culprit is the availability of money as a "store of value".

Why Money Matters

In the sort of *non-exchange* desert island economy inhabited by Robinson Crusoe, saving can take place only in terms of real wealth. The act of saving is also an act of investing. Saving and investment are not merely equal; they are the same thing. The intention to provide for the future has actually to be carried out.

In a non-monetary *barter* economy, exchange between the present and the future is possible, but awkward. Contracts have to be drawn up for "forward delivery": goods or services are *delivered now* in exchange for a promise of goods or services to be *delivered later*. The problem for savers is that they have to commit themselves to specific goods or services in advance of delivery. The necessity for forward contracts, however, ensures that the intention to provide for the future has to be transmitted through the market-place.

In a *monetary* economy, futures markets in which contracts for forward delivery can be executed do exist. But they can be bypassed. For normal saving, futures markets are not essential. There is a highly convenient alternative. The saver can accumulate some form of monetary wealth instead. The choice ranges from cash to debts of different types and maturity. All monetary claims have the same essential characteristic. They allow savers who intend to consume at some time in the future to avoid committing themselves until they are ready to make up their minds. The effect is that their intentions are not transmitted through the marketplace. Their demand for future consumption is not made effective. Instead of revealing their preferences to the market by spending, they conceal them in their wallets.

Money is an ingenious device for bypassing markets for future consumption and dispensing with contracts for forward delivery. But, in this role, it severs the link between the present and future in economic life. It is the perfect economic bypass.

As a medium of exchange, money makes the economic world go round. As a store of value, it is the root of all evil.

The Moral of the Story

The experience of the Dums and the Dees provides an instructive lesson in the macroeconomic theory of the behaviour of the economy as a whole.

A "neutral" change in the desire to save makes no difference to the volume of employment, *provided* that the cut in consumption spending is replaced by spending on real investment. But, if the cut in consumption spending is replaced by the accumulation of monetary claims, the effect on employment can be catastrophic.

The moral of the story is unmistakable.

Equilibrium *cannot* guarantee full employment, *even if markets are perfectly flexible.*

A monetary economy, where savers can conceal their intentions by accumulating monetary claims, is, notwithstanding the doctrine of the New Orthodoxy, *a multi-gear machine.*

CHAPTER 21

THE MULTI-GEAR ECONOMY

The New Economic Orthodoxy

Part II tells the story of the evolution of a religion. The outcome of two hundred years of sectarian conflict is a New Economic Orthodoxy. It is the product of a fundamentalist revival of the Classical Faith which has culminated in a return to the belief that the economy is a single-gear machine whose efficiency is entirely dependent upon the lubrication of perfect competition.

Unemployment has therefore come to be regarded solely as a problem of market imperfection or disequilibrium. The path of righteousness may not be easy, but at least it is clear — obedience to the sacred Law of Competition. The reward is equilibrium; and, according to the New Orthodoxy, equilibrium means full employment. Observe the Law of Competition, and there is no apparent need to observe anything else.

Part III flatly contradicts the Orthodox view of the economy as a single-gear machine. In their "Looking-Glass Utopia", the Dums and the Dees scrupulously observe every letter of the Law of Competition. The fact that they still suffer from unemployment demonstrates the fundamental flaw in the Orthodox argument that "the theory of unemployment ... requires a non-Walrasian model in which there is no Walrasian auctioneer continuously clearing commodity and labor markets" [Phelps (1968) p.30]. Consequently, there is no need for a *structuralist* theory which "sees informational and organizational imperfections and features at the bottom of unemployment" [1994, p.247n]. For what emerges is that, contrary to the New Orthodoxy, a monetary economy has not just one gear but many.

The Multi-Gear Economy

The various categories of unemployment can be illustrated in terms of the familiar supply and demand diagram.

In Figure 21.1 (which is a reproduction of Figure 9.1), the willingness for employment is represented by the supply curve *SS*. It indicates that more labour will be supplied, the higher the real wage. The potential demand for labour is represented by the demand curve D_PD_P. It shows the demand for labour as it would be derived from the intentions to spend money on both present goods (consumption) and future goods (investment).

The intersection of the two curves at the point P indicates that the potential equilibrium volume of employment is equal to ON_P.

Figure 21.1: The "Multi-Gear" Economy

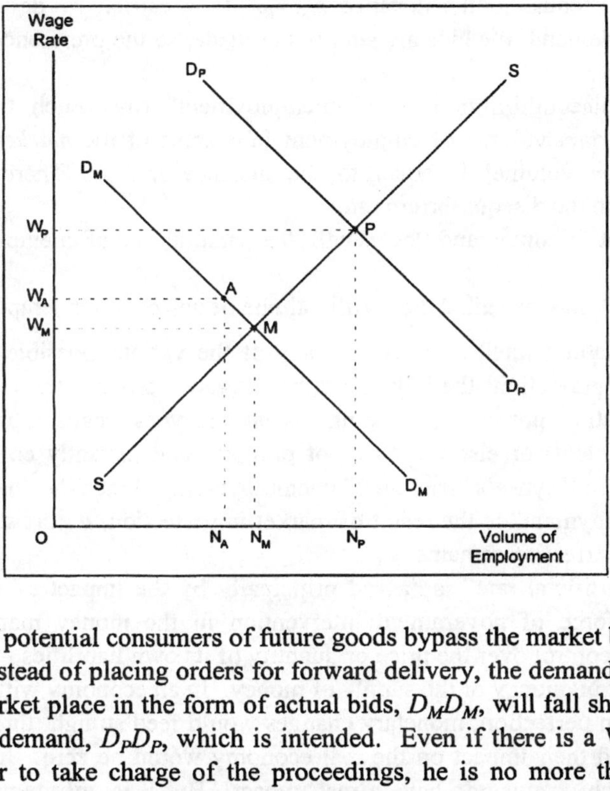

But, if potential consumers of future goods bypass the market by saving money instead of placing orders for forward delivery, the demand revealed in the market place in the form of actual bids, D_MD_M, will fall short of the potential demand, D_PD_P, which is intended. Even if there is a Walrasian auctioneer to take charge of the proceedings, he is no more than a co-ordinator of bids. If the bids actually made in the market place are represented by the demand curve D_MD_M, then the best he can do is to reach the market-clearing intersection at point M. The market equilibrium volume of employment will be no greater than ON_M.

If, however, the market is of less than Utopian perfection, the wage rate may fail to move far enough or fast enough towards W_M to enable the economy to reach even the market equilibrium at point M. It may stick at W_A so that the actual disequilibrium volume of employment is determined at point A. As long as the actual wage rate W_A remains above the market-clearing rate W_M, the actual disequilibrium volume of employment, ON_A, will remain below the market equilibrium volume, ON_M.

The Various Categories of Unemployment

The "equilibrium rate of unemployment" (by which the *market-clearing equilibrium* volume of employment falls short of the *potential equilibrium* volume) is equal to the distance $N_M N_P$. It is caused by deficiency of effective demand: the bids are simply not made, so the preferences are not revealed.

The "disequilibrium rate of unemployment" (by which the *actual disequilibrium* volume of employment falls short of the *market-clearing equilibrium* volume) is equal to the distance $N_A N_M$. There are two elements in the disequilibrium rate:

(1) what Friedman and Phelps call the "natural rate of unemployment", *plus*

(2) what may be called the "artificial rate of un-(or "over-)employment".

The "natural rate" is caused by any of the various possible forms of market imperfection: the bids are either "rigged" through the exercise of monopolistic power (producing what Keynes calls "voluntary" unemployment) or else they are not properly and instantly co-ordinated (resulting in Keynes's "frictional" unemployment). Since the "natural rate of unemployment" is the result of market imperfection, it persists as long as the imperfection remains.

The "artificial rate" is caused principally by the impact of the "non-market" force of government intervention in the money market as it exercises control over the price or quantity of its own liabilities — the rate of interest on money or the supply of money. In an economy with markets of Utopian perfection, monetary changes would feed straight through into prices, and their impact on the real economy would be zero. In the real world, such changes *do* have a real impact. But it is only temporary; it lasts as long as it takes to overcome the frictional resistances encountered in the imperfect markets of the real world.

The descent of the economy from the Paradise of Full Employment to the Real World of Unemployment is charted in Table 21.1. Because its existence is *not* recognised by the New Orthodoxy, the "market-clearing equilibrium rate of unemployment" has been shaded.

The "disequilibrium rate of unemployment" is the only type recognised by the classical economists; at its root are Mill's "maladjustments" and Pigou's "frictional resistances" (in Phelps's terminology: "informational and organizational imperfections"). This type of unemployment would be cured by the appointment of a Walrasian auctioneer.

The "market-clearing equilibrium rate of unemployment", which coincides with Keynes's "involuntary unemployment", is not recognised by the classics at all. Its root cause is deficiency of effective demand.

This type of unemployment could *not* (*pace* Leijonhufvud [1968] and Phelps [1994]) be cured by the appointment of a Walrasian auctioneer.

The major significance of a "market-clearing equilibrium rate of unemployment", is that it is not susceptible to classical remedies. Since it is unrelated to the degree of market perfection, it could occur even in a Walrasian Utopia. For a deficiency of effective demand implies, not that there is no auctioneer to co-ordinate the bids, but that there are insufficient bids to co-ordinate.

Table 21.1: The Fall From Grace

ON_P	POTENTIAL equilibrium level of employment		THE PROMISED LAND of Full Employment
	MINUS:-		
$N_M N_P$	Market-clearing equilibrium rate of unemployment		Deficiency of Effective Demand [Too low a Gear]
	EQUALS:-		
ON_M	MARKET equilibrium level of employment		
	MINUS:-		
$N_A N_M$	Disequilibrium rate of unemployment	Natural rate caused by imperfect market forces Artificial rate caused by government intervention	Deficiency of Competition [Insufficient Lubrication]
	EQUALS:-		
ON_A	ACTUAL disequilibrium level of employment		THE REAL WORLD of Full Employment

Acknowledgement of the possibility of a "market-clearing equilibrium rate of unemployment" would require a radical reappraisal of economic policy. There is little prospect of that because of the unprecedented agreement among all shades of economic opinion that there is no such thing as a "market-clearing equilibrium rate of unemployment". According to the New Orthodoxy, it is a contradiction in terms.

The Extraordinary Breadth of Sectarian Consensus

Controversy between the rival economic sects over economic policy is extremely fierce. Yet, viewed in the perspective of Table 21.1, the range of disagreement is astonishingly narrow.

The Classical economists deny the possibility of a "market-clearing equilibrium rate of unemployment"; Keynes insists on it. Table 21.1 is an accurate representation of Classical Orthodoxy, provided that the shaded area is omitted; it is an accurate representation of the Keynesian Revolution, provided that the shaded portion is reinstated. Following the exposure of the fatal flaw in Keynes's theory by the Neo-Classical Counter-Revolution, the shaded area has been removed. The New Bible has successfully obliterated all traces of its existence.

The consensus is that the shaded portion of Table 21.1 does not exist. In Figure 21.1, therefore, D_MD_M cannot diverge from D_PD_P; consequently, ON_M is identical with ON_P. The New Orthodoxy, like the Old Orthodoxy, maintains that, in a perfectly competitive Utopia, there can be no deficiency of effective demand.

According to the New Bible, the religion is split between Monetarists who claim that Keynes is guilty of asserting the possibility of an equilibrium rate of unemployment and "Keynesians" who deny that he ever meant to make such an assertion. They are united in believing that such an assertion is an error of the worst possible kind.

The Incredible Narrowness of Sectarian Conflict

The Sectarian Conflict is over that part of the disequilibrium rate of unemployment which is labelled "artificial" in Table 21.1. The divisive issue is the speed with which the real economy adjusts to monetary changes instigated by the government. Those who are labelled "Keynesian" by the New Bible take the view that the speed of adjustment is relatively slow. "Monetarists" (particularly those who support the cult of "rational expectations") believe that it is fairly fast.

This empirical difference is the reason why economists who share the same theology can advocate radically different policies. Monetary restriction is advocated by the Monetarists as a safe weapon against inflation, because they believe that its impact on the real economy is only temporary. "Keynesians" who have abandoned Keynes's theoretical position are reduced to complaining that, because the adjustment process is slow, the depressing effect on employment is likely to be prolonged.

To recur to the engineering analogy, the Sectarian Consensus is that the economy is a single-gear machine — so the only problem is lubrication.

The Multi-Gear Alternative

The experience of the Dums and the Dees in their Looking-Glass Utopia demonstrates, on the contrary, that the economy is a multi-gear machine — so lubrication is only one problem. Obedience to the Law of Competition is *necessary* to reach the Promised Land of Full Employment, but it is *not sufficient*.

Recognition of a market-clearing equilibrium rate of unemployment would focus attention on the possibility that there is a gear-lever which can be shifted — in either direction.

The implication for economic policy is that the elimination of market imperfection, so far from being the end of the problem, is only the beginning. It may also be necessary to come to terms with the possibility of a direct linkage between the fuel tap and the gear lever.

The Orthodox single-gear view of the economy (in Part II) is contradicted by the alternative multi-gear view (in Part III). The object in Part IV is to resolve the conflict in favour of the Secular Alternative. The method is to examine the rival Theologies — Classical, Keynesian, and Monetarist — and to identify the logical flaw in each one.

PART IV

WHAT'S WRONG WITH ECONOMIC THEORY?

INTRODUCTION

The Secular view of the economy as a multi-gear machine is anathema to Orthodox Theology which holds steadfastly to the "single-gear" view.

Because economics is a religion masquerading as a science, none of the rival sects are prepared to admit that their doctrine rests on an Act of Faith.

The Looking-Glass Utopia is an excellent device for penetrating the veneer of scientific respectability. In Part IV, the microeconomic foundations of the principal macroeconomic theories (Classical, Keynesian, and Monetarist) are exposed to the "acid test": the problem of a general increase in the desire to save money in an economy of Utopian perfection. All of the rival theologies fail. In no case, does the macroeconomic outcome follow logically from the microeconomic preferences. On the contrary, whenever the actual preferences of savers prove to be inconvenient, they are replaced by microeconomic assumptions invented to justify the macroeconomic conclusions they are supposed to prove.*

---

* For a diagrammatical representation of the argument in Part IV, see Sections G, H, and I of the Appendix.

CHAPTER 22

WHAT'S WRONG WITH CLASSICAL ECONOMICS?

Classical Theology

There are two major essentials of Orthodox Classical Doctrine:

1) competition is the key to full employment;
2) saving is the key to economic growth.

Classical doctrine is based on an Article of Religious Faith:

as long as markets are perfectly competitive,
there is no possibility of a deficiency of effective demand.

This belief is disguised as a scientific principle by what appears to be a logical argument to establish the *irrationality* of "hoarding".

The Classical Irrelevance: The Irrationality of Hoarding

"No man, if he can help it, will let any part of his property lie useless and run to waste. ... He will lend, not hoard it" [James Mill (1807) pp.129,133]. What is saved "is not, generally speaking, hoarded, but (through savings banks, benefit clubs, or some other channel) re-employed as capital, and consumed" [John Stuart Mill (1848) p.70].

The essential mechanism is a "perfect" capital market in which it is possible to borrow and lend without restriction. "The rate of interest will be such as to equalize the demand for loans with the supply of them. It will be such, that exactly as much as some people are desirous to borrow at that rate, others shall be willing to lend. If there is more offered than demanded, interest will fall; if more is demanded than offered, it will rise; and, in both cases, to the point at which the equation of supply and demand is re-established" [pp.637,638].

The Classical argument is clear and simple:

what is saved is lent – (otherwise interest is lost);
what is lent is borrowed – (by definition);
what is borrowed is spent – (or there is no point in borrowing).

It follows that, apart from the behaviour of misers which can safely be dismissed as irrational and insignificant, money saved is money spent.

The danger with this line of argument is that it leads straight into the quicksand of "Desert Island Economics".

The Classical Distortion: The Desert Island Fantasy

If Robinson Crusoe on his desert island wishes to save, he must abstain from consumption activities like catching fish ("present goods") and switch his efforts to investment activities like making a fishing boat and nets ("future goods"). In the monetary economies of the real world, savers are likened to unskilled Robinson Crusoes; they are not capable of producing future goods themselves, so they simply lend the money to others who are. By the time that it emerges from the desert island economics of the nineteenth-century textbooks, saving is simply a switch from spending on present consumption to spending on future consumption.

This argument is relentlessly pursued through nineteenth-century economic literature to its logical conclusion.

"In loans, as in all other money transactions, ... the money which passes" is regarded "only as the medium, and commodities as the thing really transferred — the real subject of the transaction" [Mill (1848) p.644]. "The key to the whole theory of capital is to be found in thus eliminating capital loans *in the form of numéraire* so that attention is directed exclusively to the lending of capital *in kind*" [Walras (1874) p.290]. "A loan is nothing else than a real and true exchange of present goods for future goods" [Böhm-Bawerk (1888) p.285]. "Money as such ... is of significance in the economic world only as an intermediary" [Wicksell (1898) p.29].

The nature of the subterfuge employed by the classical economists to justify their belief in the virtue of saving is exposed in Table 22.1.

Table 22.1: The "Classical Distortion"

PLANNED ALLOCATION OF RESOURCES	INITIAL EQUILIBRIUM	Actual Change in Preferences	Classical Distortion
	% of Total	*% of Total*	*% of Total*
Leisure	20	20	20
Consumption	$26\frac{2}{3}$	20 →→	20 →→
		↓	↓
Real Wealth	20	20 ↓	$26\frac{2}{3}$ ←←
Revealed in the Market Place	$66\frac{2}{3}$	60 ↓	$66\frac{2}{3}$
		↓	
Money	$33\frac{1}{3}$	40 ←←	$33\frac{1}{3}$
Total	100	100	100

The actual preferences of the Dums and the Dees as revealed in the market-place are shown in the centre column. They signal an increase in the desire for Leisure relative to Consumption and Real Wealth. Classical theology simply ignores the actual market signals and replaces them with assumptions invented to prove its own conclusions. The "Classical Distortion" of the actual preferences is shown in the right-hand column. The false assumption of no change in the desire for Leisure relative to Consumption and Real Wealth "proves" the Classical solution by the simple expedient of assuming away the problem. The actual preferences which do not support Classical religious convictions are ignored; they are replaced with assumed preferences which do.

To the classical economists, saving money simply shifts demand from consumption to investment, it does not affect demand in total. Money saved (the subject of chapter 19) is therefore treated as if it were the same thing as money spent on investment in real goods and services (the subject of chapter 18). Consequently, the Classical "theological" version of *monetary* saving in Table 22.2 is identical to the Free-Market "secular" version of *real* saving in Table 18.2.*

Table 22.2: The Impact of an Increase in the "Saving Demand" for Money: The Classical "Theological" Version

	INITIAL EQUILIBRIUM	NEW EQUILIBRIUM: CLASSICAL "Theological"	NEW EQUILIBRIUM: FREE-MARKET "Secular"
Level of Prices	£4 per unit	£4 per unit *NO CHANGE*	£3 per unit *25% FALL*
Volume of Employment	40,000 hours	40,000 hours *NO CHANGE*	36,667 hours *8⅓% FALL*
FLOW OF REAL INCOME	*units*	*units*	*units*
Production	120,000	120,000	110,000
− Consumption	−120,000	−90,000	−100,000
= SAVING	0	30,000	10,000
STOCK OF REAL WEALTH	*units*	*units*	*units*
Closing Balance	90,000	120,000	100,000
− Opening Balance	−90,000	−90,000	−90,000
= INVESTMENT	0	30,000	10,000

The Classical reassurance that an increase in the desire to save money has no impact on the volume of economic activity is therefore dangerously false.

---

* For a diagrammatical representation, see Section G of the Appendix.

The Classical Fallacy

There is nothing wrong with the logic of the Classical "what is saved is lent, what is borrowed is spent" argument. It is its relevance which is open to question.

Either effective demand can be deficient, or else it cannot; capital markets (perfect or otherwise) have no bearing on the issue.

In the Looking-Glass Utopia, all the Dums and Dees have the same time preference and the same investment opportunities. There is therefore no scope for lending and borrowing. The assumption can, however, be easily relaxed. If some individuals are more thrifty than others, the more thrifty will lend money to the less thrifty. But, if other preferences remain unchanged, that will make no difference to the rest of the equilibrium. With the same total preferences for Leisure, Consumption, and Real Wealth, the same volume of employment will be devoted to the same present and future consumption. (The only difference is that the less thrifty individuals will enjoy a higher proportion of present to future consumption than will the more thrifty individuals.)

The existence of a free market in which money can be borrowed and lent at a "perfectly flexible" rate of interest has therefore no bearing whatever on the issue of whether or not demand can be deficient.

The validity of the Classical argument becomes clear when it is related to the Free-Market "Secular" version of the impact of an increase in the "saving demand" for money; — so does its irrelevance.

The "Secular" version of the new equilibrium following an increase in the "saving demand" for money (reproduced in the right hand column of Table 22.2) confirms the classical argument in every respect. With prices reduced to £3 per unit, income from the production of 110,000 units amounts to £330,000, and expenditure on the consumption of 100,000 units amounts to £300,000. What is saved (£330,000 – £300,000 =) £30,000 is indeed spent on increasing the investment in real wealth from 90,000 units to 100,000 units.

Nevertheless, total demand — and with it the volume of output and employment — has fallen. And it has done so *without contradicting the classical argument* that what is saved out of consumption is spent on investment. The unassailable logic of the argument is overwhelming proof of its irrelevance.

The flaw in Classical Theology is not an error of logic: what is saved out of consumption is indeed spent on investment. The fallacy lies in the inference that the volume of what is saved and spent does not alter. For it is clear that, during the process of adjustment (details of which are shown in Table 19.2 of chapter 19), the volume of output which is the source of the saving and spending falls from 120,000 units to 110,000 units.

The false inference is motivated by the need to justify Classical religious convictions. The Act of Faith lies in assuming what is to be proved, namely, that demand does not fall. Incorporation of this false assumption into the analysis from the outset is the nature of the "Classical Distortion".

The problem which Classical theology overlooks is the role of money as a concealer of preferences. Savers who intend that the reduction in their present consumption shall be replaced by an increase in their future consumption fail to communicate their intentions. If they save money, without placing specific orders for forward delivery, they send misleading signals to the market. No market, however free, however flexible, and however competitive, can respond to intentions which are never signalled in the first place. Individuals will not get what they want (in terms of employment or anything else), if they fail to signal their intentions in the only way possible in a free market — with actual spending.

Classical Theology is based on the erroneous conviction that an increase in the desire to accumulate money produces exactly the same result as an increase in the desire to accumulate real wealth. *Saving and investment are not merely equal; they are one and the same thing.*

It is against the Classical desert island fantasy in which "money doesn't matter" that Keynes's *General Theory* is directed.

The Keynesian Challenge

"The conviction ... that money makes no real difference except frictionally and that the theory of production and employment can be worked out (like Mill's) as being based on "real" exchanges with money introduced perfunctorily in a later chapter, is the modern version of the classical tradition. Contemporary thought is still deeply steeped in the notion that if people do not spend their money in one way they will spend it in another. ... These conclusions may have been applied to the kind of economy in which we actually live by false analogy from some kind of non-exchange Robinson Crusoe economy, in which the income which individuals consume or retain as a result of their productive activity is, actually and exclusively, the output *in specie* of that activity. ... Those who think in this way ... are fallaciously supposing that there is a nexus which unites decisions to abstain from present consumption with decisions to provide for future consumption" [1936, pp.19-21].

Unfortunately, his *General Theory* replaces one set of religious distortions with another.

CHAPTER 23

WHAT'S WRONG WITH KEYNES'S *GENERAL THEORY*?

Keynesian Theology

There are two major essentials of Keynes's Revolutionary Doctrine:

1) although competition is necessary for full employment, it is not sufficient;
2) although saving can be a major stimulus to economic growth, saving can also be its gravest threat.

This does not deny the Classical view of real saving as "the noblest virtue". But it directly contradicts Orthodox Classical Doctrine by recognising monetary saving as "the deadliest sin".

Keynes's Revolutionary Doctrine is that

even if markets are perfectly competitive,
deficiency of effective demand remains a danger.

Although this doctrine *can* be logically proved, its presentation in the *General Theory* allows it to be portrayed as if it were dependent on its own Article of Religious Faith.

A Question of Presentation

Classical theology derives from approximately 150 years of economic scripture written by scores of different authors from the time of Adam Smith. Keynesian theology derives from a single book by a single author. *The General Theory of Employment Interest and Money* contains less than 400 pages — yet its theoretical core is more difficult to pin down. As the title of Leijonhufvud's work *On Keynesian Economics and the Economics of Keynes* implies, "there is room ... for differing interpretations" [1968, p.6].

That is putting it mildly. There is a whole literature devoted to explaining "what Keynes really meant".

The cause of the problem lies in the way the *General Theory* is presented. Although the theoretical core is perfectly sound and the empirical superstructure is highly relevant, they need (in the first instance) to be carefully and clearly segregated. Instead, they are so well integrated that it is difficult to tell them apart. Fundamental differences in interpretation are often attributable to whether any particular item is taken to be a theoretical proposition or an empirical assumption.

Contrary to Friedman's argument, "Keynes' key theoretical proposition, namely, that even in a world of flexible prices, a position of equilibrium at full employment might not exist" [1968, pp.2,3] is, in fact, valid. The object of Part III above is to demonstrate that it is Keynes's theory which stands up "in a world of flexible prices" and that it is the Classical theory which falls down. Keynes is right and his neoclassical "counter-revolutionary" critics are wrong.

Moreover, on the score of empirical relevance, even his most dedicated opponents concede that the *General Theory* constitutes one of the greatest achievements in the whole of economic literature.

What, then, is the nature of the complaint?

Keynes is vulnerable to criticism, not on the grounds of any serious error in the *General Theory*, but on the grounds of his failure to make the theory stick. The proof of that failure is the simple historical fact of a neoclassical counter-revolution which has led to the rehabilitation of classical theory, albeit with a "Keynesian" empirical superstructure.

Ironically, two of Keynes's most significant contributions to empirical relevance, the liquidity preference doctrine and the multiplier process, may be responsible. The argument in chapter 19 above demonstrates that they are *not* necessary to prove the validity of the "multi-gear" view of the economy. But, once "equilibrium with less than full employment" has been established as a theoretical possibility *in the absence of market imperfection and dynamic disequilibrium*, the next question to be addressed is empirical. How is the volume of employment determined in the real world where market imperfection and dynamic disequilibrium are facts of everyday life?

The liquidity preference doctrine and the multiplier process are both part of the empirical flesh with which Keynes clothes the theoretical skeleton. But, if they are misinterpreted as part of the theoretical core, the liquidity preference doctrine is an irrelevance and the multiplier process is a distortion.

The Keynesian Irrelevance: The Rationality of Hoarding

One of Keynes's major objections to Classical theory is "the tacit assumption that every individual spends the whole of his income either on consumption or on buying, directly or indirectly, newly produced capital goods" [1936, p.225].

In order to challenge this assumption, Keynes has to demolish the classical argument that hoarding is irrational.

He begins by restating the classical view. "Money, it is well known, serves two principal purposes. By acting as a money of account, it facilitates exchanges ... it is a convenience which is devoid of significance or real influence. In the second place, it is a store of wealth. ... But in the world of the classical economy, what an insane use to which to put it! For it is a recognized characteristic of money as a store of wealth that it is barren; whereas practically every other form of storing wealth yields some interest or profit. Why should anyone outside a lunatic asylum wish to use money as a store of wealth?" [1937, p.218].

The answer supplied by Keynes lies in "the state of liquidity preference", or "the propensity to hoard", as he sometimes calls it [p.219]. "Three divisions of liquidity-preference" are distinguished in the *General Theory*: "(i) the transactions-motive, *i.e.* the need of cash for the current transaction of personal and business exchanges; (ii) the precautionary-motive, *i.e.* the desire for security as to the future cash equivalent of a certain proportion of total resources; and (iii) the speculative-motive, *i.e.* the object of securing profit from knowing better than the market what the future will bring forth" [1936, p.170].

Although the establishment of a rational motive for hoarding is sufficient to undermine the Classical position, and although it invests Keynes's revolutionary theory with empirical relevance, it is neither necessary nor sufficient to prove the revolutionary theoretical proposition that demand can be deficient *in the absence of market imperfection*. Its interpretation as theoretical proof, gives legitimacy to the allegation made by Patinkin of a "chain of errors in Keynes's reasoning which caused him to overlook these factors" [1948, p.269]. The factors in question form the core of the "real-balance effect" argument (discussed in chapter 10 above and chapter 24 below). From his discussion of "real balances" in the *Tract*, the *Treatise* and the *General Theory* itself, it is clear that Keynes is not unaware of the argument that "incomes and ... prices necessarily change until the aggregate of the amounts of money which individuals choose to hold at the new level of incomes and prices thus brought about has come to equality with the amount of money created by the banking system" [1936, pp.84,85]. Nevertheless, it is Keynes's own lack of care in making a clear distinction between the theoretical core and the empirical superstructure which lends credibility to the accusation that he is guilty of a major oversight: the failure to take account of the "real-balance effect" of falling prices which *in freely competitive markets* accompanies an increase in the "saving demand" for money.

In place of the "dampener" of the real-balance effect, stands the famous "multiplier" by which a change in the "saving demand" for money can produce an impact greater than the initial intention. But the standard textbook treatment of the "multiplier" as part of the theoretical core of the *General Theory* rather than a particularly relevant empirical assumption requires just as great a distortion as the Classical argument that it produces no impact at all.

Keynes's Argument: The Multiplier Process

In the *General Theory*, the microeconomic assumptions underlying the macroeconomic results are not made explicit. Instead, by a master-stroke of simplification, they are summed up "in the portmanteau function "propensity to consume". ... The fundamental psychological law ... is that men are disposed, as a rule and on the average, to increase their consumption as their income increases, but not by as much as the increase in their income" [p.96].

On this basis, Keynes defines the *increase in consumption* divided by the *increase in income* as "the *marginal propensity to consume*", and he defines the "investment multiplier" as equal to 1/(1 – MPC), where MPC is the "marginal propensity to consume". The "*investment multiplier* [*k*] ... tells us that, when there is an increment of aggregate investment, income will increase by an amount which is *k* times the increment of investment" [p.115]. Applied to spending in general, this can be converted into a *spending multiplier* to cover the relationship between employment and spending.

Initially, the Dums and the Dees plan to spend 26⅔% of their resources on consumption and to hold 33⅓% in the form of money — a ratio of 4 to 5. Since saving is defined as "the excess of income over what is spent on consumption" [p.74], the marginal propensity to consume is equal to 4/9. Following the increase in their "saving demand" for money, they plan to reduce consumption spending to only 20% of their resources in order to hold 40% in the form of money — a ratio of 1 to 2; and the marginal propensity to consume changes to 1/3.

The new spending multiplier is therefore equal to $\left[\frac{1}{1 - \frac{1}{3}}\right] = 1\frac{1}{2}$.

The multiplier formula provides a simple rule of thumb for calculating the ultimate impact on income of a change in spending. In the case of the Dums and the Dees, the initial cut in aggregate consumption by 30,000 units sets off a process which, according to the multiplier formula, leads to a decrease in aggregate real income of (30,000 x 1½ =) 45,000 units.

Table 23.1 describes the process in terms of what Keynes calls "primary" and "secondary" employment. During the first round of spending following the initial cut in consumption, the "primary" fall in real income amounts to 30,000 units. But the process does not end there. Given the marginal propensity to consume of 1/3, the response to the "primary" fall in real income is a further cut in consumption during the second round of spending by (30,000 x 1/3 =) 10,000 units. This produces a "secondary" fall in real income of 10,000 units. This in turn produces a further fall in consumption leading to a further fall in real income — and so on. The multiplier process continues along the lines indicated in Table 23.1. It does not work itself out until the initial cut in consumption of 30,000 units has been "multiplied" into a fall of 45,000.

Table 23.1: The "Multiplier" Process

				'000 units
Initial Real Income				120
			'000 units	
Round 1:	{Reduction in Real Income from } {"*Primary* unemployment" due } {to initial cut in Consumption }		30	
		'000 units		
Round 2:	{Reduction in Real Income from }	10.0		
Round 3:	{"*Secondary* unemployment" }	3.3		
Round 4:	{due to successive cuts }	1.1		
Round 5:	{in Consumption }	0.4		
Round 6:	{ (at ⅓ of previous round) }	0.1		
Round 7:	{ }	0.1		
			15	
Total Reduction in Real Income				45
Final Real Income				75

The Textbook Representation of the Multiplier Model

Figure 23.1 is a typical textbook representation of the consumption function used for demonstrating the multiplier process. Real income is shown along the horizontal axis, and real expenditure is shown along the vertical axis. The dotted 45° line represents positions of equilibrium where planned income is equal to planned expenditure.

The initial consumption preferences of the Dums and Dees are represented by the consumption function, CF_1. Its slope is equal to the initial marginal propensity to consume of 4/9. Equilibrium income, Y_1, is determined at the point where the consumption function crosses the 45° line indicating that planned income is equal to planned expenditure. Initially they both amount to 120,000 units.

When the preferences change, the consumption function shifts to CF_2 and becomes flatter as the marginal propensity to consume falls to 1/3. The new equilibrium level of real income, Y_2, is 75,000 units.

The multiplier process from Y_1 to Y_2 is indicated by the dotted line which follows the progress of the rounds of spending in the direction indicated by the arrows.

As a consequence of the initial cut in consumption spending of 30,000 units, a "deflationary gap" is opened between planned income and planned expenditure. Planned income remains at 120,000 units, but planned expenditure has fallen to 90,000 units. This is indicated by the arrows which drop vertically from Y_1 to point P. But this is a position of disequilibrium. Since planned expenditure has fallen to 90,000 units, planned income also falls to 90,000 units. This is indicated by the arrows which travel horizontally from point *P* to point *Q*. But at point *Q*, there is still a deflationary gap. Planned expenditure falls to 80,000 units down the line of arrows to point *R*. The zigzag process continues until the new equilibrium is reached at Y_2, where planned income and planned expenditure are equal.

Figure 23.1: The Consumption Function and the Multiplier Process

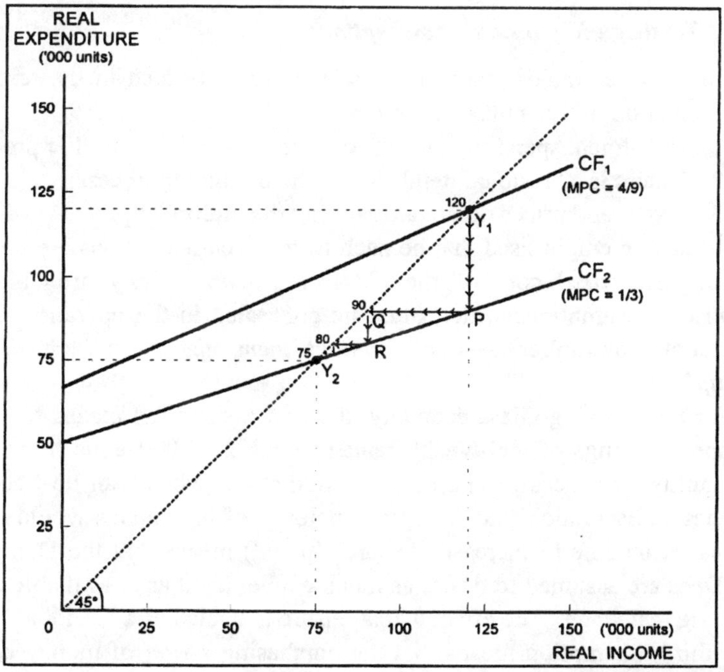

This type of diagram makes clear that the lower the marginal propensity to consume, the flatter is the consumption function and consequently the greater is the "multiplier" effect of any change in the choice between spending and saving.

The use of the multiplier formula neatly avoids the complications of microeconomic analysis. It provides a handy rule-of-thumb for assessing the impact of changes in spending. As such, it is part of the empirical superstructure of the *General Theory*. The standard textbook representation, however, gives the impression that it is part of the theoretical core. It may not be an accurate interpretation of "what Keynes really meant", but it is, perhaps, one of the most widely disseminated. Rightly or wrongly, what is written in His Name has become part of "Keynesian Theology".

It is a distortion *of* Keynes as a result of unclear presentation *by* Keynes. The ambiguity of the expression "Keynesian Distortion" seems entirely appropriate.

The extent of the "Keynesian Distortion" can be exposed only by thorough exploration of the microeconomic foundations in order to uncover the assumptions about individual preferences which are implicit in the operation of the multiplier process.

The "Textbook Keynesian" Assumptions

There are three major assumptions which are embedded in the textbook representation of the multiplier process:

(1) investment spending does not change during the multiplier process;
(2) leisure is a "residual item" during the multiplier process;
(3) wages and prices do not alter during the multiplier process.

It must be emphasised that no such restrictive assumptions are implicit in the *theoretical* core of the *General Theory*. They are "hidden" *empirical* assumptions which often lie concealed in the operation of the "textbook" multiplier* — but, *without them, the multiplier will not multiply*.

For the Looking-Glass economy, the first assumption means that total planned holdings of real wealth remain fixed at 90,000 units throughout the multiplier process. The second assumption (which can be traced to Keynes's observation that "the great majority of individuals would prefer increased income to increased leisure" [p.326]) means that the Dums and the Dees are assumed to desire as much employment as is available at the existing real wage. The effect is that leisure is treated as a "residual" item. The third assumption means that the purchasing power of money cannot alter, so that total "real balances" cannot change.

The only "active ingredients" remaining are the desire to hold cash balances and the desire to consume real goods and services.

---

* Occasionally, some of these assumptions are made explicit. "The major assumption in the multiplier model is that prices and wages are taken as given or fixed in the short run. ... Investment [is treated as] an exogenous variable, one whose level is determined outside the model" [Samuelson and Nordhaus (1995) p.449].

Disequilibrium arises because the Dums and the Dees wish to switch $6\frac{2}{3}$% of their resources out of consumption and into holdings of money. The result is excess supply of goods in the product markets, and an unsatisfied desire for cash.

The disequilibrium can be resolved by an "auction" of bids and rebids which continues until "the books balance". Equilibrium is reached only when the planned result which each individual desires at prevailing market prices is actually achieved.

The Keynesian "Auction"

With a Walrasian auctioneer in charge, the disequilibrium is resolved by cutting market prices (in the course of the *tâtonnement* process described in chapter 19). With a Keynesian auctioneer, this solution is unavailable: no alteration in prices is allowed. Instead of announcing new *prices*, the Keynesian auctioneer announces new levels of *output* on the basis of the aggregate demand revealed in the previous round, and invites a new round of bidding (out of the new *incomes*) at the unaltered prices.

Table 23.2: The Keynesian "Auction"

	Round 1	Round 2	Round 3	Round 4	Round 5	Round 6	Round 7	INITIAL
PRICE *(per unit)*	£4.00	£4.00	£4.00	£4.00	£4.00	£4.00	£4.00	£4.00
AVAILABLE RESOURCES *('000 equivalent units)*								
Time (70,000 hours)	210.0	210.0	210.0	210.0	210.0	210.0	210.0	210.0
Real Wealth (90,000 units)	90.0	90.0	90.0	90.0	90.0	90.0	90.0	90.0
Money (£600,000/Price)	150.0	150.0	150.0	150.0	150.0	150.0	150.0	150.0
Total	450.0	450.0	450.0	450.0	450.0	450.0	450.0	450.0
PLANNED ALLOCATION *('000 equivalent units)*								
Leisure (residual)	90.0	120.0	130.0	133.3	134.4	134.8	135.0	90.0
Consumption ($^1/_3$)	90.0	80.0	76.7	75.6	75.2	75.1	75.0	120.0
Real Wealth (fixed)	90.0	90.0	90.0	90.0	90.0	90.0	90.0	90.0
Money ($^2/_3$)	180.0	160.0	153.3	151.1	150.4	150.1	150.0	150.0
Total	450.0	450.0	450.0	450.0	450.0	450.0	450.0	450.0
PRODUCT MARKET *('000 equivalent units)*								
Supply (Time – Leisure)	120.0	90.0	80.0	76.7	75.6	75.2	75.0	120.0
Demand (Consumption)	90.0	80.0	76.7	75.6	75.2	75.1	75.0	120.0
Demand (+ Investment) *	0.0	0.0	0.0	0.0	0.0	0.0	0.0	0.0
Excess Supply	30.0	10.0	3.3	1.1	0.4	0.1	0.0	0.0

* Investment = Real Wealth Planned – Real Wealth Available

Round 1 results in excess supply of 30,000 units. Consequently, the "new real income" in *Round 2* is 30,000 units lower. In order to maintain the newly desired 2 to 1 relationship between real-balances and consumption, planned consumption is cut by 1/3 of the 30,000 unit reduction in real income, and planned holdings of money are cut by 2/3. That still leaves excess supply at 10,000 units. In *Round 3*, therefore, further cuts are made in the same proportions. The "Keynesian" process continues through the successive rounds of bidding and rebidding described in Table 23.2 (matching the Multiplier Process described in Table 23.1), until excess supply is eliminated and equilibrium is finally reached in *Round 7*.

The eventual equilibrium, after the "multiplier process" has worked itself out, is summarised in Table 23.3.*

The Keynesian Distortion

The Keynesian "Theological" version of the new equilibrium following an increase in the "saving demand" for money in Table 23.3 is in sharp contrast with the Free-Market "Secular" version. According to the "Secular" version, the impact of an increase in the desire to save money falls partly on the level of prices and partly on the volume of employment. According to the Keynesian version, the impact falls on the volume of employment only.

Table 23.3
The Impact of an Increase in the "Saving Demand" for Money:
The Keynesian "Theological" Version

	INITIAL EQUILIBRIUM	NEW EQUILIBRIUM	
		KEYNESIAN "Theological"	FREE-MARKET "Secular"
Level of Prices	£4 per unit	£4 per unit *NO CHANGE*	£3 per unit *25% FALL*
Volume of Employment	40,000 hours	25,000 hours *37½% FALL*	36,667 hours *8⅓% FALL*
FLOW OF REAL INCOME	*units*	*units*	*units*
Production	120,000	75,000	110,000
– Consumption	–120,000	–75,000	–100,000
= SAVING	0	0	10,000
STOCK OF REAL WEALTH	*units*	*units*	*units*
Closing Balance	90,000	90,000	100,000
– Opening Balance	–90,000	–90,000	–90,000
= INVESTMENT	0	0	10,000

* For a diagrammatical representation, see Section H of the Appendix.

The discrepancies between the two versions arise out of the three hidden assumptions concealed in Keynes's "multiplier process". Nevertheless, the free-market version is sufficient to demonstrate the possibility of stable equilibrium with less than full employment, *even in a Looking-Glass world of perfectly flexible prices*. The central proposition of the *General Theory* can therefore be proved without the necessity of the assumptions hidden in the multiplier process.

The extent of the distortion of actual preferences implicit in the multiplier process is indicated in Table 23.4.

Table 23.4: The "Keynesian Distortion"

PLANNED ALLOCATION OF RESOURCES	INITIAL EQUILIBRIUM	Actual Change In Preferences	Keynesian Distortion
	% of Total	*% of Total*	*% of Total*
Leisure	20	20	30 ←←
			↑
Consumption	26⅔	20 →→	16⅔ →→
		↓	
Real Wealth	20	20 ↓	20
Revealed in the Market Place	66⅔	60 ↓	66⅔
		↓	
Money	33⅓	40 ←←	33⅓
Total	100	100	100

The hidden assumptions are exclusive to multiplier process. They are not merely unnecessary to Keynes's central theory, they are positively damaging. The most damaging of all is the assumption of price rigidity. The stated object of the *General Theory* is to show that there is a category of unemployment which is not caused by market imperfection [1936, p.6]. Yet the "multiplier" — one of the most important mechanisms in Keynes's theory — is based on the implicit assumption of prices which are so inflexible that they cannot move at all. Prices are not just "sticky"; they are held fast in superglue.

Because it is not made clear that the multiplier is part of the empirical superstructure and not part of theoretical core, the *General Theory* is delivered into the hands of its most dedicated opponents — disciples of the classical school to whom the notion of "stable equilibrium with less than full employment" is anathema — the monetarists.

The Monetarist Challenge

The monetarist challenge to the *General Theory* is directed at Keynes's neglect of the real-balance effect. The success of what has come to be known as the "counter-revolution" in economic theory is therefore largely Keynes's own fault. By pointing out what appear to be errors in the *General Theory*, the Monetarists are able to divert attention from the fallacies in their own; and these are far more serious.

CHAPTER 24

WHAT'S WRONG WITH MONETARISM?

Monetarist Dogma: Back to the Classics

The key proposition of monetarism is that, if markets are perfectly flexible, monetary changes do not affect the volume of output and employment; they affect only the level of prices.

This is a reaffirmation of the classical doctrine enunciated by John Stuart Mill. Nevertheless, there is a significant difference in the supporting argument.

The classical attitude to hoarding cash is that it is an irrational activity confined to misers and consequently unlikely to be of significance. The neo-classical view adopted by the monetarists is slightly different. They are prepared to concede Keynes's argument that there are circumstances in which cash hoarding may take place on a significant scale. But the monetarists argue that, even if cash hoarding does take place, it will simply cause the level of prices to fall. Provided that markets are perfectly flexible, it will make no difference to the volume of output and employment.

The neo-classical conclusion of monetarist theology is therefore in complete harmony with the classical doctrine, but it is in direct conflict with the "secular" free-market result described in chapter 19.

Monetarist Analysis

Monetarist theology is crucially dependent on the real-balance effect argument. In the version developed by Don Patinkin, the existence of unemployed resources exerts a downward pressure on wages and prices. *Provided that markets are perfectly flexible*, the consequent increase in the real purchasing power of existing cash balances stimulates increased spending until effective demand has risen to absorb all the resources offered at current market rates.

"The real-balance effect ... stimulates the commodity market directly. Thus the downward shift in the commodity demand function automatically creates market forces which tend to offset it. If this demand is sufficiently sensitive to these forces, it will quickly return to a full-employment position at a lower level of wages, prices, and interest. Throughout this period of adjustment there will exist a state of excess supply in the commodity market. But due to the assumed shortness of this period, producers will react to their temporary inability to sell by simply permitting their inventories to build up. That is, they will leave their level of production unchanged" [1956, p.318].

Milton Friedman identifies the real-balance effect argument as the basis of the "counter-revolutionary" challenge. "These theoretical developments ... did undermine Keynes' key theoretical proposition, namely, that even in a world of flexible prices, a position of equilibrium at full employment might not exist. Henceforth, unemployment had again to be explained by rigidities or imperfections, not as the result of a fully operative market process" [1968, pp.2,3].

Monetarist theology is therefore founded on whatever assumptions lie concealed below the surface of the "real-balance effect" argument.

The Hidden Monetarist Assumptions

The assumptions hidden in Patinkin's analysis of the real-balance effect are the exact reverse of those hidden in Keynes's analysis of the multiplier process. Throughout Keynes's multiplier process, prices are absolutely rigid, investment is fixed, and leisure is the residual. In Patinkin's explanation of the real-balance effect (quoted above), prices are perfectly flexible, leisure is fixed, and investment ("permitting ... inventories to build up") is the residual.

The initial disequilibrium of the Looking-Glass Utopia following an increase in the "saving demand" for money to 40% of total resources is summarised in the *Round 1* column of Table 24.1. In an attempt to increase their holdings of Money from the purchasing-power equivalent of 150,000 units of product to the newly desired level of 180,000 units, the Dums and the Dees cut their total planned consumption below their total planned production so that there is excess supply in the Product Markets of 30,000 units.

Because the Monetarist auctioneer is totally committed to price flexibility, the procedure is very similar to the Walrasian auction described in chapter 19 above. In order to stimulate a reduction in the quantity supplied and an increase in the quantity demanded, the Monetarist auctioneer lowers prices in the Product Markets in steps of 25 pence per unit.

The effect of the first price reduction is shown in the *Round 2* column. The purchasing power of the available money rises to 160,000 units, with a corresponding increase in the total available resources to 460,000 units. Since desired money holdings are 40% of total resources, planned money holdings are the equivalent of 184,000 units. The actual level of 160,000 units is therefore inadequate. The collective attempt by the Dums and the Dees to close the gap is responsible for excess supply of 24,000 units in the Product Markets. As in chapter 19, it is not until *Round 5* when prices have been reduced to £3 per unit that excess supply is eliminated.

Table 24.1: The Movement (*Tâtonnement*) towards Equilibrium following an Increase in the "Saving Demand" for Money
The Monetarist "Theological" Version

	Round 1	Round 2	Round 3	Round 4	Round 5	INITIAL
PRICE *(per unit)*	£4.00	£3.75	£3.50	£3.25	£3.00	£4.00
AVAILABLE RESOURCES *('000 equivalent units)*						
Time (70,000 hours)	210.0	210.0	210.0	210.0	210.0	210.0
Real Wealth (90,000 units)	90.0	90.0	90.0	90.0	90.0	90.0
Money (£600,000/Price)	150.0	160.0	171.4	184.6	200.0	150.0
Total	450.0	460.0	471.4	484.6	500.0	450.0
PLANNED ALLOCATION *('000 equivalent units)*						
Leisure (fixed)	90.0	90.0	90.0	90.0	90.0	90.0
Consumption (20%)	90.0	92.0	94.3	96.9	100.0	120.0
Real Wealth (residual)	90.0	94.0	98.6	103.8	110.0	90.0
Money (40%)	180.0	184.0	188.5	193.9	200.0	150.0
Total	450.0	460.0	471.4	484.6	500.0	450.0
PRODUCT MARKET *('000 equivalent units)*						
Supply (Time – Leisure)	120.0	120.0	120.0	120.0	120.0	120.0
Demand (Consumption)	90.0	92.0	94.3	96.9	100.0	120.0
Demand (+ Investment) *	0.0	4.0	8.6	13.8	20.0	0.0
Excess Supply	30.0	24.0	17.1	9.3	0.0	0.0

* Investment = Real Wealth Planned – Real Wealth Available

The sole cause of the divergence between the Monetarist auction in Table 24.1 and the Free-Market auction in Table 19.2 is the fact that the Monetarist version ignores the preferences of the Dums and the Dees as revealed in the market-place. In Table 24.1, the planned allocation of resources does not reflect the actual preferences for Leisure (20% of total resources) and Real Wealth (also 20% of total resources). Instead of the actual preferences, it reflects the Monetarist assumption that "producers ... will react to their temporary inability to sell by simply permitting their inventories to build up. That is, they will leave their level of production unchanged" [Patinkin (1956) p.318]. Consequently, during each round of the bidding, planned leisure remains unchanged at the initial equivalent of 90,000 units, but inventories are allowed to build up to bringing planned investment spending up to 110,000 units. Table 24.1 is a faithful reproduction of the adjustment process assumed in Patinkin's analysis. Throughout the course of the bidding, "there exists a state of excess supply in the commodity market." As prices are reduced, "the real-balance effect stimulates the commodity market directly." "Thus the downward shift in the commodity demand function automatically creates market forces which tend to offset it." In the presence of a Walrasian auctioneer, demand is so sensitive to these forces that ultimately (in *Round 5*) "it returns to a full-employment position at a lower level of wages, prices, and interest."

The Monetarist version of final equilibrium is shown in Table 24.2. The level of prices falls by 25% (from £4 per unit to £3 per unit), but the volume of output and employment remains unchanged.*

Table 24.2: The Impact of an Increase in the "Saving Demand" for Money: The Monetarist "Theological" Version

	INITIAL EQUILIBRIUM	NEW EQUILIBRIUM	
		MONETARIST "Theological"	FREE-MARKET "Secular"
Level of Prices	£4 per unit	£3 per unit *25% FALL*	£3 per unit *25% FALL*
Volume of Employment	40,000 hours	40,000 hours *NO CHANGE*	36,667 hours *8⅓% FALL*
FLOW OF REAL INCOME	*units*	*units*	*units*
Production	120,000	120,000	110,000
− Consumption	−120,000	−100,000	−100,000
= SAVING	0	20,000	10,000
STOCK OF REAL WEALTH	*units*	*units*	*units*
Closing Balance	90,000	110,000	100,000
− Opening Balance	−90,000	−90,000	−90,000
= INVESTMENT	0	20,000	10,000

According to Monetarist "theology" two changes must occur before equilibrium can be restored:

(a) a fall in the level of prices, and

(b) a shift from consumption spending to investment spending.

By contrast with the Free-Market "secular" explanation, the Monetarist "theological" explanation refuses to admit the possibility of any reduction in the volume of output and employment.

According to the Free-Market "secular" explanation, however, although the price level adjustment is strong enough to satisfy the increased demand for "real balances", it is not strong enough *on its own* to restore

* The error in the "real-balance effect" argument is identified later on in this chapter: it ignores the wealth effect on the consumption of leisure. If preferences for leisure remain unaltered, the amount "consumed" will increase. For a diagrammatical representation, see Section I of the Appendix.

equilibrium. The change in the balance of "real" preferences, can be satisfied only by "real" changes.

The Monetarist Distortion

The nature of the subterfuge employed by the monetarists to justify their insistence that an increase in the "saving demand" for money has no impact on the level of output and employment is exposed in Table 24.3.

Table 24.3: The "Monetarist Distortion"

PLANNED ALLOCATION OF RESOURCES	INITIAL EQUILIBRIUM	Actual Change In Preferences	Monetarist Distortion
	% of Total	*% of Total*	*% of Total*
Leisure	20	20	←← 18
			↓
Consumption	$26\frac{2}{3}$	20 →→	↓ 20 →→
		↓	↓ ↓
Real Wealth	20	20 ↓	→→ 22 ↓
Revealed in the Market Place	$66\frac{2}{3}$	60 ↓	60 ↓
		↓	↓
Money	$33\frac{1}{3}$	40 ←←	40 ←←
Total	100	100	100

The actual preferences of the Dums and the Dees as revealed in the market-place are shown in the centre column. They signal an increase in the desire for Leisure relative to Consumption and Real Wealth. Monetarist theology simply ignores the actual market signals and replaces them with assumptions invented to prove its own conclusions. The "Monetarist Distortion" of the actual preferences is shown in the right-hand column. The false assumption of no change in the desire for Leisure relative to Consumption and Real Wealth "proves" the Monetarist solution by the simple expedient of assuming away the problem.

The actual preferences of the Dums and the Dees reveal a desire to devote the equivalent of 20% of their total resources to leisure. But that is inconvenient for Monetarist theology. So their actual preferences are ignored and replaced by the assumption that they wish to reduce the proportion to 18%.

Nevertheless, the argument has a certain degree of plausibility.

The monetarists are quite right to argue that, in flexible markets, an increase in the desire to hoard will have a powerful effect on the level of prices. They are also entitled to criticise Keynes for having failed to take this into account. There is, however, a fallacy in the monetarist argument, and it has its origin in Patinkin's explanation of the "real-balance effect".

The Monetarist Fallacy

In common with many classical theorists, Patinkin conducts his analysis in a manner which, though deceptively simple at the outset, ultimately turns out to be fraught with peril.

"For simplicity, it is assumed that … each individual begins … with an initial collection of goods which, like the manna of the Children of Israel, has descended upon him "from the heavens" " [1956, p.4].

There is no harm in this assumption as a device for explaining how equilibrium market prices of various different goods are established through a competitive process of barter. But it is dangerous. It is all too easy to fall into the habit of assuming a fixed volume of output in cases where the assumption is no longer legitimate.

This is precisely what happens with Patinkin's explanation of the real-balance effect.

To assume that "producers … will leave their level of production unchanged" [p.318] in the face of a fall in the demand for their product is a gross violation of free-market principles. It amounts to an assertion that producers have a desire to produce which is so overwhelming that they will do so whether there is any market for their output or not. The demand for leisure and its obverse, the supply of labour, are treated as if they were fixed at a given number of hours and not subject to the influence of market forces. This is a peculiar interpretation of free-market competition.

One of the few things upon which economists of all persuasions seem to agree is that "consumption is the sole end and purpose of all production" [Smith (1776) IV,8]. "All production is for the purpose of ultimately satisfying a consumer." "Consumption — to repeat the obvious — is the sole end and object of all economic activity" [Keynes (1936) p.46 and p.104].

Patinkin justifies his conclusion that "producers will react to their temporary inability to sell by simply permitting their inventories to build up" by reference to "the assumed shortness of [the adjustment] period".

Any reduction in output can then be blamed on lack of market flexibility.

"In the absence of sufficient interest- and price- elasticity, the adjustment process becomes a long, drawn-out one. It cannot then realistically be assumed that firms will continue producing at an unchanged level, for this would require them to accumulate inventories at ever increasing levels. Hence they must eventually take some step to bring current output — and consequently current input — into line with current sales. And this is the beginning of involuntary unemployment" [p.318].

This entirely misses the point. Where "the adjustment process becomes a long, drawn-out one", it is accepted without dispute that unemployment will be the result. The question is whether or not unemployment can occur where the adjustment process is a short, quick one. The free-market argument in chapter 19 shows that, even in a Walrasian Utopia, where the adjustment process is so short and quick that it is instantaneous, output and employment will still fall.

The assumed reaction of producers in the face of a *general fall in demand* is particularly odd when contrasted with the assumed reaction of the same producers in the face of a *relative fall in demand* for their own particular product. Yet, whatever the reaction of an individual producer to a fall in the demand for his own product happens to be, it is the same whether the fall is part of an overall decline in the total demand for all products or a fall in the demand for his own product relatively to others.

It is no criticism to observe that Patinkin is driven by the inexorable logic of his own argument to an explicit statement of the implicit assumption. It is, on the contrary, a tribute to the rigour of his analysis. Many theorists who rely on the real-balance effect argument are either unconscious of the implicit assumption or deliberately gloss over it.

Ironically, the most serious flaw in the real-balance effect argument is its failure to take full account of the real-balance effect. By increasing the purchasing power of money balances, a fall in the level of prices has a positive wealth effect. It is this enhanced wealth upon which the real-balance effect argument relies for the presumed increase in consumption spending. An unchanged desire to consume out of increased wealth implies an increase in the amount spent. But the increased wealth effect of fall in prices, must have effect on everything *including leisure.* If the consumption of goods increases in response to the increase in wealth, so also does the consumption of leisure.

In the Looking-Glass economy, the desire of the Dums and the Dees to persist in devoting 20% of their resources to the consumption of goods and 20% to the enjoyment of leisure must have the result of increasing both. In order to justify its denial of any reduction in employment, Monetarist theology has to assume a decrease in the desire for leisure.

The Absence of Challenge from the New Orthodoxy

The monetarist fallacy is obvious enough. It is understandable, though hardly excusable, that committed zealots should blind themselves to the logical flaws in their theory. The real puzzle is why the monetarist fallacy has gained acceptance as rational theory, even among the most determined opponents of monetarist policy.

Because the disregard of the real-balance effect (particularly in the textbook representation of the Keynesian multiplier process) is wholly wrong, it seems to be accepted without question that the monetarist counter-argument must be wholly right.

The New Orthodoxy is an attempt at a "synthesis" following the Keynesian revolution and the monetarist counter-revolution. It is flawed by the fallacies of both.

CHAPTER 25

WHAT'S WRONG WITH THE NEW ORTHODOXY?

The Nature of the New Orthodoxy

The New Orthodoxy is a "neo-classical synthesis" in which the Keynesian Revolution and the Monetarist Counter-revolution are regarded as part of the logical evolution of Classical Orthodoxy.

Keynes's own view of his *General Theory* points in that direction and has become part of the conventional wisdom. "Our criticism of the accepted classical theory of economics has consisted not so much in finding logical flaws in its analysis as in pointing out that its tacit assumptions are seldom or never satisfied, with the result that it cannot solve the economic problems of the actual world" [1936, p.379].

Also pointing in that direction and equally part of the conventional wisdom is Johnson's verdict on the "real-balance effect" argument. It "finally disposes of the Keynesian contention that under-employment equilibrium does not depend on the assumption of wage-rigidity. It does. ... It turns out that Keynes's theory is a special case of the classical — or rather of the neo-classical theory, since a satisfactory 'classical' theory was not worked out until after the Keynesian revolution. ... Keynes's theory started from an empirically relevant special assumption, derived some important meaningful results from it, and provided an approach which has since proved its usefulness for a wide range of problems" [1958, pp.119,120].

Samuelson's New Bible maintains the orthodox line by presenting the contrast between "Classical Analysis" and the "Keynesian Revolution" as purely empirical.

"The classical approach holds that prices and wages are flexible, so the economy moves to its long-run equilibrium very quickly. ... Changes in aggregate demand affect the price level but have no lasting impact upon output and employment. ... Wage-price flexibility provides a self-correcting mechanism that quickly restores full employment and always maintains potential output. ... Macroeconomic aggregate demand policies cannot influence the level of unemployment and real output" [Samuelson & Nordhaus (1995) pp.601,602].

"One of Keynes' great breakthroughs was to let the facts oust this beautiful but irrelevant theory" [p.565]. "Keynes' *General Theory* offered an alternative macroeconomic theory. ... Whereas the classical approach assumed flexible prices and wages ... the Keynesian approach insisted on price and wage inflexibility. ... Keynes and his followers emphasized that because wages and prices are inflexible, there is no economic mechanism that will quickly restore full employment and ensure that the economy produces at full capacity. … Through monetary or fiscal policies, the government can stimulate the economy and help maintain high levels of output and employment" [pp.602,603].

The controversy between Keynes and the Monetarists is similarly presented as a conflict over empirical assumptions.

"One of the precepts of Keynesian economics is that prices and wages are "sticky". While generally accepting the view that there is *some* inertia in wage-price setting, … monetarists think that Keynesian economists exaggerate the economy's wage-price stickiness" [p.608]. Even the empirical differences are played down. "In fact, there has been considerable convergence in views between the two schools over the last three decades, and the disputes today are ones of emphasis rather than of fundamental beliefs" [p.608].

The sectarian conflict between "Keynesians" and "Monetarists" is therefore passed off as empirical rather than theoretical — a difference of opinion over the nature of the real world. Keynesians are supposed to work on the assumption that wages and prices are sticky. Monetarists work on the assumption that wages and prices are flexible. Both rival camps are made out to be strongly united in their devotion to the old Classical dogma that perfect competition is the key to full employment.

The Classical view of the economy as a "single-gear" machine emerges as if it has no serious challenge. The only conflict which is admitted is over the quality of the lubrication.

New Orthodox Dogma

The modern version of the old "single-gear" orthodoxy is encapsulated in Patinkin's counter-revolutionary battle-cry: "Equilibrium means full employment, or, equivalently, unemployment means disequilibrium" [1956, p.328].

The conventional wisdom is that the matter has been settled beyond all reasonable doubt. It is taken for granted that, in a Walrasian Utopia, there can be no such thing as unemployment, so that "the theory of unemployment … requires a non-Walrasian model in which there is no Walrasian auctioneer continuously clearing commodity and labor markets" [Phelps (1968) p.30]. It is "characterized by the absence of a "Walrasian auctioneer" assumed to furnish, without charge and without delay, all the information needed to obtain the perfect coordination of the activities (both spot and future) of all traders" [Leijonhufvud (1968) pp.47,48].

The New Orthodoxy has spawned a plethora of "theories" on the causes of unemployment. These theories are devoted to seeking the fault or flaw which distinguishes the real world from the Walrasian Utopia. It is true that the term "unemployment equilibrium" is often used. But it is usually accompanied by a careful warning that what is meant cannot be equilibrium in the full "Walrasian" sense.

In Phelps's *structuralist theory of unemployment*, for example, it is openly admitted that "some of the terms of discourse have undergone a change of meaning. The term "equilibrium" is a case in point. ... "Labor-market equilibrium is not defined by market clearing" [1994, pp.9,10]. "The information ... does not exist and cannot be produced" [p.13]. "The enterprise economy is riddled with informational imperfections in every market" [p.86].

The error, which the *structuralist* approach shares with all the other Orthodox theories of unemployment, is not that "it sees informational and organizational imperfections and features at the bottom of unemployment" [p.247 n.14]; it is that it fails to see anything else!

The old Classical fallacy that the economy is a "single-gear" machine, which requires only "well-lubricated" markets, has been rehabilitated as the New Orthodoxy.

The Fallacy of the New Orthodoxy

The fallacy of New Orthodoxy can be exposed when all the elements of the "sectarian consensus" are subjected to the "acid test" of the Looking-Glass Utopia.

In the top half of Table 25.1, the first column shows the preferences of the Dums and the Dees underlying the initial equilibrium in the Looking-Glass Utopia. The second column shows the new preferences following an increase in the "saving demand" for money when all the Dums and the Dees plan to restrict consumption in favour of holding money. The remaining columns show the distortion of the actual preferences necessary to justify each of the rival versions.

The Classical "desert island" distortion assumes that a switch into holdings of *monetary* wealth is the same thing as a switch into spending on *real* wealth. Consequently, it recognises no impact on the level of prices or on the volume of employment.

The Keynesian "multiplier" distortion assumes no change in the level of prices so that a planned $6\frac{2}{3}$% switch into money is "multiplied" into a ($6\frac{2}{3}$% x 1½ =) 10% switch into leisure. Consequently, it recognises no impact on the level of prices but an amplified reduction in the volume of employment.

The Monetarist "real-balance effect" distortion is rather more subtle. The actual switch from consumption spending into holdings of money is fully recognised — hence the fall in the level of prices. The possibility of any adverse impact on the volume of employment is removed by the invention of a switch out of leisure into real wealth (i.e. employment in order to increase inventories) sufficient to prevent employment falling below its initial level.

The effect of these distortions is shown in the lower half of Table 25.1 which presents the alternative versions of the new equilibrium according to each of the rival "theologies".

Table 25.1
The Impact of an Increase in the "Saving Demand" for Money: The Rival Versions

	INITIAL EQUI-LIBRIUM	NEW EQUILIBRIUM			
		Free-Market "Secular"	Classical "Theology"	Keynesian "Theology"	Monetarist "Theology"
PLANNED ALLOCATION OF RESOURCES	*% of Total*	*% of Total*	*% of Total*	*% of Total*	*% of Total*
Leisure	20	20	20	30 ←	←18
				↑	↓
Consumption	26⅔	20 →	20 →	16⅔ →	↓ 20 →
		↓	↓		↓ ↓
Real Wealth	20	20 ↓	26⅔ ←	20	→ 22 ↓
Revealed in the Market Place	66⅔	60 ↓	66⅔	66⅔	60 ↓
		↓			↓
Money	33⅓	40 ←	33⅓	33⅓	40 ←
Total	100	100	100	100	100
FLOW OF REAL INCOME	*units*	*units*	*units*	*units*	*units*
Production	120,000	110,000	120,000	75,000	120,000
– Consumption	–120,000	–100,000	–90,000	–75,000	–100,000
= SAVING	0	10,000	30,000	0	20,000
STOCK OF REAL WEALTH	*units*	*units*	*units*	*units*	*units*
Closing Balance	90,000	100,000	120,000	90,000	110,000
– Opening Balance	–90,000	–90,000	–90,000	–90,000	–90,000
= INVESTMENT	0	10,000	30,000	0	20,000
LEVEL OF PRICES	£4 per unit	£3 per unit *25% FALL*	£4 per unit *NO CHANGE*	£4 per unit *NO CHANGE*	£3 per unit *25% FALL*
VOLUME OF EMPLOYMENT	40,000 hours	36,667 hours *8⅓% FALL*	40,000 hours *NO CHANGE*	25,000 hours *37½% FALL*	40,000 hours *NO CHANGE*

The attitude of the New Orthodoxy is that "all have won, and all must have prizes." Classical theory is considered appropriate for a non-monetary barter economy. Keynesian theory is considered appropriate for a monetary economy with wage and price rigidity. Monetarist theory is considered appropriate for a monetary economy with wage and price flexibility. No one is guilty of theoretical errors. There are no logical flaws, only different empirical assumptions.

This is a nice cosy view, but it is entirely false.

There are serious logical flaws in all three versions. These flaws have been discussed in detail in the three preceding chapters. But they all stem from the same fault — too much religion, not enough logic.

The rival "theologies" in Table 25.1 are all different, but they share one thing in common — a disregard of the "microeconomic foundations". In not one of the "theological" versions do macroeconomic results reflect the actual preferences of the individual Dums and Dees operating through a free-market. Instead, they reflect different sets of assumptions invented with the object of justifying alternative religious dogma.

That is what accounts for the differences in the rival versions of the new equilibrium in the Looking-Glass Utopia following a general increase in the desire to save money by restricting consumption in order to increase holdings of monetary wealth.

Classical theology insists that "money makes no difference whatsoever" so that the real transactions in a monetary economy are exactly the same as those in a barter economy. The classical solution is therefore based on the assumption that preferences have changed as they would have changed in a barter economy. In other words, the switch away from consumption is into holdings of *real* wealth.

Keynesian theology insists that "money makes all the difference" so that the impact of an increase in money saving falls wholly on output. The Keynesian solution is therefore based on the assumption that prices are absolutely rigid.

Monetarist theology insists that "money makes no real difference" so that the impact of an increase in money saving falls wholly on prices. The monetarist solution is therefore based on the assumption that quantities are absolutely rigid.

The "secular" Free-Market solution is the only one which reflects the new preferences as they actually are.

The New Orthodoxy that "equilibrium means full employment" is precisely the same as the Old Orthodoxy. It is not a rational hypothesis which rests on an appeal to logic. It is a False Dogma maintained by the device of assuming what is to be proved.

Economics, as currently practised, is hardly a science; but it has no claim even to be a religion. The basis of New Orthodoxy in economic theory is not theology; it is mythology.

To dispel the myths and to view economic theory in a proper perspective, it is necessary to enter a Looking-Glass World in which the labels mean the opposite of what they say.

PART V

ECONOMICS THROUGH THE LOOKING-GLASS

INTRODUCTION

"Theology … induces a dogmatic belief that we have knowledge where in fact we have ignorance."

Russell, *A History of Western Philosophy* (1946).

The "New Orthodoxy" is the outcome of religious conflict. And that is what is wrong with it. At every stage in the evolution of economic theology from the time of Adam Smith, faith has been allowed to take precedence over logic. And whenever rational argument has been subordinated to religious conviction, fallacies have seeped into the theoretical foundations. This has undermined the structure to such an extent that the whole edifice is unsafe.

The New Orthodoxy is a theology which has evolved out of half a century of religious conflict between the self-appointed disciples of Adam Smith and those of John Maynard Keynes.

It is a grave mistake to assume that Classical Orthodoxy, the Keynesian revolution, and the Monetarist counter-revolution are all part of a rational evolution of scientific principles. The New Orthodoxy cannot be properly understood except as the outcome of an ingenious succession of fallacies created in order to rationalise the prejudices of rival religious movements.

The account of the development of the New Orthodoxy in Part II is not, therefore, scientific history; it is religious mythology. And the mythology needs to be unravelled before the reality can be exposed.

This requires an excursion "Through the Looking-Glass", not only because the labels mean the opposite of what they say, but also because time runs backwards. The object is to unravel the history of Economic Theology (by retracing the steps taken in Part II) all the way back to Adam Smith and beyond — to the days before economics became a religion.

Perhaps the excursion will throw some light on the process by which False Dogma became reinstated as the New Orthodoxy?

CHAPTER 26

WHAT'S WRONG WITH RELIGION?

> **"And it repented the Lord that he had made man on the earth, and it grieved him at his heart. And the Lord said, I will destroy man whom I have created from the face of the earth; both man, and beast, and the creeping thing, and the fowls of the air; for it repenteth me that I have made them." [Genesis VI, 6,7].**

One of the most endearing characteristics of The Almighty is that if He makes mistakes He is not afraid to admit them. Those who claim to speak in His name are not always quite so honest.

The complaint that economics has an affinity closer to religion than to science is not an implied criticism of religion. The objection is to the way that religion is commonly practised and to doctrinaire attitudes which owe more to human vanity than to divine inspiration.

To seek after perfection is one of the finest human virtues; to claim to have found it is one of mankind's most pernicious vices. Claims to perfection are the ultimate blasphemy, for they represent man's attempt to place himself above God.

It is man's belief in the perfection of his religion which constitutes his "fatal conceit".*

The Fallible Doctrine of Infallibility

"During [the reign of Pius IX (1846-78)] the development of the modern papacy reached a kind of climax with the promulgation of the dogma of papal infallibility … the doctrinal constitution *Pastor Aeternus* ("Eternal Shepherd"), promulgated by the first Vatican Council on July 18, 1870. It asserted that "the Roman Pontiff, when he speaks *ex cathedra*, that is, when in discharge of the office of pastor and teacher of all Christians, by virtue of his supreme apostolic authority he defines a doctrine regarding faith or morals to be held by the universal Church, by the divine assistance promised to him in blessed Peter, is possessed of that infallibility with which the divine Redeemer willed that his Church should be endowed." " [*Encyclopaedia Britannica* vol.15, pp.1015,6].

Although the doctrine of Papal Infallibility is a fairly recent innovation, the dispute over the question has a long history. Abélard (a twelfth

---

* The Greek word *hubris* is very difficult to render into English. "Fatal conceit", an expression used by Friedrich Hayek for the title of his broadside against Socialism [1988], comes very close.

century theologian remembered for his illicit love-affair with Héloïse) expressed the opinion that "nothing outside the Scriptures … is infallible; even Apostles and Fathers may err" [Russell (1946) p.430].

More to the point, however, is that nothing *inside* the Scriptures is infallible. The Old Testament prophets all had human failings; Moses threw down the tablets and struck the rock. Jesus of Nazareth never claimed infallibility. In the sixth Book of Genesis, The Almighty Himself repented of the creation.

Thou Shalt Not Take in Vain

The mark of the true Prophets was humility. They considered themselves unworthy. It is not the Prophets who lay claim to infallibility but the preachers whose vanity blinds them to the injunction of the Third Commandment that "Thou shalt not take the name of the Lord thy God in vain" [Exodus XX, 7]. Those who claim infallibility set themselves above their God, for they arrogate to themselves powers which are not merely super-human but super-divine.

The doctrine of Papal Infallibility is not, however, peculiar to Roman Catholicism; it seems to contaminate the practice of *all* religions — and that includes economics.

The Communist claim to infallibility owed less to the economic theory of Karl Marx than to the obsession for power on the part of Joseph Stalin and his political heirs. In that case, the conceit has indeed proved to be fatal. The Capitalist Religion is divided between two rival sects: Monetarists who take in vain the name of Adam Smith, and Keynesians who take in vain the name of Maynard Keynes. Now that they have buried their differences by forming a Sectarian Consensus, the New Economic Orthodoxy insists on the infallibility of the New "Single-Gear" Religion. If the conceit continues unchecked, then it, too, will no doubt be fatal.

The attraction of infallibility is not only that one's own beliefs are true but that everybody else's are false. Those who take the name of the Lord in vain are not likely to be unduly troubled by a bit of false witness against their neighbour.

Thou Shalt Not Bear False Witness

Bertrand Russell's observation that "Christianity, at first, was preached by Jews to Jews, as a reformed Judaism" [1946, p.325] is borne out by the words of Jesus: "Think not that I am come to destroy the law, or the prophets: I am not come to destroy, but to fulfil" [Matthew, V, 17]. When the Pharisee asked the question: "Master, which is the great commandment in the law? Jesus said unto him, Thou shalt love the Lord thy God with all thy heart, and with all thy soul, and with all thy mind. This is the first and great commandment. And the second is like unto it, Thou shalt love thy neighbour as thyself. On these two commandments hang all the law and the prophets." [Matthew, XXII, 36-39].

That reply is a direct quotation of the moral essence of Judaism as laid down in the Old Testament. "And thou shalt love the Lord thy God with all thine heart, and with all thy soul, and with all thy might" [Deuteronomy VI, 5]. "Thou shalt love thy neighbour as thyself" [Leviticus IX, 18].

The Old Testament precept of loving one's fellow man and fellow creature is not restricted to one's neighbour. "The stranger that dwelleth with you shall be unto you as one born among you, and thou shalt love him as thyself" [Leviticus XIX,34]. It even extends to one's enemy. "If thou meet thine enemy's ox or his ass going astray, thou shalt surely bring it back to him again" [Exodus XXIII, 4]. Nor is it sufficient simply to *do* no harm. "Thou shalt not hate thy brother in thine heart ... nor bear any grudge" [Leviticus XIX,17,18].

But some of the early evangelists resented the fact that they had been pre-empted by the Jews. So they reviled the Old Testament as intolerant and passed off its message of love of mankind as their own. According to Jesus, "love thy neighbour as thyself" is the message of Judaism; according to the Church, it is the message of Christianity.

The Ninth Commandment issues the following prohibition: "Thou shalt not bear false witness against thy neighbour" [Exodus XX,16]. As a result of widespread breach of that Commandment, however, "the received view was that ... Christ had abrogated the Mosaic Law, substituting the two commandments to love God and our neighbour" [Russell (1946) p.326].

Religions based on belief in God are responsible for some of the most tragic episodes of human history — all because of breach of the third commandment. Religions based on man, like those of Hitler and Stalin, are infinitely worse; for there is no third commandment at all.

The Practice of the Economics Religion

Economics suffers from the same human failing — the arrogance of its priests. All worship the same God. Yet Old Testament Capitalism and New Testament Socialism remain unreconciled.* Within the Capitalist Faith, Protestant Keynesians and Jesuit Monetarists, who recently

* The references in this context are to the "Old (Economic) Testament" of Adam Smith and the "New (Economic) Testament" of Karl Marx. No association with the religious Scriptures is intended.

persecuted each other with accusations of blasphemy and heresy, now refuse to tolerate any challenge to their New Single-Gear Orthodoxy.

It is not the religion which is to blame but those who use it to further their own ends — who take name of their God in vain and bear false witness against their opponents. The religious bigotry which led to the Holy Inquisition in Mediaeval Spain is the same religious bigotry which is responsible for the New Inquisition in modern Economics.

The history of the descent into economic perdition caused by such sinfulness is long and harrowing. It is a tale to be told — as befits the title of this book — backwards.

CHAPTER 27

THE NEW INQUISITION

> "The Pythagorean doctrine — which is false and altogether opposed to the Holy Scripture — of the motion of the Earth, and the immobility of the Sun, which is also taught by Nicolaus Copernicus in *De revolutionibus orbium coelestium*, ... is now being spread abroad and accepted by many. ... Therefore, in order that this opinion may not insinuate itself any further to the prejudice of Catholic truth, the Holy Congregation has decreed that the said Nicolaus Copernicus, *De revolutionibus orbium*, ... be suspended until they be corrected; ... and that all other works likewise, in which the same is taught, be prohibited, as by this present decree it prohibits, condemns and suspends them all respectively. In witness whereof the present decree has been signed and sealed with the hands and with the seal of the most eminent and Reverend Lord Cardinal of St. Cecilia, Bishop of Albano, on the fifth day of March 1616."
>
> As quoted by Koestler, *The Sleepwalkers* [1959].

Four Gospels faithfully record the life and teaching of Jesus of Nazareth. Nowhere in the New Testament is there an account of any sermon on the subject of astronomy. Yet, on 22nd June 1633, the trial of Galileo ended with the pronouncement of the following sentence:

"Invoking ... the most holy name of our Lord Jesus Christ and of His most glorious Mother, ever Virgin Mary, ... we say, pronounce, sentence, and declare that you, [Galileo Galilei], ... have rendered yourself in the judgment of this Holy Office vehemently suspected of heresy, namely, of having believed and held the doctrine — which is false and contrary to the sacred and divine Scriptures — that the Sun is the centre of the world and does not move from east to west and that the Earth moves and is not the centre of the world; ... and that consequently you have incurred all the censures and penalties imposed and promulgated in the sacred canons ... against such delinquents" [as quoted by Koestler (1959) p.609].

It may not have been mentioned by Matthew, Mark, Luke, or John, but, after sixteen centuries of theological progress, the doctrine that the Earth was the centre of the universe had, somehow, become an article of Christian faith. Denial of that doctrine was condemned as a heresy contrary to the sacred and divine Scriptures.

Galileo's *Dialogo sopra i due massimi sistemi del mondo* in favour of the Copernican heliocentric view of the universe was no threat to Christianity, but it was a serious challenge to the authority of the Church. It was suppressed because it was an unpardonable affront to the dignity of the Holy Fathers who had committed themselves to the geocentric view maintained by Aristotle.

Economics has moved faster than astronomy. Only two centuries after Adam Smith's silence on the matter, it has become an Article of Faith of the New Economic Orthodoxy that Equilibrium is the centre of the economic universe and *does not move* from full employment.

The Great Betrayal

Keynes's *General Theory* is devoted to the heresy that Equilibrium is *not* the centre of the economic universe and *can move* away from full employment. His challenge to the classical orthodoxy is openly stated. "The economic system may find itself in stable equilibrium ... at a level below full employment" [1936, p.30].

The fundamental theological nature of Keynes's challenge was clearly recognised by opponents like Patinkin. "The fundamental argument of Keynes is directed against the belief that price flexibility can be depended upon to generate full employment automatically. The defenders of the classical tradition, on the other hand, still insist upon this automaticity as a basic tenet" [1948, p.252]. This found an echo in Friedman's reference to "Keynes' key theoretical proposition, namely, that even in a world of flexible prices, a position of equilibrium at full employment might not exist" [1968, p.3].

Because they had no defence against Patinkin's real-balance effect argument, the post-war generation of Keynesian theologians were compelled to accept his classical conclusion that "the possibility of the coexistence of underemployment equilibrium and flexible prices ... is an indefensible position" [1948, pp.278,279].

Having comprehensively lost the theological argument, the Keynesian theologians of the period found a way to salvage their own reputations by pretending that the dispute between Keynes and the Classics was not over fundamental theory. Instead of defending Keynes's key theoretical proposition, they simply denied that he ever made it in the first place.

The cock crowed three times; and, one after another, Keynes's disciples deserted him.

Keynes's insistence on "stable equilibrium ... with less than full employment" [1936, p.30] was simply brushed aside. Without any apparent sign of embarrassment, Tobin was able to make the comment that "what Keynes calls equilibrium should be viewed as persistent disequilibrium" [1972, p.4]. It was tantamount to "defending" Galileo on the ground that, when he said that the earth went round the sun, what he really meant to say was that the sun went round the earth.

Even more astonishing was the observation made by Axel Leijonhufvud that "there is every reason to doubt that Keynes ever set out on the quixotic quest of reconciling perfect price-flexibility with unemployment of resources" [1968, p.53n]. Keynes's quest may or may not have been quixotic, but to deny that he ever set out to reconcile perfect price-flexibility with unemployment of resources is a travesty of the truth. If Keynes had merely argued that unemployment was the result of lack of market flexibility, he would simply have been reinforcing classical doctrine. There would have been no challenge — let alone a revolution.

Economic theologians seemed to be divided between opponents of Keynes who attacked him on the ground that it was wrong to speak of stable equilibrium with less than full employment and supporters who defended him on the ground that he never meant what he said.

The Sentence

The issue has been thoroughly distorted by the nature of the verdict on Keynes subsequently delivered by the New Orthodoxy:

"Invoking ... the most holy name of our Lord Léon Walras and of His most glorious Father, Adam Smith ... we say, pronounce, sentence, and declare that you, John Maynard Keynes, ... have rendered yourself in the judgment of this Holy Office vehemently suspected of heresy, namely, of having believed and held the doctrine — which is false and contrary to the sacred and divine Scriptures — that Equilibrium may move away from full employment and is not the centre of the world; ... and that consequently you have incurred all the censures and penalties imposed and promulgated in the sacred canons ... against such delinquents."

The Holy Fathers of the New Orthodoxy have a difficult problem. Keynes, like Galileo, is recognised as a man of genius by supporters and opponents alike. How can the reputation of one of the economic religion's greatest (but, in their view, errant) Prophets be protected, when, at the same time, the True Faith must be upheld and Church Unity must be preserved?

The conflict is ingeniously resolved by the New Bible during the course of its explanation of unemployment (already quoted in chapter 12 above).

"The left-hand panel [of Figure 27.1] shows the usual picture of competitive supply and demand, with a market equilibrium at point *E* and a wage of *W*. ... In (a), wages move up or down to clear the labor market. All unemployment is involuntary. Part (b) shows what happens if wages do not adjust to clear the labor market. At the too high wage at W_H, OL_D workers are employed, but L_DL_S workers are involuntarily unemployed" [Samuelson & Nordhaus (1995, pp.564,565]

Figure 27.1: Unemployment According to the "New Orthodoxy"

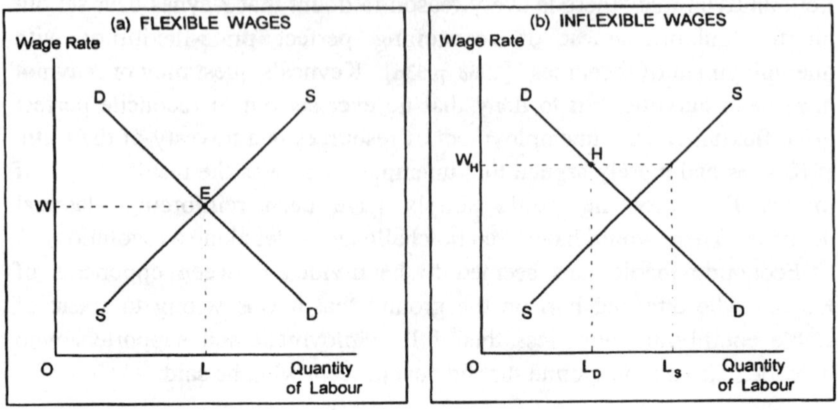

"In summary, a labor market characterized by perfectly flexible wages will not contain involuntary unemployment. Prices and wages simply float up or down until the markets are cleared. In any economy with perfectly flexible wages, widespread unemployment such as that in the 1930s or 1980s would simply not exist" [Samuelson & Nordhaus (1992) p.578].

This passage is part of a cover-up to protect Keynes's reputation and to bring him back into the Orthodox fold.

Keynes is, in fact, guilty as charged by Patinkin of the fundamental theoretical error of having ignored the real-balance effect.

In the New Bible the cover-up is engineered by means of two devices.

The first device is to define as "involuntary" the category of unemployment explicitly defined by Keynes himself as "voluntary".

"In [Figure 27.1(b)], … the labor market finds itself with too high a wage rate. Labor's price is at W_H rather than at the equilibrium or market-clearing wage of W. At the too high wage rate, there are more qualified workers looking for work than there are jobs looking for workers. The number of workers willing to work at wage W_H is … OL_S [as shown by] the supply curve, but firms want to hire only OL_D workers, as shown by the demand curve. Because the wage exceeds the market-clearing level, there is a surplus of workers. The unemployed workers represented by … L_DL_S are said to be **involuntarily unemployed**, signifying that they are qualified workers who want to work at the prevailing wage but cannot find jobs" [Samuelson & Nordhaus (1995) p.566].

But "unemployment due to the refusal or inability of a unit of labour, as a result of legislation or social practices or of combination for collective bargaining or of slow response to change or of mere human obstinacy, to accept a reward corresponding to the value of the product attributable to its marginal productivity" is placed firmly by Keynes in the category labelled "voluntary" [1936, p.6].

The second device is to explain Keynes's contribution as empirical rather than theoretical: "one of Keynes' great breakthroughs was to let the facts oust a beautiful but irrelevant theory" [Samuelson & Nordhaus (1995) p.565].

But Keynes makes clear that he objects to "the classical postulates [because] they do not admit the possibility of the third category [of unemployment in addition to "frictional" and "voluntary"] which [he defines] as "involuntary" unemployment" [p.6].

Rewriting the *General Theory* may succeed in rescuing Keynes from his own heresy, but it smacks of salvation by misrepresentation.

Unity Über Alles

The fact that some of Keynes's most distinguished disciples could pass off his *General Theory* as if it were a confirmation, rather than a denial, of the New Orthodoxy indicates how far, in spite of the scientific pretensions of its practitioners, economics remains a religion.

Whether Keynes is right or wrong is not the issue. His *General Theory* is in direct conflict with the New Orthodoxy. Out of well-meaning, but excessive, concern for Keynes's reputation and in the interests of Church unity, the proposition that the economy may find itself in stable market-clearing equilibrium with less than full employment has been "airbrushed" out of the New Bible. Instead of the heresy being reported and the error pointed out, history has been rewritten lest the faithful be "confused" by ideas "contrary to the sacred and holy scripture".

The most distressing aspect of the whole affair is that Paul Samuelson, one of the finest scholars of his generation, should have lent his authority to the decree issued by the most eminent and Reverend Lord Cardinal of St. Cecilia, Bishop of Albano (quoted at the head of this chapter).

"The Keynesian doctrine — which is false and altogether opposed to the Holy Scripture — of the motion of Equilibrium away from full employment — is now being spread abroad and accepted by many. Therefore, in order that this opinion may not insinuate itself any further to the prejudice of Economic truth, the Holy Congregation has decreed that Keynes's *General Theory* be corrected; and that all other works likewise, in which the same is taught, be prohibited, as by this present decree it prohibits, condemns and suspends them all respectively."

So thoroughly has the correction been accomplished that readers of the New Bible are not told that the *General Theory* contains the proposition of stable equilibrium with less than full employment, and that the proposition is, in the Orthodox view, mistaken; they are never informed of its existence in the first place.

It is therefore particularly regrettable that far more students of economics read Samuelson (and others) on Keynes than Keynes on Keynes. Consequently, there are holders of university degrees in Economics who are totally unaware of Keynes's challenge to the fundamental basis of the New Orthodoxy.

If only the Cardinals had possessed the wisdom to claim Martin Luther as one of their own, they might have preserved the unity of the Christian Church as effectively as the economists have patched up the schism in theirs.

The Holy Fathers of the Economic Church are, no doubt, motivated by the highest ideals, but to suppress a theory, however misguided and erroneous, is quite unpardonable.

Church unity is safe, and the debate on equilibrium economics is at an end. As long as theoretical harmony is not disturbed, empirical discord, so far from being prohibited, is positively welcomed. It provides a veneer of tolerance beneath which religious bigotry can masquerade as freedom of conscience. Empirical diversity is a useful camouflage for theoretical rigidity.

It is the Age of Conformism in economic theology.

Keynes's notion of "stable equilibrium with less than full employment" has been effectively expunged. As far as the key theoretical proposition is concerned, it is as if the *General Theory* had never been written.

Keynes certainly achieved a revolution in economic policy. But that was due to the empirical realism of the *General Theory*. The Keynesian Revolution in economic theory has not failed, it has never begun.

In plotting the courses of the Heavenly Bodies, Keynes's empirical assumptions are accepted as the most accurate guide — to an economic universe in which the general belief is that the Sun goes round the Earth.

Fifty years after its publication, the empirical superstructure provided by the *General Theory* still dominates modern macroeconomics, but the theoretical skeleton had been discarded and replaced by the Hicksian classical apparatus* within twelve months.

Why the Revolution Failed

The failure of the Keynesian revolution to deliver the killer-blow necessary to put an end to the Classical fallacy of the single-gear economy is not entirely due to religious bigotry on the part of his opponents; it is largely Keynes's own fault.

* To be discussed in the next chapter.

The parallel with Galileo is striking.

"Galileo completely evaded any astronomical or physical discussion of the Copernican system; he simply gave the impression that it was proven beyond doubt. … It must be remembered that the system which Galileo advocated was the orthodox Copernican system, designed by the canon himself, nearly a century before Kepler threw out the epicycles and transformed the abstruse paper-construction into a workable mechanical model. … Galileo blindly and indeed suicidally ignored Kepler's work to the end" [Koestler (1959), p.444]. "It was Galileo's ill-conceived crusade which had discredited the heliocentric system and precipitated the divorce of science from faith" [p.503].

Like Galileo, Keynes completely evaded the problem of tracing back to individual preferences *the microeconomic foundations* of the monetary system in which equilibrium could move away from full employment; he simply gave the impression that it was proven beyond doubt and gave a brilliant *empirical* description of how the system would work. Though he championed Malthus's *insight* for having wrestled "the great puzzle of Effective Demand" [1936, p.32, and ch.23], the *analysis* which Keynes blindly and indeed suicidally ignored to the end was that of Malthus. It was Keynes's ill-conceived crusade which discredited the Keynesian system and precipitated the divorce of science from faith.

Koestler criticises as "naively erroneous" the caricature of "Galileo's trial [as] … a showdown between 'blind faith' and 'enlightened reason' " [1959, p.432]. "The Jesuit Order was the intellectual spearhead of the Catholic Church. [It] was at that time in full retreat from Aristotle and Ptolemy, and had taken up an intermediary position regarding Copernicus. They praised and fêted Galileo, whom they knew to be a Copernican, and they kept Kepler, the foremost exponent of Copernicanism, under their protection throughout his life. … The Copernican system itself could be freely discussed and advocated as a working hypothesis, but it was unfavourably viewed to present it as established truth, because it seemed contrary to current interpretation of scripture — unless and until definite proof could be adduced in its favour" [p.433].

It would be as "naively erroneous" to caricature Keynes's treatment at the hands of the New Orthodoxy as "a showdown between 'blind faith' and 'enlightened reason'." Keynes's vision of a monetary universe with an equilibrium not necessarily at full employment was ultimately discarded, not because it ran against cherished beliefs (though it did), *but because he failed to leave a microeconomic proof strong enough to resist the subsequent reaction of his opponents* — and because as much religious bigotry was enlisted by some of his "Keynesian" successors in support of his theory as others used against it.

Once again, Koestler's observations on Galileo apply almost as well to Keynes, whose *General Theory* similarly gave "the impression that some new Luther had arisen, denying the miracles of the Bible and defying the authority of the Church" [p.446].

It is regrettable that Keynes should have suffered the same fate at the hands of the Counter-Reformation as did Galileo. But it is difficult to resist the conclusion that, to some extent at least, he got what he deserved.

CHAPTER 28

THE REVOLUTION THAT NEVER WAS*

It is not that the Emperor has no clothes. It is just that he neglects to bring them out of the wardrobe. If he catches a cold, he has only himself to blame.

Keynes's *General Theory of Employment, Interest and Money* is a most remarkable work. It is remarkable for its theoretical insight, and it is remarkable for its empirical realism, but, above all, it is remarkable for a curious omission.

It is devoted to the revolutionary Copernican proposition that there are several "possible positions of equilibrium" [1936, p.3]. Equilibrium is not the centre of the economic universe; *it moves*.

The argument that "the economic system may find itself in stable equilibrium … at a level below full employment" [p.30] is revolutionary, because it directly contradicts the conventional wisdom. It is as challenging to the New Orthodoxy today as it was challenging to the Old Orthodoxy half a century ago. If the proposition should ever be accepted, its impact on man's vision of the economic universe would be no less dramatic than the impact made by Copernicus on man's vision of the physical universe. In its repudiation of the immaculate conception cherished by the established Church, it is no less heretical.

What makes the *General Theory* unique, however, is not the revolutionary nature of the central proposition. It is that the author makes no attempt to prove it. That is to say, he makes no attempt to provide it with microeconomic foundations strong enough to withstand the inevitable Classical reaction. The result is not so much a theory which is general as a theory which is absent. This does not mean that the book should be retitled *The General Theory-that-Isn't-There of Employment, Interest and Money*; but it ought to carry a warning, prominently displayed:

Danger — No Microeconomic Foundations!

One of the principal reasons for the endless debate over the validity of the *General Theory* is that Keynes fails to provide microeconomic foundations of sufficient depth (i.e. right down to the underlying personal preferences) to protect his central proposition against the inevitability of a classical counter-attack. Instead, he devotes himself to the task of

---

* "Two propositions, widely held, are evidence that the Keynesian Revolution remains to be made: (i) the macroeconomics of the General Theory do not rest on proper microeconomic foundations, and (ii) the General Theory is the economics of disequilibrium" [Chick (1978) p.1].

explaining how the economic system will operate *on the assumption that the proposition is secure.*

The *General Theory* contains a description of how an economy behaves if demand is deficient; it contains no proof (sufficient to convince a Walrasian) showing how demand can be deficient in the first place *if markets are flexible* — i.e. in markets free from all the imperfections excluded on page 6 of the *General Theory* (together with "inexactnesses of adjustment", "miscalculation", and "unforeseen changes") as causes of the only categories of unemployment admitted by "the classical postulates". What is missing is an explanation of why any deficiency of effective demand would not be remedied by a classical adjustment in the level of prices operating through the market mechanism.

Instead of providing a proof, Keynes chooses to resurrect a corpse.

"Say's Law"

"From the time of Say and Ricardo, the classical economists have taught that supply creates its own demand. ... In J. S. Mill's *Principles of Political Economy* the doctrine is expressly set forth. ... It still underlies the whole classical theory, which would collapse without it" [1936, pp.18,19]. "Say's law ... is equivalent to the proposition that there is no obstacle to full employment" [p.26].

The orthodox interpretation of "Say's Law" is that, in a perfectly competitive economy, there can be no such thing as deficiency of effective demand. It comes in two versions. According to the simple version in John Stuart Mill's *Principles*, as long as savers are rational, they will lend at interest rather than hoard. Full employment is therefore maintained by interest rate adjustments. The more complex version traceable from Walrasian general equilibrium analysis through Wicksell and Pigou relies on the "real-balance effect" of changes in the level of prices on the real value of savings. Full employment is therefore maintained by price-level adjustments.

Both versions deny the possibility of deficiency in effective demand:

1) The Interest-Rate Version ("Mill's Doctrine"):

   Provided that markets are perfect, hoarding cannot take place.

   Argument: the rate of interest will fall until the amount which spenders are willing to borrow is brought into equality with the increased amount which savers are willing to lend.

2) The Price-Level Version (the "Real-Balance Effect" Doctrine):

   Provided that markets are perfect, hoarding, *even if it does take place*, cannot cause a deficiency of effective demand.

   Argument: the price level will fall until the amount for which producers are willing to sell their output is brought into equality with the reduced amount which savers are willing to spend.

Coup de Grace to a Corpse

By the end of the nineteenth century, Mill's doctrine had become so vulnerable to the scorn of its socialist critics (see chapter 6 above) that it had been quietly allowed to die a natural death. It was laid to rest by Alfred Marshall with the epitaph: "Though men have the power to purchase they may not choose to use it" [1890, p.591].

Keynes's liquidity preference doctrine, by providing a rational motive for hoarding, nails the coffin-lid well and truly down. The justification for this action is that "contemporary economists, who might hesitate to agree with Mill, do not hesitate to accept conclusions which require Mill's doctrine as their premiss" [1936, p.19]. This is not quite accurate. The word "require" is an anachronism. Mill's conclusions, which are as much a part of the New Orthodoxy as of the Old, no longer *required* his "Doctrine" to support them. The simple "interest rate adjustment" version of "Say's Law" had been superseded by the "price level adjustment" version *before* the *General Theory*. Since both versions led to essentially the same conclusion, it is true that many "contemporary economists" found it more convenient to stick to the simple version; but they did not *need* to do so.

The introduction of Keynes's liquidity preference doctrine certainly adds a great deal in the way of empirical relevance. But, in terms of the theoretical debate, it represents the delivery of a coup de grace to a corpse.

The fatal flaw in the *General Theory* is that it fails to defuse the "real-balance effect" version of "Say's Law". The time-bomb is allowed to continue relentlessly ticking away.

The Danger that was Ignored

Keynes's neglect of the "real-balance effect" is extremely odd. In a different context, he enlists it in support of his own arguments. "Incomes and ... prices necessarily change until the aggregate of the amounts of money which individuals choose to hold at the new level of incomes and prices thus brought about has come to equality with the amount of money created by the banking system" [1936, pp.84,85].

The conventional wisdom, which Keynes claims to challenge, relies, not on Mill's discredited dogma that hoarding (on a significant scale) cannot occur, but on the Pigovian argument that a freely operating price mechanism will prevent hoarding from resulting in a deficiency of effective demand and so causing unemployment.

The orthodox argument, inherited from Walras and Wicksell, relies on the "real-balance effect". As the desire for monetary savings increases, money is withdrawn from the commodity markets. This puts downward pressure on the general level of prices until the purchasing power of existing monetary balances has risen to the newly desired level. As long as markets are perfectly frictionless, the whole of the impact will be absorbed by price adjustments. But, if prices and incomes are not lowered far enough or fast enough, some of the impact will fall on the level of output, and this will depress the volume of employment. Unemployment is, therefore, a disequilibrium phenomenon resulting from market imperfection of one sort or another. It could not occur if markets were as perfectly frictionless as they would be in a Walrasian Utopia.

In the theology of the "old orthodoxy", unemployment is a phenomenon of disequilibrium in an imperfect world. Recessions happen only because there are obstacles in the way of the necessary wage and price adjustments.

If Keynes wishes to establish that there is an additional category of unemployment, which can occur even when there is stable equilibrium, he has to dispose of the real-balance effect argument.

Yet he seems too impatient to make the attempt either to prove his own proposition in the light of the real-balance effect or to disprove the conflicting classical proposition.

It is as if he cannot permit himself to be detained by irritating points of abstract theory when there is important work to be done. So he takes a short-cut: he does not waste time providing the microeconomic foundations vital to the defence of his proposition, he simply assumes that it is secure. Having disposed of the theory, he is then free to pursue his quest for "realism". Most of the *General Theory* is occupied with the more interesting and apparently more relevant subject of the real world.

Consequently, Keynes has only himself to blame if his theory is interpreted as a special, albeit empirically relevant, case of the classical.

The Empirical Success of the "Keynesian Revolution"

The *General Theory* is refreshingly free of the desert island economics characteristic of the traditional classical textbooks on economic theory. For having dragged economic theory out of Utopia into the Real World, Keynes has received almost universal acclaim. Even his most dedicated opponents concede that, on the score of empirical relevance, the *General Theory* marks an advance so dramatic that it deserves to be described as "revolutionary".

Yet this is surely the main criticism of the *General Theory* as a work of theory — an unusual case of damning with *great* praise.

The bulk of the *General Theory* is concerned with the explanation of the behaviour of the economic system in the real world. In the course of that description, he introduces several valuable tools of analysis. They include the *marginal efficiency of capital*, the *marginal propensity to consume*, the *consumption function and the multiplier process*, and the *liquidity preference* doctrine. Most of these tools rely on market imperfection for their operation. Without market imperfection, the multiplier will not multiply (see chapter 23 above). The influence of the money rate of interest on real investment demand, which plays a prominent part in the *General Theory*, depends on real markets being less flexible than money markets. It is because of his perception that the real world exhibits just these kinds of imperfection and dynamic disequilibrium, that Keynes achieves so much more realism than his classical predecessors.

And that is what is wrong with the *General Theory*. The beauty of its empirical superstructure obscures the nature of the theoretical skeleton. It is almost as if the validity of the (admittedly unproved) theoretical proposition is denied by the relevance of the empirical assumptions.

So great is the advance in empirical relevance that the *General Theory* would have been an outstanding work on economics without its central theoretical proposition. In fact, since the central theoretical proposition has been rejected, that is precisely what the *General Theory* has become. It is accepted as the classic work on macroeconomic theory — as long as the central theoretical proposition is discarded.

The Keynesian revolution is a Pyrrhic revolution.

The Hicksian Misrepresentation

Immediately following the publication of the *General Theory*, Hicks responded by constructing a classical model with empirical assumptions taken from the *General Theory*. "Since our purpose is comparison, I shall try to set out my typical classical theory in a form similar to that in which Mr. Keynes sets out his own theory" [1937, p.148]. The result — modestly described by Hicks as "a little apparatus" [p.156] — has become famous as the "IS/LM" model. It shows how orthodox classical theory will produce Keynesian results, if Keynes's empirical assumptions are used.

Hicks's "little apparatus" has proved so successful (particularly following its popularisation by Alvin Hansen in his *Guide to Keynes* [1953, ch.7]) that the IS/LM model has become more widely known to non-specialists than the *General Theory* itself. Macroeconomic theory has commonly been studied, not by reading Keynes's *General Theory*, but by learning the mechanics of Hicks's IS/LM apparatus instead.

Being a classical model, it naturally dispenses with Keynes's central theoretical proposition that unemployment can occur even in a Utopia from which every vestige of imperfection and disequilibrium is absent [1936, p.6]. Instead, it has market imperfection built into its theoretical foundations: the influence of the money rate of interest on real investment demand, which depends on real markets being less flexible than money markets, is part of the mechanism of the IS/LM apparatus. By contrast, Keynes's model incorporates market imperfection only in the empirical superstructure.

The IS/LM apparatus is an excellent medium through which to transmit what Hicks, in his 1937 article, describes as "my typical classical theory". But the issue has been confused by his subsequent change of mind. "I still feel that the diagram which was worked out in that article gives the most convenient summary of the Keynesian theory of Interest and Money which has yet been produced" [1950, p.137]. "It is possible ... to express the essence of the Keynes theory on a single diagram" [1957, pp.279,280].

Hicks's "typically classical theory" has mysteriously turned into a "potted version" [1967, p.vii] of Keynes's. In other words, the majority of economists have been introduced to "Keynesian" macroeconomic theory through the medium of an "apparatus" from which Keynes's central theoretical proposition has been ruthlessly eliminated.

The Theoretical Failure of the "Keynesian Revolution"

The unquestioning acceptance by the New Orthodoxy of Hicks's classical IS/LM apparatus as the *General Theory* "in pictures" is conclusive proof of the failure of the Keynesian revolution. "As early as 1937," in Davidson's view, "Hicks was publishing a 'potted version' of what he believed to be Keynes's central argument" [1972, p.xi]. According to Johnson's expression of the conventional wisdom, "the full Keynesian theory ... can be represented very conveniently by a diagram developed by Professor J. R. Hicks, which has proved so useful that it has become a standard tool of monetary theory" [1958, p.112].

"It turns out that Keynes's theory is a special case of the classical — or rather of the neo-classical theory, since a satisfactory 'classical' theory was not worked out until after the Keynesian revolution. ... Keynes's theory started from an empirically relevant special assumption, derived some important meaningful results from it, and provided an approach which has since proved its usefulness for a wide range of problems" [p.120].

The reason given by Davidson is that, whereas the ideal models of the abstract theorists "create an unbridgeable gulf between theory and practice", Keynes moves outside the Walrasian Utopia and gets to grips with the real world. "The Keynesian revolution in economics ... is based on an analysis which is the polar opposite of the neoclassical timeless equilibrium view of the world" [1972, p.14].

The verdict that the difference between Keynes and the classics is purely empirical is confirmed by the New Bible. "At the heart of the classical view is the belief that prices and wages are flexible and that wage-price flexibility provides a self-correcting mechanism that quickly restores full employment and always maintains potential output. ... Whereas the classical approach assumed flexible prices and wages ... the Keynesian approach insisted on price and wage inflexibility. ... Keynes and his followers emphasized that because wages and prices are inflexible, there is no economic mechanism that will quickly restore full employment and ensure that the economy produces at full capacity" [Samuelson & Nordhaus (1995) pp.602,603].

The New Orthodoxy has a great deal to answer for. Its misrepresentation of Keynes's theory is bad enough. Its misrepresentation of Classical theory is even worse.

CHAPTER 29

THE IMMACULATE MISCONCEPTION

Keynes's revolutionary theoretical proposition is that "the economic system may find itself in stable equilibrium ... at a level below full employment" [1936, p.30]. Deficiency of effective demand is identified as the culprit. But the absence of any serious attempt to prove that deficiency of effective demand depresses the volume of employment — rather than the level of prices — leaves the *General Theory* at the mercy of its critics.

Patinkin has no problem in reaffirming the classical doctrine with the counter-revolutionary battle-cry: "Equilibrium means full employment, or, equivalently, unemployment means disequilibrium" [1956, p.328].

In support of this view, Patinkin's argument is that deficiency of effective demand depresses the level of prices rather than the volume of output. "The dynamic groping of the absolute price level towards its equilibrium value will — through the real-balance effect — react back on commodity markets" [1956, p.183].

Yet this argument is not decisive. The demonstration of a price effect, however large, does not constitute conclusive proof that there is no employment effect *at all*. It is Keynes's failure to admit any price effect, however small, which leaves his *General Theory* defenceless and makes Patinkin's argument appear fatal.

Consequently, the belief that "equilibrium means full employment" is now enshrined in the Holy Writ adopted by the New Orthodoxy. The notion of stable market-clearing equilibrium with less than full employment is regarded, by Keynesians and Monetarists alike, as a contradiction in terms. Opponents of Keynes claim that he was wrong to suggest the possibility; supporters claim that he never really meant it.

The outcome is a reincarnation of Walras' Immaculate Conception in a modern version presented by Leijonhufvud.

But it may not be quite what Walras had in mind.

The Pseudo-Walrasian Revival

"Keynes," in the interpretation offered by Leijonhufvud, "departed from the postulates of Classical doctrine on only one point. ... His model is characterized by the absence of a "Walrasian auctioneer" assumed to furnish, without charge and without delay, all the information needed to obtain the perfect coordination of the activities (both spot and future) of all traders" [1968, pp.47,48].

The key to the analysis is the absence of "false trading".

Leijonhufvud takes as his "point of departure" "the standard illustration of the hypothetical Walrasian auction process. ... A price is "*crié au hazard*" and an auctioneer registers the buy and sell offers. If he finds that, in the aggregate, there is excess demand at the called price, a higher price is called out; if excess supply is registered, a lower price is tried. The process is repeated until a market-clearing price is found. *Only then are actual exchanges allowed to be carried out.* Thus, in a market operating on such rules, no "false trading" is ever carried out. Such markets always clear" [p.75].

This is a perfectly accurate description of the tâtonnement process envisaged by Walras. Since, "the *tâtonnement*," is regarded, "as consuming *no* time" [p.75], the Walrasian auctioneer operates like a computer of infinite speed and accuracy.

If a Walrasian auctioneer is not present, discrepancies between planned and actual transactions are liable to occur. Such discrepancies are needed to drive the multiplier process described in chapter 23 above.

Clower infers from this a "dual decision hypothesis" which he claims "Keynes either had ... at the back of his mind, or most of the *General Theory* is theoretical nonsense" [1965, p.290].

The trouble with the "dual decision hypothesis" is that it is a *disequilibrium* explanation. It is therefore entirely consistent with the classical tradition which insists on some form of imperfection or disequilibrium as the sole cause of unemployment. If Keynes actually did have such an explanation "at the back of his mind", the *General Theory* would be another explanation in the classical mould. The nonsense would consist in claiming any theoretical departure, let alone a revolution.

Discrepancies between planned and actual transactions are always liable to occur during the process of response to economic change. A "dual-decision hypothesis" can be used equally well to explain the repercussions following a change in the demand for cornflakes.

This type of disequilibrium is due to the absence of central co-ordination. Since it could not occur in the presence of a Walrasian auctioneer, Leijonhufvud prefers the general explanation.

"There is no *deus ex Machina* to straighten things out, no Walrasian auctioneer to ensure that prices tell the truth (and nothing but the truth) about how resources can and ought to be allocated" [1968, p.85].

That sentence is vitally important: it underpins the New Orthodoxy. It finally settles the key theoretical question: can unemployment occur when the economy is in equilibrium in the full Walrasian sense? The Classical answer is "no", but the proof is unsatisfactory. Keynes's answer is "yes", but his proof is non-existent. Patinkin's answer is "no", and his proof —

the real-balance effect argument — is sufficient to support the rehabilitation of Classical economics as the New Orthodoxy. The victory of the Counter-revolution is symbolised by the readiness of a Keynesian of Leijonhufvud's stature to sign away Keynes's belief in the possibility of "stable equilibrium with less than full employment".

The sentence is worth repeating.

"There is no *deus ex Machina* to straighten things out, no Walrasian auctioneer to ensure that prices tell the truth (and nothing but the truth) about how resources can and ought to be allocated" [p.85].

It is worth repeating because what it describes is a travesty of the role of the Walrasian auctioneer. The impression which it gives of the operation of a free-market economy is totally misleading.

The Immaculate Misconception

The auctioneer envisaged by Walras in the *Elements of Pure Economics* does not ensure that prices tell the truth about how resources *ought to be allocated.*

The analogy which Leijonhufvud draws between the Walrasian Auctioneer and the *deus ex Machina* of Greek Tragedy is most unfortunate. It is the divine knowledge of the god who descends which allows him to see into the minds of the characters themselves and enables him to resolve all their problems. A Walrasian auctioneer is, as his name implies, an auctioneer. To invest him with divine powers is to turn him from being an impersonal agent for clearing the market into a commissar who claims to know what is best for the consumer.

In the Walrasian system, the auctioneer deals with effective demand and effective offer. He is a co-ordinator of bids, not a reader of minds. If he does his job efficiently — that is to say, if markets are perfect — resources will be allocated in response to the bids. If the bids are unwise or immoral, the allocation of resources will be unwise or immoral.

If people eat too much, drink too much, smoke too much, and read the wrong sort of literature, it is not evidence of imperfect markets, it is evidence of imperfect people. The auctioneer may not "approve", but he has no say in the matter. He is there to accept bids, not to question them. A perfect market is impersonal.

The same applies if people save too much.

The problem for the Dums and the Dees, in chapter 22 above, is that there is a general increase in the desire to restrict consumption in favour of saving money. The result is a reduction in bids in the market place. Effective demand for present consumption falls, and is replaced by an intention to increase future consumption. But the intention is not translated into actual bids; preferences are not revealed; demand is not made effective in the market place.

The fall in employment below the desired level occurs not because there is no one (like a Walrasian auctioneer) to co-ordinate the bids, it occurs because there are insufficient bids to co-ordinate.

In the saga of the Dums and the Dees, a *deus ex Machina* can guarantee a happy ending. Divine inspiration allows him to see that all the individuals are bidding "wrongly". He can remedy deficiency of effective demand by ignoring the under-bidding in the market place and substituting the bids which his divine insight tells him they *ought* to have made for their own good. A *deus ex machina* is therefore able to give them what they really want by *ignoring* their bids. He refuses to allocate resources according to the bids *actually* made. Instead, he allocates resources according to the bids which *should* have been made. A mere mortal cannot do this. A Josef Stalin might pretend that he can, but an *auctioneer* most definitely cannot. He is blind to the motives and needs of the bidders. He cannot overrule their bids. He gives them what they bid for. If they fail to bid for what they want, it is their own fault; there is nothing that an auctioneer, however talented, can do.

Deficiency of effective demand is a symptom, not of incompetent auctioneering, but of bad bidding. Improving the flexibility of the market cannot remedy this particular fault.

The market is a channel of communication between consumers and producers. Normally, it is the *only* channel of communication between consumers and producers. If the channel of communication is imperfect, the signals are liable to be distorted. But that can be remedied by removing the market imperfection. When effective demand is deficient it is not because the signals are being distorted; it is because they are not being transmitted in the first place.

If savers who intend to spend more in the future do not enter the market with the bids to make their intentions effective, they transmit misleading signals. No streamlining of the transmission mechanism can correct a wrong signal.

The modern counterpart of the Walrasian auctioneer is a giant computer into which all producers and consumers enter their offers and demands. If demand is deficient, the reason could be that the computer is not working properly. The reason could also be that the users are not keying-in accurate information about their own intentions.

The Subversion of the Walrasian Auctioneer

With his conception of the economy as a vast auction, Walras succeeds in constructing an idealised form of the market-place.

What Leijonhufvud achieves with his subversion of the role of the Walrasian auctioneer is an idealised form of central planning.

Leijonhufvud commits a very grave error in claiming that a Walrasian auctioneer is able to "ensure that prices tell the truth (and nothing but the truth) about how resources can and ought to be allocated" [p.85]. An auctioneer cannot give the bidders what they really want. He can give them only what they bid for.

If Leijonhufvud's *deus ex machina* is able to give the bidders what they really want, he is a divinely inspired central planner not a free market auctioneer. The economy envisaged by Leijonhufvud is not a Free Market Utopia but a Socialist Paradise.

At the hands of Leijonhufvud, the Walrasian Utopia has undergone a not-so-subtle transformation. The apotheosis of the market place has become the apotheosis of central planning.

The "Fatal Conceit"

There is little doubt that if the Almighty were to take personal charge of the allocation of resources He would make a pretty good job of it.

Central planners who believe they can do just as well suffer from what Hayek [1988] calls "the fatal conceit" of Socialism. Having cut themselves off from the information generated by the market, they are forced to rely on divine guidance. Those who deny the existence of the Almighty in spiritual matters, can hardly complain if He gets His own back by denying them Divine inspiration in economic affairs.

The availability of information is a crucial reason for the superiority of a free-market economy over a centrally planned bureaucracy in the efficient allocation of resources. But, although a perfect market guarantees equilibrium, it does not guarantee full employment.

To equate the Walrasian auctioneer with a *deus ex machina* is the "fatal conceit" of Capitalism.

But, if a free-market economy of the Utopian perfection envisaged by Léon Walras cannot guarantee full employment. Patinkin's "counter-revolutionary" battle-cry "equilibrium means full employment" begins to sound a little hollow. Yet, it is no more than a modern version of "Say's Law". The trouble with "Say's Law", however, is that, on closer examination, it turns out to be a myth.

CHAPTER 30

THE MYTH OF "SAY'S LAW"

The first acquaintance which most economists make with "Say's Law" is in a passage on page 18 of Keynes's *General Theory*:

"From the time of Say and Ricardo the classical economists have taught that supply creates its own demand; ...

In J. S. Mill's *Principles of Political Economy* the doctrine is expressly set forth:

> What constitutes the means of payment for commodities is simply commodities. Each person's means of paying for the productions of other people consist of those which he himself possesses. All sellers are inevitably, and by the meaning of the word, buyers. Could we suddenly double the productive powers of the country, we should double the supply of commodities in every market; but we should, by the same stroke, double the purchasing power. Everybody would bring a double demand as well as supply; everybody would be able to buy twice as much, because every one would have twice as much to offer in exchange.[1]

[1]*Principles of Political Economy*, Book III. chap. xiv. § 2."

"The doctrine ... still underlies the whole classical theory, which would collapse without it" [1936, p.19]. "Say's law ... is equivalent to the proposition that there is no obstacle to full employment" [p.26].

This must be true. It is written in the New Bible.

"Before Keynes wrote the *General Theory* ... the major economic thinkers generally adhered in good times to the classical view of the economy. ... Their analysis revolved around **Say's Law of markets** ... [which] states that overproduction is impossible by its very nature ... supply creates its own demand" [Samuelson & Nordhaus (1995) p.601].

It is a relief, for once, to find something over which there is so little controversy. Say's Law is the ultimate authority for the view that the economy is a single-gear machine; and the Classical economists were imbued with Say's Law. They had it for breakfast, they had it for lunch, and they had it again for tea.

That, at any rate, is the impression conveyed by modern literature.

And yet, there is something which is not quite right.

It is customary for physicists, if they wish to discuss Newton's Third Law of Motion, to quote Newton. Literary critics, who wish to discuss Shakespeare's Merchant of Venice, quote Shakespeare.

Economics, it seems, is different.

Keynes wishes to challenge "Say's Law". Which author does he quote? Not Jean-Baptiste Say, but John Stuart Mill. And, within the economics profession, it passes almost without comment.

Curious!

Even curiouser: if "Say's Law" is central to the classical tradition, how come that it is not mentioned by Walras, Marshall, or Pigou?* Why is it almost as difficult to find references to "Say's Law" in the fifty years of economic literature *before* the *General Theory* as it is to avoid them in the fifty years *after*?

In 1936, apparently, after half a century or so languishing in the footnotes of economic literature, Jean-Baptiste Say became an overnight failure — as the one who had led everyone astray. And he managed this signal achievement without a single word from his own works ever having been quoted.

Keynes's choice of John Stuart Mill as the authority for "Say's Law" rather than Jean-Baptiste Say is, however, not altogether surprising.

Say doesn't Say what they Say Say Says

What has become known as "Say's Law" is derived from the following passages from his *Treatise*.

"A man who applies his labour to the investing of objects with value by the creation of utility of some sort, can not expect such a value to be appreciated and paid for, unless where other men have the means of purchasing it. Now, of what do these means consist? Of other values of other products, likewise the fruits of industry, capital, and land. Which leads us to a conclusion that may at first sight appear paradoxical, namely, that it is production which opens a demand for products" [1803, p.133].

"It is worth while to remark, that a product is no sooner created, than it, from that instant, affords a market for other products to the full extent of its own value. When the producer has put the finishing hand to his product, he is most anxious to sell it immediately, lest its value should diminish in his hands. Nor is he less anxious to dispose of the money he may get for it; for the value of money is also perishable. But the only way of getting rid of money is in the purchase of some product or other. Thus, the mere circumstance of the creation of one product immediately opens a vent for other products" [pp.134,135].

* It is not mentioned by Keynes's father, John Neville Keynes, in his *Scope and Method of Political Economy* even though he comments on theories of "the causes of commercial depression, and the impossibility of general over-production" [1890, p.107].

There is nothing in those two paragraphs which implies that supply creates its *own* demand, there is merely the observation that it "opens a vent for *other* products".

This is simply a reminder of the principle of effective demand. As Say puts it in his *Catechism of Political Economy*, "there is no other effective demand than that which is accompanied by the offer of a price" [1815, pp.27,28]. People cannot buy *your* products from *you*, unless they have the money; and they cannot earn the money, unless you buy *their* products from *them*. The message is addressed to those who think that protection from competition is the road to prosperity (and it needs repeating to those economists who are afflicted by the dangerous modern habit of blithely assuming shifts in demand that "come from nowhere").

Is the principle of Effective Demand — important though it may be — all there is to "Say's Law"?

The man who should know is Jérôme-Adolphe Blanqui (not to be confused with his more famous brother Louis who was the Red sheep of the family). His *History of Political Economy in Europe* has a special significance because of his relationship with Jean-Baptiste Say, first as protégé, and subsequently as successor in the Chair of Political Economy at the Conservatoire des Arts et Métiers in Paris. An attitude towards Smith and Say which borders on hero-worship is revealed by his references to "Adam Smith, the master of us all" [1837, p.355], and "J. B. Say, … the most indefatigable athlete of the science, and next to Adam Smith its most illustrious propagator" [p.450].

Say's Law of Effective Demand

In Blanqui's *History*, Say's Law is revealed in all its glory.

"What assures immortal renown to the French writer is his *théorie des débouchés*, (literally, *theory of outlets i.e.*, openings for sale of products; generally translated, *theory of markets. — Trans.*), which gave the last blow to the exclusive system and hastened the fall of the colonial régime. This fine theory, wholly founded on most careful observation of facts, has proved that nations pay for products only with products, and that all the laws which forbid them to buy, prevent them from selling" [1837, p.444].

"The restrictive system could no longer be maintained before the overpowering arguments by which J. B. Say provoked its destruction" [p.445].

Precisely!

Say's Theory of Markets is an argument for free trade against protection. It states that competition will *not cause* general unemployment. It does not state that competition will *prevent* general unemployment.

There is a difference. It is the difference between claiming that wearing a hat will not cause baldness and claiming that wearing a hat will prevent baldness.

Blanqui goes on to quote Say's observation that "a nation in relation to another nation, is in the same condition as a province in its relation to another province, or a city in its relation to the country; it is interested in seeing them prosper, and sure of profiting by their opulence." He adds, by way of a footnote, that "it would be as absurd to attempt to impoverish a people with whom we trade, as it would be in a tradesman to wish for the insolvency of a rich and frequent customer" [p.445].

Perhaps the neatest summary of Say's Law of Effective Demand is a remark made in 1421 by Thomas Moncenigo, the Doge of Venice. "What will you sell to the Milanese," said the doge, "when you shall have ruined them? What will they be able to give you in exchange for your products?" [Blanqui (1837) p.206].

The point is emphasised in Say's *Catechism*. "So far from that which another man, or another people gains, being a loss to you, their gains are favourable to you; that it is only necessary for you to produce, not that which they produce easier than you, but that which they cannot fail to demand from you by means of their products; and that wars, entered into for commerce, will appear so much the more senseless as we become better informed" [1815, pp.105,106].

If Say's Theory of Markets is intended to be no more than a strongly worded statement of the Principle of Effective Demand, then is the modern interpretation of "Say's Law" simply a figment of Keynes's imagination?

Not entirely. It is actually an error of logic committed by someone else.

Mill's Doctrine of Full Employment

The author of "Say's Law" is not a Frenchman called Jean-Baptiste Say. He is a Scotsman called James Mill — whose relationship with his son, John Stuart, was not unlike that of Leopold Mozart with his son, Wolfgang.

In *Commerce Defended*, James Mill rides to the rescue of "the immortal Smith" [1807, p.95] against an outrageous attack perpetrated by William Spence. Mill quotes the anti-saving argument from Spence's *Britain Independent of Commerce*. " 'Let us make the supposition that [savers] … were to be convinced by the arguments of Dr. Smith, that the practice of parsimony is the most effectual way of accumulating national riches, and should save. … Is it not self-evident that [those] … , who had been accustomed to receive this sum, would have their power of consuming diminished? ... It is clear then that [it is upon] expenditure, not parsimony, ... that the production of national wealth depends' " [p.126].

Mill dismisses this argument with contempt. "Let not Mr. Spence ... be alarmed. Let him rest in perfect assurance, that the whole annual produce of the country will always be very completely consumed, whether [they] ... choose to spend or to accumulate. ... No man, if he can help it, will let any part of his property lie useless and run to waste" [p.129]. "Even Mr Spence allows that he will lend, not hoard it. Let us suppose that he lends it to the linen manufacturer in his neighbourhood. To what use in his hands is it immediately applied? to the augmentation unquestionably of his business. ... He employs the carpenters, blacksmiths, and other necessary artisans ... , and he hires an additional number of weavers. In this manner the [money of the saver] ... is as completely consumed as ever it was" [p.133].

Mill does not let the matter rest there. He moves on to "another idea the explication of which ... exposes the fallacy of certain notions current in this country. ... The Economistes [now known as Physiocrats] and their disciples express great apprehensions ... lest the production of commodities should be too rapid" [1807, pp.134,135].

It is this "other idea" which is instantly recognisable as the orthodox interpretation of "Say's Law". And its introduction is not marred by undue modesty.

"No proposition ... in political economy seems to be more certain than this which I am going to announce, how paradoxical soever it may at first sight appear; and if it be true, none undoubtedly can be deemed of more importance. The production of commodities creates, and is the one and universal cause which creates a market for the commodities produced" [p.135].

This bears at least a passing resemblance to Say's "conclusion that may at first sight appear paradoxical, namely, that it is production which opens a demand for products" [1803, p.133]. What is more, the rest of Mill's argument reads deceptively like an English translation from Say's French.

"When goods are carried to market what is wanted is somebody to buy. But to buy, one must have the wherewithal to pay. ... But wherein consist the collective means of payment of the whole nation? Do they not consist in its annual produce, in the annual revenue of the general mass of its inhabitants? But if a nation's power of purchasing is exactly measured by its annual produce, as it undoubtedly is; the more you increase the annual produce, the more by that very act you extend the national market, the power of purchasing and the actual purchases of the nation. Whatever be the additional quantity of goods therefore which is at any time created in any country, an additional power of purchasing, exactly equivalent, is at the same time created" [1807, p.135].

"The demand of a nation is always equal to the produce of a nation. This indeed must be so; for what is the demand of a nation? The demand of a nation is exactly its power of purchasing. But what is its power of purchasing? The extent undoubtedly of its annual produce. The extent of its demand therefore and the extent of its supply are always exactly commensurate. ... How great soever that annual produce may be it always creates a market to itself" [pp.136,137].

There is therefore no question about it. *James Mill*, at least, certainly believes that supply creates its own demand; and it looks as if Say has a very good case against him under the Copyright Act. But Mill's argument contains a fatal *non-sequitur* which Say's does not.

The *non-sequitur* occurs in the passage where Mill argues that "if a nation's power of purchasing is exactly measured by its annual produce, as it undoubtedly is; the more you increase the annual produce, the more by that very act you extend the national market, the power of purchasing and the actual purchases of the nation" [p.135]. It does not follow that "the power of purchasing" is automatically converted into "actual purchases". As Alfred Marshall points out, "though men have the power to purchase they may not choose to use it" [1890, p.710].

In the Authorised Version of the Free-Trade Bible, John Stuart Mill dutifully stands up for his father's doctrine; and the fatal *non-sequitur* is ignored. "It is an error to suppose ... that a commercial crisis is the effect of a general excess of production. It is ... a temporary derangement of markets. ... The permanent decline in the circumstances of producers, for want of markets, ... is a conception to which the nature of a commercial crisis gives no support" [1848, p.561]. The possibility of "deficiency of demand" would imply that "there is a third thing to be considered — how a market can be created for produce. ... A theory so essentially self-contradictory cannot intrude itself without carrying confusion into the very heart of the subject. ... It is but justice to two eminent names to call attention to the fact that the merit of having placed this most important point in its true light belongs principally, on the Continent, to the judicious J. B. Say, and in this country to Mr. James Mill; who ... set forth the correct doctrine with great force and clearness in an early pamphlet ... entitled *Commerce Defended*" [pp.562,563].

John Stuart Mill's verdict is now part of the New Orthodoxy. Consequently, Jean-Baptiste Say's valid argument that free competition is *no threat* to full employment has become identified with James Mill's invalid doctrine that free competition is a *guarantee* of full employment.

And that, Ladies and Gentlemen of the Jury, is the case for the Prosecution against the New Orthodoxy. The charge is wilful misrepresentation.

The Case for the Defence

All that the Defence has to do, in order to prove that the orthodox interpretation of "Say's Law" is correct, is to show that "*supply always creates its own demand: general over-production is an impossibility*" is the message intended by Jean-Baptiste Say.

Chief witness for the defence is Jérôme-Adolphe Blanqui. In commenting on Say's attitude to unemployment, he states that "the glutting of the markets seemed to him only the consequence of commercial restrictions" [1837, p.450].

Exhibit A, in support of the proposition that effective demand cannot be deficient, is a passage from Say's own *Treatise*. "Even when money is obtained with a view to hoard or bury it, the ultimate object is always to employ it in a purchase of some kind ... for money, as money, has no other use than to buy with" [1803, p.133n]. This is known (among those who like their metaphors well and truly mixed) as a smoking gun straight out of the horse's mouth.

Exhibit B is a collection of Say's *Letters to Mr. Malthus on the Cause of the Stagnation of Commerce.** The pessimistic view of saving as a cause of economic stagnation, which Malthus urges in his *Principles of Political Economy*, is firmly rebutted in the second of Say's *Letters*. "As to riches accumulated, without being reproductively consumed, such as the sums amassed in the miser's coffers, neither *Smith* nor I, nor any one, undertakes their defence; but they cause very little alarm; first, because they are always very inconsiderable, compared with the productive capital of a nation; and secondly, because their consumption is only suspended. All treasures get spent at last, productively or otherwise" [1820, pp.37,38].

But an awkward question is posed by Malthus in the first edition of his *Principles*. "What ... would become of the demand for commodities, if all consumption except bread and water were suspended for the next half-year? What an accumulation of commodities! *Quels débouchés!* What a prodigious market would this event occasion!" [*Principles* (1st ed.) as quoted by

* Thomas Robert Malthus was a promising clergyman who became a Professor of Political Economy. Unable to come to terms with this misfortune, he turned into an arch-pessimist of almost Malthusian proportions. His dire predictions of impending doom caused by the population increasing faster than the means of subsistence are said to have been responsible for provoking Thomas Carlyle's famous description of economics as the "dismal science".

Keynes (1936) p.364]. Say's answer is to criticise the supposition of "an extravagant fast from mere wantonness, and without any object whatever" as an "exaggeration [which] itself is an error when the nature of things itself presents continually increasing obstacles to the supposed excess, and thus renders the supposition inadmissible" [1820, p.40].

The Defence rests its case.

The Summing-Up

At first sight, Blanqui's evidence looks very strong indeed. Say certainly argues that commercial restrictions are a cause of unemployment. Indeed, he argues that they are the *main* cause of unemployment. He does not, however, argue that they are the *sole* cause of unemployment. Blanqui, out of misguided loyalty, may have doctored the evidence ever-so-slightly in order to maintain his mentor's reputation with orthodox opinion.

Whatever the reservations about Blanqui's commentary, however, Exhibit A — in Say's own handwriting — looks conclusive. It is impossible to deny that "even when money is obtained with a view to hoard or bury it, the ultimate object is always to employ it in a purchase of some kind" [1803, p.133n]. But the word *ultimate* is of crucial significance. Changing "ultimate" into "immediate" would turn the statement into an assertion that a deficiency of effective demand is impossible. As it stands, however, the statement implies not only that a deficiency of effective demand is possible, but that it can persist for an indefinite period.

Surely this objection is taken care of by Say's reassurance in Exhibit B? "The sums amassed in the miser's coffers ... cause very little alarm; first, because they are always very inconsiderable ... and secondly, because their consumption is only suspended" [1820, pp.37,38]. That is absolutely true; but does it not carry the implication that, if considerable and prolonged, "the sums amassed in the miser's coffers" *would* cause alarm? In other words, Say's reassurance is intended, not as a *theoretical argument* that a deficiency of effective demand is impossible, but as an *empirical assumption* that a deficiency of effective demand is unlikely.

This view is reinforced by Say's dismissal of Malthus's supposition of "an extravagant fast from mere wantonness" as "inadmissible" [p.40]. By refusing to debate this possibility, on the grounds that it will never happen, Say is virtually conceding the argument to Malthus; and it is particularly odd in the light of James Mill's comprehensive victory over William Spence on precisely the same point.

If Say really believes in the orthodox version of "Say's Law" as strongly as James Mill (which is the essence of the case being tried), why does he not use against Malthus the same argument which Mill uses so effectively against Spence? Why, if he possesses what (to a believer in "Say's Law") is a knockout punch, does he refuse to get into the ring? (And why, since Keynes quotes Malthus's question, does he fail to mention Say's answer?)

The Verdict

The New Bible contains a reference to **"Say's Law of markets** ... [which] states that overproduction is impossible by its very nature ... supply creates its own demand" [Samuelson & Nordhaus (1995) p.601]. The verdict towards which the evidence seems to point, however, is that this representation of "Say's Law" should be convicted on two counts:

1) it is not Say's – its author is James Mill,
and 2) it is not a Law – it is an error of logic.

Although *James Mill's Doctrine* states that supply always creates its *own* demand: general over-production is *impossible*, *Say's Theory of Markets* states that supply always creates potential demand *for other products*: general over-production is *unlikely*.

The arguments used by Say and James Mill look very close; both employ the principle of effective demand to reach the same conclusion, namely, that unemployment is not a significant problem for a competitive economy. But the closeness is deceptive; their differences are fundamental. Mill uses the principle of effective demand to argue that a deficiency of effective demand is *impossible*; Say uses it to argue that a deficiency of effective demand is *unlikely*. Say's belief in full employment is based on an empirical assumption; Mill's belief in full employment is based on a theoretical proposition.

The arguments used by Say and Malthus look far apart; and they lead to diametrically opposite conclusions. Malthus believes that unemployment is a serious problem even for a competitive economy. But the distance is deceptive; their differences are empirical rather than theoretical. Say does not dispute the anti-saving argument in principle; his quarrel with Malthus is not over the theoretical possibility of a deficiency of "effectual demand", it is over the extent of Malthusian pessimism.

According to James Mill: a deficiency of effective demand is theoretically impossible, therefore there is *no* danger of unemployment as long as the economy is perfectly competitive.

According to Say: a deficiency of effective demand is empirically unlikely, therefore there is *little* danger of unemployment as long as the economy is perfectly competitive.

According to Malthus: a deficiency of effective demand is empirically probable, therefore there is *serious* danger of unemployment even if the economy is perfectly competitive.

Table 30.1: Three Views of a Perfectly Competitive Economy

	DEFICIENCY OF EFFECTIVE DEMAND	DANGER OF UNEMPLOYMENT
James MILL	Theoretically Impossible	None
Jean-Baptiste SAY	Empirically Unlikely	Insignificant
Robert MALTHUS	Empirically Probable	Serious

Mill treats the economy as a single-gear machine, whereas both Say and Malthus treat it as a multi-gear machine. Say and Malthus are therefore in the same theoretical camp. Where they differ is over their empirical assumptions. Say is confident that the machine will normally operate in top gear. Malthus fears that it will not.

What's in a Name?

Suppose the jury accepts that Say is not responsible for the orthodox version of the Law which bears his name and finds the New Orthodoxy guilty of misrepresentation, does it really matter? After all, "a stench by any other name would smell as foul", whether or not it was Shakespeare who said so.* Is the identity of the author of "Say's Law" of any greater relevance?

The answer is that the matter is of more than mere historical significance.

Jean-Baptiste Say is one of the most distinguished founder-members of the classical school of economic theory. Adam Smith may be its most revered philosopher; but it is Say's analysis (rather than that of Smith, Ricardo, or John Stuart Mill) which has stood the test of time. If his vision of the economy is indeed as a multi-gear machine, and if that vision has been buried under the myth of "Say's Law", the consequence is false theory. The consequence of false theory is bad policy; and the cost of the damage inflicted by bad policy is probably incalculable.

There is a further cause for concern.

It is easy to pin the blame for "Say's Law" on James Mill or David Ricardo; and many have done so. But they are only the front-men. The mastermind is surely the author of these passages from *The Wealth of*

* *Romeo and Juliet* Act II, Scene 2, line 43 (first draft).

Nations. "Money can serve no other purpose besides purchasing goods. ... The man who buys, does not always mean to sell again, but frequently to use or to consume; whereas he who sells, always means to buy again. ... It is not for its own sake that men desire money, but for the sake of what they can purchase with it" [1776, IV,1]. "What is annually saved is as regularly consumed as what is annually spent, and nearly in the same time too; but it is consumed by a different set of people" [II,3].

The suspicion must be that the guilty party is not in Court and that Adam Smith is the person ultimately responsible for the single-gear view of the economy. If that is so, how much confidence can be placed in the Truth of the original Revelation?

CHAPTER 31

THE REVELATION THAT NEVER WAS

The name of the religion is still Free Trade. But Mount Sinai is not in Scotland, Adam Smith is no Moses, and the Walrasian Utopia is not the Promised Land.

"The publication in 1776 of *The Wealth of Nations* by Adam Smith," is identified by the New Bible, "as the birthdate of modern economics" [Samuelson & Nordhaus (1989) p.824]. No less an authority than the *Encyclopaedia Britannica* confirms that "the effective birth of economics as a separate discipline may be traced to the year 1776, when the Scottish philosopher Adam Smith published *An Inquiry into the Nature and Causes of the Wealth of Nations*."

This is not entirely accurate.

1776 marks the birth of the belief in the economy as a single-gear machine. It also marks the suppression of the previous belief in the economy as a multi-gear machine — a belief which is such anathema to the New Orthodoxy that economists before 1776 are either dismissed as being of little consequence or portrayed merely as the "forerunners" of Adam Smith.

Is it possible that the *Wealth of Nations* conceals as much as it reveals?

The Tablet that got Left Behind

If it can be said that the economic revelation is inscribed on two tablets of stone, then it has to be recognised that, when Adam Smith came down from the mountain, he was carrying only one.

The tablet he brought with him contains the commandments on competition. The one he left behind contains the commandments on circulation. The Law of Competition has become the foundation of the Free-Market religion. The Law of Circulation has largely been ignored.

Smith's sojourn is no myth. It actually took place during the years 1763 to 1766 — not on Mount Sinai, but, rather closer to home — in France. It was there that he came face to face, not exactly with the Almighty, but with a group of statesmen and philosophers known as the Physiocrats — "a pretty considerable sect, distinguished in the French republic of letters by the name of The Economists" [1776, IV,9].

The French Connection

The leading figure in the ranks of the Physiocrats is generally acknowledged to be François Quesnay, whose influence at the court of Louis XV owed something to his position as personal physician to Madame Pompadour. His reputation with posterity owes more to the publication in 1758 of his *Tableau Économique*, which is regarded by many as the first real essay in economic analysis (as opposed to economic philosophy).

Quesnay shows in his *Tableau* how the annual revenue of the nation is produced and distributed. He then emphasises that it will be achieved only on the basis of certain assumptions. These assumptions are set out under the title of "Extrait des Économies Royales de M. de Sully" (suggested by the translators as possibly "due to the influence of Mirabeau, who ... had drawn the public's attention to the thirty-six maxims which Sully had addressed to Henry IV in 1604"). Later they came to be known, under the label given by Mirabeau, as the "Maximes Générales du Gouvernement économique" [1758, trans. note 46 p.9].

According to the *Physiocrats*, economic wealth has its origin in the land and the activity of "agriculture ... where," in the words of Quesnay, "the most energetic competition results in the expansion of the wealth of Nations with large territories" [1758, p.13n].

The importance of competition is emphasised in the twenty-second maxim which states:

> "22. That each person is free to cultivate in his fields such products as his interests, his means, and the nature of the land suggest to him, in order that he may extract from them the greatest possible product. Monopoly in the cultivation of landed property should never be encouraged, for it is detrimental to the general revenue of the Nation." [p.16].

There are two things worth noting about the twenty-second maxim. The first is its unqualified advocacy of free competition. The second is its position at number twenty-two.

The first of the Maxims is

> "1. That the whole of the ... revenue enters into the annual circulation, and runs through it to the full extent of its course; and that it is never formed into monetary fortunes, or at least that those which are formed are counterbalanced by those which come back into circulation; for otherwise these monetary fortunes would check the flow of a part of this annual revenue of the Nation, and hold back the money stock or finance of the kingdom, to the detriment of the return of

> the advances, the payment of the artisans' wages, the reproduction of the revenue, and the taxes" [p.3].

Maxims number five and six state

> "5. That the proprietors and those engaged in remunerative occupations are not led by any anxiety, unforeseen by the Government, to give themselves over to sterile saving, which would deduct from circulation and distribution a portion of their revenues or gains" [p.4].
>
> "6. That the administration of finance, whether in the collection of taxes or in the expenditure of the Government, does not bring about the formation of monetary fortunes, which steal a portion of the revenue away from circulation, distribution, and reproduction" [p.4].

In short, the Physiocrats had their commandments set out on two tablets of stone: the first dealt with circulation,
the second dealt with competition.

The Scottish Enlightenment

Although Smith criticises Quesnay's "agricultural system of political economy" because it "represents the produce of land as the sole source of the revenue and wealth of every country", his overall verdict is favourable. "This system, however, with all its imperfections, is, perhaps, the nearest approximation to the truth that has yet been published upon the subject of political economy. ... In representing the wealth of nations as consisting, not in the unconsumable riches of money, but in the consumable goods annually reproduced by the labour of the society; and in representing perfect liberty as the only effectual expedient for rendering this annual reproduction the greatest possible, its doctrine seems to be in every respect as just as it is generous and liberal" [1776, IV, 9].

Why, then, does Smith, having enthusiastically seized the tablet marked competition, leave behind the tablet marked circulation?

The reason is the error in his analysis — an early manifestation of the "classical fallacy" discussed in chapter 22 above. Smith argues that "what is annually saved is as regularly consumed as what is annually spent, and nearly in the same time too; but it is consumed by a different set of people" [II,3]. Consequently, he has no need to worry about circulation; and saving, instead of being deplored as "sterile", is an activity to be positively encouraged.

"As the capital of an individual can be increased only by what he saves, ... so the capital of a society, which is the same with that of all the individuals who compose it, can be increased only in the same manner. ...

An augmentation of fortune is the means by which the greater part of men propose and wish to better their condition. ... The most likely way of augmenting their fortune is to save and accumulate" [II,3].

Smith's conclusion that "every prodigal appears to be a public enemy, and every frugal man a public benefactor" [II,3] is in direct conflict with Quesnay's condemnation of "the formation of monetary fortunes, which steal a portion of the revenue away from circulation, distribution, and reproduction" [1758, p.4].

The fact that Smith's doctrine can be encompassed in a single commandment — "free competition" — gives it a twofold attraction.

To believers in "natural liberty", freedom in economic affairs has a powerful philosophical appeal. To philosophers in the quest for a single unifying theme, a single commandment has an overwhelming intellectual appeal.

It is perhaps the intellectual elegance of Smith's doctrine that blinds modern economists both to the fallacy of classical economics and to the validity of what had gone before.

In the religion of economics, Sir William Petty in the role of Abraham is probably more convincing than Adam Smith in the role of Moses.

The English Patriarch

Sir William Petty, like Quesnay, was a physician; and, like Quesnay, he was keen to apply his knowledge of the human body to the economy of society. "Anatomy is not only necessary in Physicians, but laudable in every Philosophical person whatsoever" [1672, p.129]. What is more, he must have been profoundly influenced by the revolutionary advance in medical science made by William Harvey whose treatise on the Circulation of the Blood was published in 1628.

A century before Quesnay, Petty was preoccupied with the circulation of money through the economy.

"As the most thriving Men keep little or no Money by them, but turn and wind it into various Commodities to their great Profit, so may the whole Nation also; which is but many particular Men united" [1682, p.446]. "A hundred pound passing a hundred hands for Wages, causes 10000l. worth of Commodities to be produced, which hands would have been idle and useless, had there not been this continual motive to their employment" [1662, p.36].*

* Hobbes makes explicit use of the anatomical metaphor in *Leviathan*: "Mony the Bloud of a Common-wealth ... passeth from Man to Man, within the Common-wealth; and goes round about, Nourishing (as it passeth) every part thereof" [1651, p.174].

In suggesting a cure for unemployment, Petty makes "profligate" recommendations which run directly counter to Smith's exhortations to parsimony and frugality.

"Money ... expended on Entertainments, magnificent Shews, triumphal Arches, &c.... is a refunding the said moneys to the Tradesmen who work upon those things; which Trades though they seem vain and onely of ornament, yet they refund presently to the most useful; namely, to Brewers, Bakers, Taylours, Shoemakers, &c." [1662, p.33].

The persistence of this type of heresy is such an affront to the established Church that, even after the lapse of two centuries, John Stuart Mill is provoked by the outrage into massive retaliation.

"The utility of a large government expenditure, for the purpose of encouraging industry, is no longer maintained. Taxes are not now esteemed to be "like the dews from heaven, which return again in prolific showers." It is no longer supposed that you benefit the producer by taking his money, provided you give it to him again in exchange for his goods. There is nothing which impresses a person of reflection with a stronger sense of the shallowness of the political reasonings of the last two centuries, than the general reception so long given to a doctrine which, if it proves anything, proves that the more you take from the pockets of the people to spend on your own pleasures, the richer they grow; that the man who steals money out of a shop, provided he expends it all again at the same shop, is a benefactor to the tradesman whom he robs, and that the same operation, repeated sufficiently often, would make the tradesman's fortune" [1844, pp.47,48].

Mill names no names, but to whom can "the political reasonings of the last two centuries" be traced, if not to Petty? Mill's refusal to mention him by name is illuminating. Heretical ideas must be buried — and the grave must be left unmarked. For those (like Malthus) weak or stupid enough to persist with such heresies, there is to be no place of pilgrimage.

Even more significant, given the length and importance of the discussion in his *Essays on Some Unsettled Questions of Political Economy* [1844], is that no mention of the controversy is made in the *Principles* [1848]. It is presumably too dangerous and inflammatory.

Keynes's summing-up of the episode is masterly.

"Malthus ... had vehemently opposed Ricardo's doctrine that it was impossible for effective demand to be deficient; but vainly. For, since Malthus was unable to explain clearly (apart from an appeal to the facts of common observation) how and why effective demand could be deficient or excessive, he failed to furnish an alternative construction; and Ricardo conquered England as completely as the Holy Inquisition conquered Spain. Not only was his theory accepted by the city, by statesmen and by the academic world. But controversy ceased; the other point of view completely disappeared; it ceased to be discussed. The great puzzle of Effective Demand with which Malthus had wrestled vanished from economic literature. You will not find it mentioned even once in the whole works of Marshall, Edgeworth, and Professor Pigou, from whose hands the classical theory has received its most mature embodiment. It could only live on furtively, below the surface, in the underworlds of Karl Marx, Silvio Gesell or Major Douglas" [1936, p.32].

The legacy of Smith's "revelation" of the Law of Competition is the "concealment" of the Law of Circulation.

CHAPTER 32

THE LOST COMMANDMENT: THE LAW OF CIRCULATION

The most effective critic of "Say's Law" is not Keynes but an obscure clerk employed by a French assurance society in the late eighteenth century. His inspiration is reputed to be derived from a copy of Adam Smith's *Wealth of Nations* presented to him by the director of the society.*

In a treatise (which is now almost totally neglected), the influence of Adam Smith is clearly visible. One passage in the *Wealth of Nations* seems to have made a powerful impression. "Money can serve no other purpose besides purchasing goods. ... The man who buys, does not always mean to sell again, but frequently to use or to consume; whereas he who sells, always means to buy again. ... It is not for its own sake that men desire money, but for the sake of what they can purchase with it" [1776, IV,1].

Although many celebrated economists use this passage to justify "Say's Law", the obscure clerk has the temerity to voice dissent.

"Values once produced may be devoted, either to the satisfaction of the wants of those who have acquired them, or to a further act of production. They may also be withdrawn both from unproductive consumption and from reproductive employment, and remain buried or concealed. The owner of values, in so disposing of them ... withholds from industry the profits it might make by the employment of that value. ... A hoard of specie locked up in a strong box, or buried in the earth ... however considerable in amount, ... yield[s] no sort of benefit whatever, being in fact little else than a mere precautionary deposit."

This early anticipation of the Keynesian multi-gear economy comes with a warning that the danger is particularly acute in times of crisis when "the general distrust and uncertainty of the future induce people of every rank ... to withdraw a part of their property from the greedy eyes of power: and value can never be invisible, without being inactive."

Heedless of the warning, David Ricardo persists with the single-gear vision of the economy by establishing the orthodox version of "Say's Law" in his *Principles of Political Economy, and Taxation*. "Productions are always bought by productions, or by services; money is only the medium by which the exchange is effected. Too much of a particular commodity may be produced, of which there may be such a glut on the

* See Ingram (1888) pp.163,164.

market, as not to repay the capital expended on it; but this cannot be the case with respect to all commodities" [1817, pp.291,292].

The response of the ex-clerk takes the form of a blistering attack on "Say's Law".

"Mr. Ricardo insists ... that all capital saved is always employed, because the interest is not suffered to be lost. On the contrary, many savings are not invested, when it is difficult to find employment for them, and many which are employed are dissipated in ill-calculated undertakings. Besides, Mr. Ricardo is completely refuted ... by our present circumstances, when capitals are quietly sleeping in the coffers of their proprietors."

This attack on "Say's Law" is consistent with its author's noble ambition to save the science of economics from degenerating into a religion. "I submit only to the decrees of eternal reason, and am not afraid to declare it: Adam Smith has not embraced all the phenomena of the production and consumption of wealth; but he has done so much that we ought to feel the deepest gratitude for his exertions."

Nevertheless, the tone of the neglected treatise is positive. Smith's Law of Competition is enthusiastically welcomed and endorsed — but without the usual religious awe. It is made perfectly clear that, while the Law of Competition is necessary for economic prosperity, it is not sufficient by itself. There is another law which must also be observed. It is the law recognised by Quesnay and the Physiocrats — a law which is the very antithesis of Say's Law — the Law of Circulation.

The Law of Circulation

The Law of Circulation is implicit in the following sentence in the ex-clerk's neglected treatise: "No act of saving subtracts in the least from consumption, provided the thing saved be re-invested or restored to productive employment."

The corollary of that statement is its negative form: *"every act of saving may subtract from consumption, unless the thing saved is re-invested or restored to productive employment."*

That is the Law of Circulation — the second tablet which Smith left behind, but which is equally essential to economic prosperity.

The name of the obscure clerk, as the reader will probably have guessed, is Jean-Baptiste Say. His *Treatise on Political Economy* is still, with the exception of a few quotations (often out of context), shamefully neglected.

If anything deserves the title of "Say's Law", it is not the proposition that effective demand *cannot* be deficient, it is the proposition that it *can*.

Jean-Baptiste Say is in a direct line of intellectual descent from François Quesnay. The "Law" which emerges from Say's *Treatise* is not the myth of orthodox tradition that there is no obstacle to full employment. It is precisely the opposite. "Say's Law of Circulation" is the "lost" commandment of Petty and Quesnay. It is also the key theoretical proposition at the heart of Keynes's *General Theory*.

Jean-Baptiste Say is a victim of religious intolerance. His Law of Circulation has been denied recognition in the same way as the Old Testament injunction to "love thy neighbour as thyself". It is a casualty of the jealousy of quarrelsome priests.

A Casualty in the Crossfire of Religious Conflict

The allegation made by Keynes that Say is the author of a Law, which "is equivalent to the proposition that there is no obstacle to full employment" [1936, p.26] is, on the available evidence, a travesty of the truth. Yet the same allegation is made by John Stuart Mill, and it remains entrenched in the New Orthodoxy.

Mill is the Defender of a Classical Faith which believes that the only law that matters is the Law of Competition. In his reading of the Gospel according to Say, he claims to have found complete vindication of the eternal Classical truth, namely, that obedience to the law of competition *alone* is sufficient to ensure full employment. To Keynes, seeking a direct confrontation with classical doctrine, Mill's distortion of Say's Law is a gift from heaven. It could not have suited his purpose more exactly if he had invented it himself — which, as a matter of fact, is largely what he did.

Mill's tampering with the evidence seems quite deliberate. The evidence, which is openly examined in his *Essays on Some Unsettled Questions of Political Economy* [1844], is carefully suppressed and removed from the *Principles* [1848]. There is nothing sinister about Mill's motives. He is acting purely in the interests of protecting the free-trade religion. And the most effective way of dealing with heresy is not to criticise its faults, but to deny its existence.

Keynes's motives are equally innocent; and it is unfair to accuse him of creating a classical "strawman". To make "Say's Law" the centrepiece of classical orthodoxy without quoting Say himself may be inexcusable; yet one can sympathise with Keynes's predicament. He arrives at the tournament as the Challenger — mounted on a magnificent white charger — resplendent in gleaming armour — impatient to launch himself against the Classical Champion. Dimly discernible through the swirling mist is the outline of the classical horse — without a rider. The Classical Champion is nowhere to be seen. It is extremely frustrating.

Faced with a riderless horse, Keynes is desperate for an opponent who is the acknowledged champion of the classical single-gear view of the economy. And he frankly admits his dilemma. "Professor Pigou's theory of unemployment ... is the only attempt with which I am acquainted to write down the classical theory of unemployment precisely" [1936, p.279]. But a not-very-well-known infant theory is hardly a worthy opponent; it cannot convincingly be called out to do combat as the representative of a widespread tradition with a history going back to at least 1776. Jean-Baptiste Say, on the other hand, the earliest of the established disciples of Adam Smith, is a much more respectable opponent.

It suits both rival theologies — Classical and Keynesian — to hold up Say as the Champion of the classical single-gear economy. "Say's Law" satisfies both Mill's desire for a flawless ideal and Keynes's desire for a clear target. "Say's Law" makes a magnificent banner. Theorists can cheerfully die at the barricades fighting either for it or against it. A series of qualifying footnotes would spoil the effect.

Say's Law of Circulation, based on a multi-gear view of the economy, stands no chance. It perishes in the crossfire of religious conflict.

In the heat of the battle, however, Keynes unfortunately dispatches one of the few English economists (apart from Lauderdale*) whose work is capable of challenging the classical single-gear doctrine on its own ground.

Malthus: Villain or Hero?

Malthus's criticism is as applicable to the New Orthodoxy as to the Old, but the nice thing about his *Principles of Political Economy* is that it is full of helpful hints. There is one for John Stuart Mill: "theoretical writers in Political Economy, from the fear of appearing to attach too much importance to money, have perhaps been too apt to throw it out of their consideration in their reasonings" [1820, p.324n]. There is another for Milton Friedman: "theoretical writers are too apt, in their calculations, to overlook these intervals [of adjustment]; but eight or ten years, recurring not unfrequently, are serious spaces in human life" [p.437].

Keynes's tone is unnecessarily condescending. "Malthus ... had vehemently opposed Ricardo's doctrine that it was impossible for effective

* *An Inquiry into the Nature and Origin of Public Wealth* [1804], by James Maitland, 8th Earl of Lauderdale, is hostile to Adam Smith in particular and to classical economic theory in general. His "tendency to extremes" is too much even for Malthus [1820, p.314n], and he is not mentioned in John Stuart Mill's *Principles*.

demand to be deficient; but vainly. For, since Malthus was unable to explain clearly (apart from an appeal to the facts of common observation) how and why effective demand could be deficient or excessive, he failed to furnish an alternative construction" [1936, p.32].

In the light of the subsequent counter-revolution, it is clear that Keynes's own vehement opposition to the classical doctrine is equally vain — and for the very same reason. Since the *General Theory* contains no microeconomic foundations based on individual preferences explaining how and why effective demand can be deficient or excessive, it, too, fails to furnish an alternative construction.

The irony is that Malthus — the person on the wrong side of the barricade on competition — is the one who actually *does* point the way to an alternative construction. For he describes as a "fundamental error ... the not taking into consideration the influence of so general and important a principle in human nature, as indolence or love of ease" [1820, p.320]. It is by taking on the appearance *in the market-place* of an increase in "indolence or love of ease" that the desire to save money causes deficiency of effective demand. Malthus, however, fails to convince. Keynes who does convince — is the one who fails to provide the alternative construction.

Keynes is lucky. Although his *General Theory* is a Grin without a Cat, the onlookers are so captivated by the seductiveness of the Grin that they do not seem to mind that, in the eyes of some of its neo-classical critics, it has no visible means of theoretical support.

It is Malthus's misfortune to have produced a Cat without a Grin — a creature with such a bad-tempered scowl on its face that it has been able to attract nothing other than a few well-aimed kicks.

The result is that the Law of Competition has become the single principle of the New Orthodoxy. The Law of Circulation has been quietly forgotten.

The Triumph of the Single-Gear Vision of the Economy

The Article of Faith is that equilibrium is the centre of the economic universe; it cannot move away from full employment. Any deviation from full employment is believed to be a deviation from equilibrium. The economy is regarded as a single-gear machine. If the machine fails to operate at its full employment potential, it is taken as evidence that what is lacking is the lubricant of competition.

Nowadays, followers of the Capitalist faith, whether their Sectarian allegiance is Classical, Keynesian, or Monetarist, are unable to recognise that the economy is a multi-gear machine. It is forbidden by their religion.

The fundamental error of this belief is the root cause of the failure of many capitalist economies to achieve full employment without inflation or price stability without unemployment. It is also the cause of failure to secure freedom in international trade without massive imbalances.

Such is the power of religious dogma that these failures are, almost without exception, blamed on breaches of the Law of Competition, whereas they are, in the main, the consequence of breaches of Law of Circulation. They are therefore impervious to improvements in competition.

This is the nature of the "fatal conceit" (to borrow Hayek's expression) of the New Orthodoxy in economic theory.

The journey from Adam Smith to the present day seems to have run into the dead-end of single-gear economics. *The Wealth of Nations*, however, is an excellent point of departure. Perhaps it is simply that we have been travelling in the wrong direction?

PART VI

BACK TO THE FUTURE

INTRODUCTION

"There was a young lady named Bright,
Who could travel much faster than light;
She set off one day
In a relative way,
And returned on the previous night."*

The thing that people find most puzzling about Einstein's *Theory of Relativity* is the proposition that a body, which moves faster than light, goes backwards in time. Although some have attempted to reproduce this experiment (in circular accelerators like the CERN cyclotron near Geneva and the M25 motorway round London), few have succeeded.

There is only one known exception.

The journey made by economic theory from Adam Smith in 1776, through Mill, Marshall, Pigou, etc. to Milton Friedman is a two hundred year detour which arrives, two decades before it set out, at David Hume in 1752.

No disrespect is intended to Albert Einstein, but Lewis Carroll is a lot easier to follow. In the Looking-Glass world, there is no need to rush; time itself runs backwards. The White Queen first puts on a bandage; next, she screams; finally, she pricks her finger.

Looking-Glass chronology takes some getting used to, but it is the only way that the history of economic thought makes any sense. And there are other benefits besides. The disappointing result of setting off from Adam Smith and travelling forwards indicates a more promising direction for making progress in economics: to set off from Adam Smith and travel backwards.

---

* There are many variations on this well-known limerick. The *Oxford Dictionary of Quotations* attributes the original version to Arthur Buller, *Punch* 19th December 1923.

CHAPTER 33

DAVID HUME (1711 - 1776)

Economic theory has come a long way in the two centuries following the mythical Revelation to Adam Smith. Milton Friedman is not without his critics; but few would deny the excellence of his monetary analysis. It is just that David Hume's, published twenty years before the *Wealth of Nations*, is even better.

By Looking-Glass chronology, however, it is clear that Hume is not original.

Back to Friedmanite Monetary Theory

Hume, like Friedman, is a no-nonsense quantity theorist. "The prices of commodities are always proportioned to the plenty of money" [1752b, p.33]. "The quantity of specie [i.e. coinage], when once fixed, though ever so large, has no other effect, than to oblige every one to tell out a greater number of those shining bits of metal, for clothes, furniture or equipage, without encreasing any one convenience of life" [1752c, p.48].

Hume is very fond of Friedman's "helicopter" type of analogy.* "Suppose, that, by a miracle, every man in GREAT BRITAIN should have five pounds slipt into his pocket in one night. ... This money, however abundant, ... would only serve to encrease the prices of every thing, without any farther consequence" [1752c, p.51]. "Suppose four-fifths of all the money in GREAT BRITAIN to be annihilated in one night, ... what would be the consequence? Must not the price of all labour and commodities sink in proportion? ... Again, suppose, that all the money of GREAT BRITAIN were multiplied fivefold in a night, must not the contrary effect follow? [1752d, pp.62,63].

But there are occasions when the quantity theory of money appears to be contradicted by the facts. "It is certain, that, since the discovery of the mines in AMERICA, industry has encreased in all the nations of EUROPE. ... In every kingdom, into which money begins to flow in greater abundance than formerly, every thing takes a new face: labour and industry gain life; the merchant becomes more enterprising, the manufacturer more diligent and skilful, and even the farmer follows his plough with greater alacrity and attention. This is not easily to be accounted for, if we consider only the influence which a greater abundance

* See chapter 17, Part I above.

of coin has in the kingdom itself, by heightening the price of commodities, and obliging every one to pay a greater number of these little yellow or white pieces for every thing he purchases" [1752b, p.37].

Hume's resolution of this paradox is the same as Friedman's: it is simply a question of the period necessary for adjustment.

"To account, then, for this phenomenon, we must consider, that though the high price of commodities be a necessary consequence of the encrease of gold and silver, yet it follows not immediately upon that encrease; but some time is required before the money circulates through the whole state, and makes its effect be felt on all ranks of people. … It is only in this interval or intermediate situation, between the acquisition of money and rise of prices, that the encreasing quantity of gold and silver is favourable to industry" [1752b, pp.37,38].

Hume's explanation of the dynamics of the process is lifted straight from Friedman's Presidential Address to the American Economic Association (discussed in chapter 11 above).

"When any quantity of money is imported into a nation, it is not at first dispersed into many hands, but is confined to the coffers of a few persons, who immediately seek to employ it to advantage. … They are thereby enabled to employ more workmen than formerly, who never dream of demanding higher wages, but are glad of employment from such good paymasters. If workmen become scarce, the manufacturer gives higher wages, but at first requires an encrease of labour; and this is willingly submitted to by the artisan, who can now eat and drink better, to compensate his additional toil and fatigue. He carries his money to market, where he finds every thing at the same price as formerly, but returns with greater quantity and of better kinds, for the use of his family. The farmer and gardener, finding, that all their commodities are taken off, apply themselves with alacrity to the raising more: and at the same time can afford to take better and more cloths from their tradesmen, whose price is the same as formerly, and their industry only whetted by so much new gain. It is easy to trace the money in its progress through the whole commonwealth; where … it must first quicken the diligence of every individual, before it encrease the price of labour. And that the specie may encrease to a considerable pitch, before it have this latter effect, appears, amongst other instances, from the frequent operations of the FRENCH king on the money; where it was always found, that the augmenting of the numerary value did not produce a proportional rise of the prices, at least for some time" [1752b, pp.38,39].

"Unemployment," according to Friedman, "is an inevitable side effect of an effective policy to damp down inflation … because of the time that it takes for the tapering off of total demand to be recognised by employers and employees for what it is, and for contractual arrangements to be readjusted to the new situation" [1974b]. Hume does not disagree. "There is always an interval before matters be adjusted to their new situation; and this interval is as pernicious to industry, when gold and silver are diminishing, as it is advantageous when these metals are encreasing. … The poverty, and beggary, and sloth, which must ensue, are easily foreseen" [1752b, p.40].

In view of the slavishness with which Hume follows Friedman's monetary theory, it is no surprise that the monetary policy adopted by Hume is what may be called "Orthodox Friedmanite".

Back to Friedmanite Monetary Policy

"From the whole of this reasoning we may conclude, that it is of no manner of consequence, with regard to the domestic happiness of a state, whether money be in a greater or less quantity. The good policy of the magistrate consists only in keeping it, if possible, still encreasing"[1752b, pp.39,40], perhaps by following Friedman's advice and "adopting publicly the policy of achieving a steady rate of growth in a specified monetary total" [1968, p.16].

It would be unfair to suggest that Hume makes no advance *at all* on Friedman's analysis. After all, two hundred Looking-Glass years of progress must count for something — and indeed they do. For the significant original contribution made by Hume is his recognition of the effect that a period of temporary adjustment is likely to have on underlying tastes and technology.

Hume grabs old-fashioned twentieth-century "monetarism" by the scruff of the neck and drags it "kicking and screaming" into the eighteenth.

The Modernisation of Friedmanite Doctrine

Hume's starting point is the basic monetary philosophy of late twentieth-century orthodoxy. "Money, when encreasing, gives encouragement to industry, during the interval between the encrease in money and rise of the prices" [1752d, p.68n]. That accounts for the "ratcheting upwards" of prices as demand and supply chase each other up the type of inflationary spiral described in chapter 11 above. During this interval, however, the "temporary" increase in activity can be instrumental in changing permanent habits.

If monetary expansion "must first quicken the diligence of every individual, before it encrease the price of labour", and if "the merchant becomes more enterprising, the manufacturer more diligent and skilful", those skills and attitudes, once acquired, do not simply disappear after the period of adjustment. Production technology and consumer tastes may never be the same again.

Improvements in technology, which occur under the stimulus to enterprise and innovation, are not normally reversed. Expectations, which are raised as consumers acquire new appetites and become accustomed to a higher standard of living, are not easily lowered. In terms of the traditional diagrams used in ch.11, it is not simply a question of the same real demand and supply curves shifting upwards in nominal terms; they may shift in real terms outwards to the right.

Hume's point is that, after the period of adjustment, economic activity does not necessarily return to its previous level, with increased prices being the only lasting result. There may also be some permanent expansion in the volume of activity. "No other satisfactory reason can be given, why all prices have not risen to a much more exorbitant height, … besides that more commodities are produced by additional industry" [1752b, p.44].

Although Hume does not abandon the single-gear view of the economy, he takes an enlightened view which recognises its organic nature; exercise can stimulate growth. The economy is still a single-gear machine, but an increase in its speed can, in certain circumstances, change the size of the engine.

Time Really Does Run Backwards

Sceptics, who are inclined to doubt the proposition that time can run backwards, have only to compare Milton Friedman's monetary analysis with David Hume's. If that is not sufficient, there is further evidence scattered all the way through Hume's *Essays* on economics.

His statement that "every thing in the world is purchased by labour" [1752a, p.11] clearly derives from the labour theory of value of Adam Smith and Karl Marx.

The language in which he repeats Say's Principle of Effective Demand demonstrates an intimate acquaintance with Say's *Treatise*. "States are in the same position as individuals. A single man can scarcely be industrious, where all his fellow-citizens are idle. The riches of the several members of a community contribute to encrease my riches, whatever profession I may follow. They consume the produce of my industry, and afford me the produce of theirs in return" [1758, p.79]. "Were our narrow and malignant politics [of protection] to meet with success, … what would be the consequence? They could send us no commodities: They could take none from us" [p.81].

His commitment to the twentieth century ideal of a European Community is unequivocal. "Not only as a man, but as a BRITISH subject, I pray for the flourishing commerce of GERMANY, SPAIN, ITALY, and even FRANCE itself" [1758, p.82].

Can there be any doubt about the target of this next comment? "In general, all poll-taxes, even when not arbitrary, which they commonly are, may be esteemed dangerous" [1752e, p.86].

To suggest that Hume's writings are not influenced by the lessons of late twentieth-century history would be to stretch credulity beyond all reasonable bounds.

Nineteenth- and twentieth-century economic theory cannot be logically explained if time runs forwards; eighteenth- and seventeenth-century economic theory cannot be logically explained unless time runs backwards.

This chapter contains conclusive proof that the long journey *forwards* in time from Adam Smith's *Wealth of Nations* of 1776 to Milton Friedman's Presidential Address of 1968 on *The Role of Monetary Policy* still leaves monetary economics well short of its position in Hume's *Essays* of 1752.

The next few chapters cannot fail to convince even the most hardened sceptic that the journey *backwards* in time from Adam Smith is one of steady and consistent progress.

CHAPTER 34

ANNE ROBERT JACQUES TURGOT (1727 - 1781)

The next stop on the backward journey from Adam Smith is eighteenth-century France — a country in dire economic straits desperately trying to recover from the success of Louis XIV.

The role of the White Queen, destined to apply the bandages before the fatal lacerations inflicted by the Revolution of 1789, is played by Anne Robert Jacques Turgot, Finance Minister to Louis XVI from 1774 until his dismissal (for being too good at his job) in 1776.

According to Looking-Glass chronology, Turgot's *Reflections on the Formation and the Distribution of Riches* [1770] trail the *Wealth of Nations* by six years.

Like Smith, Turgot attributes the development of society to the economic benefits derived from specialisation and the division of labour. "Each man ... if he were reduced to his own field and his own labour, would consume much time and trouble to be very badly equipped in every respect, and would cultivate his land very badly. ... Each by devoting himself to a single kind of work succeeded much better in it" [1770, p.6]. "Reciprocal want has led to the exchange of what people have for what they have not" [p.28]. "This circulation, ... by the reciprocal exchange of wants, renders men necessary to one another and forms the bond of the society" [p.7].

Like Smith, Turgot identifies the use of money as the stimulus to commerce. "The more money came to stand for everything else, the more possible did it become for each person, by devoting himself entirely to the kind of cultivation or industry he had chosen, to relieve himself of all care for the satisfaction of his other wants, and to think only how he could obtain as much money as possible by the sale of his fruits or his labour, very sure that by means of this money he can get all the rest. It is thus that the employment of money has prodigiously hastened the progress of Society" [p.42].

Like Smith, Turgot observes that "the mere Workman, who has only his arms and his industry, has nothing except in so far as he succeeds in selling his toil to others ... [who have] the choice among a great number of Workmen. ... The Workmen are therefore obliged to lower the price, in competition with one another. ... The wages of the workman are limited to what is necessary to procure him his subsistence" [p.8].

The Looking-Glass influence of Karl Marx is apparent in Turgot's emphasis on the class divisions in society.

"The whole Class occupied in supplying the different wants of the Society with the vast variety of industrial products finds itself, so to speak, subdivided into two orders: ... possessors of large capitals* which they make profit from by setting men at work, by means of their advances; and the second order, which is composed of simple Artisans who have no other property but their arms, who advance only their daily labour, and receive no profit but their wages" [p.54].

On the question of money, Turgot is a straightforward quantity theorist. He uses the familiar Friedmanite "helicopter" type of argument (taking meticulous care over redistributional effects).

"Suppose there comes into the State ... *a second million* ounces of silver, and that this increase is distributed to every purse in the same proportion as the first million, so that the man who before had two ounces of silver now has four. ... Commodities will be paid for more dearly; ... it will be necessary to give a good deal more silver, and perhaps *two ounces* instead of one" [pp.75,76].

In a letter to Hume, dated March 25th 1767, Turgot repeats the orthodox Friedmanite argument that "in every complicated machine there are frictions which delay the results most infallibly demonstrated by theory. Even in the case of a fluid perfectly homogeneous, it takes time for the level to be restored; but with time it always is restored. It is the same with the equilibrium of the values which we are examining" [reprinted in 1770, p.109].

This seems to confirm Turgot as an orthodox monetarist. Yet there are passages in the *Reflections* where he shows signs of trying to break free from the single-gear view of the economy.

Turgot's comment that "it would not be safe to interrupt the labours of an enterprise once set on foot, and they could not be taken up again just when one wished" [p.59] suggests that the eighteenth century administrator has a keener appreciation of business reality than many twentieth-century academics, chancellors, and Monetary Policy Committee members. But it is the following passage which seems to open the way to a multi-gear view of economy.

"It is ... *the circulation of money* ... which gives life to all the labours of the society, which maintains movement and life in the body politic, and which is with great reason compared to the circulation of blood in the animal body. For if, by any disorder, be it what it may, in the sequence of

---

* According to a note by the translator [p.56n], Turgot uses the term "Capitalistes Entrepreneurs".

expenditures on the part of the different classes of society, the Entrepreneurs cease to get back their advances with the profit they have a right to expect from them, it is evident that they will be obliged to reduce their undertakings; that the amount of labour, the amount of consumption of the fruits of the earth, the amount of production and the amount of revenue will be reduced in like measure; that poverty will take the place of wealth, and that the common Workmen, ceasing to find employment, will fall into the extremest destitution" [p.63].

There is just a hint there of some cause (in addition to "frictions which delay the results") which is responsible for the disruption of circulation. But it is difficult to be certain.

It takes another dozen Looking-Glass years before the emergence of someone who has circulation, as it were, in his blood — the court physician to Madame Pompadour.

CHAPTER 35

FRANÇOIS QUESNAY (1694 - 1774)

Quesnay's *Tableau Économique*, published in 1758, is unique in its emphasis on the circulation of wealth through the body of the economy. In the words of the Marquis de Mirabeau: "There are three marvellous inventions in the world, *writing, money and the Tableau Economique*" [quoted in Blanqui (1837) p.357].

In spite of his commitment to the Physiocratic doctrine that land, rather than labour, is the ultimate source of value, Quesnay is clearly a devoted disciple of Adam Smith.

The Looking-Glass debt to Adam Smith is obvious from Quesnay's insistence on the Law of Competition. "Absolute freedom of trade should be maintained; for the management of domestic and foreign trade, which is the most reliable, the most precise, and of the greatest benefit to the whole nation, is complete freedom of competition."*

Quesnay's major advance beyond Smith comes with his statement of the Law of Circulation in the first of his maxims (quoted once before in ch.31) "that the whole of the ... revenue enters into the annual circulation, and runs through it to the full extent of its course; and that it is never formed into monetary fortunes, or at least that those which are formed are counterbalanced by those which come back into circulation; for otherwise these monetary fortunes would check the flow of a part of this annual revenue of the Nation, and hold back the money stock or finance of the kingdom, to the detriment of the return of the advances, the payment of the artisans' wages, the reproduction of the revenue, and the taxes" [1758, p.3].

Quesnay's condemnation of "sterile saving, which would deduct from circulation and distribution a portion of their revenues or gains" [p.4], follows logically from the Law of Circulation. But it marks a clean break with Classical Orthodoxy. It is a repudiation of Adam Smith's view that "capitals are increased by parsimony, and diminished by prodigality and misconduct. ... Every prodigal appears to be a public enemy, and every frugal man a public benefactor" [1776, II,3].

---

* This is a home-made translation of "QU'ON maintienne l'entiere liberté du commerce: CAR LA POLICE DU COMMERCE INTÉRIEUR ET EXTÉRIEUR LA PLUS SURE, LA PLUS EXACTE, LA PLUS PROFITABLE A LA NATION ET A L'ÉTAT, CONSISTE DANS LA PLEINE LIBERTÉ DE LA CONCURRENCE" [1758, trans. note 46, p.11].

It marks the establishment of a multi-gear view of the economy in the mainstream of economic thought.

Commenting on the progress of economic theory, Blanqui observes that "after Quesnay came Turgot; after Turgot, Adam Smith; science henceforth marches with giant steps" [1837, p.365].

But see what happens when that comment is recast in a Looking-Glass perspective. "After Smith comes Turgot; after Turgot, François Quesnay; science henceforth marches with giant steps which are even greater."

For, after the Physiocrats, come the businessmen.

CHAPTER 36

RICHARD CANTILLON (1680? - 1734)

Richard Cantillon, author of the *Essai Sur La Nature Du Commerce*, is a bit of a mystery. He was either a Frenchman living in England who wrote in French; or else he was an Englishman living in France who wrote in English — and was translated into French. But he might have been an Irishman (which sounds a reasonable compromise). After a successful career in Paris as a banker (or was it as a swindler?), he retired to England with a hard-earned fortune and the good wishes of grateful clients; or else he fled to England with his ill-gotten gains after evading the law-suits of his ruined victims. He died in a fire while reading in bed by the light of a wobbly candle; or else he got himself stabbed after an injudicious complaint to an over-sensitive chef.

He owes his vaguely Malthusian reputation to the quotability of a single memorable sentence. "Men multiply like Mice in a barn if they have unlimited means of subsistence" [1732, p.83]. But his *Essay on the Nature of Trade* is praised by Jevons as "the first systematic Treatise on Economics"* — a compliment which turns out to be even more apt in the Looking-Glass world where time runs backwards.

The Importance of Competition

On the multi-gear economic skeleton inherited from the Physiocrats, Cantillon puts some flesh.

The hero of the piece is a character called the "entrepreneur".† "These Entrepreneurs can never know how great will be the demand in their City, nor how long their customers will buy of them since their rivals will try all sorts of means to attract customers from them. All this causes so much

* Stanley Jevons's article on Richard Cantillon is reprinted on pp.333-360 of the translation, and it is followed by Henry Higgs's account of his strange life and death. Cantillon's *Essay* is thought to have been written between 1730 and his death in 1734. (To split the difference, 1732 is used for references in the text.)

† The term first appears in Say's *Treatise* [1803]; it is used sparingly by Turgot in his *Reflections* [1770]; but by the 1730s it is apparently so common that Cantillon is able to make frequent reference to the "entrepreneur" with full confidence in his readers' familiarity with the term.

In the quotations, the original French "entrepreneur" (literally "enterpriser" — a businessman who risks *his own* capital) is retained in preference to the term "undertaker" favoured by the translator. Cantillon includes farmers within his definition: "Le Fermier est un Entrepreneur" [p.46].

uncertainty among these Entrepreneurs that every day one sees some of them become bankrupt" [1732, p.51].

In this competitive atmosphere, "prices are fixed by the proportion between the produce exposed for sale and the money offered for it" [p.13]. But the state of supply and demand, "often depends upon the eagerness or easy temperament of a few Buyers or Sellers" [p.119].

Unable to break free from the obsession with intrinsic value, however, Cantillon combines Smith's labour theory with Quesnay's land theory. "The Price and Intrinsic Value of a Thing in general is the measure of the Land and Labour which enter into its Production" [p.27] — or, in Marxist terminology, the land and labour "socially necessary" for its production. This raises the question why "it often happens that many things which have actually this intrinsic value are not sold in the Market according to that value" [p.29]. For Cantillon admits that "if the Farmers in a State sow more corn than usual, much more than is needed for the year's consumption, the real and intrinsic value of the corn will correspond to the Land and Labour which enter into its production; but as there is too great an abundance of it and there are more sellers than buyers the Market Price of the Corn will necessarily fall below the intrinsic price or Value" [pp.29,31].

Cantillon is able to achieve a reconciliation between intrinsic value and market value because he sees clearly that the process is demand driven. Production follows demand in markets full of competing entrepreneurs. "They will not fail to change from year to year the use of the land till they arrive at proportioning their production pretty well to the consumption of the Inhabitants" [p.63]. "But the impossibility of proportioning the production of merchandise and produce in a State to their consumption causes a daily variation, and a perpetual ebb and flow in Market Prices. However in well organised Societies the Market Prices of articles whose consumption is tolerably constant and uniform do not vary much from the intrinsic value" [p.31].

What gives Cantillon the edge over Smith and Marx is his use of marginal analysis in describing the formation of market prices by the bargaining between buyers and sellers. In an illustration [1732, pp.119,121] (based, no doubt, on Böhm-Bawerk's "marginal pairs" [1888]), the market price is determined at the point where the enjoyment derived by the least enthusiastic consumer is just sufficient to cover the costs incurred by the most reluctant producer.

Ultimately, however, "intrinsic value" theories have a nasty habit of turning out to be circular arguments.

The Quantity Theory of Money

On the question of money, Cantillon is an enlightened quantity theorist. In place of the crude Friedmanite "helicopter" arguments presented by twentieth-century academics and nineteenth-century philosophers, there is an eighteenth-century businessman's practical appreciation of the importance of the velocity of circulation.

"An increase of actual money causes in a State a corresponding increase of consumption which gradually brings about increased prices" [p.163]. But Cantillon insists that it is always necessary to take into account "la vîtesse de sa circulation" [p.130] — the "velocity of circulation." "An acceleration or greater rapidity in the circulation of money in exchange, is equivalent to an increase of actual money up to a point" [p.161].

"Money will be valued according to the quantity of it in circulation proportionably to its power of exchange against all other merchandise and produce, and their value will be arrived at roughly by the altercations of the Markets" [p.177]. It depends how "this new quantity of money will spread itself [and how it influences] the rapidity in the circulation of money" [p.177]. "The proportion of the dearness which the increased quantity of money brings about in the State will depend on the turn which this money will impart to consumption and circulation" [p.179].

The issue is complicated by commercial credit. "When there is great confidence in the Banks and in book credits less money will suffice, as also when the rapidity of circulation is accelerated in any other way" [p.149]. "The new money gives a new turn to consumption and even a new speed to circulation. But it is not possible to say exactly to what extent" [p.181]. "By doubling the quantity of money in a State the prices of products and merchandise are not always doubled" [p.177].

Cantillon does not assume that activity will automatically return to normal after an interval of monetary adjustment. In this he is in advance even of Hume.

Although Hume's single-gear vision of the economy is more enlightened than that of the nineteenth and twentieth centuries, it is still a single-gear vision. Like John Stuart Mill, whenever the theoretical going gets tough, he runs for cover. Time and again, in his writings on economics, Hume takes refuge in the nineteenth-century argument that the number of shining bits of metal cannot make any real difference. This enables him to expose the common fallacy that changes in the quantity of money automatically affect the rate of interest.

"It is in vain ... to look for the cause of the fall or rise of interest in the greater or less quantity of gold and silver, which is fixed in any nation"

[1752c, pp.48,49]. "High interest arises from *three* circumstances: A great demand for borrowing; little riches to supply that demand; and great profits arising from commerce: And these circumstances are a clear proof of the small advance of commerce and industry, not of the scarcity of gold and silver" [p.49]. "This money, however abundant, ... would only serve to encrease the prices of every thing, without any farther consequence. ... The overplus of borrowers above that of lenders continuing still the same, there will follow no reduction of interest. That depends upon another principle; and must proceed from an encrease of industry and frugality, of arts and commerce" [p.51].

Valuable though Hume's contribution undoubtedly is, Cantillon's is far more realistic.

"Just as the Prices of things are fixed in the altercations of the Market by the quantity of things offered for sale in proportion to the quantity of money offered for them, or, what comes to the same thing, by the proportionate number of Sellers and Buyers, so in the same way the Interest of Money in a State is settled by the proportionate number of Lenders and Borrowers" [1732, p.199]. "It is a common idea ... that the increased quantity of currency in a State brings down the price of Interest there, because when Money is plentiful it is more easy to find some to borrow. This idea is not always true or accurate" [p.213]. "If the abundance of money in the State comes from the hands of money-lenders it will doubtless bring down the current rate of interest by increasing the number of money-lenders: but if it comes from the intervention of spenders it will have just the opposite effect and will raise the rate of interest by increasing the number of Entrepreneurs who will have employment from this increased expense, and will need to borrow to equip their business in all classes of interest" [p.215].

In terms of the "equation of exchange", $MV = PT$,* the crude twentieth-century classical approach is to apply the "ceteris paribus assumption" to V and to T, so that a change in quantity of money produces a proportional increase in the level of prices. Cantillon points out that the method of changing M may affect V, so that the change in P is not necessarily proportionate.

That still leaves open the question of changes in T, the level of activity.

The Multi-Gear Economy

Coming close on the heels of Quesnay and the Physiocrats, Cantillon shares their view of the economy as a multi-gear machine. His suggestion

* See p.142 above.

for stimulating employment has a curiously old-fashioned Keynesian flavour.

"If enough employment cannot be found to occupy ... persons ... upon work useful and profitable to the State, I see no objection to encouraging employment which serves only for ornament or amusement. ... How little soever the labour of a Man supplies ornament or even amusement in a State it is worth while to encourage it unless the Man can find a way to employ himself usefully" [pp.91,93].

As Cantillon is one of the first of Adam Smith's Looking-Glass successors to recognise the Law of Circulation, it is a shame that his work is marred by two serious breaches of the Law of Competition.

The first comes at the end of his discussion of foreign trade. This is particularly regrettable, because the discussion begins in a most promising fashion.

Foreign Trade

One of the lingering superstitions, which is said to have originated in the beliefs of the primitive ancients who lived in the twentieth century, is the strange notion that imports are bad and exports are good. To Cantillon, foreign trade is no different from any other kind of trade. The advantage consists in the goods and services which are received (or imported); the disadvantage consists in the goods and services which have to be paid (or exported) in exchange.*

Because he believes that land is the scarcest factor of production, he is dismayed at the "great amount of produce of the Land ... withdrawn from the subsistence of the French" [p.77] and exported in return for foreign frippery. "When the Nobility and Proprietors of Land draw from Foreign Manufactures their Cloths, Silks, Laces, etc. and pay for them by sending to the Foreigner their native produce they diminish extraordinarily the food of the People and increase that of Foreigners who often become Enemies of the State" [p.75]. "But if Gold and Silver be attracted from abroad in exchange for the Labour of the People, such as Manufactures and articles which contain little of the produce of the soil, this will enrich the State in a useful and essential manner" [p.91].

Because he is convinced of the benefit of buying from abroad, he favours the accumulation of currency reserves. "As Gold and Silver can always buy [imports], even from the Enemies of the State, Gold and Silver

* Cantillon, however, is clearly under the influence of his Looking-Glass predecessor, James Mill. "Whatever advantage is derived from trading with [foreign countries], consists in what is received from them, not in what is sent; because that, if not followed by a return, would be altogether a loss" [1821, p.317].

are the true reserve Stock of a State, and the larger or smaller actual quantity of this Stock necessarily determines the comparative greatness of Kingdoms and States" [pp.89,91]. Nevertheless, he refuses to countenance government intervention by means of currency controls. "Those who have practical knowledge of [trade] ... are rightly astonished that those who govern States ... have so little knowledge of the nature of exchanges as to forbid the export of bullion and specie of gold and silver. The only way to keep them in a State is so to conduct foreign trade that the balance is not adverse to the State" [p.267].

So far, Cantillon's free-trade credentials sound impeccable. The cause of the blot on his copy-book is either a severe bout of acute xenophobia or else a mistranslation of Clausewitz's dictum. The result is an apparent belief that "foreign trade is nothing but a continuation of war with the admixture of different means".

Although he emphasises the advantage of foreign trade, Cantillon seems to imply that the advantage is not mutual. For he claims that the burden of having to export is of no benefit "unless an equally considerable amount of produce be brought back in exchange" [p.77].

If only one party gains, international trade is an opportunity to exploit or be exploited by others, and the sole object of the exercise is to do unto foreigners before they do unto you. Consequently, Cantillon's advice sounds suspiciously protectionist. "In order that the consumption of the Manufactures of a State should become considerable in foreign parts, these Manufactures must be made good and valuable by a large consumption in the interior of the State. It is needful to discourage all foreign Manufactures and to give plenty of employment to the inhabitants" [p.91].

The other skeleton in Cantillon's cupboard is a remedy for inflation reminiscent of the wildest interventionist excesses of ancient twentieth-century Friedmanites. "The Prince or the Legislator ought to withdraw money from circulation ... and try to retard its circulation, ... so as to forestall the too great dearness of its articles" [p.185].

It is, however, necessary to make allowances. After all, there is still a full Looking-Glass century to elapse before the emergence of true free-traders like Malynes, Misselden, and Mun. On the other hand, the age of wholehearted acceptance of the multi-gear economy is not far away.

CHAPTER 37

BERNARD MANDEVILLE (1670 - 1733)

" . . . whilst Luxury
Employ'd a Million of the Poor,
And odious Pride a Million more.
Envy it self and Vanity
Were Ministers of Industry;
Their darling Folly, Fickleness
In Diet, Furniture, and Dress,
That strange ridic'lous Vice, was made
The very Wheel that turn'd the Trade.
. . . .
Thus every Part was full of Vice,
Yet the whole Mass a Paradice."
[*The Fable of the Bees*, pp.67,68].

Books on economics do not normally become popular best-sellers. One of the few exceptions is *The Fable of the Bees* written by Bernard Mandeville, a doctor of medicine (born and educated in Holland) who practised in London. *The Fable* started life in 1705 as a short satirical poem which attracted little attention. Several editions later, with the addition of a series of explanatory *Remarks*, it had grown into a large book.*

It might have been forgotten, but for an incredible stroke of good fortune. In 1723, it was condemned by a Grand Jury, denounced in the press, and attacked from the pulpit. With that sort of publicity, it could not fail.

The flavour of the book is conveyed by its subtitle: *Private Vices, Publick Benefits*. It is easy to see why its application to conventional morality might give offence to the conventionally moral.

"Honour is ... directly opposite to Religion. The one bids you bear Injuries with Patience, the other tells you if you don't resent them, you are

* According to the editor's introduction [pp.9-11], the work first "appeared as an anonymous sixpenny pamphlet in 1705 and was called *The Grumbling Hive: or, Knaves Turn'd Honest*. ... In 1714, ... [it was] reissued ... along with a series of twenty prose remarks under the title of *The Fable of the Bees: or, Private Vices, Publick Benefits* ... [at] less than half the length to which it would eventually grow. After another interval of nine years, ... Mandeville published in 1723 a new edition ... which had been greatly expanded. ... The following year, 1724, *The Fable of the Bees* reached its final form ... including 'A Vindication of the Book' ."

The year 1714 is used for references in the text, since that is the date of the first publication of the poem with the addition of the explanatory prose remarks. Quotations are from the final version, which includes replies to criticism.

not fit to live. Religion commands you to leave all Revenge to God, Honour bids you trust your Revenge to no body but your self, even where the Law wou'd do it for you. Religion plainly forbids Murther, Honour openly justifies it. Religion bids you not shed Blood upon any account whatever, Honour bids you fight for the least Trifle. Religion is built on Humility, and Honour upon Pride. How to reconcile them must be left to wiser Heads than mine" [1714, pp.232,233].

His remedy for priests who meddle in politics instead of attending to their pastoral duties is that "the Clergy [be] allow'd no greater Share in State Affairs than our Saviour has bequeathed them in his Testament" [p.142].

And there are others who are not always treated with the respect to which they believe they are entitled. "Most of the Common Council of the City would make but very indifferent Foot Soldiers; and … if your Horse was to be compos'd of Aldermen, … a small Artillery of Squibs would be sufficient to rout them" [p.144].

Another source of irritation is his habit of exposing all kinds of human weakness. Targets include men who "love out of Vanity; they take delight in a Handsome Wife, as a Coxcomb does in a Fine Horse, not for the use he makes of it, but because it is His" [p.237].

Protesting that his book has "been condemn'd by thousands who never saw a word of it" [p.58], Mandeville declares that the object of his remarks is that "the People, who continually find Fault with others, by reading them, would be taught to look at home, and examining their own Consciences, be made asham'd of always railing at what they are more or less guilty of themselves" [p.55].

A suspicion that the loudest complaints about traffic congestion tend to come from the two-car family is detectable in his reply to those who grumble about "the stinking Streets of *London*" [p.58]. "What offends them is the result of the Plenty, great Traffick and Opulency of that mighty City. … If we mind the Materials of all sorts that must supply such an infinite number of Trades and Handicrafts, as are always going forward; the vast quantity of Victuals, Drink and Fewel that are daily consum'd in it, and the Waste and Superfluities that must be produc'd from them; the multitudes of Horses and other Cattle that are always dawbing the Streets, the Carts, Coaches and more heavy Carriages that are perpetually wearing and breaking the Pavement of them, and above all the numberless swarms of People that are continually harrassing and trampling through every part of them … it is impossible *London* should be more cleanly before it is less flourishing" [p.57].

The author is probably justified in concluding that "it is chiefly Self Love that has gain'd this little Treatise ... so many Enemies; every one looks upon it as an affront done to himself, because it detracts from the Dignity, and lessens the fine notions he had conceiv'd of Mankind" [p.240].

The exposure of hypocrisy always has a ready audience, but a work is unlikely to achieve real popularity unless it is in tune with the spirit of the times.

The reason for interest in *The Fable of the Bees* (both then and now) is that it reflects the everyday concerns of the eighteenth-century man in the eighteenth-century street.

Top of the list is the creeping commercialisation of health care.

> "Physicians valued Fame and Wealth
> Above the drooping Patient's Health" [p.65].

Next come the lawyers and accountants who

> "Examin'd and survey'd the Laws;
> As Burglars Shops and Houses do;
> To find out where they'd best break through" [p.65].

Although this type of sentiment tends to go down well with the general public, it is not calculated to win applause from those professions, which, instead of striving to close loopholes in the law, seek to profit from exploiting them.

Mandeville voices the popular anxiety about the menace from vicious dogs. "Those of a true fighting Breed, being voracious Creatures, both Male and Female, will fasten upon any thing, and suffer themselves to be kill'd before they give over" [p.217].

And he is deeply concerned about the lack of opportunity for women in society. "*Miss* is scarce three Years old, but she's spoke to every Day to hide her Leg, and rebuk'd in good Earnest if she shews it; whilst *Little Master* at the same Age is bid to take up his Coats, and piss like a Man" [p.97].

Perhaps most remarkable of all is his sensitivity to the distress likely to be caused by sexual harassment, — particularly as practised by wives who do not "scruple to Employ the most tender Minutes of Wedlock ... and act the Harlots with their Husbands! Nay, she is worse than Whore, who impiously profanes and prostitutes the Sacred Rites of Love to Vile Ignoble Ends; that first excites to Passion and invites to Joys with seeming Ardour, then racks our fondness for no other purpose than to extort a Gift, whilst full of Guile in Counterfeited Transports she watches for the Moment when Men can least deny" [p.238].

But he is refreshingly frank in admitting that men can be just as bad: — "if a Man should tell a Woman, that he could like no body so well to propagate his Species upon, as her self, and that he found a violent Desire that Moment to go about it, and accordingly offer'd to lay hold of her for that Purpose" [p.105].

Mandeville is a sincere campaigner for animal rights. "If it was not for this Tyranny which Custom usurps over us, … Men of any tollerable good Nature could never be reconcil'd to the killing of so many Animals for their daily Food, as long as the bountiful earth so plentifully provides them with varieties of vegetable Dainties" [p.191]. "In such perfect Animals as Sheep and Oxen, in whom the Heart, the Brain and Nerves differ so little from ours, and in whom the Separation of the Spirits from the Blood, the Organs of Sense, and consequently Feeling itself, are the same as they are in Human Creatures, I can't imagine how a Man not hardned in Blood and Massacre, is able to see a violent Death, and the Pangs of it, without Concern" [p.192].

To illustrate his point, Mandeville delivers a moving rebuke to the Merchant who, having been cornered by a talking lion, pleads for his life "reasoning from the excellency of Man's Nature and Abilities".

"Oh Vain and Covetous Animal, (*said the Lyon*) whose Pride and Avarice can make him leave his Native Soil, where his natural Wants might be plentifully supply'd, and try rough Seas and dangerous Mountains to find out Superfluities, why should you esteem your Species above ours? … 'Tis only Man, mischievous Man, that can make Death a sport, Nature taught your Stomach to crave nothing but Vegetables; but your violent fondness to change, and greater eagerness after Novelties, have prompted you to the Destruction of Animals without Justice or necessity. … Your squeamish Stomach … won't so much as admit of the most tender Parts of them, unless above half the Concoction has been perform'd by artificial Fire before hand. … Ungrateful and perfidious Man feeds on the Sheep that Cloaths him, and spares not her innocent young ones, whom he has taken into his care and custody. If you tell me the Gods made Man Master over all other Creatures, what Tyranny was it then to destroy them out of wantonness?" [pp.194-197].

It goes without saying that a man with such a deep understanding of women and animals is able to bring to bear a penetrating insight into the principles of economics.

At what is now called the "microeconomic level", Mandeville is a firm believer in market forces. He goes so far as to recommend that they should be harnessed in the fight against crime. "Where Six or Seven Thousand Sailors arrive at once … that have seen none but their own Sex for many Months together, how is it to be suppos'd that honest Women should walk the Streets unmolested, if there were no Harlots to be had at reasonable Prices" [pp.127,128].

If this sounds a little too permissive for the twentieth century, Mandeville's defence may be worth considering. "It is Wisdom in all Governments to bear with lesser Inconveniencies to prevent greater. If Courtezans and Strumpets were to be prosecuted with as much Rigour as some silly People would have it, what Locks or Bars would be sufficient to preserve the Honour of our Wives and Daughters?" [p.127].

The most remarkable achievement of *The Fable of the Bees*, however, is in the field of macroeconomics.

With the benefit of Looking-Glass hindsight, Mandeville is able to reconcile Say's *Treatise* [1803] with Keynes's *General Theory* [1936].

He opens with an accurate statement of Say's "Theory of Markets". "Buying is Bartering, and no Nation can buy Goods of others that has none of her own to purchase them with" [1714, pp.138,139]. His commitment to Free Trade and the Law of Competition does not, however, blind him to the importance of the Law of Circulation.

The Fable is full of practical examples of the operation of the Keynesian "multiplier" process. "A Highwayman having met with a considerable Booty, gives a poor common Harlot, he fancys, Ten Pounds to New Rig her from Top to Toe; is there a Spruce Mercer so Conscientious that he will refuse to sell her a Thread Sattin, tho' he knew who she was? ... The Sempstress, the Linnen-draper, all must get something by her, and a hundred different Tradesmen dependent on those she laid her Money out with, may touch part of it before a Month is at an end" [p.120].

The threat to employment from the disruption of circulation, if there is a reduction in effective demand, is clearly spelled out. "Frugality is ... an idle dreaming Virtue that employs no Hands, and therefore very useless in a trading Country, where there are vast numbers that one way or other must all be set to Work" [pp.134,135]. "As this prudent Œconomy, which some People call *Saving*, is in Private Families the most certain Method to encrease an estate, so some imagine, that ... the same Method, if generally pursued ... will have the same effect upon a whole Nation, and that, for Example, the *English* might be much richer than they are, if they would be as frugal as some of their Neighbours. This, I think, is an Error" [p.199].

Adam Smith is not mentioned by name, but there can be no doubt as to the target of Mandeville's criticism. There is, of course, nothing wrong with Smith's common-sense observation that "what is prudence in the conduct of every private family, can scarce be folly in that of a great kingdom" [1776, IV,2]. A nation saves when it manages to produce more than it consumes; and when it saves, it is able to accumulate real wealth. This Mandeville does not deny; what he challenges is the false implication that the nation as a whole saves when private families do nothing more than simply cease to spend. Mandeville will not allow the reader to forget that the error lies in ignoring the adverse effect on production.

Because he is writing at the beginning of the eighteenth century, Mandeville is able to take for granted the generally accepted view of unemployment as a profound social evil. "The Death of half a Million of People could not cause a tenth part of the disturbance to the Kingdom, that the same number of Poor unemploy'd would certainly create, if at once they were to be added to those, that already one way or other are a Burthen to the Society" [1714, p.237]. He reminds his readers that when people are out of work, it is not always for want of trying. "We ought not to confound those who remain unemploy'd for want of an Opportunity of exerting themselves to the best Advantage, with such as for want of Spirit, hug themselves in their Sloth, and will rather starve than stir" [p.250].

Mandeville, is therefore convinced that "the great Art then to make a Nation happy, and what we call flourishing, consists in giving every body an Opportunity of being employ'd" [pp.211,212]. But, with the historical lesson of the 1970s before him, he is not tempted by simple-minded policies of government spending. First of all, he does not entertain a very high opinion of politicians. "Unhappy is the People, and their Constitution will be ever precarious, whose Welfare must depend upon the Virtues and Consciences of Ministers and Politicians" [p.206]. More significantly, he is highly conscious of the dangers of inflation. Like Cantillon, he blames the decline of British industry during the 1970s and 1980s on monetary excess encouraged by the discovery of North Sea Oil.

"*Britain* was a fertile Country, where Trade and Manufactures flourish'd and had a knowing industrious People to boast of. But as soon as ... that Ocean of Treasure came rowling in upon them, it took away their Senses, and their Industry forsook them. ... Gold and Silver [from North Sea Oil] ... have made all Things dear, and most Nations of *Europe* Industrious, except their Owners. ... And thus by *too much Money*, ... *Britain* is from a fruitful and well peopled Country, with all its mighty Titles and Possessions, made a Barren and empty Thorough fair, thro' which Gold and Silver pass from *the North Sea* to the rest of the World, and the Nation, from a rich, acute, diligent and laborious, become a slow, idle, proud and beggarly People" [pp.210,211].*

The quantity of money may have been the occasion of much discussion in the twentieth and the nineteenth centuries, but by Mandeville's time it is commonplace that "the quantity of circulating Coin in a Country ought

* For Looking-Glass purposes, "Britain" takes the place of "Spain" and "North Sea Oil" takes the place of "American Gold and Silver".

always to be proportion'd to the number of Hands that are employ'd" [p.209].

And it is clearly implied that the "proportioning" is not to be done by the government, but is to be left to market forces.

There can be no doubt of Mandeville's faith in the Law of Competition. He is an upholder of Adam Smith's philosophy that "it is not from the benevolence of the butcher, the brewer, or the baker, that we expect our dinner, but from their regard to their own interest. We address ourselves, not to their humanity but to their self-love, and never talk to them of our own necessities but of their advantages" [1776, I,2]. True, he gives it a satirical twist. "No Society can be rais'd, subsist in their Wealth and Power for any considerable Time without the Vices of Man" [1714, p.239]. But that is entirely consistent with his declared object of opening the readers' eyes and forcing them to face the truth whether they like it or not.

It is the same with his commitment to the Law of Circulation.

"In a very Virtuous Age ... no body would dress above his Condition ... or overreach his Neighbour to purchase Finery, and consequently there would not be half the Consumption, nor a third part of the People employ'd as now there are" [p.151]. "This Emulation and continual striving to outdo one another, ... or at least the consequence of it, ... sets the Poor to Work, adds Spurs to Industry, and incourages the skilful Artificer to search after further Improvements" [p.154]. "If an Ill-natur'd Miser, who ... spends but Fifty Pounds a Year, ... should be Robb'd of Five Hundred or a Thousand Guineas, it is certain that as soon as this Money should come to Circulate, the Nation would be the better for the Robbery" [p.119].

Free-market enthusiasts, who are outraged by this warts-and-all caricature of their true-love, condemn *The Fable of the Bees* as an incitement to vice and dishonesty. That is to miss the point. The object of Mandeville's scorn is not freedom of competition but the beatification of Adam Smith.

Mandeville's magnificent achievement cannot be praised too highly. After two and a half Looking-Glass centuries, he succeeds in purging economic theory of its religious overtones. In *The Fable of the Bees*, freedom of competition is essential for economic efficiency, but it is not the solution to all economic problems. Private enterprise is not a religion, nor is competition a god. The message is unmistakable: the market place is a human institution; it has its faults. Far better to come to terms with them, than to pretend that they do not exist.

The funny thing about satire is that what really hurts is the truth. Without it, satire cannot work. If it is false, it loses its bite. Mandeville arouses hostility, not for being economical with the truth, but for being over-generous. *The Fable of the Bees* is therefore highly illuminating for what it reveals about its readers. A constantly recurring theme is the link between consumption and employment (and its corollary, the link between saving and unemployment). Writing early in the eighteenth century, a popular satirist is able to ridicule the operation of a multi-gear economy, only because he is confident that his audience takes it for granted that a competitive economy is a multi-gear machine.

The next encounter on the Looking-Glass journey is with someone who cannot wait to get his hands on the gear-lever.

CHAPTER 38

JOHN LAW (1671 - 1729)

John Law, a Scottish financier who settled in London, is in a class of his own.

In 1694, he fled abroad after killing his opponent in a duel over an *affair de coeur*. In 1720, having engineered one of the most spectacular financial collapses of all time, he fled back home again.

Swashbuckling on that scale is sufficient, in itself, to place him in the very front rank of economists. But there is one outstanding quality which raises him above all the rest: he is neither an academic nor a philosopher. This quality illuminates the whole of his *Money and Trade Considered*, and it shines out in the very first paragraph of the very first chapter.

Law's Microeconomic Theory

"Goods have a Value from the Ufes they are apply'd to; And their Value is Greater or Leffer, not fo much from their more or lefs valuable, or neceffary Ufes: As from the greater or leffer Quantity of them in proportion to the Demand for them. *Example.* Water is of great ufe, yet of little value; Becaufe the Quantity of Water is much greater than the Demand for it. Diamonds are of little ufe, yet of great Value, becaufe the Demand for Diamonds is much greater, than the Quantity of them" [1705, p.4].

Apart from its superiority over Adam Smith's treatment of the paradox of value, there is nothing remarkable about that statement. It is a routine repetition of the principles of supply and demand which can be found in almost every book ever written on the subject. The truly remarkable aspect of that paragraph — the part that contains the brilliant insight — is the full-stop at the end.

It is a full-stop that few other economists are able to achieve. They rush off on a futile search for the philosopher's stone of intrinsic value. Some like Smith and Marx claim to find it in labour; others like Quesnay and the Physiocrats claim to find it in land. It is as if those for whom economics is still a religion are driven by an obsession to justify the perfection of their concept of value. Law, with the Looking-Glass benefit of Mandeville's message, is no longer bound by the constraints of religion.

James Maitland, 8th Earl of Lauderdale, — an anachronism whether time runs backwards or forwards — is one of the few admirers of Smith's *philosophy* with the perception to recognise that most of Smith's economic *analysis* is rubbish and the honesty to say so. He is also one of the few to take Law's side. "There is no fuch thing as intrinfic value" [1804, p.21]. "After this philofopher's ftone many have been in fearch; and not a few, diftinguifhed for their knowledge and their talents, have imagined that in *Labour* they had difcovered what conftituted a real measure of value. ... Mr. LAW'S Treatife on Money, publifhed in Scotland in 1705, feems to convey an accurate idea of the nature of value" [p.23].

To a businessman like John Law — indeed, to anyone who is not a philosopher looking for a grand unifying theory — a market price is a market price. It is not a sign from heaven, nor is it a repository of divine justice. It is simply an indication of the intensity of human desire relative to the means of satisfaction. There is no need to pretend that it is fair and just any more than that the ebb and flow of the tide are fair and just. Nevertheless, a market price is a similarly indispensable aid to economic navigation.

It is difficult to overemphasise the historic significance of this breakthrough in the development of economic thought. It marks the acknowledgment that, however crucial the market-place may be as a disseminator of economic information, it is not a dispenser of social justice.

But that is nothing by comparison with Law's second great contribution: his vision of the economy as a multi-gear machine.

Law's Macroeconomic Theory

Like countless economists, Law makes uses of the proverbial desert island as a simplification of a complex economy. But, in a literature literally littered with littoral illustrations, Law's desert island is different. It is a desert island on which "there are 300 Poor or Idle, who live by Charity" [1705, p.97].

And that is what makes it one of the most significant passages in the whole of economic literature.

When John Law, businessman and financier, indulges in hypothetical speculation, his thoughts are concentrated on the real world, where, as it says in the Bible , "the poor shall never cease out of the land" [Deuteronomy XV,11]; "for ye have the poor always with you" [Matthew XXVI,11].

When academics and philosophers contemplate a desert island economy, they think of Robinson Crusoe. And their conception of Robinson Crusoe is like the famous illustration on the title page of Hobbes's *Leviathan*: a large figure of the sovereign which, on closer inspection, turns out to be composed of minuscule figures of all the citizens. Since a single Robinson Crusoe is fully employed, the preconception is established that a large composite Robinson Crusoe made up of millions of individuals will, as long as communications (i.e. markets) are perfect, also be fully employed.

Instead of following the classical tradition which views the economy as a complex version of a single-gear desert island, Law views the desert island as a simplified version of a multi-gear economy. He argues that "if a Money were eftablif't to pay the Wages of Labour, the 300 Poor might be imployed in manufacturing" [1705, p.98]. "The Paper Money propos'd being always equal in Quantity to the Demand, the People will be employ'd, the Country improv'd, Manufacture advanc'd, Trade Domeftick and Forreign will be carried on, and Wealth and Power attained" [p.102].

This expression of faith in spending as the key to revitalising industry indicates (according to Looking-Glass chronology, at least) that John Law owes just as much to Maynard Keynes as David Hume owes to Milton Friedman.

"Domeftick Trade depends on the Money. A greater Quantity employes more People than a leffer Quantity. A limited Sum can only fet a number of People to Work proportion'd to it, and 'tis with little fuccefs Laws are made, for Employing the Poor or Idle in Countries where Money is fcarce; Good Laws may bring the Money to the full Circulation 'tis capable of, and force it to thofe Employments that are moft profitable to the Country: But no Laws can make it go furder, nor can more People be fet to Work, without more Money to circulate fo, as to pay the Wages of a greater number. They may be brought to work on Credit, and that is not practicable, unlefs the Credit have a Circulation, fo as to fupply the Workman with neceffaries; If that's fuppos'd, then that Credit is Money, and will have the fame effects, on Home, and Forreign Trade" [p.13].

John Law might be less than welcome at the British Treasury; but he could be sure of a receptive audience in Japan's Ministry of Trade and Industry. "Without fome Addition to the Money, 'tis not to be fuppos'd next years Export can be equal to the laft: It will leffen as Money has leffen'd; a part of the People then imploy'd being now idle; not for want of Inclination to work, or for want of Imployers, but for want of Money to imploy them with" [p.35].

Law, with the benefit of over two Looking-Glass centuries of progress in economic thought, is clearer than Keynes that full employment can be achieved without Government intervention. The optimum quantity of money, "being always equal in Quantity to the Demand", would be determined by the market through the agency of the banking system.

"The ufe of *Banks* has been the beft Method yet practis'd for the increafe of Money. ... [A Bank] is a fecure Place, where Merchants may give in Money, and have credit to trade with. Befides the convenience of eafier and quicker Payments, thefe Banks faves the Expenfe of Cafheers, the Expenfe of Bags and Carriage, loffes by bad Money, and the Money is fafer than in the Merchants Houfes, for 'tis lefs lyable to Fire or Robbery, the neceffary Meafures being taken to prevent them" [p.36].

But he warns against the dangers of bank failure caused by excessive creation of credit.

"The whole Sum for which Credit is given, ought to remain there, to be ready at demand. ... So far as they lend they add to the Money, which brings a Profit to the Country, by imploying more People, and extending Trade. ... But the Bank is lefs fure, and tho none fuffer by it, or are apprehenfive of Danger, its Credit being good; Yet if the whole Demands were made, or Demands greater than the remaining Money, they could not all be fatisfied, till the Bank had called in what Sums were lent. The certain good it does, will more than ballance the hazard, tho once in two or three years it failed in payment; providing the Sums lent be well fecured" [p.37].

He also gives due warning of the inflationary dangers of expanding the supply of money beyond the demand.

"If Money were given to a People in greater Quantity than there was a Demand for, Money would fall in its value; but if only given equal to the Demand, it will not fall in value" [p.117].

In view of his subsequent career, these warnings ring out like those of a man on the edge of a precipice who calls out: "Don't fall over the aaaaaaagggghhhhh ...... "

Law's Macroeconomic Practice

The smell left by the collapse of Law's "creative banking" schemes (amid bitter recriminations and accusations of fraud and swindle) still lingers. Respectable economic opinion keeps its distance — it holds its nose and hurries on.

J. S. Mill does not take the risk of contaminating his *Principles* with even a mention of Law's name. In an index which lists almost half a column of various different laws, Samuelson's *Economics* has no place for John. Marshall, who makes no mention of Law in the *Principles* or *Industry and Trade*, refers to him in *Money Credit and Commerce* as "that reckless, and unbalanced but most fascinating genius" [1923, p.41n]. Described by Taussig as "the Scotch schemer and adventurer" [1911, p.387], and by Galbraith as "perhaps the most innovative financial scoundrel of all time" [1987, p.143], John Law seems to have gone down as the Guy Fawkes of economic history: a rebel against orthodox theory who is held up as a shocking example of unorthodox practice — a dreadful warning to others.

An account of the rise and fall of John Law is presented by Jérôme-Adolphe Blanqui in his *History of Political Economy in Europe.* Blanqui's Great Crash of 1721 is not quite as entertaining as Galbraith's Great Crash of 1929; but it is not at all bad.

The "Mississippi Scheme"

Blanqui sets the scene with an envious comment on the development of banking in seventeenth-century England and Holland. "The banks of circulation, especially the Bank of England, gave a more active impulse to all industries, and labor entered upon a new era. ... France alone ... had remained behind; ... while England and Holland, under the auspices of credit, gave birth to marvels" This he contrasts with "the sad diminution of the productive power of France in these deplorable times. ... When Louis XIV died ... the public debt amounted then to more than three milliards, and bankruptcy seemed imminent" [1837, pp.334,335].

Enter our hero.

"It was at this time that John Law made the proposition of a bank of circulation and discount and laid the first foundations of credit in our country. ... He had had a near view of what activity of circulation can do for a country. ... It seemed to him that by assuring to a country the possession of a quantity of money sufficient to command labor, it could be made to attain the highest degree of wealth and power. Now, banks of circulation allowed the place of money to be supplied by credit, which procured for paper the value and utility of coin; and, as there were no limits to the issue of paper money, the public wealth appeared to him henceforth protected against all obstructions. Such was the error of Law: the exaggeration of a good principle. ... He had not considered that money, whether in specie or in paper, must always be proportioned to the quantity of values in way of circulation by exchange, and that money could not give rise to manufactures among a people, without pre-existing labor. The increase of money, without a corresponding increase of exchangeable values, would only cause the prices of things to rise, instead of increasing the real wealth of a nation. But the vast and sure genius of Law had comprehended from the beginning the necessity of furnishing capital to labour, at a low rate" [1837, pp.335,336].

On "the effects produced by Law's bank [at Paris]," Blanqui quotes Dutot: "Abundance soon spread through the cities and the rural districts: ... it awakened industry, it restored the value of all landed property ... ; it lowered the interest on public funds, ... it crushed out usury, ... it caused edifices to be erected in city and country, and the old ones which were falling to ruins, to be repaired, lands to be cultivated" [p.337n].

So far, so good; and, up to that point, Law's operations have Blanqui's approval.

"The success was ... complete and ... decisive. ... Thus Law had realized in less than two years [1716 to 1718] the most brilliant utopias of public and private credit. He had obtained, on an immense scale, results which are still, after a hundred years, centered in a few commercial cities; he had reached, at one single stroke, the end of a course which would have seemed to require several successive generations" [p.338].

It is when Law goes beyond that point, that Blanqui becomes highly critical.

"The bank of circulation established at Paris no longer sufficed for the ambition of Law. ... The mania for colonization, which was then general, afforded him an opportunity to found a commercial company on the banks of the Mississippi. Thus was born the West India Company, with a capital ... composed of ... shares ... under form of notes transferable by endorsement. ... But the safety of the enterprise really depended on the success of the colonial trade of the company. ... Finally, December 4, 1718, two years and a half after its foundation, the bank of Law was declared a royal bank, and ... the king took upon himself henceforth the responsibility for the security of the notes" [pp.338-340]. "Never have theories more adventurous had at their service a power more absolute" [p.342].

Blanqui reserves his strongest criticism for the scheme which he describes as "the most seductive of all; namely, the payment of the public debt" [p.342]. "The shares, almost as soon as issued, rose to three, four, and even ten times their nominal value. ... The French were at a loss where to invest their money, so eager were they to obtain at any price titles to the new loan. ... The folly went so far, that shares rose to thirty times the capital, and speculations in public funds absorbed, as a gulf, all the savings of the rich and poor, in less than a few months. There were soon not enough gold and silver laces at the stores to deck the new aristocracy which sprang from this effervescence of the purse; and the six hundred thousand shares of the India Company came to represent more than ten imaginary milliards. One should have been a witness of some financial infatuations of the present time, to have an idea of the delirium of the time of Law, and the complete blindness into which the mania for speculation had plunged the most reasonable people" [pp.342,3].

The collapse was inevitable. "There was no longer any security possible for a capital carried up to more than ten milliards ... even if the Mississippi had been a veritable Eldorado. ... It was soon necessary to impose by authority a multitude of measures which should have been the result of confidence; and from this moment confidence was shaken. Law supposed the bank notes could be sustained by edicts which forbade their conversion, at Paris, into gold and silver. ... But these vain expedients only hastened the consummation of the catastrophe. ... Then came senseless measures: [including] a prohibition against wearing gems and diamonds, lest people should buy them in exchange for bank-bills. ... The decline in the shares went on, nevertheless, rapidly, to the great despair of the unfortunates who had exchanged real estate for fictitious wealth" [pp.344].

In all the main essentials, Law's Mississippi Scheme is the same as every other boom-and-bust financial speculation, from the South Sea Bubble to the Great Crash of 1929, — conclusive proof that financiers, at any rate, *do* learn from history. The secret of financial perpetual motion never seems to change. You spend lots of money that you haven't got — on shares in property which doesn't really exist. The share price shoots upwards (in obedience to the laws of supply and demand); which means that the shares can be used as security to borrow more money to buy more shares. Rising demand boosts the share price, and the rising share price boosts the demand — *ad infinitum* or *ad carcerem*,* whichever is the sooner.

Galbraith's comments on the Great Crash of 1929 serve equally well to summarise the success and failure of the Mississippi Scheme. "In 1929 the discovery of the wonders of the geometric series struck Wall Street with a force comparable to the invention of the wheel" [1954, p.83]. "Geometric series are equally dramatic in reverse" [p.85].

Blanqui blames the ultimate disaster, not on Law, but on "the avidity of courtiers and the folly of speculators. The shares had already risen to a rate which neither the securities offered by the company, nor even the most exaggerated chances of profit, justified. Operations were no longer anything but gambling. ... The public reaped, in truth, what they had sown. Was it not they who had caused the prices of shares to rise to an exaggerated figure, and who had thus artificially increased their value, so as to render impossible the payment of interest proportionate to a capital so enormous!" [1837, pp.341 and 346]. Galbraith is more succinct: "Men have been swindled by other men on many occasions. The autumn of 1929 was, perhaps, the first occasion when men succeeded on a large scale in swindling themselves" [1954, p.146].

No less breathtaking than Law's Mississippi Scheme is Blanqui's attitude towards it.

---

* A Latin word meaning "gaol".

The "Classical" Verdict on "Keynesian" Excess

Blanqui is a classical economist commenting on the downfall of a Keynesian. Now Blanqui is not just any old classical economist; he is the fervent disciple and hero-worshipper of Say. And Law is not just any old Keynesian. He is the perpetrator of a scheme which Keynes, even in his wildest imaginings, would never have contemplated; and the scheme ended after two years in total ruin.

It is instructive to compare the Monetarist view of Keynes's success with Blanqui's view of Law's failure.

The Monetarist attitude to the twenty-five Keynesian years of low inflation and low unemployment from 1945 until 1970 can be summed up fairly accurately by the adaptation of an old story:

In his youth, the Keynesian was a bit of a tearaway. "Mark my words," said the Monetarist, "that lad will come to a sticky end." As an adult, the Keynesian turned out to be something of a playboy. "Mark my words," said the Monetarist, "that man will come to a sticky end." When, at last, the Keynesian died in his bed at the age of ninety-three, "There you are," said the Monetarist, "I told you he'd come to a sticky end."

What does Blanqui (who is more classical than the Monetarists) have to say about Law (who is more Keynesian than Keynes) and his spectacular achievement (the collapse of the French banking system and the virtual bankruptcy of the economy)?

A disciple of Say's is entitled to indulge in a certain amount of gloating. Instead of adopting the expected I-told-you-so attitude, however, Blanqui makes excuses on Law's behalf. "Confidence was general; the error of Law lay in the abuse of it. The regent led him into this by degrees, in the intention of paying off the national debt; and he forced him, to use the expression of a contemporary [Dutot], "to raise seven stories on foundations that he had laid for only three." " [1837, p.347]. "If Law had remained faithful to the true principles of credit which he had so well developed in his *Considerations on Money*, he would have raised France ... to the first rank among financial powers, and perhaps prevented the terrible catastrophes by which the latter part of the eighteenth century was agitated" [p.346].

"Such was the error of Law: the exaggeration of a good principle" [p.336].

No believer in the modern version of what is supposed to be "Say's Law" could seriously describe Law's fiasco as the "exaggeration of a good principle" (nor could he refer to Law's "vast and sure genius"). Those are not exactly the words which would fall from the lips of a twentieth-century monetarist.

From a believer in a multi-gear economy, however, the verdict is not quite so odd. The "good principle" is to get the economy into top gear. The "exaggeration" is the delusion that the machine can subsequently be made to go even faster by pouring in more fuel. The reality is that monetary excess will overheat and ultimately blow-up the engine.

This is not inconsistent with Say's own views.

"A national debt of moderate amount, the capital of which should have been well and judiciously expended in useful works, might indeed be attended with the advantage of providing an investment for minute portions of capital, in the hands of persons incapable of turning them to account, who would probably keep them locked up. ... This is perhaps the sole benefit of a national debt" [1803, p.481].

But there are obvious dangers.

"Public credit affords such facilities to public prodigality, that many political writers have regarded it as fatal to national prosperity. For, say they, when governments feel themselves strong in the ability to borrow, they are too apt to intermeddle in every political arrangement, and to conceive gigantic projects, that lead sometimes to disgrace, sometimes to glory, but always to a state of financial exhaustion" [p.483]. A case in point is "the monstrous breach of faith on the part of the French government in 1721, in regard to its paper-money and the Mississippi share-holders" [p.483].

Law's achievement is far more valuable than merely to have bankrupted the French economy. He has some claim to be recognised as a pioneer.

The Achievement of John Law

In the Looking-Glass perspective (apart from some early attempts by Keynes), John Law is the first to have taken the theory of the multi-gear economy and put it into practice. The ultimate failure of his experiment is no less instructive than its early success. For it demonstrates the difficulty of labouring under a handicap from which few commercial enterprises ever recover — enthusiastic government support.

As a result of Law's practical experiment with the multi-gear theory, it is clear that an economy *can* change gear, and, when necessary, *should* change gear.

The question is: whose hand should be on the gear-lever?

A clue to the answer can be found in the work of one of Britain's greatest philosophers.

CHAPTER 39

JOHN LOCKE (1632 - 1704)

In *Some Considerations of the Consequences of the Lowering of Interest, and Raising the Value of Money*, John Locke gets straight to the point.

"The firft thing to be confider'd, is, Whether the Price of the Hire of Money can be regulated by *Law*. And to that I think, generally fpeaking, one may fay, 'tis manifeft it cannot" [1691, p.1].

Not bad for a first page.

The rest of the book merely demonstrates the excellence of seventeenth-century economics. But those two sentences contain everything that needs to be said about the conduct of monetary policy.

All that remains is to have them carved in stone over the entrance of the British Treasury. If the stone is massive, and if it is designed to fall on the head of any passing Chancellor of the Exchequer who believes that he himself or a Monetary Policy Committee, rather than the market, is to be the judge of the price and quantity of money, then so much the better.

The principle demonstrated practically by John Law is argued philosophically by John Locke. The economy *can* change gear, and, when necessary, *should* change gear. But the gear-lever has to be kept out of the "intermeddling" hands of governments (however well-intentioned) and policy committees (however independent).

This is not yet a positive solution, but it clears the ground for the economist, to whom all the rest — from the twentieth century, to the nineteenth century, to the eighteenth century — are merely forerunners.

CHAPTER 40

SIR WILLIAM PETTY (1623 - 1687)

John Law and Bernard Mandeville can be regarded as iconoclasts who defy the authority of the economic Church. Sir William Petty goes further. He simply refuses to recognise economics as a religion and treats it as a science instead.

Having dropped a hint in the title of his *Political Arithmetick*, he explains the nature of his scientific revolution in the preface. "I have taken the course ... to express my self in Terms of *Number, Weight*, or *Measure*; ... leaving those [Arguments] that depend upon the mutable Minds, Opinions, Appetites, and Passions of particular Men, to the Consideration of others" [1676, p.244].

Although Petty is a deeply religious man who often refers to the Scriptures, he is also an emancipated man who believes in liberty of conscience. And he adopts the same attitude towards the study of economics. His criticism of "Hypocrites, especially such as abuse holy Religion to cloak and vizzard worldly ends" [1662, p.71], is a rebuke to those who break the third commandment. It is also a reproach to those who indulge in the twentieth century habit of settling economic issues, not on their own merits, but in obedience to some doctrine based on an act of faith.

Whereas the twentieth century is an age of intolerance in the study of economics, the seventeenth century is an age of enlightenment.

The problems which Petty discusses are not far removed from those of the present day. They include: the poll-tax — inner city decay — unemployment — inflation — crime — privatisation — and the Irish Question. The main difference is that Petty is able to discuss them free from the constraints imposed by economic theology.

The Poll-Tax

Commenting on the poll-tax fiasco "in which ... great mistakes were committed" [1662, p.34], Petty is highly critical of "the simple Poll-money upon every head of all mankinde alike. ... The evil of this way is, that it is very unequal; men of unequal abilities, all paying alike" [p.62]. "Council-charge" modifications based on property values are not, in his opinion, a great deal of help. "The Poll-moneys which have been leavied of late have been wonderfully confused; as taxing some rich single persons at the lowest rate; ... making ... some to pay according to their Estates, the same to be valued by those that know them not" [p.62].

The Inner-Cities

Petty expresses great concern over the problem of urban decay, particularly in "such excessive and overgrown Cities [as] *London*. … The dwellings of the West end are so much the more free from the fumes, steams, and stinks of the whole Easterly Pyle" [1662, pp.40,41]. He complains that buildings in the inner cities are neglected "until they become fundamentally irreparable, at which time they become either the dwelling of the Rascality, or in process of time return to waste and Gardens again. … This we see in *London*, where the Noblemens ancient houses are now become Halls for Companies or turned into Tenements" [p.41]. Petty does "not doubt but that five hundred years hence, the King's Pallace will be near *Chelsey*, and the old building of *Whitehall* converted to uses more answerable to their quality" [p.42]. Whether that includes becoming "the dwelling of the Rascality" he is too polite to say.

The Market

Petty's views on the economy are clearly influenced by his medical background. "Anatomy is not only necessary in Physicians, but laudable in every Philosophical person whatsoever" [1672, p.129]. He is therefore conditioned to be highly sceptical about government intervention. "As wiser Physicians tamper not excessively with their Patients, rather observing and complying with the motions of nature, then contradicting it with vehement Administrations of their own; so in Politicks and Oconomicks the same must be used" [1662, p.60].

As evidence of the futility of trying to beat the market, he cites "the vanity and fruitlessness of making Civil Positive Laws against the Laws of Nature" [p.48].

Crime

Petty's views on crime and punishment are market-related.

"The State by killing, mutilating, or imprisoning their members, do withall punish themselves; wherefore such punishments ought (as much as possible) to be avoided and commuted for pecuniary mulcts, which will encrease labour and publick wealth" [1662, p.68]. "Nor does the Gospel specifie any punishment in this world, onely declaring they shall not be received into the joyes of the next" [p.70].

The notion that the State should be kept out of the business of punishment is a fundamentalist interpretation of a well-known Biblical injunction. "To me *belongeth* vengeance" [Deuteronomy, XXXII, 35]. "Vengeance *is* mine; I will repay, saith the Lord" [Romans, XII, 19].

Petty's idea that the responsibility of the State should be restricted to the protection of its citizens is motivated neither by misplaced compassion for the offender nor by disregard of the victim.

Those guilty of violent crime would have to be imprisoned, not as a punishment, but for the protection of their fellow citizens.

Those guilty of economic crime, instead of being kept in jail at the state's expense and without compensation to the victim, would be compelled to work (for the rest of their lives, if necessary) until they had made full restitution to their victims.

Privatisation and the Irish Question

What sets Petty out from other economists, is the strength of his commitment to full-blooded privatisation — not the milk-and-water privatisation of a few monopolies popular in the 1980s — but the mother of all privatisation proposals.

His solution to the problem of Ireland is simple. Sell it!

"I have heard many Wise Men ... bewailing the vast losses of the *English*, in preventing and suppressing Rebellions in *Ireland*, and considering how little profit hath returned, either to the King or Subjects of *England*, for their Five Hundred Years doing and suffering in that Country; ... wish that ... *Island* were sunk under Water" [1676, p.285,286]. Petty replies "that the benefit of those wishes, may practically be obtained, without sinking that vast Mountainous Island under Water, ... if [it] may be sold for Money" [pp.286,287].

True to the principle of expressing himself "in Terms of *Number, Weight*, or *Measure*", Petty undertakes a careful analysis of the costs and benefits. His seventeenth-century scientific approach to privatisation which relies on monetary calculations is in stark contrast with the twentieth century doctrinaire approach which relies on economic theology.

Having estimated the advantage of getting out of Ireland at "about Sixty nine Millions, Three Hundred thousand Pounds" [p.288], he is able to calculate the expected profit to be made on the transaction. "If any Prince willing to inlarge his Territories, will give any thing more than Six ½ Millions or half the present value for the said relinquished Land, which are estimated to be worth Thirteen Millions; then the whole profit, will be above Seventy Five Millions, and Eight Hundred 600*l*" [p.289].

Economic rationality does not blind him to political reality. Anxieties are relieved with a cast-iron reassurance. "But if any Man shall object, that it will be dangerous unto England, that Ireland should be in the hands of any other Nation, ... whoever shall purchase it ... shall not be more able to annoy England, than now in its united condition" [p.289].

Although Petty admits that it is all a dream, he points out that "the greatest absurdities of Dreams, are but a Preposterous and Tumultuary contexture of realities" [p.286]. And there is no doubt of his attachment to the general principle. "If the *Relict Lands*, and the *immovables* left behind upon them, may be sold for Money; ... then I conceive that the whole proposal will be a pleasant and profitable Dream indeed" [p.287].

It is worth remembering that another of Petty's far-fetched proposals is to "keep all Accompts in a way of Decimal Arithmetick, which hath been long desired for the ease and certainty of Accompts" [1682, p.447].

Inflation

On the subject of money, Petty's writings show what great strides have been made during three Looking-Glass centuries.

"There is a certain measure, and proportion of money requisite to drive the trade of a Nation, more or less then which would prejudice the same" [1662, p.35].* The effect of credit means that "where there are Banks of Money also, there less money is necessary to drive the Trade" [p.36]. The "right" quantity of money depends on the "velocity of circulation" which Petty calls "revolutions and circulations" [1664, p.112].

A medical metaphor comes in useful when trying to determine what quantity is "right". "Money is but the Fat of the Body-politick, whereof too much doth as often hinder its Agility, as too little makes it sick" [p.113].

On the dangers of too much money, he follows the Quantity Theory. "Suppose one shilling were proclaimed to be worth two, what other effect could this have, then the raising of all Commodities unto a double price?" [1662, p.87]. The resulting inflation "amounts to no more then a Tax, upon such People unto whom the State is indebted, or a defalkation of what is due; as also the like burthen upon all that live upon Pensions, established Rents, Annuities, Fees, Gratuities, &c" [p.84]. He emphasises the immorality of such a policy. It "is a very pitiful and unequal way of Taxing the people; and 'tis a sign that the State sinketh, which catcheth hold on such Weeds as are accompanied with the dishonour of impressing a Princes Effigies to justifie Adulterate Commodities, and the Breach of Publick Faith, such as is the calling a thing what it really is not" [p.91].

---

* This may have been derived from Adam Smith's observation that "the value of goods annually bought and sold in any country requires a certain quantity of money to circulate and distribute them to their proper consumers, and can give employment to no more. The channel of circulation necessarily draws to itself a sum sufficient to fill it, and never admits any more" [1776, IV,1].

He ridicules the absurdity of increasing the quantity of money in an effort to achieve prosperity. "If the wealth of the Nation could be decupled by a Proclamation, it were strange that such proclamations have not long since been made by our Governours" [1682, p.442].

In answer to the rhetorical question "Is there any way to know how much Money is sufficient for any Nation?" [p.446], he provides a calculation based upon the total expenses and their frequency. In other words, the "right" quantity of money is not something to be determined by the arbitrary authority of a government minister (however enlightened) or even of a central banker (however independent); it depends entirely on the market.

Unemployment

Because he takes the seventeenth-century view of the economy as a multi-gear machine, he recognises that commercial freedom, though necessary for economic efficiency, is not enough. Obedience to the Law of Competition has to be accompanied by respect for the Law of Circulation. Unemployment can be caused by lack of spending.

"A hundred pound passing a hundred hands for Wages, causes 10000l. worth of Commodities to be produced, which hands would have been idle and useless, had there not been this continual motive to their employment" [1662, p.36]. "As the most thriving Men keep little or no Money by them, but turn and wind it into various Commodities to their great Profit, so may the whole Nation also; which is but many particular Men united" [1682, p.446]. In the words of Adam Smith, "what is prudence in the conduct of every private family, can scarce be folly in that of a great kingdom" [1776, IV,2].

Petty's views on economic policy are founded on the belief that "the greatness and glory of a Prince lyeth ... in the number, art, and industry of his people, well united and governed" [1662, p.22]. But he does not regard economics as a religion, nor does he see himself as the defender of a faith. Consequently, he has no difficulty in admitting what has been the experience in all countries in every period of history: unemployment is not merely an economic problem, it is also a social evil.

"Causes of Civil War are also, that the Wealth of the Nation is in too few mens hands, ... the allowing Luxury in some, whilst others needlessly starve" [p.23]. "Beggary and Theevery, that is a sure livelihood for men wanting imployment" [p.37].

He does not thereby imply that unemployment is an excuse for crime. On the contrary, he wishes to see "the lazy and thievish restrained and punished by the Minister of Justice" [p.29]. In the seventeenth-century spirit of frankness, he does not use crime as an excuse for the evasion of responsibility towards the unemployed. He accepts, as an obligation, the necessity that "we finde out certain constant Employments for all other indigent people" [p.29]. To the question "what shall these Employments be?", he answers, "such as were reckoned as the sixth Branch of the Publick Expence, *viz.* making all High-wayes so broad, firm, and eaven, as whereby the charge and tedium of travelling and Carriages may be greatly lessened" [p.29].

There is a Looking-Glass echo of Keynes's *General Theory* in Petty's suggestion that any work is better than nothing. " 'Tis no matter if it be employed to build a useless Pyramid upon *Salisbury Plain*, bring the Stones at *Stonehenge* to *Tower-Hill*, or the like; for at worst this would keep their mindes to discipline and obedience, and their bodies to a patience of more profitable labours when need shall require it" [1662, p.31].*

"Money ... expended on Entertainments, magnificent Shews, Triumphal Arches, &c... . is a refunding the said moneys to the Tradesmen who work upon those things; which Trades though they seem vain and onely of ornament, yet they refund presently to the most useful; namely, to Brewers, Bakers, Taylours, Shoemakers, &c" [p.33].† "Better to burn a thousand mens labours for a time, then to let those thousand men by non-employment lose their faculty of labouring" [p.60].

Petty's great achievement is the establishment of the multi-gear view of the economy in the mainstream of economic thought. But the credit for working out the policy implications without falling into the errors of the ancient Keynesians must go to his Looking-Glass successors.

---

* "If the Treasury were to fill old bottles with bank-notes, bury them at suitable depths in disused coal-mines which are then filled up to the surface with town rubbish, and leave it to private enterprise on well-tried principles of *laissez-faire* to dig the notes up again ... there need be no more unemployment. ... It would, indeed, be more sensible to build houses and the like; but if there are political and practical difficulties in the way of this, the above would be better than nothing" [Keynes (1936) p.129].

† It is widely believed that this is the passage which infuriated John Stuart Mill (see p.242 above).

CHAPTER 41

THE "MERCANTILISTS"

The Looking-Glass journey ends in the early 1600s.

Gloriana

The reign of the woman, who had dominated British Politics for so long, had just ended. A staunch believer in her own supremacy over Parliament, she was noted for an autocratic manner which was not always popular with her subjects; and, while her strength of character was respected, her stridency of tone and adoption of masculine political tactics were often the subject of criticism. Although her successor[*] professed to continue in her tradition, he brought to politics a style which was softer and more conciliatory.

In her formative years, the previous monarch had come under the influence of the "New Learning" (particularly on the subject of economics). Her predecessors had drained the treasury by their extravagance. By contrast, she favoured public parsimony, trade liberalisation, and the abolition of monopolies. These aims were achieved more often in appearance than in substance, and the public finances had to be bolstered by revenue from the sale of state assets. Throughout a reign constantly plagued by troubles in Ireland and squabbles with the clergy, she was always able to rely on the loyal support of her faithful adviser, Cecil.[†]

Her moment of greatest peril came after she had encouraged (by a combination of diplomatic feebleness and expenditure cuts in naval defence) a Spanish-speaking autocrat, with whom she was in dispute, to imagine that he could mount a successful invasion. Her reputation was saved by a glorious victory achieved by the gallantry of British troops and the brilliance of their commanders.[‡]

In the aftermath of that victory, her popular support rose to heights rarely enjoyed by so absolute a monarch. But, as memories of military glory gradually faded, economic preoccupations began to reassert themselves.

---

[*] James VI of Scotland and I of England.

[†] William Cecil, 1st Baron Burghley.

[‡] The force which defeated the Spanish Armada in the summer of 1588 was under the command of the Lord High Admiral, Lord Howard of Effingham, on board the *Ark Royal*. Second-in-command was Sir Francis Drake on board the *Revenge*. John Hawkyns and Martin Frobisher both received knighthoods for distinguished service.

Abroad, there were commercial disputes with many European states — particularly the Dutch. At home, there was popular discontent with a system of taxation which enabled the better-off to avoid paying their fair share. The end of her reign was marked by the recurrence of economic difficulties, and "their social impact was exacerbated by increased poverty and vagrancy. ... The Poor Laws ... offered limited parish relief but did not innovate. Furthermore, the motivation behind the ... legislation was the fear of vagrancy and urban insurrection ... rather than genuine human concern for the living conditions of the poor" [*The Oxford Illustrated History of Britain* p.276].

"It is plain that her own propaganda, the cult of Gloriana, her sheer longevity, ... and the lucky defeat of the Armada have beguiled us into joining a crescendo of adulation that ignores the simple fact that she quietly allowed England to become ungovernable" [p.264].*

Business was bad; lawlessness was rife; the country was going to the dogs. The 1620s were, in short, every bit as bad as the early 1990s.

Elizabethan "short-termism" had undermined Britain's ability to compete in overseas markets. The legacy of the poor housekeeping which characterised her reign was a severe economic recession and a huge deficit on Britain's 1622 balance of trade — calculated by Edward Misselden [1623, p.129] to be as much as £298,878.07.02.

Against this unpromising background, there took place a great flowering of economic theory; and many of the most ancient fallacies (some dating as far back as the twentieth century) were finally rejected. It is no coincidence that, for the first time in Looking-Glass history, economics was in the hands of practical businessmen.†

The Era of the Free-Traders

The early seventeenth-century writers on economics are practical businessmen who take great pride in their profession. They seem only too eager to sign themselves "merchant", and they show no sign of the defensiveness characteristic of their twentieth-century counterparts. Misselden displays their typical self-confidence in declaring that "merchants are of high account in all parts of the world, in times of peace,

* On the plus side, it has to be remembered that, only two years after the death of Elizabeth I, Britain produced the only national hero whose exploits are still generally celebrated — Guy Fawkes, who received *The Most-Promising-Amateur-of-1605 Award* for his attempt to blow-up the Houses of Parliament.

† Their Looking-Glass obligation to the philosopher John Locke is so strong, however, that some of the passages from which their inspiration is most obviously derived are quoted in footnotes throughout this chapter.

and in times of warre. Merchants are wont to be fupported of Kings and Princes, cherifhed of Nobles, favoured of States-men, honoured of all men, difgrac't of none: becaufe the ftrength of Kingdomes, the revenue of Princes, the wealth of every Cõmon-wealth, hath a Correlation with this Noble Profeffion" [1623, pp.17,18]. "There's none more fit to make a minifter for a King, then an expert and iudicious Merchant" [p.19].

Their devotion to the cause of free trade is reflected in the title of Edward Misselden's *Free Trade or the Meanes to Make Trade Florish* and Gerard Malynes's *The Maintenance of Free Trade*, both published in 1622.

The degree of unanimity on this issue is somewhat obscured by the intense rivalry between Malynes and Misselden for the favour of King James. The problem which preoccupies them both is, as usual, the recession. "For what," asks Misselden rhetorically, "is at this time more enquired after then the *Caufes* of the *Decay of Trade*?" [1622, p.4].

In order to distance himself from Malynes, Misselden over-emphasises the importance of the foreign trade deficit. In order to criticise Misselden, Malynes over-emphasises the importance of the exchange rate.

Some people relish criticism; some even thrive on it. Edward Misselden is not one of them. The subtitle of *The Circle of Commerce*, published the following year in indignant reply, includes the words "in defence of free Trade: *Oppofed* To *Malynes*"; and the title page charmingly carries a quotation from Proverbs 26, 4: "*Anfwer not a foole according to his folly*".

Lest the reader should miss the point, hardly a page is written without some personal insult to Malynes. Some of the flavour of Misselden's invective is contained in his appeal for "fupport ... against the *Malignitie* of one *Malynes* onely, amongft thoufands of better inftructed and affected perfons. Whofe palate being fallen, is become fo farre out of tafte, that he can relifh no meats not cook't by himfelf" [1623, p.4]. "Himfelf, his fubiect, much more his rude ftile, and vnmannerly manner of writing, deferue contempt rather then the honour of an anfwer" [p.4]. "Its pitty fuch ftuffe as this fhould paffe the Preffe" [p.14]. "Alas poore man, how fhall hee fpeake *Ingenioufly* or wittily, that hath no *Genius* at all?" [p.16]. "It is an ill bird, that foules his owne neft" [p.16]. "All *Malynes* Pamphlet from one end to the other, is piec't together with ftollen ftuffe" [p.29]. "Hee muft *Maligne*, or not be *Malynes*" [p.43]. "Thus you fee this *Sophifter* how he chops Logicke!" [p.68]. "*Malynes* hath ledde vs a wilde-goofe race" [p.68]. "Telling vs a tale, of a Cocke and a Bull" [p.70]. "But not willing to be Cenforious, I fhall leaue him and it, to the fentence of the wife" [p.145].*

Taking Disraeli's advice very much to heart,† Misselden explains that his book is a "iuft defence" against charges made "to no leffe, then *The Maiefty* of fo great *A King*. But I haue thought it my happines *ô Cæsar*, to haue anfwered before *Thee*, of all thefe things, whereof I am accufed and maligned of *Malynes*: For my Lord *The King*, is as an angell of God. Before whom I fhall euer acknowledge, my want of knowledge" [p.145].

As a result of all this nonsense, Misselden is not always taken seriously. This is a pity. Admittedly, the bath-water is pretty murky, but the baby has some fine qualities. There is a great deal which late twentieth-century academics can learn from early seventeenth-century businessmen — even one as embarrassing as Edward Misselden.

Freedom of Competition

One hundred and fifty Looking-Glass years after the *Wealth of Nations*, and with his own business experience as a merchant, Misselden is a sincere believer in the "invisible hand". "Is not gaine the end of trade? Is not the publique involved in the private, and the private in the publique? What elfe makes a Common-wealth, but the private-wealth, if I may fo fay, of the members thereof in the exercife of *Commerce* amongft themfelues, and with forraine Nations?" [1623, p.17].

"And trade hath in it fuch a kinde of naturall liberty in the courfe and vfe thereof, as it will not indure to be fors't by any" [p.112].‡ "Without that ill tincture of *Monopoly*, the KINGS *high way of trade* fhould be opened vnto all" [1622, p.55]. Monopoly is "a diuerting of *Commerfe* from the naturall courfe and vfe thereof, into the hands of fome few, to their benefit, and others preiudice" [p.55]. "*Monopoly is a kind of Commerce, in buying, felling, changing, or bartering, vfurped by a few, and fometimes but by one perfon, and foreftalled from all others, to the Gaine of the Monopolist, and to the Detriment of other men*" [p.57]. "The parts then of a *Monopolie* are twaine. The reftraint of the libertie of *Commerce* to fome one or few: and the fetting of the price at the pleafure of the *Monopolian* to his priuate benefit, and the preiudice of the publique. ... It is againft *Equitie*, that one Member of a *Common-wealth* fhould bee more free then another of equall ranke and condition. And what can be more contrary to *Publique*

* This is what is known in late twentieth-century political terminology as "concentrating on the issues".

† "Everyone likes flattery; and when you come to Royalty you should lay it on with a trowel."

‡ "Things muft be left to find their own Price" [Locke (1691) p.51].

Vtility, then that fome one or few perfons, fhould fway the price of any thing vfefull to the *Common-wealth*, to their owne *Enriching*, and the *Common loffe* of other men?" [pp.57,58].

He is, however, prepared to condone "*Reftraint of the Publicke Libertie*" in certain special cases. "If any man inuent a new Art, beneficiall to the *Common-wealth*, hee may haue a Patent to vfe that Arte folely, with reftraint of all others for feuen yeares: as well in recompence of his induftry, as for the incouragement of others to ftudie and inuent things profitable for the publique *Symbiofis*" [pp.59,60]. "A *Reftraint* of the *Publique Liberty* ... is alwayes to be allowed, when the fame is recompenced with a *Publique Vtility*" [p.67].

In general, however, he relies on freedom of competition, arguing that the exploitation of monopoly in commodities can be prevented if "there is fuch a multitude of Traders of them; and euery man is at liberty to buy or fell, without any rule by any generall order, or meanes to hold one price" [p.70].

Because their acceptance of competitively established prices is genuine and not invested with religious significance, the seventeenth-century merchants (unlike many of their Looking-Glass predecessors) do not waste time on the futile search for a theory of value.*

Misselden's severest criticism, however, is reserved for the ancient monopoly privatisations of the 1980s. "The greateft fufpition of *Monopoly* in *Corporations*, is in fuch as Trade in *Ioint ftockes*. Whereof if there be any that tradeth in a *Ioint ftocke*, and hath the *Sole* buying or felling of any *Commodity*, and buy and fell the fame *Iointly*, as by one perfon or common factor, fuch is guilty of *Monopoly*" [1622, p.70]. "By [*Monopolies*], this *Common-wealth* is depriued of that true liberty of Trade, which belongeth to all the fubiects: when the Commodity of fome few, is preferred to the publique good" [p.100].

Malynes expresses the same opinion. "A Society may become to be *A Monopoly* in effect, when fome few Merchants haue the whole managing of a *Trade*, to the hurt of a Common-wealth, when many others might alfo

---

* Their objection to theories of value like Adam Smith's is clearly influenced by John Locke's observation that "there is no fuch Intrinfick Natural fettled Value in any Thing, as to make any affign'd quantity of it, conftantly worth any affigned quantity of another" [1691, p.66].

Locke's treatment of the Paradox of Value is similar to John Law's. "What more ufeful or neceffary things are there to the Being or Well-being of Men, than Air and Water, and yet thefe have generally no Price at all, nor yield any Money: Becaufe their quantity is immenfly greater than their vent in moft places of the World. But as foon as ever Water ... comes any where to be reduced into any proportion to its confumption, it begins prefently to have a Price, and is fometimes fold dearer than Wine" [p.63,64].

Traffique and negotiate for the Common good" [1622, pp.68,69]. And he is equally critical of "*Reftraint of the freedome of commerce to fome one or few, and the fetting of the price, at the pleafure of one or few; to their priuate benefits, and the preiudice of the Common-Wealth*" [p.69].

Enlightened "Monetarism"

Any reasonably experienced early seventeenth-century merchant is well aware of the quantity theory of money.* Malynes is no exception. "The *Moneyes of Chriftendome*, which haue their ebbing and flowing, doe fhew their operation vpon Commodities, making by *Plenty*, the price thereof deare, or by *Scarcity* better cheape" [1622, p.36]. Thomas Mun, in *England's Treafure by Forraign Trade*, agrees that "plenty or scarcity of mony in a Common-wealth doth make all things dear or good cheap" [1628, p.39].

In discussing the evils of inflation, Misselden points out "the ineuitable loffe that thereby will fall, *Generally* vpon all men in the endearing of all things; and *Particulerly* vpon *Landlords* and *Creditors*, in their rents and contracts" [1622, p.106]. As a partial remedy, he revives an old-fashioned Friedmanite recommendation for the indexation of contractual obligations. "For *Landlords and Creditors*, their loffe is eafie to be preuented by *Prouifo*, that the *Contracts* made before the raifing of the *Monies* fhall be paide at the value the *Money* went at, when the *Contracts* were made" [p.107].

However, the seventeenth-century merchants do not subscribe to a quantity theory as crude as that current in the twentieth and nineteenth centuries; they are sufficiently sophisticated to recognise the operation of Law of Circulation from their own practical business experience.

The Law of Circulation

The importance of the Law of Circulation is emphasised by Malynes. "Since money was inuented and became the firft wheele which ftirreth the wheele of *Commodities* and inforceth the *Action*. ... [circulation is stimulated by] Merchants by exchange in the fale of commodities and negotiation of monyes, without which, commodities lie dead in all markettes" [1622, p.6]. He also makes clear that one of the main threats to employment is a deficiency of effective demand. "*The Want of Money* ... ,

* John Locke's Looking-Glass influence as a quantity theorist is particularly obvious. "The intrinfick Value of Silver and Gold ufed in Commerce is nothing but their *quantity*" [1691, p.31]. But the importance of the velocity of circulation is emphasised. "The ... *Proportion of Money* to Trade ... depends not barely on the quantity of Money, but the quicknefs of its Circulation" [p.33].

is the firft caufe of the *Decay of Trade*, for without money, Commodities are out of requeft" [p.37]. Misselden refers to the problem in terms of the (by now) well-worn medical analogy. "And thus the *Hepatites*, or Liuer veine of this *Great body* of ours being opened, & fuch profufions of the *Life bloud* let out" [1622, p.10].*

As a businessman conscious of the importance of circulation, Misselden endorses Keynes's ancient view that "it is worse, in an impoverished world, to provoke unemployment than to disappoint the *rentier*" [1923, p.40], by pointing out that "it is much better for the *Kingdome*, to haue things deare with plenty of *Money*, whereby men may liue in their feuerall callings: then to haue things cheape with want of *Money*, which now makes euery man complaine" [1622, p.107].

But the advantages of free-competition over monopoly, the inflationary consequences of excessive money supply, and the depressing effects of a deficiency of effective demand, are not new. The great contribution made by the practical businessmen of the early seventeenth century is the final disposal of the ancient twentieth-century fallacies on the question of foreign trade.

Enlightened Free-Trade

By contrast with the superstitious mysticism of the late twentieth-century, economics in the 1620s is a fully-fledged science. Gone are the religious dogma. The free-trade argument is more sophisticated. It comes from the pens of practical businessmen who are well versed in the Law of Circulation and who are governed by science rather than religion. Consequently, they are able to learn from history and to profit from examples like that of twentieth-century Japan. Their understanding of the mutual advantage of foreign trade is derived, not from textbook theory, but from personal experience, "the beft Schoole-mafter of mans life" [Malynes (1622) p.86].

To Misselden, foreign trade is all part of the grand design. "And to the end there fhould be a *Commerce* amongft men, it hath pleafed *God* to inuite as it were, one Country to traffique with another, by the variety of

* "There being a certain proportion of Money neceffary for driving fuch a proportion of Trade, fo much Money of this as lies ftill, leffens fo much of the Trade" [Locke (1691) p.14]. "The Neceffity of a certain Proportion of Money to Trade … lyes in this, That Money in its Circulation driving the feveral Wheels of Trade" [p.30]. "It matters not … whether the Money be in *Thomas* or *Richards* Hands, provided it be fo order'd, that, whoever has it, may be encouraged to let it go into the current of Trade, for the improvement of the general ftock, and wealth of the Nation" [p.100]. "That [Money] which is not let loofe into *Trade*, is all one whil'ft Hoarded up, as if it were not in Being" [p.121].

things which the *One hath*, and the *other hath not*: that fo that which is wanting to the *One*, might be fupplied by the *Other*, that all might haue fufficient" [1622, p.25]. On this at least Malynes is in complete agreement. "God caufed nature to diftribute her benefites, or his blefsings to feuerall *Climates*, fupplying the barrenneffe of fome things in one countrey, with the fruitfulneffe and ftore of other countries, to the end that inter-changeably one Common-weale fhould liue with an other" [1622, p.58].

"Comparative advantage" is not a term used by Misselden. Nonetheless, he is clearly aware of the benefits of free trade even to a nation with no natural advantage in any area of production. "Let vs confider the ftate of the *Netherlands*, in what a miferable cafe thofe people were, if they receiued not fupply from all other *Nations*. They haue *Nothing* of their owne, and yet they feeme to poffeffe *All things*, in the *Supply* they receiue from *All the World*" [1622, pp.26,27].

"It is the maxim of every prudent master of a family," according to Adam Smith, "never to attempt to make at home what it will cost him more to make than to buy. The taylor does not attempt to make his own shoes, but buys them of the shoemaker. ... What is prudence in the conduct of every private family, can scarce be folly in that of a great kingdom. If a foreign country can supply us with a commodity cheaper than we ourselves can make it, better buy it of them with some part of the produce of our own industry, employed in a way in which we have some advantage" [1776, IV,2].

Following the example of John Locke,* Misselden borrows Adam Smith's "family" analogy in order to provide a simple guide to good-housekeeping for the whole nation.

"A *Common-wealth* is like vnto a *Family*, the *Father* or Mafter whereof ought to fell more then he buyeth. ... Otherwife his *Expence* being greater then his *Reuenue*, he muft needs come behind hand" [1622, pp.12,13]. The Micawberian consequences of a foreign trade deficit are obvious. "The *General remote* caufe of our want of money, is the *great Exceffe* of this *Kingdom*, in confuming the *Commodities* of *Forreine Countries* [p.11].

To politicians looking for a simple method of staunching the outflow of precious metals, the "bullionist" solution has an obvious appeal — simply pass a law prohibiting the export of bullion.

Exchange controls, however, even if applied with the full rigour of the law, are unlikely to be successful for the reasons given by John Locke.†

---

* " 'Tis with a *Kingdom*, as with a *Family*. Spending lefs than our own Commodities will pay for, is the fure and only way for the Nation to grow Rich" [Locke (1691) p.118].

† And also by Richard Cantillon, see pp.267,268 above.

"Laws made againft Exportation of Money or Bullion, will be all in vain. Reftraint, or Liberty in that matter, makes no Country Rich or Poor: As we fee in *Holland*; which had plenty of Money under the free liberty of its Exportation; and *Spain*, in great want of Money under the fevereft penalties againft carrying of it out" [1695, pp.36,37]. Like all attempts to rig the market, "which way ever it fucceeds it proves either prejudicial or ineffectual. If the defign of your Law take place, the Kingdom lofes by it: If the inconvenience be felt and avoided, your Law is eluded" [1691, p.167].

To merchants engaged in foreign trade, exchange controls spell the ruin of their business. Consequently, they are fervent supporters of Locke's cry for liberty. One of the most effective replies to the Bullionists is Thomas Mun's observation that "if we only behold the actions of the husbandman in the seed-time when he casteth away much good corn into the ground, we will rather accompt him a mad man than a husbandman: but when we consider his labours in the harvest which is the end of his endeavours, we find the worth and plentiful encrease of his actions" [1628, p.19].

"The ordinary means therefore to encrease our wealth and treasure is by *Forraign Trade*, wherein wee must ever observe this rule; to sell more to strangers yearly then wee consume of theirs in value" [p.5] "by making our commodities which are exported yearly to over ballance in value the foraign wares which wee consume" [p.14].

This Micawberian obsession with a favourable balance of trade, which is characteristic of the early seventeenth-century businessmen, is traceable to John Locke's proposition that "whenever the whole of our Foreign Trade and Confumption exceeds our Exportation of Commodities, our Money muft go to pay our Debts fo contracted. ... Our Coin and Treafure ... can be reftor'd only by an over-balance of our whole Exportation, to our whole Importation of confumable Commodities" [1695, p.36].

The Importance of the Balance of Trade

Because of the importance which he attaches to the balance of trade, Misselden is anxious that it should be properly measured. "For as a paire of Scales or Ballance, is an Inuention to fhew vs the waight of things, whereby we may difcerne the heauy from the light, and how one thing differeth from another in the Scale of waight: So is alfo this *Ballance of Trade*, an excellent and politique Inuention, to fhew vs the difference of waight in the *Commerce* of one Kingdome with another: that is, whether the Natiue Commodities exported, and all the forraine Commodities Imported, doe ballance or ouerballance one another in the *Scale of Commerce*. If the Natiue Commodities exported doe waigh downe and exceed in value the forraine Commodities imported; it is a rule that neuer faile's that then the Kingdome growe's rich, and profper's in eftate and ftocke: becaufe the ouerplus thereof muft needs come in, in treafure. But if the Forraine Commodities imported, doe exceed in value the Natiue Commodities exported; it is a manifeft figne that then trade decayeth, and the ftocke of the Kingdome wafteth apace: becaufe the ouerplus muft needs goe out in treafure" [1623, pp.116,117].

Misselden is clearly shocked by the results of his calculations:

The Ballance of Trade of the Kingdome ...
from Chriftmas An.1621 to Chriftmas An. 1622, as followeth. ...

		li.	*fh.*	*d.*
The Totall Importations amount to	–	2619315.	00.	00
The Totall Exportations	–	2320436.	12.	10
The Remainder fheweth, that there is more imported this yeare then was Exported, by the fumme of	–	0298878.	07.	02

"So then wee fee it to our griefe, that wee are fallen into a great *Vnder-ballance of Trade* with other Nations. Wee felt it before in fenfe; but now we know it by fcience: wee found it before in operation; but now wee fee it in fpeculation: Trade alas, faile's and faint's, and we in it" [1623, pp.129,130].

To anyone who understands the operation of the Law of Circulation in a multi-gear economy, the adverse consequences of a trade deficit are obvious — a reduction in the volume of economic activity. After nearly four centuries of Looking-Glass progress, Misselden's cry of anguish bemoaning the return to the bad old days of the 1990s is heartrending.

"If all the *Caufes* of our *Vnder-ballance of Trade*, might be contracted in two words, furely they might be reprefented, in two extremities of the Kingdome at this day: *Pouerty*, alas, and *Prodigality*. The *Poore* fterue in the ftreets for want of labour: The *Prodigall* excell in exceffe. ... What's the fruit of thefe things? The Sunne blufheth to fee ... vnheard of monftruous murtherers of thefe times. ... He that's *Idle*, is fit for any *Evill*: He that's *Prodigall*, is a prey to the *Deuill*. ... If the people of this Kingdome were numbred from *Dan* to *Berfheba*, I am perfwaded, there were neuer more people, neuer leffe employment: neuer more *Idlenes*, neuer fo much *Exceffe*!" [1623, pp.132-134].

The contrast with that paragon of economic virtue — the Netherlands — fills Misselden with envy. "The *Low Countries* doe feeme to be an *Epitome* of all the Reft. Which certainly for *Policy* and *Induftry*, may read a Lecture to all the other people of the world. There you fhall fee, their Gates ftand wide open: you may carry out as much mony as you will: It is there held no *Paradoxe*, to let money goe out, and yet not to want it within: becaufe they haue an Eie to the *Ballance of Trade*; whereby they are affured, that although it may goe out at one dore, yet it will come in at another. But there you fhall fee no *Exceffe* in fuperfluous confumptions of forraine Commodities. No *Proiects*, nor *Proiectors*, but for the Common-good. All kinde of *Manufactures* inuented, that will fit the times, and pleafe the mindes of forrain Nations. ... Frugality, induftry, policy, all working together for the publike. ... And this is a liuing *Precept*, a Patterne, a Forme, a plat-forme for our Imitation, for the encreafe of our *Exportation* and this will reftore our ancient *Ballance of Trade*" [pp.134,135].*

In spite of the evils of an adverse balance of trade, however, the seventeenth-century businessmen, unlike some of their twentieth-century ancestors (and even Richard Cantillon), are able to resist the temptation of protectionism.

The appropriate remedy for a breach of the Law of Circulation can never be a breach of the Law of Competition. As Thomas Mun points out, the erection of protective trade barriers only makes matters worse; it invites retaliation. "Whatsoever (in this kind) we shall impose upon strangers here, will presently be made a Law for us in their Countreys" [1628, p.35]. "Such a restriction must of necessity destroy much trade" [p.36]. Protectionism is therefore counter-productive and will not lead to the goal of a surplus. "This gain is no way to be accomplished but by the overballance of our trade, and this overballance is made less by restrictions: therefore such restrictions do hinder the increase of our treasure" [p.37].

In view of the importance which the seventeenth-century businessmen attach to a foreign trade surplus, it is an object lesson to the twentieth century to see how strongly they reject measures to restrict competition, and how strongly they advocate measures to promote its effectiveness.

The Importance of Effective Competition

Misselden identifies two threats to a nation's ability to compete effectively in overseas markets. One is too *much* restriction of competition; the other is too *little*. These threats lie "in the *Forme* of Trade, as it is *too ftrict*, or *too loofe*. *Too ftrict*, in refpect of *Monopolies*, ... *too loofe*, in the diforderly Trade of the fubiects out of *Gouernment*" [1692, p.90]. Consequently, a chapter devoted to criticising the "*Abufe* of

* Misselden complains that the country is flooded with their tourists. "Looke vpon *Norwich, Colchefter*, ... and other Citties peopled with the Dutch. There you fhall fee at Home, what you might feeke Abroad" [1623, p.135].

Gouernment, by way of *Monopoly*," is followed by another chapter in which "it now remaineth briefely to fhew the *Too Loofe Vfe* thereof, by *Vngouerned Trade*" [p.73].*

An objection to excessive restriction is unremarkable in a book entitled *Free Trade*; but an objection to excessive freedom is quite a surprise. Even more so is his criticism of the argument "that this their better thriuing is becaufe euery man is at libertie to be a *Merchant* at his pleafure" as a "*Fallacy*" [p.79]. It is no wonder that Misselden has acquired a reputation as a protectionist.

However, it is inadvisable to jump to conclusions before examining the context.

Misselden points out the "the benefit of *Gouernment* it felfe. For thereby the *Common-wealth* hath beene much aduantaged. ... This will be yet more perfpicuous, if we caft our eye firft vpon the feueral *Societies of Merchants* which trade *vnder Gouernment*: and then on thofe which trade *without Gouernment* [pp.73,74]. In the first category he places the great trading companies, like the "Merchants Aduenturers", the "Eaft India Company", and the "Mufcouy Company"; and he documents their achievements "none of all which they had euer beene able to haue done as particular men, in a loofe, diftracted, and diforderly trade" [p.76].

"Hauing anfwered the obiections againft *Corporations*, of *Merchants* and *Gouerned Trades*, and fhewed the many and manifold benefits arifing to the *Common-wealth* thereby: It is now eafie to fhew the Iniury and Inconuenience to this *Common-wealth* by the want of *Gouernment in Trade*. Thofe that Trade without *Order* and *Gouernment*, are like vnto men, that make *Holes* in the bottome of that *Ship*, wherein themfelues are *Paffengers*" [pp.84,85].

The Dutch — the Japanese of the 1620s — are quite different; and Misselden is clearly impressed by their sense of solidarity. "For they wifely confider, that their intereft is inuolued in the *Publique*: where, in our *Nation*, men commonly preferre their *Particular*, to the *Common-good*" [p.84].

In a Looking-Glass perspective, Misselden's attitude is easily understandable. He is deeply influenced by the tragic historical example of Britain's "High Fidelity Sound" industry. In the 1950s and 1960s, the British Hi-Fi Industry consisted of many small family businesses. They were hard-working and enterprising; they took pride in the high quality of their workmanship and in the individuality of their designs; and they were

* In this context, the term "government" has no political connotations; it is not a reference to *the* government. The term implies co-ordination between traders rather than a "free-for-all".

dedicated to providing unstinting service to their customers. Ranged against them were the big bureaucratic trading corporations of Japan, sponsored by the all-powerful Ministry of Trade and Industry.

What became of the valiant band of British hedgehogs which sallied forth (under the banner SMALL IS BEAUTIFUL) to take on the might of a handful of Japanese steam-rollers?

— Stains on the concrete!

Misselden's remedy for "diforderly trade" is to imitate the ancient Japanese example "by reducing of the ftragling trade ... into *Gouernment*; whereby they also might goe in Fleetes, as other Gouerned Companies doe" [1622, p.111].*

From an old-fashioned twentieth-century viewpoint, to organise vessels together in convoy looks like restraint of competition. But that is not Misselden's intention. Had the British Hi-Fi industry of blessed memory gone in convoy, it might have survived instead of resting in peace.†

Misselden is a businessman. He takes the world as it is — not as the theorists would like it to be. In a world full of steam-rollers, it is pointless to encourage hedgehogs to use their weight. Competition from a few large living firms is more effective than from a lot of small dead ones. Recognition of this awkward fact of commercial life does not make him a protectionist. It means that he is a realist.

The trouble is that this line of argument can be taken too far. His criticism of "the clamour of fome who preferred their owne liberty, to the vtility of the publique" [p.86] is absolutely lethal to freedom of trade. It can be used to justify almost any restrictive or monopolistic practice in restraint of trade; and it leads directly to the Ministry of Central Planning.

Misselden is free-trader of the "level playing-field" persuasion; and "level playing-field" arguments are dangerously seductive. They are advertised with the claim that they promote the cause of effective competition. Too often, they can kill it.

---

* Although Misselden fails to acknowledge his Looking-Glass sources, it is not difficult to see where this idea comes from:

"The trading company provided the essential links by skillfully organizing a large number of small enterprises to produce for the export market. The relationship between the trading companies and the small firms subsequently came to be known as *Keiretsu*. (*Kei* means ... group and *retsu* means arranged in order, so that Keiretsu suggests an organization that is hierarchically well ordered.)" [M. Y. Yoshino: *Japan's Multinational Enterprises*. Harvard University Press: Cambridge Mass. 1976, p.7].

† The story did have a happy ending. By the 1990s, the survivors had recovered to restore Britain's reputation for the highest quality audio equipment in the world. A large part of the mass market, however, seemed to have been lost.

If too many hedgehogs are getting squashed, the answer is not to restrict the freedom of the victims, it is to curb the monopolistic power of the steam-rollers.

If there are doubts about Misselden's adherence to the Law of Competition, however, there can be none about his commitment to the Law of Circulation. His anguish over the 1622 trade deficit, is not a superficial "bullionist's" concern over loss of treasure, it is a sensible businessman's despair over loss of trade. "So then wee fee it to our griefe, that wee are fallen into a great *Vnder-ballance of Trade* with other Nations. ... Trade alas, faile's and faint's, and we in it" [1623, pp.129,130].

And so the Looking-Glass journey ends in the 1620s with the question which preoccupies the 1990s. "For what," asks Misselden, "is at this time more enquired after then the *Caufes* of the *Decay of Trade*?" [1622, p.4] — or, to put it another way: Is the age of full employment really over? — Is full employment dead?

EPILOGUE

IS FULL EMPLOYMENT DEAD?

What free-market microeconomic policy hath given, interventionist macroeconomic policy hath taken away.

The Market-Place and Society

The market-place is a lot older than capitalism; it was in full swing when Plato wrote *The Republic.*

"A state comes into existence because no individual is self-sufficing; we all have many needs. ... We call in one another's help to satisfy our various requirements. ... If one man gives to another what he has to give in exchange for what he can get, it is because each finds that to do so is for his own advantage. ... No two people are born exactly alike. There are innate differences which fit them for different occupations. ... And will a man do better at working at many trades, or keeping to one only? ... The conclusion is that more things will be produced and the work be more easily and better done, when every man is set free from all other occupations to do, at the right time, the one thing for which he is naturally fitted" [380 BC, pp.54-56].

"How are the various sets of producers to exchange their products? ... Obviously, they must buy and sell. That will mean having a market-place, and a currency to serve as a token for purposes of exchange" [pp.56-57].

Two thousand years separate Plato from Adam Smith, but their views are strikingly close.

"When the division of labour has been once thoroughly established, it is but a very small part of a man's wants which the produce of his own labour can supply. He supplies the far greater part of them by exchanging that surplus part of the produce of his own labour, which is over and above his own consumption, for such parts of the produce of other men's labour as he has occasion for" [Smith (1776) I,4].

Very few people "stand on their own two feet".

Trade and commerce have liberated mankind from that necessity — a necessity from which no other creature has managed to escape. "Each animal is still obliged to support and defend itself, separately and independently, and derives no sort of advantage from that variety of talents with which nature has distinguished its fellows. ... Nobody ever saw a dog make a fair and deliberate exchange of one bone for another with another dog" [Smith (1776) I,2].

Robinson Crusoe may have stood on his own two feet. The rest of us stand in shoes made by other people. As Confucius might have said: "man who stands on own two feet, goes barefoot."

It is a view which transcends the barriers of time and politics. "The great multiplication of the productions of all the different arts, in consequence of the division of labour, ... occasions, in a well-governed society, that universal opulence which extends itself to the lowest ranks of the people" [Smith (1776) I,1]. "Just as a certain number of simultaneously employed labourers are the material pre-requisites for division of labour in manufacture, so are the number and density of the population ... a necessary condition for the division of labour in society" [Marx (1867) p.352]. "Differences among individuals increase the power of the collaborating group beyond the sum of individual efforts. Synergetic collaboration brings into play distinctive talents that would have been left unused had their possessors been forced to strive alone for sustenance" [Hayek (1988) p.80].

Hayek's observation that "it is misleading to treat ... 'society' animistically, or to personify it by ascribing to it a will, an intention, or a design" [p.113] is a necessary reminder that social and economic changes cannot be regarded as good or bad for "society" or for "the economy" without recognition of the different impact on different individuals. It is not intended to provide an excuse for breaching the mutual obligations which bind the members of a free-market economy. It is certainly no excuse for those who pose as champions of economic freedom to claim that "there is no such thing as society". At the very heart of the free-market philosophy of Adam Smith himself is the recognition that "all the members of human society stand in need of each other's assistance" [1759, p.124].

The market is not an alternative to the social contract; it is its very essence.

And so the Looking-Glass journey has come full circle — back to the opening declaration of the Prologue.

Inflation, Unemployment, and the Social Contract

In societies where the division of labour has been carried so far in the interests of the community as a whole that each member is economically dependent on every other, it is an implied term of the social contract that every individual who is willing to work should have the right to do so. It is also an implied term of the social contract, in societies where monetary claims are used as a means of exchange, that those claims should be fully honoured.

Inflation and unemployment are breaches of the social contract.

Just as assault and theft are crimes by individuals against society, so inflation and unemployment are crimes by society against individuals. Unemployment robs them of their income; inflation robs them of their savings.

It is the duty of every responsible government to protect its citizens from this kind of breakdown of economic law and order.

The New "Single-gear" Economic Orthodoxy has failed so miserably that "the search for a way to resolve the cruel dilemma of needing high unemployment to contain inflation continues to be one of the most pressing concerns of modern macroeconomics" [Samuelson & Nordhaus (1995) p.597].

Is Full Employment Dead?

The single-gear fallacy lurks behind the chilling obituary (quoted in chapter 1 above): "the age of full employment is over ... the price ... quite simply ... accelerating and ultimately explosive inflation ... is too high" [*The Times*, 10th April 1975].

Advertised as the new economic realism, it is the old economic nonsense in disguise. For over a quarter of a century, the "natural rate hypothesis" has contaminated all the "expert" economic advice. Because they have to draw their economic advice from the same infected pool, politicians of all parties have fallen victim.

Changes of government make no difference. In Britain, the Old Tory economic battle-cries have been taken up with even greater fervour by New Labour:

(1) *market flexibility* as the sole cure for unemployment;
(2) *monetary restriction* as a safe cure for inflation.

In making markets more flexible, the microeconomic *laissez-faire* policy of the 1980s has been a spectacular success. Even the most hostile critics have been forced to concede that unions are less intransigent, firms are more competitive, and the government is less intrusive. Markets have become more flexible than at any time since the Second World War. Compared with the 1960s, the *natural rate* of unemployment must have fallen dramatically. If the *actual rate* of unemployment has risen, it is not because microeconomic *laissez-faire* policy has not been a success, but because macroeconomic interventionist policy has been a disaster.

It is a disaster because it is based on one of the most absurd self-contradictions in the history of economic policy. Markets are to be set free. Yet the most important market-price of all — the rate of interest —

is to be determined, not by market forces, but by a Monetary Policy Committee of the Bank of England.

To release the economy from the chains holding it back from free competition only to confine it in a monetary cage is responsible for perpetuating the unnecessarily high unemployment and low growth which, over the past two decades, have robbed the British economy of at least one third of its potential GDP. Who better to pronounce the verdict than Adam Smith?

> "It is the highest impertinence and presumption … , in kings and ministers, to pretend to watch over the œconomy of private people, and to restrain their expence" [1776, II,3].

But the full extent of the disaster has been covered-up by a ceaseless flow of propaganda from economic spin-doctors whose virtuosity would have dazzled George Orwell.

'Nineties Newspeak and the "Goldilocks Economy"

In the Bad Old Days of over-mighty unions, inefficient industry, and interfering government, when unemployment climbed towards one million, "Britain wasn't working". In 'Nineties Newspeak, those were the days of "over-employment". Following the economic miracle of the 1980s, unemployment of less than one and half million is a cause for congratulation.

In the Bad Old Days, inflation was "out of control" when it reached an annual rate of 3% — the rate at which money loses more than two-thirds of its purchasing power over the period of a forty year career. In 'Nineties Newspeak, an annual rate of 3% is "on target".

In the Bad Old Days, a rate of economic growth of less than 4% was "miserably low". In 'Nineties Newspeak, a rate of economic growth of more than 3% is "dangerously high".

As Britain approaches the second millennium, inflation is nearly "down" to what used to be regarded as a crisis level. Unemployment has been "reduced" to more than three times what used to be regarded intolerably high. The annual rate of economic growth has been "increased" to less than half of what used to be regarded as miserable. Britain's GDP is less than two-thirds of its potential. In 'Nineties Newspeak, it is hailed as a brilliant economic success and dubbed the "Goldilocks economy".

Lions led by Donkeys?

Current economic strategy is reminiscent of military strategy during the First World War, when millions of lives were uselessly sacrificed on the altar of false military dogma. Politicians of all parties seem as helpless now in the hands of the economists as they were then in the hands of the generals. Now, as then, the fault lies, not with the politicians, but with their advisers who are so blinded by religious zeal that they refuse to see the flaws in their dogma.

The danger of single-gear monetary intervention to control inflation is not the risk of failure but the certainty of success. Like trench warfare, if pursued with sufficiently callous disregard for the troops, it, too, will result in victory. But the tragic waste of economic life may, in the long run, be self-defeating. A temporary respite from the ravages of inflation, secured by destroying the capacity to produce without curbing the desire to consume, may leave the economy permanently weaker.

The world recession, the muddle over currency alignments, the retreat into protectionist clubs masquerading as Free Trade Areas, Common Markets, or Currency Unions, which risk provoking the next war through well-intentioned but poorly conceived efforts to prevent a recurrence of the last one, are largely the consequence of applying single-gear economics to the problems of multi-gear economies. The abject failure of Orthodox single-gear economic policy to protect the newly liberalised economies of Russia and Eastern Europe from inflation and unemployment has brought free-market economics into disrepute. Nothing could have produced a more dangerous set-back to the cause of political and economic democracy. And it is the inadequacy of single-gear economics which is responsible for the fear that world recovery will spark off another round of world inflation.

The Tyranny of Single-Gear Economics

In Britain, the high unemployment and low growth of the early 1990s is blamed on "the years of Conservative rule"; in France, it is blamed on "the years of Socialist rule". But economies are not subject to the "rule" of politicians. In the sphere of economics, no one lives under Conservative or Socialist rule. Whatever the political label of their government, in most parts of the world people are living under the tyranny of single-gear economics.

Full employment can be achieved — but only at the risk of increasing inflation; and price stability can be achieved — but only at the risk of increasing unemployment. Single-gear economics can provide no mechanism to halt the endless cycle of high unemployment alternating with rapid inflation. During some phases of the cycle, there may well be the "Goldilocks" coincidence of relatively low levels of both inflation and unemployment. But to sing the praises of single-gear economic policy for that reason makes no more sense than to commend the reliability of a stopped clock because twice in every twenty-four hours it happens to be precisely correct.

Single-gear economics is a modern illustration of Keynes's "analogy between the sway of the classical school of economic theory and that of certain religions" [1936, pp.350,351]. No politician dare resist. In its anxiety to demonstrate its New Economic Responsibility, both before and after its election in May 1997, one of the main preoccupations of Britain's New Labour government has been to confirm its commitment to the single-gear economic policy of its predecessor.

The New Politics looks suspiciously like the Old Economics.

As Lady Bracknell might have put it: "to lose one major political party to the tyranny of single-gear economic fundamentalism may be regarded as a misfortune; to lose two looks like carelessness."

The Multi-Gear Alternative

The lesson of the journey *Through the Looking-Glass* is that a return to the "multi-gear" common sense of the seventeenth century would make the installation of a mechanism for ending the cycle a practical possibility. It would require the removal from the government (or any other non-market authority — however benign its intentions) of discretionary power over interest rates or exchange rates. In its place would stand a *laissez-faire* macroeconomic policy for allowing a "multi-gear" economy to operate in the "market-determined" gear.

Over three centuries have elapsed since a deputation of French businessmen confronted Colbert with their famous demand for economic freedom: "*Laissez-nous faire!*". The plea from the millions of unemployed in the world's dole queues is the same: "*Let us work!*".

Not until monetary interventionism is repudiated in favour of monetary freedom, will there be an end to the nonsense of having to curb economic growth during periods of high unemployment for fear of rekindling inflation.

The problem with inflation has never been how to control it, but how to do so *without causing unemployment*. Similarly, the problem with unemployment is not how to control it, but how to do so *without causing inflation*. The "multi-gear" theory outlined in *Economics Through the Looking-Glass* points towards a non-interventionist macroeconomic policy driven by market forces — the economic equivalent of automatic traffic lights operated by the flow of traffic rather than a (government or central bank) policeman. The extension of *laissez-faire* into macroeconomic policy is therefore not a device for avoiding government responsibility for economic law and order; it is the means of fulfilling it.

The multi-gear alternative is to allow the market-determined volume of economic activity to be carried on at market-determined rates of interest and at market-determined rates of exchange.

A mechanism designed to prevent a *laissez-faire* macroeconomic policy from degenerating into a spiral of uncontrollable inflation is described in the next volume — *Full Employment Without Inflation in a "Multi-Gear" Economy.* Once that mechanism is in place, the gear-lever can be allowed to move freely, thereby enabling the economy to get closer to its full employment potential.

The Restoration of Full Employment

Full employment (once the automatic commitment of every British political party) is not a luxury — an extravagance which must be put off until it can be "afforded". It is a basic economic necessity.

Yet the topsy-turvy Wonderland of single-gear economics is full of free-market economists who dare not trust the market. They fear that the pace of economic growth set by market forces may be "unsustainable" and could bring the economy "dangerously close to full employment". Market forces cannot, in their opinion, be trusted with money. At the first sign of decent economic growth, their impulse is always the same: to slam on the "monetary brakes".

The high and persistent level of unemployment produced by policies of monetary restriction is not simply a question of social injustice, it is a monumental economic inefficiency.

The growing demand for better transport, education, healthcare, crime-prevention, and pensions cannot be met simply by cutting out waste or by redistributing wealth. Nor can unemployment be cured simply by retraining. The only way of generating real resources and genuine jobs is to allow economic activity to rise to its full potential. The question is not whether an annual growth rate is "unsustainable" if it is above 3%, but whether it is "unsustainable" if it is below 6%.

Rapid growth and full employment are impossible without inflation until macroeconomic policy is prised from the grip of the High Priests of the New Economic Orthodoxy and returned to the market-place. It is not the mould of politics which needs breaking but the mould of economics. If the stranglehold of the Orthodox Economic Religion can, at last, be broken, it may be possible to discard the interventionist single-gear economics of the New Economic Orthodoxy and return to the non-interventionist multi-gear economics of Adam Smith's predecessors.

Towards a Laissez-Faire Macroeconomic Policy

In the 1960s, before the free-market revolution, Britain, France and Germany had unemployment rates of less than 2%. In 1997, a proposal from the European Commission to adopt a "target" to cut Europe's unemployment rate from 11% to 7% over the next five years is described by *The Economist* as "ambitious" [November 15th 1997, p.118].

Are today's self-styled free-market economists trying to bring back Marxism? Are they trying to prove that "capitalist production ... requires for its free play an industrial reserve army [of unemployed "surplus" labour] ... kept in misery in order to be always at the disposal of capital ... a mass of human material always ready for exploitation" [Marx (1867) pp.635,487,632]?

An unemployment rate of 7% is ambitious only in the context of an interventionist single-gear policy of monetary restriction to control inflation. Full employment is not dead, but it requires more than deregulation of the market for labour; it requires deregulation of the market for money. Inflation must be kept under control; but the single-gear policy of monetary intervention must be abandoned, if the old target of 2% unemployment is to be realistic.

In the 1960s, the complaint used to be that government ministers lacked the political courage to follow the advice of the monetary experts. In the 1990s, the question is whether or not they have the political courage to reject it.

If they are prepared to abandon the notion of controlling inflation by monetary restriction and turn instead to the free-market alternative, the New Politics need not turn out to be the same Old Economics.

Laissez-faire means more than freedom to compete; it means freedom to work. For New Politicians of any party, what slogan could be more appropriate?

APPENDIX

THE MICROECONOMIC FOUNDATIONS OF MACROECONOMIC EQUILIBRIUM

The volume of employment in a large economy is the result of millions of different choices made by millions of different individuals. The macroeconomic outcome cannot properly be considered in isolation from its microeconomic foundations. The desired level of employment — the "full employment" potential — depends on consumer tastes and production technology. Whether or not the full employment potential is achieved depends on how accurately the economic signals are transmitted through the channels of communication — the markets.

Orthodox theory maintains that, so long as the channels of communication are perfect, "*market-clearing* equilibrium" in the full Walrasian sense is a guarantee of full employment.

In Parts III and IV, the device of a Looking-Glass Utopia is used to demonstrate that the Orthodox view is wrong by proving that unemployment can occur even in markets of Utopian perfection. The numerical illustrations used in the text are deliberately simplified in order to establish the main principles.

In this Appendix, the argument in the text is presented in more general terms by the use of "four-quadrant" diagrams which are designed to keep the microeconomic foundations of macroeconomic equilibrium constantly in view.*

---

* This discussion, which is not essential to the main argument, assumes an acquaintance with indifference curve analysis.

SECTION A: Resource Allocation for a Single Individual: Microeconomic Choice (Chapter 15)

The planned allocation of Tweedledum's resources is represented in Figure A.1, which is divided into four quadrants. The two upper "real" quadrants cover the economic activity of *production*; the two lower "monetary" quadrants cover the economic activity of *exchange*. The "path" chosen by Tweedledum is indicated by the arrows.

(1) EMPLOYMENT: "exchanging" (Leisure) Time for Goods

The choice between leisure and employment is shown in the upper-right EMPLOYMENT Quadrant. Time is measured up the vertical axis; Product A is measured along the horizontal axis. The total time available to Tweedledum (for the choice between employment and leisure) is equal to *OT* [70 hours].*

The *employment opportunity boundary, TA*, is a straight line to reflect the simplifying assumption that his physical productivity is constant [3 units per hour]. It shows how he can "convert" his time into output of Product A by moving (i.e. employing himself) along the boundary from *T* [70 hours of Leisure + 0 units of A] to *A* [0 hours of Leisure + 210 units of A].

Figure A.1: The Four-Dimensional Decision

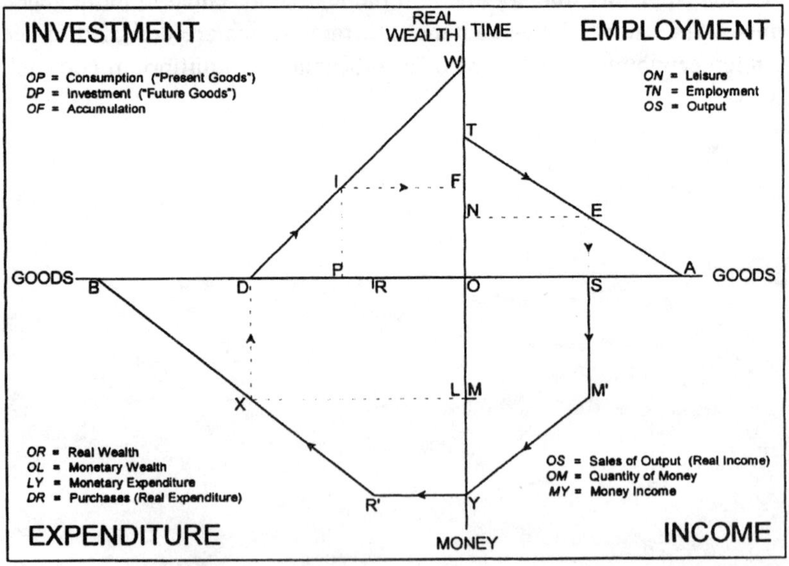

* The figures in square brackets are corresponding figures from the numerical illustrations in the text.

Tweedledum's decision to move from point *T* to point *E* in the EMPLOYMENT Quadrant (indicated by an arrow) represents the choice of leisure amounting to *ON* [30 hours] and employment amounting to *TN* [40 hours]; the resulting output amounts to *OS* [120A].

The market opportunities for buying and selling are shown in the two lower "monetary" quadrants.

(2) INCOME: exchanging Goods for Money

The choice between Product A and money is shown in the lower-right INCOME Quadrant. Product A is measured along the horizontal axis, and Money is measured down the vertical axis. In addition to his supply of output *OS* [120A], Tweedledum also has a stock of monetary wealth *OM* [£600] accumulated during previous periods. This money balance enables him to start at point *M'* in the INCOME Quadrant.

The *earning opportunity boundary*, *M'Y*, is a straight line on the assumption that markets are perfectly competitive with a uniform price [£4 per unit]. It shows how he can "convert" his output into money by further movement (representing sales of Product A) along the boundary from *M'* [120A + £600] to *Y* [0A + £1,080].

Because Tweedledum has no desire to consume Product A himself, he moves all the way to point *Y*, where he sells his entire output of Product A and receives a money income of *MY* [(120A @ £4=) £480]. The total amount of money available for spending then amounts to *OY* [(£600+£480=) £1,080].

(3) EXPENDITURE: exchanging Money for Goods

The choice between holding money and spending it is shown in the lower-left EXPENDITURE Quadrant. Money is measured down the vertical axis, and Product B is measured along the horizontal axis. In addition to his total money available *OY* [£1,080], Tweedledum also has a stock of real wealth *OR* [90B] accumulated during previous periods. This accumulation of Product B enables him to start at point *R'* in the EXPENDITURE Quadrant.

The *spending opportunity boundary*, *R'B*, is a straight line on the assumption that markets are perfectly competitive with a uniform price [£4 per unit]. It shows how he can "convert" money into goods by further movement (representing purchases of Product B) along the boundary from *R'* [£1,080 + 90B] to *B* [360B + £0].

The initial assumption is that Tweedledum chooses to maintain his money balances unchanged: his desire for liquidity *OL* is exactly equal to *OM*. He therefore moves to point *X*, which represents the decision to hold an amount equal to *OL* [£600] and to spend an amount equal to *LY* [(£1,080-

£600=) £480]. This is sufficient to purchase *DR* [(£480/£4=) 120B] which represents Tweedledum's demand for Product B. That leaves him with available goods amounting to *OD* [(90B+120B=) 210B].

(4) INVESTMENT: "exchanging" Present Goods for Future Goods

The choice between holding goods and consuming them is shown in the upper-left INVESTMENT Quadrant. Present consumption of Product B is measured along the horizontal axis; future consumption is measured up the vertical axis.

The total goods available to Tweedledum (for the choice between present and future consumption) amount to *OD* [210B]. The *investment opportunity boundary*, *DW*, is a straight line with a 45° slope to reflect the simplifying assumption that the real rate of return on investment is zero. It shows how he can "convert" present consumption into future consumption by moving (i.e. investing) along the boundary from *D* [210B present + 0B future] to *W* [0B present + 210B future]. By abstaining from present consumption, he is able to accumulate a stock of real wealth.

The initial assumption is that Tweedledum chooses to maintain his stock of real wealth unchanged. He therefore moves to point *I*, which represents the decision to consume *OP* [120B] *now* and *DP* [90B] *in the future*. At 0%, *DP* accumulates to *OF* [90B] which represents the accumulation of real wealth which is available for the next period.

If the closing stock of real wealth *OF* is greater (smaller) than the opening stock of real wealth *OR*, Tweedledum's real saving is positive (or negative), and his accumulation of real wealth rises (or falls). Figure A.1 reflects the assumption that his real wealth remains the same [90B].

The planned allocation of Tweedledum's resources includes:-

(a) the enjoyment of a FLOW of consumption *during* the period:
ON [30 hours of Leisure] PLUS *OP* [120B units of Goods];

(b) the maintenance of an unchanged STOCK of wealth *at the end* of the period:
OM [£600 of Money] PLUS *OF* [90B units of Goods] (= *OR*).

The choices made by Tweedledee (who produces Product B and consumes Product A), can also be represented by Figure A.1 — provided that the axes for Product A and Product B are switched.

The four quadrants represent different dimensions of a single decision, resolved simultaneously — and not four decisions resolved in sequence. (The arrowed path merely indicates how the four dimensions fit together.) The upper ("real") quadrants reflect technological opportunities for production or investment; the lower ("monetary") quadrants reflect market opportunities for exchange by selling or buying.

SECTION B: Resource Allocation in a Perfectly Competitive Economy: Macroeconomic Equilibrium (Chapter 16)

Resource allocation for the whole economy is determined by the individual choices of its inhabitants. In the Looking-Glass Utopia, there are 1,000 individuals (500 replicas of Tweedledum and 500 replicas of Tweedledee). Figure A.2 below is a representation of their aggregate choices. It is the same as Figure A.1 above which represents the choice of a single individual — with two exceptions: (1) the scale of every axis is multiplied by 1,000, and (2) the horizontal axis in the right-hand quadrants represents goods (of both varieties) supplied, and the horizontal axis in the left-hand quadrants represents goods (of both varieties) demanded.

With the prices of both products at the market-clearing level of £4 per unit, aggregate supply and aggregate demand are equal. There are no unwanted supplies and no unsatisfied demands in any market. The economy is in "full employment" equilibrium with each individual achieving the "desired" level of employment:

Leisure	*ON*	[30,000 hours]
Employment	*TN*	[40,000 hours]
Aggregate Supply	*OS*	[120,000 units]
Aggregate Demand	*DR*	[120,000 units]

Figure A.2: Full Employment (Market-Clearing) Equilibrium

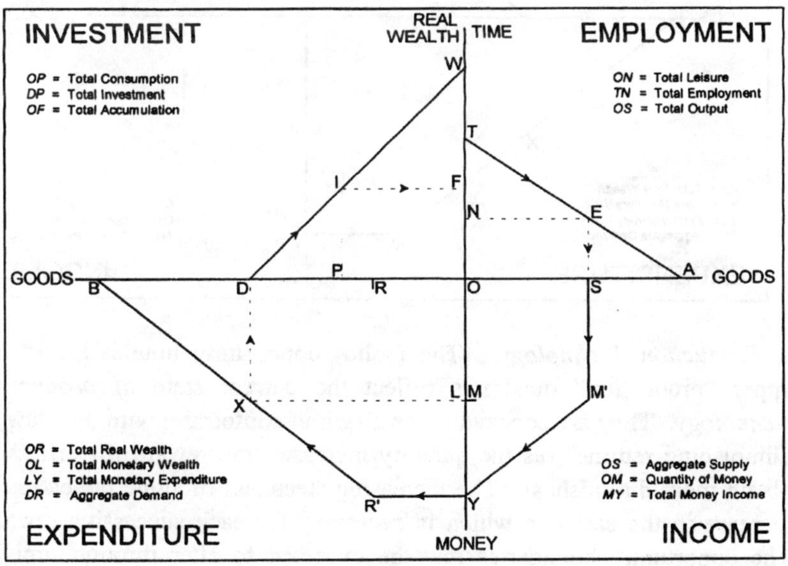

The Looking-Glass Simplification

Although the "four-quadrant" diagram in Figure A.2 is designed for the purpose of keeping the microeconomic foundations of macroeconomic equilibrium constantly in view, it contains two major over-simplifications:

1) the straight-line opportunity boundaries in the upper "production" quadrants are drawn on the assumption that physical productivity is constant;
2) there is no indication of the reason for the choices (at *E*, *Y*, *X*, and *I*) in each of the four quadrants.

Figure A.3 below is an amended version which is designed to remedy both deficiencies. The *ability* to engage in economic activity is represented by solid *opportunity boundaries*; the *willingness* to do so is represented by broken *indifference curves*.

Figure A.3: Full Employment (Market-Clearing) Equilibrium

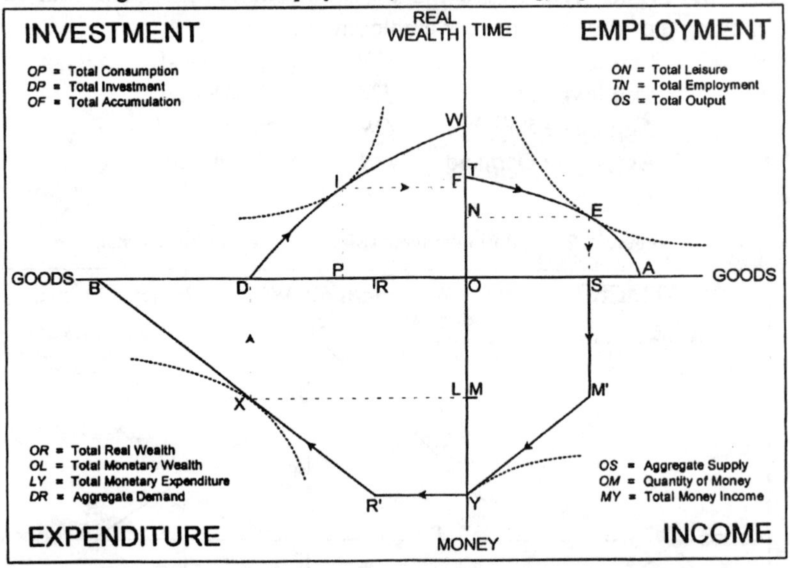

Production Technology: The (solid) opportunity boundaries in the upper "production" quadrants reflect the current state of *production technology*. They are concave to the origin in conformity with the "law of diminishing returns" (as the quantity increases, the reward for efforts to obtain more diminishes). The increasing steepness of slope indicates the increase in the sacrifice which is necessary for each successive reward. The opportunity boundaries may be expected to alter through time in response to technological progress as increasingly efficient methods of production cause them to expand.

Market Competition: The (solid) opportunity boundaries in the lower "exchange" quadrants reflect the current state of *market competition*. They are straight lines in order to represent the terms of exchange in perfectly competitive markets. The uniformity of slope indicates that, whatever is bought or sold, the market price of every unit is the same for everybody. The slope of the market boundaries (though constant throughout their length) may be expected to alter through time as market-clearing equilibrium prices change in response to changes in tastes and technology.

Consumer Tastes: The (broken) indifference curves in all four quadrants reflect the current state of *consumer tastes*. Each indifference curve (linking the various combinations which produce a given level of satisfaction) is convex to the origin in conformity with the "law of diminishing marginal satisfaction" (as the quantity increases, the desire for more diminishes). The reducing steepness of slope indicates the reduction in the sacrifice which is acceptable for each successive reward. A complete picture of consumer tastes would require a contour map of indifference curves, with each contour (radiating from the origin) representing a higher level of satisfaction. The only indifference curve displayed in each quadrant, however, is the one which touches the opportunity boundary. Lower "contours" are irrelevant, because they are less desirable; higher "contours" are irrelevant because they are unattainable. The indifference map can be expected to change through time in response to changes in preferences.

The Attainment of Maximum Satisfaction: In every quadrant, the indifference curves represent the *willingness* to engage in production or exchange; the opportunity boundaries represent the *ability* to do so. As long as the indifference curves are steeper than the opportunity boundaries, the sacrifice which is acceptable is greater than the sacrifice which is necessary. Consequently, there is an incentive to move from *T* to *E* in the EMPLOYMENT Quadrant, from *S* to *Y* in the INCOME Quadrant, from Y to *X* in the EXPENDITURE Quadrant, and from *D* to *I* in the INVESTMENT Quadrant. But, when the indifference curves become flatter than the opportunity boundaries, the willingness to sacrifice is less than the need to sacrifice. Consequently, there is no incentive for further movement in any of the quadrants.

The points of tangency represent the choices expected to produce the highest attainable level of satisfaction for each individual at the market-clearing prices. Since the total quantities demanded in all markets are equal to the total quantities supplied, and all individuals achieve their "desired" level of employment, Figure A.3 is a picture of an economy in full employment equilibrium.

It is in the nature of the multi-dimensional character of general economic equilibrium that it cannot be represented adequately in a two-dimensional diagram. The four quadrants do not represent a sequence of separate two-way choices; they represent the different dimensions of a single four-way choice. An invention, for example, which expands the opportunity boundary in the INVESTMENT Quadrant by increasing or improving investment opportunities, also expands the opportunity boundary in the EMPLOYMENT Quadrant. Similarly, changes in tastes which alter the indifference map in one quadrant may affect the indifference map in another.

The Looking-Glass Simplification: The diagrams in the rest of the Appendix represent the simplified numerical illustrations in the text. The assumption of constant marginal productivity reduces the opportunity boundaries in the upper "production" quadrants to straight lines, and the assumption of fixed % preferences makes indifference curves unnecessary.

The simplification in no way detracts from the general argument. Actual preferences have no significance in themselves. The important question is the extent to which preferences (whatever they happen to be) are accurately reflected in the market. For this purpose, the simplification has the advantage of throwing into sharp relief the different effects of different types of change.

SECTION C: An Increase in the Quantity of Money (Chapter 17, Pt.I)

The initial disequilibrium following a 25% increase in the quantity of money from OM to OM_2 is shown in Figure A.4(a).*

As there is no change in tastes, the allocation of this increase of MM_2 in total resources is allocated on the basis of existing preferences. Plans are made to increase Leisure by NN_D, to increase Consumption by DD_D, to increase Real Wealth by FF_D, and to keep the increase in Money to LL_D (by spending L_NM_2 of the increased quantity). The attempt to enjoy more leisure than before reduces the aggregate supply of goods and services by S_DS. The attempt to spend more money than before increases the aggregate demand for goods and services by D_DD. The result is excess demand in the product markets.

As prices are raised during the "Walrasian auction" in response to the pressure of the "bids", the price lines in the lower "monetary" quadrants become steeper. Each price rise reduces excess demand so that the disequilibrium becomes smaller and smaller until it is totally eliminated. The new equilibrium is shown in Figure A.4(b) and summarised in Table A.4.†

Table A.4: The Impact of a 25% Increase in the Quantity of Money

	INITIAL EQUILIBRIUM		NEW EQUILIBRIUM	
FLOW OF REAL INCOME	*Figure A.2*	*units*	*Figure A.4(b)*	*units*
Production	OS	120,000	OS	120,000
– Consumption	– OP	–120,000	– OP	–120,000
= SAVING	OS – OP	0	OS – OP	0
STOCK OF REAL WEALTH	*Figure A.2*	*units*	*Figure A.4(b)*	*units*
Closing Balance	DP	90,000	DP	90,000
– Opening Balance	– OR	–90,000	– OR	–90,000
= INVESTMENT	DP – OR	0	DP – OR	0
LEVEL OF PRICES	MY/OS	£4 per unit	M_2Y_2/OS	£5 per unit *25% RISE*
VOLUME OF EMPLOYMENT	TN	40,000 hours	TN	40,000 hours *NO CHANGE*

The letters indicate positions in the diagrams.
The figures are the corresponding units in the numerical illustration in the text.

* "Disequilibrium" choices are indicated by $_D$ subscripts. For ease of comparison, the initial equilibrium is indicated by the dotted boundaries.

† The Tables are numbered to match the corresponding diagrams.

Figure A.4(a)
25% Increase in the Quantity of Money: Initial Disequilibrium

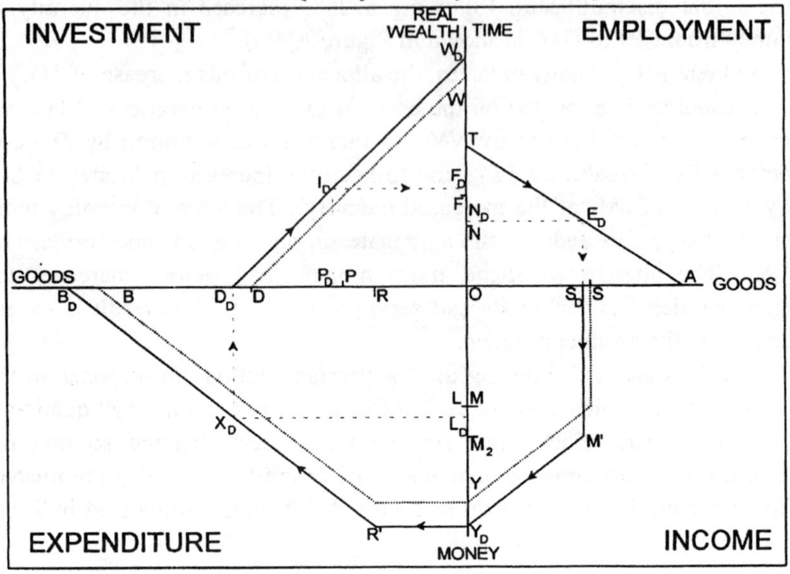

Figure A.4(b)
25% Increase in the Quantity of Money: New Equilibrium

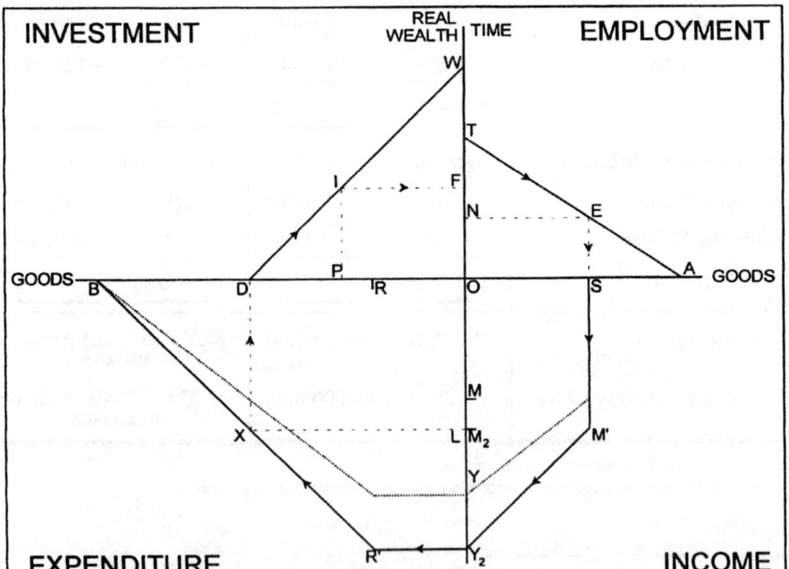

Effect on prices: 25% rise indicated by steepening of price lines.
Effect on employment: ZERO.

SECTION D: An Increase in the "Liquidity Demand" for Money (Chapter 17, Pt.II)

The initial disequilibrium following an increase in the "liquidity demand" for money is shown in Figure A.5(a).

The increase in the preference for holding Money is at the expense of a proportional reduction in the preferences for everything else. Plans are made to reduce Leisure by NN_D, to reduce Consumption by DD_D, to reduce Real Wealth by FF_D, and to obtain the desired increase in Money of LL_D by cutting spending. The attempt to enjoy less leisure than before increases the aggregate supply of goods and services by S_DS. The attempt to spend less money than before reduces the aggregate demand for goods and services by D_DD. The result is excess supply in the product markets.

As prices are lowered during the "Walrasian auction" in response to the pressure of the "bids", the price lines in the lower "monetary" quadrants become flatter. Each price cut reduces excess supply so that the disequilibrium becomes smaller and smaller until it is totally eliminated when prices have fallen far enough to raise the purchasing power of the existing quantity of money (the "real balances") to the newly desired level. The new equilibrium is shown in Figure A.5(b) and summarised in Table A.5.

Table A.5: The Impact of an Increase in the "Liquidity Demand" for Money

	INITIAL EQUILIBRIUM		NEW EQUILIBRIUM	
FLOW OF REAL INCOME	*Figure A.2*	*units*	*Figure A.5(b)*	*units*
Production	OS	120,000	OS	120,000
– Consumption	– OP	–120,000	– OP	–120,000
= SAVING	OS – OP	0	OS – OP	0
STOCK OF REAL WEALTH	*Figure A.2*	*units*	*Figure A.5(b)*	*units*
Closing Balance	DP	90,000	DP	90,000
– Opening Balance	– OR	–90,000	– OR	–90,000
= INVESTMENT	DP – OR	0	DP – OR	0
LEVEL OF PRICES	MY/OS	£4 per unit	MY_2/OS	£3 per unit *25% FALL*
VOLUME OF EMPLOYMENT	TN	40,000 hours	TN	40,000 hours *NO CHANGE*

The letters indicate positions in the diagrams.
The figures are the corresponding units in the numerical illustration in the text.

Figure A.5(a)
Increase in the "Liquidity Demand" for Money: Initial Disequilibrium

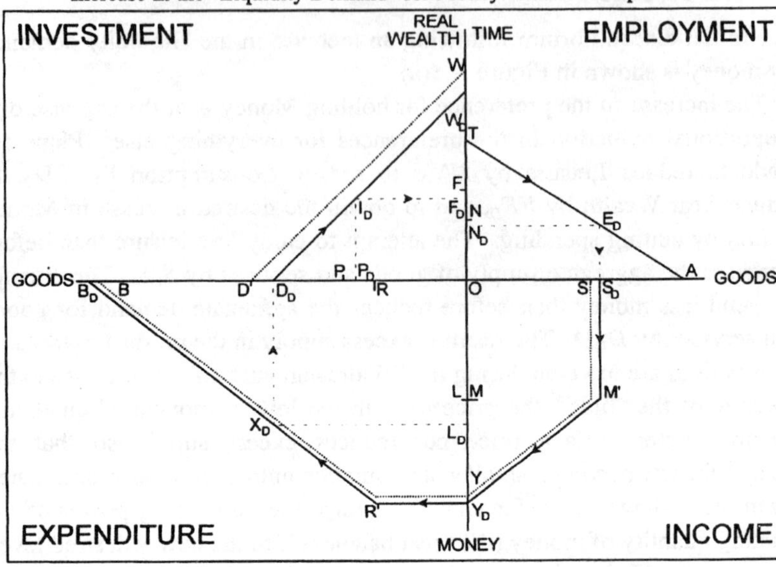

Figure A.5(b)
Increase in the "Liquidity Demand" for Money: New Equilibrium

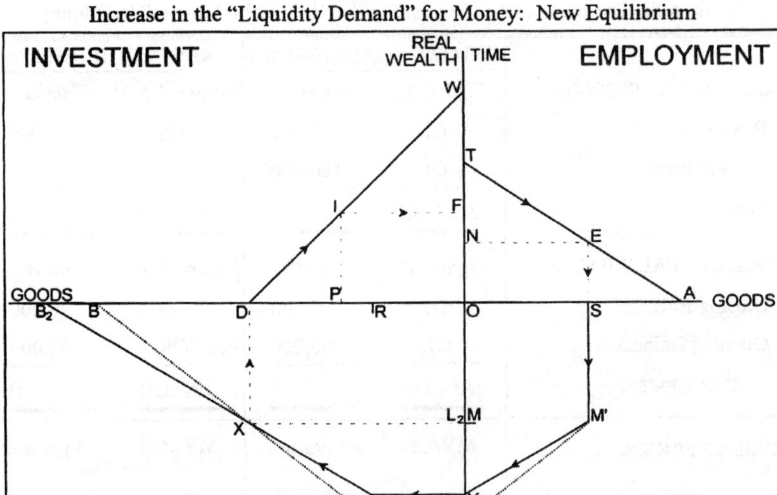

Effect on prices:	25% fall indicated by flattening of price lines.
Effect on employment:	ZERO.

SECTION E: An Increase in the "Saving Demand" for Real Wealth (Chapter 18)

The initial position following an increase in the "saving demand" for real wealth is shown in Figure A.6.

The decision to save an additional PP_2 by adding FF_2 to the stock of real wealth is reflected in the plan to increase movement along the investment opportunity boundary from I to I_2. Plans are made to cut PP_2 from spending on Consumption and to add it to spending on Investment. The replacement of consumption spending by investment spending leaves effective demand unchanged. Apart from the switch from "present goods" to "future goods", equilibrium is undisturbed. Aggregate demand *DR* remains equal to aggregate supply *OS.* The economy remains in equilibrium and continues to enjoy full employment — the achievement of the desired volume of employment — of *TN.*

The new equilibrium is shown in Figure A.6 and summarised in Table A.6.

Table A.6: The Impact of an Increase in the "Saving Demand" for Real Wealth

	INITIAL EQUILIBRIUM		NEW EQUILIBRIUM	
FLOW OF REAL INCOME	*Figure A.2*	*units*	*Figure A.6(b)*	*units*
Production	OS	120,000	OS	120,000
– Consumption	– OP	–120,000	– OP_2	–90,000
= SAVING	OS – OP	0	OS – OP_2	30,000
STOCK OF REAL WEALTH	*Figure A.2*	*units*	*Figure A.6(b)*	*units*
Closing Balance	DP	90,000	DP_2	120,000
– Opening Balance	– OR	–90,000	– OR	–90,000
= INVESTMENT	DP – OR	0	DP_2 – OR	30,000
LEVEL OF PRICES	MY/OS	£4 per unit	MY/OS	£4 per unit *NO CHANGE*
VOLUME OF EMPLOYMENT	TN	40,000 hours	TN	40,000 hours *NO CHANGE*

The letters indicate positions in the diagrams.
The figures are the corresponding units in the numerical illustration in the text.

Figure A.6
New Equilibrium following an Increase in the Desire to Save Real Wealth

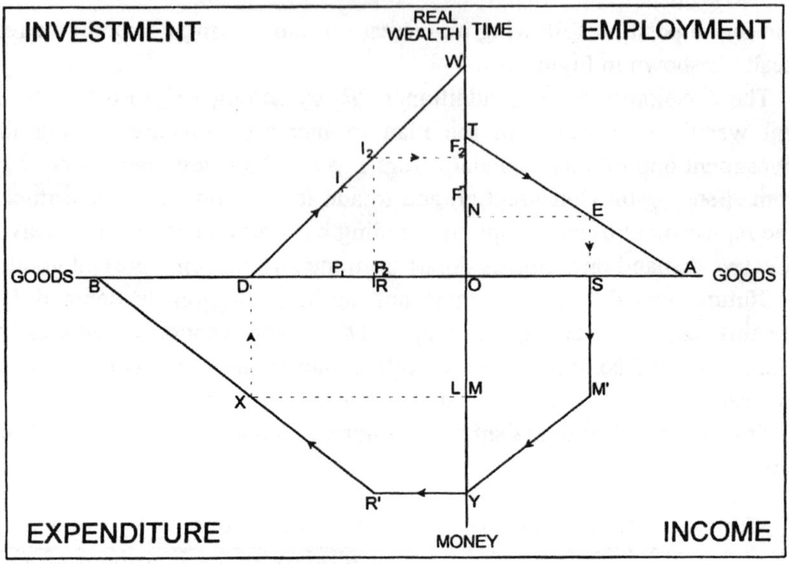

Effect on prices: ZERO.
Effect on employment: ZERO.

SECTION F: An Increase in the "Saving Demand" for Money (Chapter 19)

The initial disequilibrium following an increase in the "saving demand" for money is shown in Figure A.7(a).

The decision to save an additional PP_2 by adding LL_2 to the stock of monetary wealth is reflected in the plan to restrict movement along the spending opportunity boundary from X to X_D. The planned cut in total consumption again amounts to PP_2. But, by contrast with the saving of real wealth, there is no corresponding increase in investment spending. Instead of the shift from I to I_2 in the INVESTMENT quadrant of Figure A.6 which simply switches PP_2 from one kind of spending (on present consumption) to another kind of spending (on future consumption), the shift from X to X_2 in the EXPENDITURE quadrant of Figure A.7(a) switches PP_2 out of spending altogether.

That is the only intended difference. *There is no change in the general preference for consumption (present and future) relative to leisure.* The decision to save is "neutral": the employment decision remains at *E*. Total employment plans still remain at *TN*, and total production is still planned at *OS*. The problem is that these plans can no longer be achieved.

Since the increase in the preference for holding Money is at the expense only of Consumption, planned Leisure remains at *ON*. The attempt to maintain the same level of employment as before *leaves the aggregate supply* of goods and services unchanged at *OS*. The attempt to obtain the desired increase in Money of LL_D by spending less money than before reduces the aggregate demand for goods and services by D_DD. The result is excess supply in the product markets.

As prices are lowered during the "Walrasian auction" in response to the pressure of the "bids", the price lines in the lower "monetary" quadrants become flatter. Each price cut reduces excess supply so that the disequilibrium becomes smaller and smaller until it is totally eliminated when prices have fallen far enough to raise the purchasing power of the existing quantity of money (the "real balances") to the newly desired level. By contrast with a change in the "liquidity demand" for money, price adjustments are not sufficient *on their own* to restore equilibrium after a change in the "saving demand". The reason is that, unlike a change in "liquidity demand", a change in "saving demand" alters the balance of "real" preferences, and can be satisfied only by "real" changes.

The result is unemployment of NN_2. The volume of employment actually achieved TN_2 falls short of the desired level *TN*. The new equilibrium is shown in Figure A.7(b) and summarised in Table A.7.

Table A.7: The Impact of an Increase in the "Saving Demand" for Money

	INITIAL EQUILIBRIUM		NEW EQUILIBRIUM	
FLOW OF REAL INCOME	*Figure A.2*	*units*	*Figure A.7(b)*	*units*
Production	OS	120,000	OS_2	110,000
– Consumption	– OP	–120,000	– OP_2	–100,000
= SAVING	OS – OP	0	OS_2–OP_2	10,000
STOCK OF REAL WEALTH	*Figure A.2*	*units*	*Figure A.7(b)*	*units*
Closing Balance	DP	90,000	D_2P_2	100,000
– Opening Balance	– OR	–90,000	– OR	–90,000
= INVESTMENT	DP – OR	0	D_2P_2–OR	10,000
LEVEL OF PRICES	MY/OS	£4 per unit	MY_2/OS_2	£3 per unit *25% FALL*
VOLUME OF EMPLOYMENT	TN	40,000 hours	TN_2	36,667 hours *8⅓% FALL*

The letters indicate positions in the diagrams.
The figures are the corresponding units in the numerical illustration in the text.

Figure A.7(a)
Initial Disequilibrium following an Increase in the "Saving Demand" for Money

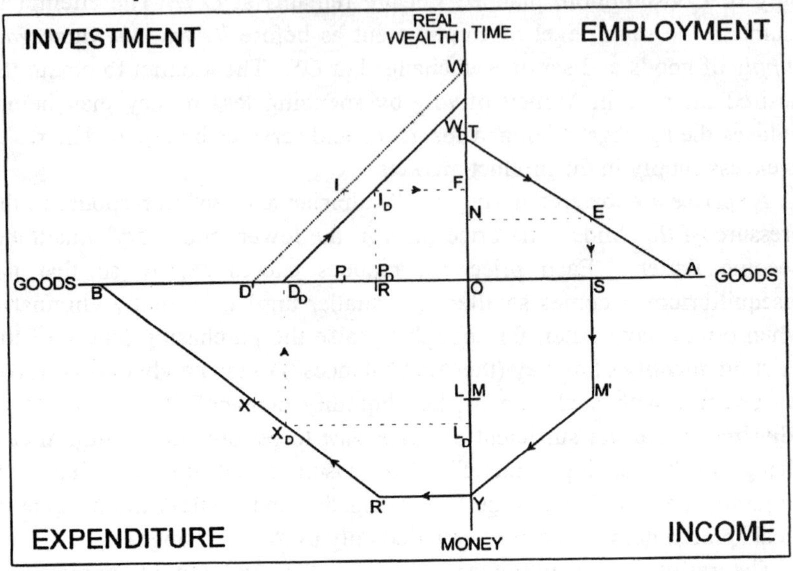

Figure A.7(b)
New Equilibrium following an Increase in the "Saving Demand" for Money: The Free-Market "Secular" Version

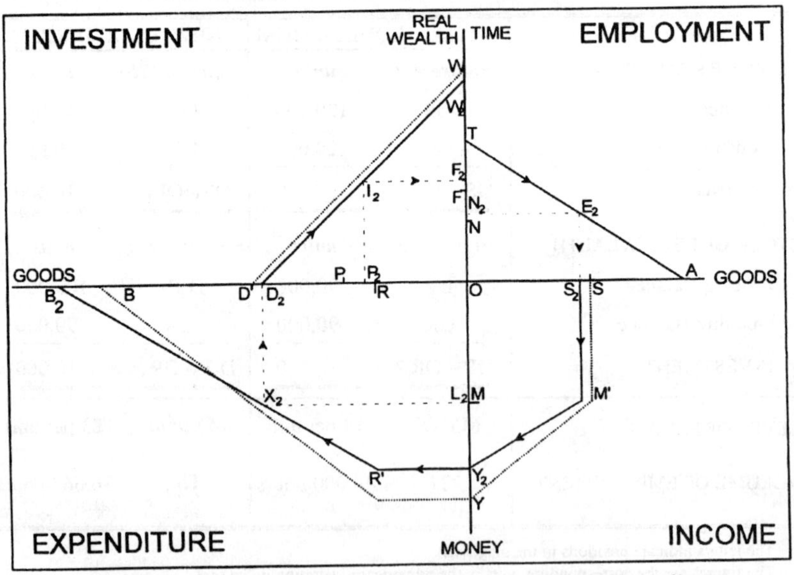

Effect on prices:	25% fall indicated by flattening of price lines.
Effect on employment:	$8\frac{1}{3}$% reduction amounting to NN_2.

The Acid Test

The object of the first part of this Appendix has been to demonstrate that the macroeconomic results of various changes cannot adequately be explained except on the basis of their microeconomic causes.

The object of the next part is to show that, by failing to keep the microeconomic foundations constantly in view, all the rival "economic theologies" give a seriously distorted view of the macroeconomic impact of an increase in the desire to save money.

The "secular" free-market version of the new equilibrium is presented in Figure A.7(b) and Table A.7 above. It demonstrates that the macroeconomic impact of an increase in the pure "saving demand" for money (i.e. in the desire to cut spending on present consumption in order to save money for the purpose of future consumption) is TWOFOLD:

(1) a reduction in the level of prices; and

(2) a fall in the volume of employment below the "desired" level.

But the Looking-Glass Utopia is not subject to any form of market imperfection or dynamic disequilibrium whatsoever. NN_2 is therefore the market-equilibrium level of unemployment.

The rest of this Appendix is devoted to a comparison of the erroneous versions given by the rival "economic theologies".

SECTION G: An Increase in the "Saving Demand" for Money: Classical Theology (Chapter 22)

In Figure A.8 below, the initial market-clearing equilibrium is indicated by the "decisions" at *E*, *Y*, *X*, and *I*. Aggregate demand *DR* is initially equal to aggregate supply *OS*. The Classical version of the new equilibrium following an increase in the "saving demand" for money discloses no more than a movement from *I* to I_2. The only change recognised by Classical "theology" is the replacement of present consumption PP_2 by future consumption FF_2. Aggregate demand *DR* remains equal to aggregate supply *OS*. Consequently there is no change either in the level of prices or in the volume of employment.

A summary of the Classical version is presented in Table A.8.

Figure A.8 and Table A.8 are exactly the same as Figure A.6 and Table A.6 above which show the consequences of accumulating real wealth. Classical "desert island" economics treats saving money as the same thing as spending it on real wealth. Examination of the microeconomic foundations exposes the Classical distortion of the actual microeconomic preferences which is designed to produce the macroeconomic result required to confirm the Classical Article of faith that equilibrium means full employment.

Figure A.8
The Impact of an Increase in the "Saving Demand" for Money:
The Classical "Theological" Version

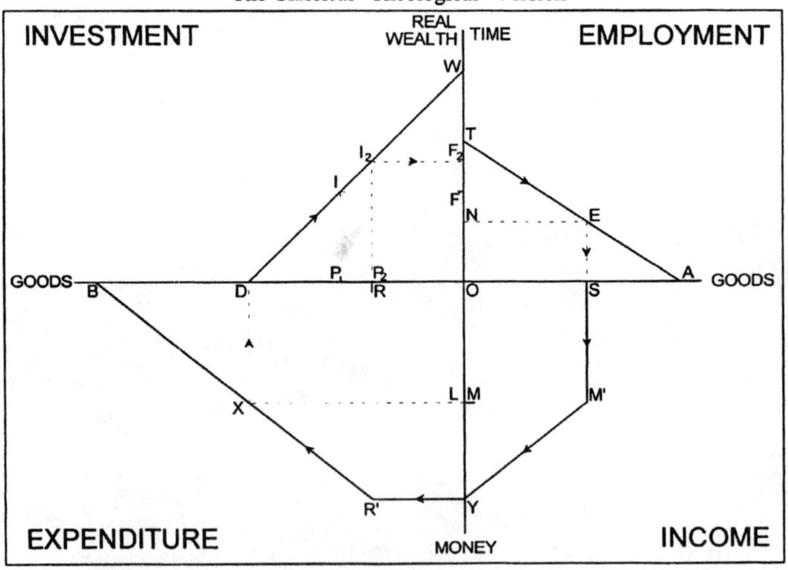

Effect on level of prices: ZERO.
Effect on volume of employment: ZERO.

Table A.8
The Impact of an Increase in the "Saving Demand" for Money:
The Classical "Theological" Version

	INITIAL EQUILIBRIUM		NEW EQUILIBRIUM	
FLOW OF REAL INCOME	*Figure A.2*	*units*	*Figure A.8*	*units*
Production	OS	120,000	OS	120,000
– Consumption	– OP	–120,000	– OP_2	–90,000
= SAVING	OS – OP	0	OS – OP_2	30,000
STOCK OF REAL WEALTH	*Figure A.2*	*units*	*Figure A.8*	*units*
Closing Balance	DP	90,000	DP_2	120,000
– Opening Balance	– OR	–90,000	– OR	–90,000
= INVESTMENT	DP – OR	0	DP_2 – OR	30,000
LEVEL OF PRICES	MY/OS	£4 per unit	MY/OS	£4 per unit *NO CHANGE*
VOLUME OF EMPLOYMENT	TN	40,000 hours	TN	40,000 hours *NO CHANGE*

The letters indicate positions in the diagrams.
The figures are the corresponding units in the numerical illustration in the text.

SECTION H: An Increase in the "Saving Demand" for Money: Keynesian Theology (Chapter 23)

In Figure A.9 below, the initial market-clearing equilibrium is indicated by the "decisions" at *E*, *Y*, *X*, and *I* on the "outer circuit". (The initial positions of boundaries which change are indicated by dotted lines.) The initial (dashed) Consumption Function CF_1 reflects a Marginal Propensity to Consume of $^4/_9$. Aggregate demand *DR* is initially equal to aggregate supply *OS*.

In the standard textbook representation of the Keynesian version of the increase in the "saving demand" for money, the Consumption Function shifts to CF_2 reflecting a Marginal Propensity to Consume of $^1/_3$. The expenditure decision taken at X_D means a cut in aggregate demand of DD_D. But, as aggregate supply remains unaltered, the economy is in disequilibrium (hence the use of the subscript $_D$).

The arrowed zigzag path from X (on the "outer circuit") to X_D and on to X_2 (on the "inner circuit") corresponds to the arrowed zigzag path in the "multiplier" diagram in Figure 23.1 (of chapter 23 above). The vertical part of the path reflects the fall in income (as the economy "ratchets" inwards on to a narrower circuit). The diagonal part of the path reflects the matching reduction in expenditure. The process continues until the economy has contracted on to the solid lines of the "inner circuit".

The position of the equilibrium "inner circuit" is determined at the intersection of the Consumption Function CF_2 and the fixed Real-Balance Function *RBF* which remains unchanged throughout the multiplier process. X_2 is the new equilibrium position: total resources have contracted sufficiently for the desired increase in the proportion held in the form of money to be satisfied by existing real balances.

The final market-clearing equilibrium is indicated in Figure A.9 by the "decisions" taken at E_2, Y_2, X_2, and I_2 in each of the four quadrants. The reduced aggregate demand D_2R is equal to the reduced aggregate supply OS_2.

The hidden assumptions are clearly exposed by the contrast between the initial equilibrium (on the "outer circuit") and the final equilibrium (on the "inner circuit").

Hidden assumption (1) — that investment spending does not change — requires a fixed Investment Function *IF* in the INVESTMENT quadrant.

Hidden assumption (2) — that wages and prices do not change — requires a fixed Real-Balance Function *RBF* in the EXPENDITURE quadrant.

Hidden assumption (3) — that Leisure is a residual — requires an Employment Function which shifts from EF_1 to EF_2 in order to accommodate the changes in the other three quadrants.

The final result is the same as the conventional representation of the multiplier process in Figure 23.1. Figure A.9 shows the microeconomic assumptions necessary to support the Keynesian explanation of how an intended cut in consumption of DD_D is multiplied into an actual cut of DD_2. An increase in the desire to cut consumption in order to save money is responsible for an unintended fall in employment of NN_2.

Figure A.9
The Impact of an Increase in the "Saving Demand" for Money:
The Keynesian "Theological" Version

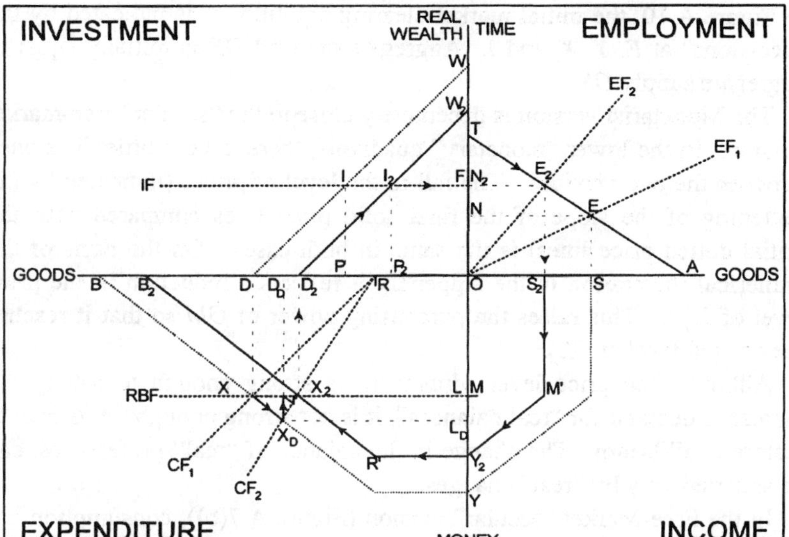

Effect on level of prices: ZERO.
Effect on volume of employment: 37½% FALL indicated by NN_2.

Table A.9
The Impact of an Increase in the "Saving Demand" for Money:
The Keynesian "Theological" Version

	INITIAL EQUILIBRIUM		NEW EQUILIBRIUM	
FLOW OF REAL INCOME	*Figure A.2*	*units*	*Figure A.9*	*units*
Production	OS	120,000	OS_2	75,000
– Consumption	– OP	–120,000	– OP_2	–75,000
= SAVING	OS – OP	0	OS_2–OP_2	0
STOCK OF REAL WEALTH	*Figure A.2*	*units*	*Figure A.9*	*units*
Closing Balance	DP	90,000	D_2P_2	90,000
– Opening Balance	– OR	–90,000	– OR	–90,000
= INVESTMENT	DP – OR	0	D_2P_2–OR	0
LEVEL OF PRICES	MY/OS	£4 per unit	MY_2/OS_2	£4 per unit *NO CHANGE*
VOLUME OF EMPLOYMENT	TN	40,000 hours	TN_2	25,000 hours *37½% FALL*

The letters indicate positions in the diagrams.
The figures are the corresponding units in the numerical illustration in the text.

SECTION I: An Increase in the "Saving Demand" for Money: Monetarist Theology (Chapter 24)

In Figure A.10, the initial market-clearing equilibrium is indicated by the "decisions" at *E*, *Y*, *X*, and *I*. Aggregate demand *DR* is initially equal to aggregate supply *OS*.

The Monetarist version is deceptively close to the "secular" free-market version. In the lower "monetary" quadrants, there is very little difference between the two versions. The fall in the level of prices (indicated by the flattening of the slope of the final solid price lines compared with the initial dotted price lines) is the same in both cases. On the basis of the numerical illustration in the Appendix it reflects a reduction in the price level of 25%. This raises the purchasing power of *OM* so that it reaches the desired level at OL_2.

Although the price level adjustment is strong enough to satisfy the increased demand for "real balances", it is not strong enough *on its own* to restore equilibrium. The change in the balance of "real" preferences, can be satisfied only by "real" changes.

In the Free-Market "secular" version (Figure A.7(b)), consumption has to fall by PP_2, real wealth has to rise by FF_2, and leisure has to rise by NN_2. But if leisure has to rise by NN_2, the level of employment must fall by NN_2. In the Monetarist "theological" version (Figure A.10), there is a switch from consumption spending to investment spending within an unchanged total. The reason why total spending is unchanged is the hidden assumption that there is no change in the desired consumption of leisure.

The difference arises solely from the assumption that "producers ... will react to their temporary inability to sell by simply permitting their inventories to build up. That is, they will leave their level of production unchanged" [Patinkin (1956) p.318]. Consequently, planned leisure remains unchanged at *ON*, and inventories are allowed to build up bringing planned investment spending up to DP_2.

The monetarist version of final equilibrium in Figure A.10 is a faithful reproduction of the adjustment process assumed in Patinkin's analysis. Throughout the course of the bidding, "there exists a state of excess supply in the commodity market." As prices are reduced, "the real-balance effect stimulates the commodity market directly." "Thus the downward shift in the commodity demand function automatically creates market forces which tend to offset it." In the presence of a Walrasian auctioneer, demand is so sensitive to these forces that ultimately "it returns to a full-employment position at a lower level of wages, prices, and interest."

Figure A.10
The Impact of an Increase in the "Saving Demand" for Money:
The Monetarist "Theological" Version

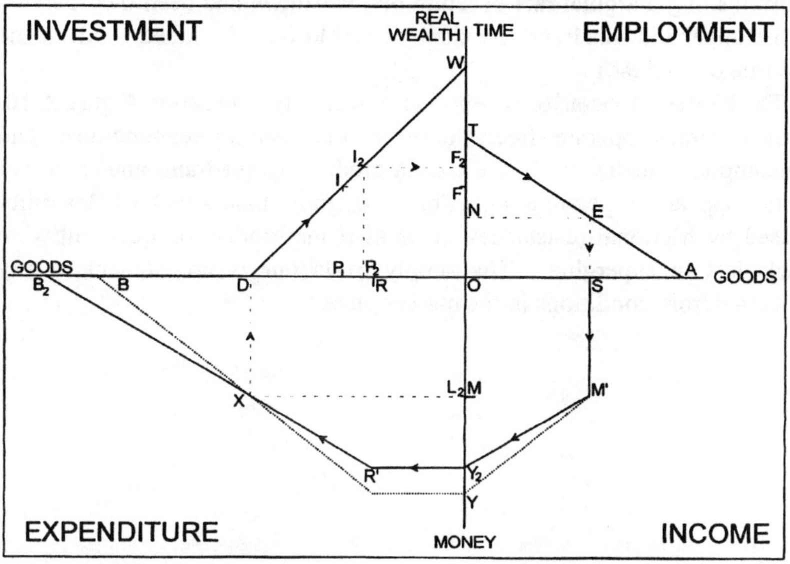

Effect on level of prices:	25% FALL indicated by flattening of price lines.
Effect on volume of employment:	ZERO.

Table A.10
The Impact of an Increase in the "Saving Demand" for Money:
The Monetarist "Theological" Version

	INITIAL EQUILIBRIUM		NEW EQUILIBRIUM	
FLOW OF REAL INCOME	*Figure A.2*	*units*	*Figure A.10*	*units*
Production	OS	120,000	OS	120,000
– Consumption	– OP	–120,000	– OP_2	–100,000
= SAVING	OS – OP	0	OS – OP_2	20,000
STOCK OF REAL WEALTH	*Figure A.2*	*units*	*Figure A.10*	*units*
Closing Balance	DP	90,000	DP_2	110,000
– Opening Balance	– OR	–90,000	– OR	–90,000
= INVESTMENT	DP – OR	0	DP_2 – OR	20,000
LEVEL OF PRICES	MY/OS	£4 per unit	MY_2/OS	£3 per unit *25% FALL*
VOLUME OF EMPLOYMENT	TN	40,000 hours	TN	40,000 hours *NO CHANGE*

The letters indicate positions in the diagrams.
The figures are the corresponding units in the numerical illustration in the text.

The level of prices falls (by 25%), but the volume of output and employment remains unchanged. (And if the more realistic assumption of a diminishing marginal rate of return on investment had been incorporated in the upper left quadrant, the changes would have included a fall in the real rate of interest.)

The hidden Monetarist assumptions are clearly exposed in Figure A.10. Market forces operate freely only in the income, expenditure, and consumption quadrants. In the crucial production quadrant, market forces do not appear to operate at all. This is far more than a lack of flexibility caused by frictional resistances. It is as if the production quadrant were stuck fast in superglue. The supply of labour is not subject to any influence from conditions in the market place.

BIBLIOGRAPHY*

BASTIAT, Frederic
1845 *Economic Sophisms*. Trans. A. Goddard. New York: Foundation for Economic Education, 1964.

BLANQUI, Jérôme-Adolphe
1837 *History of Political Economy in Europe*.
4th ed. 1859. Trans. E. J. Leonard, 1880. New York: Kelley, 1968.

BÖHM-BAWERK, Eugen von
1888 *The Positive Theory of Capital*. Trans. W. Smart, 1891. New York: Stechert, 1930.

BROWN, Arthur Joseph
1955 *The Great Inflation, 1939-1951*. London: Oxford University Press.

CANTILLON, Richard
1732 *Essai sur la Nature du Commerce en Général*. London: 1755, trans. H. Higgs, 1931. New York: Kelley, 1964.

CHICK, Victoria
1978 "The Nature of the Keynesian Revolution: A Reassessment", *Australian Economic Papers*, June 1978.

CLOWER, Robert Wayne
1965 "The Keynesian Counter-Revolution: A Theoretical Appraisal". In Clower [1969].
1969 *Monetary Theory*. Harmondsworth: Penguin.

COURNOT, Augustin
1838 *Researches into the Mathematical Principles of the Theory of Wealth*.
Trans. N. T. Bacon, 1897. New York: Kelley, 1960.

DAVIDSON, Paul
1972 *Money and the Real World*. London: Macmillan.

ENOCK, Arthur Guy
1951 *This War Business*. London: The Bodley Head.

FISHER, Irving
1911 *The Purchasing Power of Money*. Revised ed. 1913. New York: Kelley, 1985.
1930 *The Theory of Interest*. New York: Kelley, 1986.

* For the sake of chronology, the "reference" date preceding each title is that of the first edition. Quotations are taken from the latest edition indicated. (E.g. 1776 is the year used for references to Adam Smith's *Wealth of Nations*, but quotations are from an edition published in 1976.)

FRIEDMAN, Milton
1962 *Price Theory*. 2nd ed. Chicago: Aldine Publishing Company, 1976.
1968 "The Role of Monetary Policy", *American Economic Review*, March 1968.
1969 *The Optimum Quantity of Money and Other Essays*. London: Macmillan.
1970 *The Counter-Revolution in Monetary Theory*. London: Institute of Economic Affairs.
1974a *Monetary Correction*. London: Institute of Economic Affairs.
1974b Letter to *The Economist*, September 28, 1974.

GALBRAITH, John Kenneth
1954 *The Great Crash 1929*. Harmondsworth: Penguin, 1961.
1987 *A History of Economics*. Harmondsworth: Penguin, 1989.

HANSEN, Alvin Harvey
1953 *A Guide to Keynes*. New York: McGraw-Hill.

HAYEK, Friedrich August
1988 *The Fatal Conceit: The Errors of Socialism*. London: Routledge.

HICKS, John Richard
1937 "Mr. Keynes and the "Classics"; a Suggested Interpretation", *Econometrica*, April 1937.
1950 *A Contribution to the Theory of the Trade Cycle*. Oxford: Oxford University Press, 1950.
1957 "A Rehabilitation of "Classical" Economics?", *Economic Journal*, June 1957.
1967 *Critical Essays in Monetary Theory*. Oxford: Oxford University Press.

HOBBES, Thomas
1651 *Leviathan, or the Matter, Forme & Power of a Common-wealth Ecclesiasticall and Civill*. Cambridge: Cambridge University Press, 1991.

HUME, David
1752a *Of Commerce*. }
1752b *Of Money*. }
1752c *Of Interest*. } In *David Hume: Writings on Economics*
1752d *Of the Balance of Trade*. } ed. Eugene Rotwein,
1752e *Of Taxes*. } London: Nelson, 1955.
1752f *Of Public Credit*. }
1758 *Of the Jealousy of Trade*. }
1776 Letter to Turgot, September 1776. In Turgot [1770].

INGRAM, John Kells
1888 *A History of Political Economy*. 2nd ed. London: A & C Black, 1907.

JEVONS, William Stanley
1871 *The Theory of Political Economy*. 5th ed. New York: Kelley, 1965.

JOHNSON, Harry G.
1958 "Monetary Theory and Keynesian Economics", *Pakistan Economic Journal*, June 1958. In Johnson [1962].
1962 *Money, Trade and Economic Growth*. Cambridge Mass.: Harvard University Press.

KALDOR, Nicholas
1972 "The Irrelevance of Equilibrium Economics", *Economic Journal*, December 1972.

KEYNES, John Maynard
1923 *A Tract on Monetary Reform*. London: Macmillan.
1930 *A Treatise on Money*. London: Macmillan.
1936 *The General Theory of Employment, Interest and Money*. London: Macmillan.
1937 "Alternative Theories of the Rate of Interest", *Economic Journal*, June 1937. In Clower [1969].

KEYNES, John Neville
1890 *The Scope and Method of Political Economy*. 4th ed. 1917. New York: Kelley, 1986.

KOESTLER, Arthur
1959 *The Sleepwalkers*. Harmondsworth: Penguin, 1964.

LAUDERDALE, James Maitland, 8th Earl of
1804 *An Inquiry Into the Nature and Origin of Public Wealth*. 2nd ed. 1819, ed. Morton Paglin 1962. New York: Kelley, 1966.

LAW, John
1705 *Money and Trade Considered*. New York: Kelley, 1966.

LAYARD, Richard; NICKELL, Stephen; and JACKMAN, Richard
1991 *Unemployment: Macroeconomic Performance and the Labour Market*. Oxford: Oxford University Press.

LEIJONHUFVUD, Axel
1968 *On Keynesian Economics and the Economics of Keynes*. New York: Oxford University Press.

LOCKE, John
1691 *Some Considerations of the Consequences of the Lowering of Interest, and Raising the Value of Money*. 2nd ed. 1696. New York: Kelley, 1989.
1695 *Further Considerations Concerning Raising the Value of Money*. 2nd ed. 1696. New York: Kelley, 1989.

MALTHUS, Rev. Thomas Robert
1820 *Principles of Political Economy*. 2nd ed. 1836. New York: Kelley, 1966.

MALYNES, Gerard
1622 *The Maintenance of Free Trade*. New York: Kelley 1971.

MANDEVILLE, Bernard
1714 *The Fable of the Bees*. 1725 edition (ed. P. Harth 1970). Harmondsworth: Penguin, 1989.

MARSHALL, Alfred
1890 *Principles of Economics*. 8th ed. London: Macmillan, 1920.
1892 *Elements of Economics of Industry*. 3rd ed. London: Macmillan, 1907.
1923 *Money Credit and Commerce*. London: Macmillan.

MARX, Karl
1867 *Capital: A Critical Analysis of Capitalist Production*. 3rd ed. trans. S. Moore and E. Aveling, ed. F. Engels, 1887. Moscow: Foreign Languages Publishing House, 1961.

MENGER, Carl
1871 *Principles of Economics*. Trans. J. Dingwall and B. F. Hoselitz. New York: New York University Press, 1981.

MILL, James
1807 *James Mill: Selected Economic Writings*, ed. D. Winch. London: Oliver & Boyd, 1966.

MILL, John Stuart
1844 *Essays on Some Unsettled Questions of Political Economy*. London: London School of Economics and Political Science, 1948.
1848 *Principles of Political Economy*. 7th ed. 1871, ed. W.J.Ashley. London: Longmans, Green, and Co., 1909.

MISSELDEN, Edward
1622 *Free Trade or the Meanes to Make Trade Florish*. New York: Kelley, 1971.
1623 *The Circle of Commerce or the Ballance of Trade*. New York: Kelley, 1971.

MUN, Thomas
1628 *England's Treasure by Forraign Trade*. 1st ed. (posthumous) 1664. New York: Kelley, 1986.

ORMEROD, Paul
1994 *The Death of Economics*. London: Faber.

PATINKIN, Don
1948 "Price Flexibility and Full Employment" *American Economic Review*. In *Readings in Monetary Theory*, ed. F. A. Lutz and L. W. Mints. London: George Allen and Unwin, 1952.
1956 *Money, Interest, and Prices*. 2nd ed. New York: Harper and Row, 1965.

PETTY, William
1662 *A Treatise of Taxes and Contributions*. }
1664 *Verbum Sapienti*. } *The Economic Writings of Sir William*
1672 *The Political Anatomy of Ireland*. } *Petty* ed. C. H. Hull. Cambridge 1899.
1676 *Political Arithmetick*. } New York: Kelley, 1986.
1682 *Quantulumcunque concerning Money*. }

PHELPS, Edmund S.
1968 "Money-Wage Dynamics and Labor-Market Equilibrium" *Journal of Political Economy*, July/August. In Phelps [1979].
1994 *Structural Slumps: The Modern Equilibrium Theory of Unemployment, Interest, and Assets*. Cambridge Mass.: Harvard University Press.

PIGOU, Arthur Cecil
1913 *Unemployment.* London: Williams & Norgate.
1933 *The Theory of Unemployment.* London: Macmillan.

QUESNAY, François
1758 *Tableau Économique.* Trans. M. Kuczynski and R. L. Meek. London: Macmillan 1972.

RAYMAN, Robert Anthony
1975 *Price Stability and Full Employment.* London: PEP.

RICARDO, David
1817 *On the Principles of Political Economy, and Taxation.* 3rd edition 1821. In *The Works and Correspondence of David Ricardo*, ed. P. Sraffa. Cambridge: Cambridge University Press, 1951.

RUSSELL, Bertrand
1946 *A History of Western Philosophy.* 2nd ed. London: Allen & Unwin, 1961.

SAMUELSON, Paul Anthony and NORDHAUS, William D.
1995 *Economics.* (1st ed. 1948; 13th ed. 1989; 14th ed. 1992; 15th ed. 1995). New York: McGraw-Hill.

SANDILANDS COMMITTEE
1975 *Report on Inflation Accounting*, (Cmnd. 6225). London: HMSO.

SAY, Jean-Baptiste
1803 *A Treatise on Political Economy.*
4th ed. Trans. C. R. Prinsep, 1821, rev. C. C. Biddle, 1880. New York: Kelley, 1971.
1815 *Catechism of Political Economy.* Trans. J. Richter, 1821. New York: Kelley, 1967.
1820 *Letters to Mr.Malthus.* Trans. J. Richter, 1821. New York: Kelley, 1967.

SMITH, Adam
1759 *Theory of Moral Sentiments.* London: George Bell & Sons, 1880.
1776 *An Inquiry into the Nature and Causes of the Wealth of Nations.*
5th ed. 1789 ed. Edwin Cannan 1904. Chicago: Chicago University Press, 1976.*

TAUSSIG, Frank William
1911 *Principles of Economics.* 4th ed. New York: Macmillan, 1939.

TOBIN, James
1972 "Inflation and Unemployment" *American Economic Review*, March 1972.

* In view of the large number of different editions, quotations from the *Wealth of Nations* are identified, not by page numbers, but by a Book reference (in Roman numerals) followed by a Chapter reference (in Arabic numerals).

TURGOT, Anne Robert Jacques
1770 *Reflections on the Formation and the Distribution of Riches*. Trans. W. J. Ashley, 1898. New York: Kelley, 1971.

WALRAS, Léon
1874 *Elements of Pure Economics*. 4th ed. 1900 trans. W. Jaffé, 1953. Philadelphia: Orion, 1984.

WICKSELL, Knut
1898 *Interest and Prices*. Trans. R. F. Kahn, 1936. New York: Kelley, 1965.

INDEX